Modern Continental

LITERARY
CRITICISM

GOLDENTREE BOOKS

O. B. HARDISON, JR.
The University of North Carolina
EDITOR

Modern Continental
LITERARY
CRITICISM

NEW YORK

APPLETON-CENTURY-CROFTS
EDUCATIONAL DIVISION
MEREDITH CORPORATION

PREFACE

THE PRESENT ANTHOLOGY is intended for students of continental literature and also for those who wish to know more about the European background of English and American criticism. The volume extends from Kant's *Critique of Judgment* (1790) to Jacques Maritain's *Situation of Poetry* (1955). No period in the history of criticism is richer or more varied. By the same token, no period is more difficult to represent adequately in an anthology. Of necessity, important figures must be omitted and others represented by selections which fail to do justice to the full scope of their work. In the hope of minimizing this problem, I have observed the following editorial principles:

(1) Each selection is significant in itself and has influenced subsequent criticism. Often its influence has extended beyond the Continent to England and America, and where it has, the fact is noted in the headnote to the selection. There will be differences of opinion about the wisdom of omitting certain authors and essays, but there will, I hope, be agreement that all of the selections included have clear title to the space given them.

(2) Each selection is long enough to present the author's ideas in a systematic way. Short, isolated selections have been avoided in the belief that they distort rather than clarify. Likewise, no essays have been included which concentrate on works of national rather than European prominence, for it is axiomatic that to understand a critical essay the reader must know the work being discussed.

(3) Each selection illustrates a major tradition of European criticism. For this reason priority has been given to authors who initiated movements or gave them definitive formulation. Of the later Kantians, for example, Schelling has been chosen rather than Fichte or the Schlegels because of the importance of his "nature philosophy" to German and English romanticism.

(4) Longer selections have been given subheadings in order to facilitate comprehension. Notes added by the present editor are followed by "Ed." in parentheses.

It is a pleasure to acknowledge here several debts of gratitude. I wish to thank Professor Alfred Engstrom of the University of North Carolina at Chapel Hill for his luminous translations of Gautier, Baudelaire, Verlaine, and Maurras, and for many helpful suggestions. I am equally grateful to Professor James Patty of Washington and Lee University for his suggestions and his translation of Breton's *Surrealist Manifesto*. To my colleagues in the English Department of the University of North Carolina and to the graduate students in my class in modern criticism, I am especially indebted for unfailing interest and many useful suggestions. Finally, I wish to thank my wife for many hours of devoted assistance.

O. B. H.

Chapel Hill, North Carolina

CONTENTS

* Selections from longer works

Part II: POSITIVISM AND HUMANISM

° Selections from longer works

Part III: AESTHETICISM

* Selections from longer works

Part IV: PSYCHOLOGY AND ANTHROPOLOGY

FRIEDRICH NIETZSCHE

SIGMUND FREUD

CARL G. JUNG

Part V: NEW DIRECTIONS

CHARLES MAURRAS

ANDRÉ BRETON

JEAN-PAUL SARTRE

JACQUES MARITAIN

* Selections from longer works

Introduction

THE HISTORY of modern continental criticism is in large measure the history of three broad critical traditions: the aesthetic, the scientific, and the humanistic. In the past one hundred and fifty years critics have occasionally attempted to combine these traditions, but the most striking fact about them has been their tendency to resist combination. Each has its own sources, its own prophets, and its own subspecies; and each has, from its inception, been opposed to the other two.

The postulates of aesthetic criticism were established by Kant in the *Critique of Judgment* (1790). Directly or indirectly, all later aesthetic criticism is indebted to his work. Despite variations in terminology and emphasis, such key ideas as the shaping force of the imagination, the uniqueness of the aesthetic category, and the "purposiveness without purpose" of the art object are still invoked by twentieth-century critics. Aesthetic criticism has important things to say about the psychology of the creative process, the nature of the art work, and the function of criticism. However it is committed to the idea that aesthetic knowledge is different in kind from other types of knowledge such as science and ethics. When the critic discusses the work of art in terms of moral effect, conformity to literary "rules," or environmental influence, he has ceased to be an aesthetic critic, for he is attributing to the work a purpose beyond itself.

Kant's theories won immediate acceptance in Germany. A whole library of works on aesthetics, varying from brilliant to unintelligible, was published in Germany between 1790 and 1825. Fichte, Schelling, Solger, and Hegel discussed aesthetics from the point of view of the professional philosopher, while Schiller, August and Friedrich Schlegel, Jean-Paul Richter, and others wrote from the standpoint of the practicing artist or literary scholar. In 1817 Coleridge's *Biographia Literaria* was published in England, and aestheticism was launched on its international career.

During the nineteenth century several distinct varieties of aesthetic criticism emerged. The French aesthetes and their

English brethren converted the philosophical concept of "purposiveness without purpose" into the polemical slogan of "art for art's sake" and used it to attack the philistinism of their society. Gautier's preface to *Mademoiselle de Maupin* (1835) represents the first phase of French aestheticism. A later development, encouraged both by scientific scepticism and the romantic cult of the subjective, was impressionistic criticism. According to Kant, judgments of taste have "subjective universality." In the preface to *La Vie littéraire* (1888) Anatole France announced that beauty is wholly subjective. The critic, no matter how objective he pretends to be, can only record his impressions as he wanders entranced among the masterpieces. Like "art for art's sake," impressionism results from the exaggeration of one element of the aesthetic position at the expense of all the rest. It is a convenient strategy for witty authors like Anatole France and Oscar Wilde. Often the impressions of sensitive readers have proved useful to critics. But as a theory, impressionism is the denial that criticism is possible, and it has little to contribute to the organized investigation of literature.

The most important phase of French aestheticism was the symbolist movement initiated by Baudelaire. Among its sources are Swedenborg, from whom Baudelaire derived the theory of correspondences, Flaubert, whose obsession with technique anticipates Mallarmé, and Neo-Platonism. However, the decisive influence is Kantian, and most particularly the tradition extending from Coleridge to Poe and from Poe to Baudelaire. Poe's "Poetic Principle" and "Philosophy of Composition" provided Baudelaire with a way of harmonizing transcendental vision with a hardheaded, precise approach to poetic technique. Baudelaire's principal successors were Verlaine and Mallarmé. Following them, the symbolist aesthetic passed into the decadence of the *fin de siècle,* to be refurbished in the twentieth century by Yeats, T. S. Eliot, and Paul Valéry.

Toward the end of the nineteenth century what may be called "philosophic aestheticism" was being revived. Bergson and Croce were both professional philosophers who had been profoundly influenced by Hegel and through him, Kant. Working independently they applied their theories to literature, and both continue to have enthusiastic followers at the present time.

Among contemporary aesthetic critics the "new critics" are especially important. For them the aesthetic approach provides a justification for concentrating on the art work itself rather than its environment or the life of its author. Although there are almost as many varieties of "new criticism" as there are critics, most of them have drawn on the Kantian doctrine (usually *via* Coleridge) of organic unity, and they have been extremely successful in the field of the "close reading" of poems and prose works. Recently, a Jungian variety of aesthetic criticism has emerged. Jung's "collective unconscious" is a priori. Its archetypal myths and symbols are categories which make experience meaningful. Their function resembles that of the Kantian imagination. The alliance between Jung and aesthetic criticism has produced much stimulating discussion of archetypes, the mythic basis of genres such as tragedy and epic, and literary symbolism. It is fair to say that at present the influence of Jung has eclipsed that of Freud, and that Jung's popularity is evidence of the continuing vitality of the aesthetic tradition.

Kant's philosophy was, by his own admission, a reaction against the British empiricists of the eighteenth century. His *Critiques*, however, did little to diminish the prestige of empiricism in England and France. A host of discoveries in the physical and biological sciences appeared to vindicate empiricism philosophically; while inventions such as the steam engine and the power loom popularized science among those who stood to benefit from the industrial revolution. Dazzled by the success of the physical sciences, Bentham, Comte, Marx, Spencer, and others attempted to formulate a science of society. Their theories seem inadequate from the perspective of the twentieth century, but at the time they generated much enthusiasm.

Not unnaturally, many critics attempted to apply science to the analysis of literature. The varieties of scientific criticism have in common the assumption that the literary work can be "explained" by laws as rigorous in their way as the laws of chemistry or biology. Scientific criticism is thus deterministic. Its subspecies are produced by the fact that different critics invoke radically different kinds of "law." Sociological critics emphasize general cultural influences such as religion, politics, or economics. Literary historians emphasize sources and literary traditions.

Psychological critics emphasize biography, especially personal experiences affecting the author's mental outlook. Practicing novelists like Zola justify their work by showing that it conforms to approved scientific theory. There are, of course, many other variations. At times the critic moves from environment to art work, while at other times he may use the art work to explain the environment. And at times he may combine several methods. For example, most literary histories combine the sociological with the specifically literary approach.

Whatever its method, scientific criticism is committed to going beyond the literary work for its materials. Aesthetic criticism can be rigorous. It can even speak of "laws." But its laws are those operating within the literary work. Each work establishes its own laws, which have nothing to do with the "laws" of evolution or psychology, with literary rules, or with intentions, sources, or influences. The aesthetic and scientific schools are thus fundamentally opposed. The debate between them extends from the romantic period to the twentieth century, from the romantic attack on "scientism" to Croce's rejection of historical criticism and W. K. Wimsatt's critique of the intentional fallacy. At present, peaceful coexistence rather than reconciliation of differences seems the only way to end hostilities.

The earliest scientific criticism was sociological. It was based upon what passed for scientifically established cultural traits produced by such factors as heredity, climate, and social institutions. Giambattista Vico (*The New Science,* 1725), J. G. Herder (*Ideas on the History of Man,* 1784), and Montesquieu (*Spirit of the Laws,* 1748) anticipated various aspects of the method, but it was not until Madame de Staël's *Literature Considered in Its Relation to Social Institutions* (1800) that scientific criticism came into its own. Stendhal, Sainte-Beuve, and Ernest Renan contributed to the development of the method. Taine's *History of English Literature* (1864) provided a definitive formulation of its theory and an example of its application on a large scale.

Even before Taine's *History* Germany had been developing its own form of scientific criticism. The Grimm brothers, Verner, Scherer, and the "jung Grammatiker" laid the foundations of scientific linguistics. Their brilliant success encouraged the idea that criticism could be an exact science (*Strengwissenschaft*).

Between 1860 and 1910 German scholarship gained world-wide renown, and the German university system was widely imitated, especially in America. German-oriented scholarship was (and continues to be) committed to a heavy emphasis on philology in the narrow sense of linguistics and textual criticism. However it also entered the field of literary history. Among works illustrating the Germanic tradition are Boeckh's *Encyklopädie und Methodologie der Philologischen Wissenschaft* (1877), Skeat's seven-volume *Chaucer* (1894–97), Chambers' *The Medieval Stage* (1903), and Creizenach's *Geschichte des neuren Dramas* (1893–1916).

Two further developments occurred in French criticism after Taine. Both of them were encouraged by Darwin's *Origin of Species* (1859). Dissatisfied with the tendency of literary history to lose itself in a large number of vaguely defined cultural influences, Brunetière argued that literary influences should have priority over all others. Moreover, he asserted, literary influences are evolutionary. They form a sequence of "periods" initiated by significant literary "events" such as Pascal's *Provincial Letters* or Chateaubriand's *Genius of Christianity*. Brunetière applied his theory to a limited topic in *The Evolution of Literary Genres* (1890), and to general literary history in his *Manual of French Literature* (1897). Criticism of fiction also went through a scientific phase during the later nineteenth century. While literary historians emphasized the evolutionary aspect of Darwin's theory, Zola and his fellow Naturalists emphasized its mechanics. Naturalism assumes that man is the creature of forces over which he has little control. Beneath its civilized veneer society is a Darwinian jungle. Life is a struggle for survival in which the weak are inevitably losers. If the novelist is to hold the mirror up to life, he must be as dispassionate as the biologist dissecting a dead animal in the laboratory. Novels should be scientific experiments demonstrating the operation of natural law on the lives of the characters. Zola's *Experimental Novel* (1880) is a classic statement of the Naturalistic position.

Probably the most sensational forms of scientific criticism are Marxist and Freudian criticism. Marxist literary history is based on the assumption that literature, like all other aspects of a culture, is conditioned by the "mode of production" of its age.

Its postulates were formulated by Marx and Engels in the nineteenth century, but its chief works were written after 1920, usually by avowed Communists. Most of them are crude propaganda; however a few Marxists, like Christopher Caudwell, have shown genuine (if sporadic) insight. Freudian criticism has been considerably more successful. After a series of tentative starts extending from David Hartley's *Observations on Man* (1749) to William James and Havelock Ellis, the principles of clinical psychology were established by Freud in the early years of the twentieth century. Freud himself wrote essays applying psychology to poetic diction, characterization, plot structure, symbolism, and biography. Most later Freudian criticism has concentrated on the personal elements in the art object, and its major works have been literary biographies.

Today scientific criticism extends in a broad spectrum from philology, historical scholarship, and sociological criticism to history of ideas, history of genres and forms, biography, and Freudian criticism. It has frequently been guilty of excess and its practitioners have at times seemed hostile to aesthetic values, but its achievements far outweigh its deficiencies.

The humanistic tradition in criticism is harder to define than either the aesthetic or the scientific. Humanistic critics are often opposed on principle to systematic formulations of their beliefs. Perhaps the most typical features of humanistic criticism are its ideal of culture and its didactic tendency. Both of these are characteristic of renaissance humanism, but it would be false to equate renaissance and nineteenth-century attitudes. Nineteenth-century humanism is an attempt to cope with conditions peculiar to the age—the rise of science, the alienation of the artist, the emergence of mass culture, and the crisis produced by the decay of traditional values. Most humanists have been deeply interested in politics and education. They have advocated a strong state governed by an elite and sustained by an educational system based on the liberal arts. They have opposed aestheticism because of the excesses of the romantics and also because of its opposition to the ethical interpretation of literature. They have been equally hostile to scientific criticism on the grounds that it denies free will, considers ethical values illusory, and encourages a scholarship devoted to dead trivialities.

Perhaps because he lived before the pressures of nineteenth-century life had become acute, Goethe is the most attractive of the humanistic critics. His life and work set standards which have been touchstones for most later humanists. He was one of the first modern critics to condemn romanticism as a kind of sickness and to oppose to it the sweetness and light of classicism. Throughout his life he resisted the clamorous demands of nationalism. He was familiar with the great works of Italian, French, and English literature as well as the classics, and upheld the ideal of world literature against the growing tendency toward specialization in the literature of one age or nation. He believed that the artist should contribute to the moral health of society, but he did not allow this belief to blunt his sensitivity to the work of his contemporaries.

Among later humanistic critics Sainte-Beuve and Matthew Arnold seem closest to the spirit of Goethe. Charles Maurras and Irving Babbitt are in the humanistic tradition, but both men frequently allowed their reforming zeal to override their critical judgment. Tolstoy's *What is Art?* and (in certain respects) Nietzsche's *Birth of Tragedy* are examples of humanism run wild. In both the critic has become a messianic reformer who condemns contemporary art as a degenerate farce and summons writers to the promised land. Nietzsche's vision of Dionysian joy is, of course, poles apart from Tolstoy's ideal of piety, simplicity, and sincerity. However the difference in nirvanas is less significant than the similarity of the impulse which produced the visions. In the twentieth century it has been Marxists who most frequently have assumed the messianic stance. To their great embarrassment the Communist nirvana is open to inspection, whereas the nirvanas of Nietzsche and Tolstoy exist only in the world of the mind.

When humanism has avoided the messianic temptation, it has been a positive force in modern criticism. It has helped to correct the excesses of both scientific and aesthetic criticism. It has had a particularly constructive effect on education. During the early twentieth century, literary study tended to vacillate between extreme impressionism and pedantic Germanic scholarship. The humanists undertook to reform this situation and with considerable success. Both in Europe and the United States humanism continues to be an important force. It is therefore of considerable significance that Jacques Maritain has devoted his best critical work to reconciling aesthetic criticism with traditional Catholic values. Although not all readers agree that he has been successful, if he has, his achievement is bound to influence criticism in the future.

In the present volume aestheticians, scientific critics, and humanists speak for themselves. The selections fall in roughly chronological order, but this order has been modified to permit natural groupings of critics. The first section represents German criticism during its greatest age. Kant, Schelling, and Schiller illustrate the aesthetic position, while Goethe speaks for the humanists. The second section begins with Sainte-Beuve, whose work contributed to the evolution of both humanistic and scientific criticism. Taine, Brunetière, Zola, Marx, and Engels illustrate the ramifications of scientific criticism; while Tolstoy carries humanism to an unhumanistic extreme. In the third section the ramifications of aestheticism are illustrated by Gautier, Baudelaire, Verlaine, and Mallarmé among the artists, and Bergson and Croce among the philosophers. The fourth section contains selections from Nietzsche, Freud, and Jung, all of whom are interested in the irrational elements in literature; and the fifth section presents four diverse but typical twentieth-century critical statements by Charles Maurras, André Breton, Jean-Paul Sartre, and Jacques Maritain.

✿✿   ✿✿   ✿✿

A headnote accompanies each selection. The reader will find the following list a useful supplement to the works cited in the headnotes:

M. H. Abrams, *The Mirror and the Lamp* (New York, 1953); G. W. Allen and H. H. Clark, eds., *Literary Criticism: Pope to Croce* (New York, 1941); I. Babbitt, *Masters of Modern French Criticism* (Boston, 1912), and *Rousseau and Romanticism* (Boston, 1930); B. Bosanquet, *A History of Aesthetic* (New York, 1934); C. Brooks and W. K. Wimsatt, *Literary Criticism: a Short History* (New York, 1957); S. Hyman, *The Armed Vision* (New

York, 1948); A. Lehmann, *The Symbolist Aesthetic in France,* 1885–1895 (Oxford, 1950); G. Michaud, *Message poétique du symbolisme* (Paris, 1947); H. A. Needham, *Le développement de l'esthétique sociologique en France et en Angleterre au XIXe siècle* (Paris, 1926); M. Raymond, *From Baudelaire to Surrealism* (New York, 1949); G. Saintsbury, *A History of Criticism* (London, 1900–1904); F. Vial, *Idées et doctrines littéraires du XIXe siècle* (Paris, 1931); E. Vivas and M. Krieger, eds., *The Problems of Aesthetics* (New York, 1957); R. Wellek, *A History of Modern Criticism* (New Haven, 1955—first two volumes only); R. Wellek and A. Warren, *Theory of Literature* (New York, 1949).

Part I

GERMAN IDEALISM

Immanuel Kant

[1724–1804]

꧁

KANT'S "COPERNICAN REVOLUTION" in philosophy was initiated in
1781 with the publication of the *Critique of Pure Reason,* one of the
seminal books in the history of modern thought. In it, Kant examined
the conditions of empirical knowledge. In the *Critique of Practical
Reason* (1788) he examined the conditions of moral knowledge. The
Critique of Judgment (1790) considers the faculty which mediates
between pure and practical reason and is subdivided into aesthetic
judgment and teleological judgment. Despite its difficulty, Kant's
analysis of aesthetic judgment is a landmark in the history of modern
criticism.

In opposition to the British empirical philosophers, especially Locke
and Hume, Kant insisted that knowledge must begin with an understanding of the mind rather than of experience. Roughly speaking,
the mind is a receptor mechanism which must impose certain forms
or "categories" on the data which it receives before they can be perceived. These categories (*e.g.,* space and time) are a priori. They
exist prior to experience and, indeed, are the preconditions of experience. Combined with sense-data they produce the phenomenal world
(*Erscheinung,* literally *appearance*) which, in its totality, is called
Nature. Man is limited to knowledge of the phenomenal world and
of the necessary preconditions of its existence (transcendental knowledge). Everything beyond these limits is transcendent, hence un-
knowable. This includes the thing in itself (*Ding an sich,* that is,
reality) and the world of pure spirit, the Noumenal world. Statements about reality or pure spirit are conjectures which can neither
be verified nor disproved.

In Kant's system the imagination is the faculty which synthesizes
sense data; hence it is the "ground" of perception. Judgment (*Urteils-
kraft*) is the faculty which relates a perceived event or object to a
purpose. Teleological judgment looks beyond the objects for its purpose, as when the fall of a stone is related to the law of gravity or an act
of self-sacrifice to the concept of moral duty. Aesthetic judgment
finds the purpose of the object in the object itself, a concept suggested by the definition of beauty as "purposiveness without purpose"

3

(*Zweckmässigkeit ohne Zweck*). Thus aesthetic judgment is a unique way of knowing the phenomenal world. The art object, considered aesthetically, is devoid of any utilitarian function, whether of sense gratification, education (as in mnemonic poetry), or moral instruction. Judgments of taste are subjective—they cannot be verified by reference to ulterior systems—but they are also universal since the aesthetic sense is common to all men. Finally, since beauty is its own excuse for being, it becomes for Kant a symbol of morality.

Kant's influence may be observed in the present volume in the criticism of Schiller, Schelling, the French Symbolists, Croce, Bergson, and Maritain. Coleridge considered Kant his means of deliverance from the British empiricists. The *Biographia Literaria* has made Kant a living influence in British and American criticism down to the present time.

Kant's major works are readily available in English translation. His aesthetic is examined by H. Cassirer, *Commentary on Kant's Critique of Judgment* (London, 1938); B. Dunham and T. Greene, in *The Heritage of Kant* (Princeton, 1939); and I. Knox, *The Aesthetic Theories of Kant, Hegel, and Schopenhauer* (New York, 1936). For Kant's influence see especially R. Wellek, *Immanuel Kant in England, 1793–1838* (Princeton, 1931).

Sections I and II of the present selection are from the *Critique of Pure Reason*, trans. by John Watson, in *The Philosophy of Kant as Contained in Extracts from his own Writings* (Glasgow, 1901). The remaining selections are from *The Critique of Judgment*, trans. by J. H. Bernard (London, 1892). This translation is available in an inexpensive reprint in the Hafner Library of Classics (New York, 1951).

CRITIQUE OF PURE REASON

I. TRANSCENDENTAL AESTHETIC

SENSATION is the actual affection of our sensibility, or capacity of receiving impressions, by an object. The perception which refers itself to an object through sensation, is *empirical perception*. The undetermined object of such a perception is a *phenomenon* (Erscheinung).

That element in the phenomenon which corresponds to sensation I call the *matter*, while that element which makes it possible

that the various determinations of the phenomenon should be arranged in certain ways relatively to one another is its *form*. Now,
that without which sensations can have no order or form, cannot
itself be sensation. The matter of a phenomenon is given to us
entirely *a posteriori*, but its form must lie *a priori* in the mind,
and hence it must be capable of being considered by itself apart
from sensation.

This pure form of sensibility is also called *pure perception*.
Thus, if from the consciousness of a body, I separate all that the
understanding has thought into it, as substance, force, divisibil-
ity, etc., and all that is due to sensation, as impenetrability, hardness, colour, etc.; what is left over are extension and figure.
These, therefore, belong to pure perception, which exists in the
mind *a priori*, as a mere form of sensibility, even when no sensation or object of sense is actually present.

The science of all the *a priori* principles of sensibility I call
Transcendental Æsthetic, in contradistinction from the science
of the principles of pure thought, which I call *Transcendental
Logic*.

In Transcendental Æsthetic we shall first of all isolate sensibility, abstracting from all that the understanding contributes
through its conceptions, so that we may have nothing before us
but empirical perception. In the next place, we shall separate
from empirical perception all that belongs to sensation; when
there will remain only pure perception, or the mere form of
phenomena, the sole element that sensibility can yield *a priori*.
If this is done, it will be found that there are two pure forms of
sensible perception, which constitute principles of *a priori* knowledge, namely, Space and Time.

II. IMAGINATION

There must be something which makes the reproduction of
phenomena possible at all, something which is the *a priori* ground
of a necessary synthetic unity. That this is so, we may at once
see, if we reflect that phenomena are not things in themselves,
but are merely the play of our own ideas, and therefore at bottom
determinations of the inner sense. Now, if we can show that

even our purest *a priori* perceptions can yield knowledge, only in so far as they involve such a combination as makes a thorough-going synthesis of reproduction possible, we may conclude that this synthesis of imagination, being prior to all experience, rests upon *a priori* principles. We must then assume a pure transcendental synthesis as the necessary condition of all experience, for experience is impossible unless phenomena are capable of being reproduced. Now, if I draw a line in thought, or think of the time from one day to another, or even think of a certain number, it is plain that I must be conscious of the various determinations one after the other. But if the earlier determinations —the prior parts of the line, the antecedent moments of time, the units as they arise one after the other—were to drop out of my consciousness, and could not be reproduced when I passed on to the later determinations, I should never be conscious of a whole; and hence not even the simplest and most elementary idea of space or time could arise in my consciousness.

The synthesis of reproduction is therefore inseparably bound up with the synthesis of apprehension. And as the synthesis of apprehension is the transcendental ground of the possibility of all knowledge—of pure *a priori* as well as empirical knowl-edge—the reproductive synthesis of imagination belongs to the transcendental functions of the mind, and may therefore be called the transcendental faculty of imagination.

CRITIQUE OF JUDGMENT

III. TASTE IS DISINTERESTED

THE SATISFACTION which we combine with the representation of the existence of an object is called "interest." Such satisfaction always has reference to the faculty of desire, either as its deter-mining ground or as necessarily connected with its determining ground. Now when the question is if a thing is beautiful, we do not want to know whether anything depends or can depend on the existence of the thing, either for myself or for anyone else, but how we judge it by mere observation (intuition or reflection). If anyone asks me if I find that palace beautiful which I see before me, I may answer: I do not like things of that kind which are made merely to be stared at. Or I can answer like that Iroquois Sachem, who was pleased in Paris by nothing more than by the cook shops. Or again, after the manner of Rousseau, I may rebuke the vanity of the great who waste the sweat of the people on such superfluous things. In fine, I could easily convince myself that if I found myself on an uninhabited island without the hope of ever again coming among men, and could conjure up such a splendid building by my mere wish, I should not even give myself the trouble if I had a sufficiently comfortable hut. This may all be admitted and approved, but we are not now talking of this. We wish only to know if this mere representation of the object is accompanied in me with satisfaction, however indifferent I may be as regards the existence of the object of this representation. We easily see that, in saying it is *beautiful* and in showing that I have taste, I am concerned, not with that in which I depend on the existence of the object, but with that which I make out of this representation in myself. Everyone must admit that a judgment about beauty, in which the least interest mingles, is very partial and is not a pure judgment of taste. We must not be in the least prejudiced in favor of the existence of the things, but be quite indifferent in this respect, in order to play the judge in things of taste.

IV. TASTE AS THE JUDGMENT OF THE FORM OF PURPOSIVENESS

Every purpose, if it be regarded as a ground of satisfaction, always carries with it an interest—as the determining ground of the judgment—about the object of pleasure. Therefore no subjective purpose can lie at the basis of the judgment of taste. But also the judgment of taste can be determined by no representation of an objective purpose, i.e. of the possibility of the object itself in accordance with principles of purposive combination, and consequently by no concept of the good, because it is an aesthetical and not a cognitive judgment. It therefore has to do with no *concept* of the character and internal or external possibility of the object by means of this or that cause, but

merely with the relation of the representative powers to one
another, so far as they are determined by a representation.

Now this relation in the determination of an object as beautiful is bound up with the feeling of pleasure, which is declared
by the judgment of taste to be valid for everyone; hence a
pleasantness [merely] accompanying the representation can as
little contain the determining ground [of the judgment] as the
representation of the perfection of the object and the concept
of the good can. Therefore it can be nothing else than the subjective purposiveness in the representation of an object without
any purpose (either objective or subjective), and thus it is the
mere form of purposiveness in the representation by which an
object is *given* to us, so far as we are conscious of it, which constitutes the satisfaction that we without a concept judge to be
universally communicable; and, consequently, this is the determining ground of the judgment of taste.

V. VARIETY AND REGULARITY
IN JUDGMENTS OF TASTE

The regularity which leads to the concept of an object is
indeed the indispensable condition (*conditio sine qua non*) for
grasping the object in a single representation and determining
the manifold in its form. This determination is a purpose in
respect of cognition, and in reference to this it is always bound
up with satisfaction (which accompanies the execution of every,
even problematical, design). There is here, however, merely
the approval of the solution satisfying a problem, and not a free
and indefinite purposive entertainment of the mental powers
with what we call beautiful, where the understanding is at the
service of imagination, and not *vice versa*.

In a thing that is only possible by means of design—a building, or even an animal—the regularity consisting in symmetry
must express the unity of the intuition that accompanies the
concept of purpose, and this regularity belongs to cognition.
But where only a free play of the representative powers (under
the condition, however, that the understanding is to suffer no
shock thereby) is to be kept up, in pleasure gardens, room

decorations, all kinds of tasteful furniture, etc., regularity that shows constraint is avoided as much as possible. Thus in the English taste in gardens or in bizarre taste in furniture, the freedom of the imagination is pushed almost near to the grotesque, and in this separation from every constraint of rule we have the case where taste can display its greatest perfection in the enterprises of the imagination.

All stiff regularity (such as approximates to mathematical regularity) has something in it repugnant to taste; for our entertainment in the contemplation of it lasts for no length of time, but it rather, in so far as it has not expressly in view cognition or a definite practical purpose, produces weariness. On the other hand, that with which imagination can play in an unstudied and purposive manner is always new to us, and one does not get tired of looking at it. Marsden, in his description of Sumatra, makes the remark that the free beauties of nature surround the spectator everywhere and thus lose their attraction for him. On the other hand, a pepper garden, where the stakes on which this plant twines itself form parallel rows, had much attractiveness for him if he met with it in the middle of a forest. And he hence infers that wild beauty, apparently irregular, only pleases as a variation from the regular beauty of which one has seen enough. But he need only have made the experiment of spending one day in a pepper garden to have been convinced that, if the understanding has put itself in accordance with the order that it always needs by means of regularity, the object will not entertain for long—nay, rather it will impose a burdensome constraint upon the imagination. On the other hand, nature, which there is prodigal in its variety even to luxuriance, that is subjected to no constraint of artificial rules, can supply constant food for taste.

VI. A DEFINITION OF ART

(1) Art is distinguished from nature as doing (*facere*) is distinguished from acting or working generally (*agere*), and as the product or result of the former is distinguished as work (*opus*) from the working (*effectus*) of the latter.

By right we ought only to describe as art, production through freedom, i.e., through a will that places reason at the basis of its actions. For although we like to call the product of bees (regularly built cells of wax) a work of art, this is only by way of analogy; as soon as we feel that this work of theirs is based on no proper rational deliberation, we say that it is a product of nature (of instinct), and as art only ascribe it to their Creator.

If, as sometimes happens, in searching through a bog we come upon a bit of shaped wood, we do not say, this is a product of nature, but of art. Its producing cause has conceived a purpose to which the plank owes its form. Elsewhere too we should see art in everything which is made, so that a representation of it in its cause must have preceded its actual existence (as even in the case of the bees), though without the effect of it even being capable of being *thought*. But if we call anything absolutely a work of art, in order to distinguish it from a natural effect, we always understand by that a work of man.

(2) Art regarded as human skill differs from science (as *can* from *know*) as a practical faculty does from a theoretical, as technique does from theory (as mensuration from geometry). And so what we *can* do, as soon as we merely *know* what ought to be done and therefore are sufficiently cognizant of the desired effect, is not called art. Only that which a man, even if he knows it completely, may not therefore have the skill to accomplish belongs to art. . . .

(3) Art also differs from handicraft; the first is called "free," the other may be called "mercenary." We regard the first as if it could only prove purposive as play, i.e., as occupation that is pleasant in itself. But the second is regarded as if it could only be compulsorily imposed upon one as work, i.e., as occupation which is unpleasant (a trouble) in itself and which is only attractive on account of its effect (e.g. the wage). . . .

But it is not inexpedient to recall that, in all free arts, there is yet requisite something compulsory or, as it is called, mechanism, without which the spirit, which must be free in art and which alone inspires the work, would have no body and would evaporate altogether; e.g. in poetry there must be an accuracy and wealth of language, and also prosody and measure. [It is not inexpedient, I say, to recall this], for many modern educators

ich he is indebted to his genius does
has come by his ideas; and he has not
ke at pleasure or in accordance with
ate it to others in precepts that will
imilar products. (Hence it is probable
is derived from *genius*, that peculiar
irit given to a man at his birth, from
original ideas proceed.) (4) Nature, by
oes not prescribe rules to science but to
far as it is to be beautiful art.

ATIVE IMAGINATION

etical sense, is the name given to the ani-
the mind. But that by means of which
tes the soul, the material which it applies
is what puts the mental powers purposively
such a play as maintains itself and strength-
wers in their exercise.
that this principle is no other than the faculty
thetical ideas. And by an aesthetical idea I
representation of the imagination which oc-
ought, without however any definite thought,
being capable of being adequate to it; it conse-
be completely compassed and made intelligible
e easily see that it is the counterpart (pendant)
dea, which conversely is a concept to which no
epresentation of the imagination) can be adequate.
ation (as a productive faculty of cognition) is
in creating another nature, as it were, out of the
actual nature gives it. We entertain ourselves
experience becomes too commonplace, and by it
experience, always indeed in accordance with ana-
, but yet also in accordance with principles which
igher place in reason (laws, too, which are just as
us as those by which understanding comprehends
nature). Thus we feel our freedom from the law of
(which attaches to the empirical employment of

believe that the best way to produce a free art is to remove it from all constraint, and thus to change it from work into mere play.

VII. THE BEAUTIFUL IN ART

There is no science of the beautiful, but only a critique of it; and there is no such thing as beautiful science, but only beautiful art. For as regards the first point, if it could be decided scientifically, i.e. by proofs, whether a thing was to be regarded as beautiful or not, the judgment upon beauty would belong to science and would not be a judgment of taste. And as far as the second point is concerned, a science which should be beautiful as such is a nonentity. . . .

If art which is adequate to the *cognition* of a possible object performs the actions requisite therefor merely in order to make it actual, it is *mechanical* art; but if it has for its immediate design the feeling of pleasure, it is called *aesthetical* art. This is again either *pleasant* or *beautiful*. It is the first if its purpose is that the pleasure should accompany the representations [of the object] regarded as mere *sensations;* it is the second if they are regarded as *modes of cognition.*

Pleasant arts are those that are directed merely to enjoyment. Of this class are all those charming arts that can gratify a company at table, e.g. the art of telling stories in an entertaining way, of starting the company in frank and lively conversation, of raising them by jest and laugh to a certain pitch of merriment; when, as people say, there may be a great deal of gossip at the feast, but no one will be answerable for what he says, because they are only concerned with momentary entertainment, and not with any permanent material for reflection or subsequent discussion. . . .

On the other hand, beautiful art is a mode of representation which is purposive for itself and which, although devoid of [definite] purpose, yet furthers the culture of the mental powers in reference to social communication.

The universal communicability of a pleasure carries with it in its very concept that the pleasure is not one of enjoyment, from mere sensation, but must be derived from reflection; and thus aesthetical art, as the art of beauty, has for standard the reflective judgment and not sensation.

VIII. BEAUTIFUL ART RESEMBLES NATURE

In a product of beautiful art, we must become conscious that it is art and not nature; but yet the purposiveness in its form must seem to be as free from all constraint of arbitrary rules as if it were a product of mere nature. On this feeling of freedom in the play of our cognitive faculties, which must at the same time be purposive, rests that pleasure which alone is universally communicable, without being based on concepts. Nature is beautiful because it looks like art, and art can only be called beautiful if we are conscious of it as art while yet it looks like nature.

For whether we are dealing with natural or with artificial beauty, we can say generally: *That is beautiful which pleases in the mere act of judging it* (not in the sensation of it or by means of a concept). Now art has always a definite design of producing something. But if this something were bare sensation (something merely subjective), which is to be accompanied with pleasure, the product would please in the act of judgment only by mediation of sensible feeling. And again, if the design were directed toward the production of a definite object, then, if this were attained by art, the object would only please by means of concepts. But in both cases the art would not please *in the mere act of judging*, i.e. it would not please as beautiful but as mechanical.

Hence the purposiveness in the product of beautiful art, although it is designed, must not seem to be designed, i.e. beautiful art must *look* like nature, although we are conscious of it as art. But a product of art appears like nature when, although its agreement with the rules, according to which alone the product can become what it ought to be, is *punctiliously* observed, yet this is not *painfully* apparent; [the form of the schools does not obtrude itself]—it shows no trace of the rule

author of a product for wh
not know himself how he
the power to devise the
a plan, and to communi
enable them to produce
that the word "genius"
guiding and guardian s
whose suggestion these
the medium of genius,
art, and to it only in s

a
be
Ge
whi

W
merel
we are
to be
already
word here
as arts of

For ever
first instance
as possible.
the judgment
any rule whic
therefore has a
product is possi
the rule accordin
since at the same t
some precedent ru
mony of its facultie
only possible as a pr

We thus see (1) th
which no definite rule
what can be learned b
first property. (2) But
sense, its products must
consequently ought not
serve as a standard or rule
not describe or indicate sci
products, but it gives the ru

X. CRE

Spirit, in an aesth
mating principle of
this principle anim
to that [purpose],
into swing, i.e. int
ens the mental p
Now I maintain
of presenting *aes*
understand that
casions much th
i.e. any *concept*
quently cannot
by language.
of a *rational*
intuition (or r
The imagi
very powerfu
material tha
with it whe
we remold
logical law
occupy a
natural to
empirical
associatio

imagination), so that the material supplied to us by nature in accordance with this law can be worked up into something different which surpasses nature.

Such representations of the imagination we may call *ideas,* partly because they at least strive after something which lies beyond the bounds of experience and so seek to approximate to a presentation of concepts of reason (intellectual ideas), thus giving to the latter the appearance of objective reality, but especially because no concept can be fully adequate to them as internal intuitions. The poet ventures to realize to sense, rational ideas of invisible beings, the kingdom of the blessed, hell, eternity, creation, etc.; or even if he deals with things of which there are examples in experience—e.g. death, envy and all vices, also love, fame, and the like—he tries, by means of imagination, which emulates the play of reason in its quest after a maximum, to go beyond the limits of experience and to present them to sense with a completeness of which there is no example in nature. This is properly speaking the art of the poet, in which the faculty of aesthetical ideas can manifest itself in its entire strength. But this faculty, considered in itself, is properly only a talent (of the imagination).

XI. REMARKS ON POETRY

We may describe beauty in general (whether natural or artificial) as the expression of aesthetical ideas; only that in beautiful art this idea must be occasioned by a concept of the object, while in beautiful nature the mere reflection upon a given intuition, without any concept of what the object is to be, is sufficient for the awakening and communicating of the idea of which that object is regarded as the expression.

If, then, we wish to make a division of the beautiful arts, we cannot choose a more convenient principle, at least tentatively, than the analogy of art with the mode of expression of which men avail themselves in speech, in order to communicate to one another as perfectly as possible not merely their concepts but also their sensations. This is done by *word, deportment,* and *tone* (articulation, gesticulation, and modulation). It is only by the combination of these three kinds of expression that communication between the speaker [and his hearers] can be complete. For thus thought, intuition, and sensation are transmitted to others simultaneously and conjointly.

There are, therefore, only three kinds of beautiful arts: the arts of *speech*, the *formative* arts, and the art of the *play of sensations* (as external sensible impression).[1] . . .

The arts of speech are *rhetoric* and *poetry*. *Rhetoric* is the art of carrying on a serious business of the understanding as if it were a free play of the imagination; *poetry*, the art of conducting a free play of the imagination as if it were a serious business of the understanding.

The *orator*, then, promises a serious business, and in order to entertain his audience conducts it as if it were a mere *play* with ideas. The *poet* merely promises an entertaining play with ideas, and yet it has the same effect upon the understanding as if he had only intended to carry on its business. The combination and harmony of both cognitive faculties, sensibility and understanding, which cannot dispense with each other but which yet cannot well be united without constraint and mutual prejudice, must appear to be undesigned and so to be brought about by themselves; otherwise it is not *beautiful* art. Hence, all that is studied and anxious must be avoided in it, for beautiful art must be free art in a double sense. It is not a work like a mercenary employment, the greatness of which can be judged according to a definite standard, which can be attained or paid for; and again, though the mind is here occupied, it feels itself thus contented and aroused without looking to any other purpose (independently of reward). . . .

Of all the arts *poetry* (which owes its origin almost entirely to genius and will least be guided by precept or example) maintains the first rank. It expands the mind by setting the imagination at liberty and by offering, within the limits of a given concept, amid the unbounded variety of possible forms accordant therewith, that which unites the presentment of this concept

---

[1] The arts of speech are rhetoric and poetry; the formative arts are subdivided into the plastic arts (sculpture and architecture) and painting; and the arts dealing with "play of sensations" are music and "the art of color." (Ed.)

with a wealth of thought to which no verbal expression is completely adequate, and so rising aesthetically to ideas. It strengthens the mind by making it feel its faculty—free, spontaneous, and independent of natural determination—of considering and judging nature as a phenomenon in accordance with aspects which it does not present in experience either for sense or understanding, and therefore of using it on behalf of, and as a sort of schema for, the supersensible. It plays with illusion, which it produces at pleasure, but without deceiving by it; for it declares its exercise to be mere play, which however can be purposively used by the understanding. Rhetoric, in so far as this means the art of persuasion, i.e. of deceiving by a beautiful show (*ars oratoria*), and not mere elegance of speech (eloquence and style), is a dialectic which borrows from poetry only so much as is needful to win minds to the side of the orator before they have formed a judgment and to deprive them of their freedom. . . .

XII. BEAUTY AS THE SYMBOL OF MORALITY

Intuitions are always required to establish the reality of our concepts. If the concepts are empirical, the intuitions are called *examples*. If they are pure concepts of understanding, the intuitions are called *schemata*. . . .

All *hypotyposis* (presentation, *subjectio sub adspectum*), or sensible illustration, is twofold. It is either *schematical*, when to a concept comprehended by the understanding the corresponding intuition is given, or it is *symbolical*. In the latter case, to a concept only thinkable by the reason, to which no sensible intuition can be adequate, an intuition is supplied with which accords a procedure of the judgment analogous to what it observes in schematism, i.e. merely analogous to the rule of this procedure, not to the intuition itself, consequently to the form of reflection merely and not to its content.

There is a use of the word *symbolical* that has been adopted by modern logicians which is misleading and incorrect, i.e. to speak of the *symbolical* mode of representation as if it were opposed to the *intuitive*, for the symbolical is only a mode of the

intuitive. The latter (the intuitive, that is), may be divided
into the *schematical* and the *symbolical* modes of representation.
Both are hypotyposes, i.e. presentations (*exhibitiones*), not mere
characterizations or designations of concepts by accompanying
sensible signs which contain nothing belonging to the intuition
of the object and only serve as a means for reproducing the
concepts, according to the law of association of the imagination,
and consequently in a subjective point of view. These are either
words or visible (algebraical, even mimetical) signs, as mere
expressions for concepts.

All intuitions which we supply to concepts *a priori* are therefore either *schemata* or *symbols,* of which the former contain
direct, the latter indirect, presentations of the concept. The
former do this demonstratively; the latter by means of an
analogy (for which we avail ourselves even of empirical intuitions) in which the judgment exercises a double function, first
applying the concept to the object of a sensible intuition, and
then applying the mere rule of the reflection made upon that
intuition to a quite different object of which the first is only the
symbol. Thus a monarchical state is represented by a living
body if it is governed by national laws, and by a mere machine
(like a hand mill) if governed by an individual absolute will;
but in both cases only *symbolically.* For between a despotic
state and a hand mill there is, to be sure, no similarity; but
there is a similarity in the rules according to which we reflect
upon these two things and their causality. This matter has not
been sufficiently analyzed hitherto, for it deserves a deeper
investigation; but this is not the place to linger over it. . . .

Now I say the beautiful is the symbol of the morally good,
and that it is only in this respect (a reference which is natural
to every man and which every man postulates in others as a
duty) that it gives pleasure with a claim for the agreement
of everyone else. By this the mind is made conscious of a certain
ennoblement and elevation above the mere sensibility to pleasure received through sense, and the worth of others is estimated
in accordance with a like maxim of their judgment. That is the
intelligible to which, as pointed out in the preceding paragraph,
taste looks, with which our higher cognitive faculties are in
accord, and without which a downright contradiction would

arise between their nature and the claims made by taste. In this faculty the judgment does not see itself, as in empirical judging, subjected to a heteronomy of empirical laws; it gives the law to itself in respect of the objects of so pure a satisfaction, just as the reason does in respect of the faculty of desire. . . .

A reference to this analogy is usual even with the common understanding [of men], and we often describe beautiful objects of nature or art by names that seem to put a moral appreciation at their basis. We call buildings or trees majestic and magnificent, landscapes laughing and gay; even colors are called innocent, modest, tender, because they excite sensations which have something analogous to the consciousness of the state of mind brought about by moral judgments. Taste makes possible the transition, without any violent leap, from the charm of sense to habitual moral interest, as it represents the imagination in its freedom as capable of purposive determination for the understanding, and so teaches us to find even in objects of sense a free satisfaction apart from any charm of sense.

Friedrich Wilhelm Joseph von Schelling

[1775–1854]

ᴇᴪᴖ᷎ᴪᴖ

Fʀɪᴇᴅʀɪᴄʜ Sᴄʜᴇʟʟɪɴɢ learned Kantian philosophy from Fichte. His principal works are *Ideas for a Philosophy of Nature* (1797) and *System of Transcendental Idealism* (1800). Today he is considered a sentimentalizer of Kant. He taught that nature is a vital, organic whole which can be known by aesthetic intuition. His "nature philosophy" (*Naturphilosophie*) has pantheistic tendencies and betrays the influence of Spinoza and the mystics. However, it made the artist a leader in the quest for reality, and it appeared to rescue nature from the limbo of the *Ding an sich*. For both reasons Schelling was immensely popular among romantic artists. Chapter XII of Coleridge's *Biographia Literaria* is a close paraphrase of sections of Schelling's *System*, and his "On Poesy or Art" is indebted to "On the Relation of the Plastic Arts to Nature," which Schelling delivered as a lecture to the Royal Academy of Munich on October 12, 1806.

Translated selections from Schelling are available in D. S. Robinson, ed., *An Anthology of Modern Philosophy* (New York, 1931). For comment see: E. Hirsch, *Wordsworth and Schelling* (New Haven, 1960); H. Knittermeyer, *Schelling und die Romantische Schule* (Munich, 1929). The debt of Coleridge to Schelling is stressed by Herbert Read, *The True Voice of Feeling* (London, 1953).

The present selections are from "On the Relation of the Plastic Arts to Nature," trans. by J. Elliott Cabot, in *The German Classics* (New York, 1913), V, 106–36.

ON THE RELATION OF THE PLASTIC ARTS TO NATURE

I. ART AND IMITATION

Pʟᴀsᴛɪᴄ ᴀʀᴛ, according to the most ancient expression, is silent Poetry. The inventor of this definition no doubt meant thereby that the former, like the latter, is to express spiritual thoughts—conceptions whose source is the soul; only not by speech, but, like silent Nature, by shape, by form, by corporeal, independent works.

Plastic Art, therefore, evidently stands as a uniting link between the soul and Nature, and can be apprehended only in the living centre of both. Indeed, since Plastic Art has its relation to the soul in common with every other art, and particularly with Poetry, that by which it is connected with Nature, and, like Nature, a productive force, remains as its sole peculiarity; so that to this alone can a theory relate which shall be satisfactory to the understanding, and helpful and profitable to Art itself.

We hope, therefore, in considering Plastic Art in relation to its true prototype and original source, Nature, to be able to contribute something new to its theory—to give some additional exactness or clearness to the conceptions of it; but, above all, to set forth the coherence of the whole structure of Art in the light of a higher necessity.

But has not Science always recognized this relation? Has not indeed every theory of modern times taken its departure from this very position, that Art should be the imitator of Nature? Such has indeed been the case. But what should this broad general proposition profit the artist, when the notion of Nature is of such various interpretation, and when there are almost as many differing views of it as there are various modes of life? Thus, to one, Nature is nothing more than the lifeless aggregate of an indeterminable crowd of objects, or the space in which, as in a vessel, he imagines things placed; to another, only the soil from which he draws his nourishment and support; to the inspired seeker alone, the holy, ever-creative original energy of the world, which generates and busily evolves all things out of itself.

The proposition would indeed have a high significance, if it taught Art to emulate this creative force; but the sense in which it was meant can scarcely be doubtful to one acquainted with the universal condition of Science at the time when it was first brought forward. Singular enough that the very persons who denied all life to Nature should set it up for imitation in Art! To them might be applied the words of a profound writer: [1] "Your lying philosophy has put Nature out of the way; and why do you call upon us to imitate her? Is it that you may renew the pleasure by perpetrating the same violence on the disciples of Nature?" . . . .

Nor was there any change in the main view of the relation of Art to Nature, even when the unsatisfactoriness of the principle began to be more generally felt; no change, even by the new views and new knowledge so nobly established by John Winckelmann.[2] He indeed restored to the soul its full efficiency in Art, and raised it from its unworthy dependence into the realm of spiritual freedom. Powerfully moved by the beauty of form in the works of antiquity, he taught that the production of ideal Nature, of Nature elevated above the Actual, together with the expression of spiritual conceptions, is the highest aim of Art. . . .

Who can say that Winckelmann had not penetrated into the highest beauty? But with him it appeared in its dissevered elements only: on the one side as beauty in idea, and flowing out from the soul; on the other, as beauty of forms.

But what is the efficient link that connects the two? Or by what power is the soul created together with the body, at once and as if with one breath? If this lies not within the power of Art, as of Nature, then it can create nothing whatever. This vital connecting link, Winckelmann did not determine; he did not teach how, from the idea, forms can be produced. Thus Art went over to that method which we would call the retrograde, since it strives from the form to come at the essence. But not thus is the Unlimited reached; it is not attainable by mere enhancement of the Limited. Hence, such works as have had their beginning in form, with all elaborateness on that side, show, in token of their origin, an incurable want at the very point where we expect the consummate, the essential, the final. The miracle by which the Limited should be raised to the Unlimited, the human

---

[1] J. G. Hamann, *Hellenistische Briefe*, I, 189.

[2] Johann Winckelmann (1717–1768), German archeologist and art historian whose writing on classical art influenced Schelling, Schiller, Goethe, and other German romantics. Schelling's concept of grace in art (below, pp. 26–28) is influenced by Winckelmann's *Reflections on the Painting and Sculpture of the Greeks: With . . . An Essay on Grace in Works of Art* (Eng. trans. by Fuselli, 1787). (Ed.)

become divine, is wanting; the magic circle is drawn, but the spirit that it should inclose, appears not, being disobedient to the call of him who thought a creation possible through mere form.

II. IDEALIZING ART

It was long ago perceived that, in Art, not everything is performed with consciouness; that, with the conscious activity, an unconscious action must combine; and that it is of the perfect unity and mutual interpretation of the two that the highest in Art is born.

Works that want this seal of unconscious science are recognized by the evident absence of life self-supported and independent of the producer; as, on the contrary, where this acts, Art imparts to its work, together with the utmost clearness to the understanding, that unfathomable reality wherein it resembles a work of Nature.

It has often been attempted to make clear the position of the artist in regard to Nature, by saying that Art, in order to be such, must first withdraw itself from Nature, and return to it only in the final perfection. The true sense of this saying, it seems to us, can be no other than this—that in all things in Nature, the living idea shows itself only blindly active; were it so also in the artist, he would be in nothing distinct from Nature. But, should he attempt consciously to subordinate himself altogether to the Actual, and render with servile fidelity the already existing, he would produce *larvæ*, but no works of Art. He must therefore withdraw himself from the product, from the creature, but only in order to raise himself to the creative energy, spiritually seizing the same. Thus he ascends into the realm of pure ideas; he forsakes the creature, to regain it with thousandfold interest, and in this sense certainly to return to Nature. This spirit of Nature working at the core of things, and speaking through form and shape as by symbols only, the artist must certainly follow with emulation; and only so far as he seizes this with genial imitation has he himself produced anything genuine. For works produced by aggregation, even of forms beautiful in themselves, would still be destitute of all beauty, since that, through which the work on the whole is truly beautiful, cannot be mere form. It is above form—it is Essence, the Universal, the look and expression of the indwelling spirit of Nature.

Now it can scarcely be doubtful what is to be thought of the so-called idealizing of Nature in Art, so universally demanded. This demand seems to arise from a way of thinking, according to which not Truth, Beauty, Goodness, but the contrary of all these, is the Actual. Were the Actual indeed opposed to Truth and Beauty, it would be necessary for the artist, not to elevate or idealize it, but to get rid of and destroy it, in order to create something true and beautiful. But how should it be possible for anything to be actual except the True; and what is Beauty, if not full, complete Being?

What higher aim, therefore, could Art have, than to represent that which in Nature actually *is?* Or how should it undertake to excel so-called actual Nature, since it must always fall short of it?

III. PARTICULARITY AND FORM

Determinateness of form is in Nature never a negation, but ever an affirmation. Commonly, indeed, the shape of a body seems a confinement; but could we behold the creative energy it would reveal itself as the measure that this energy imposes upon itself, and in which it shows itself a truly intelligent force; for in everything is the power of self-rule allowed to be an excellence, and one of the highest.

In like manner most persons consider the particular in a negative manner—*i. e.*, as that which is not the whole or all. Yet no particular exists by means of its limitation, but through the indwelling force with which it maintains itself as a particular Whole, in distinction from the Universe.

This force of particularity, and thus also of individuality, showing itself as vital character, the negative conception of it is necessarily followed by an unsatisfying and false view of the characteristic in Art. Lifeless and of intolerable hardness would be the Art that should aim to exhibit the empty shell or limitation of the individual. Certainly we desire to see not merely the individual, but, more than this, its vital Idea. But if the artist has seized the inward creative spirit and essence of the Idea, and sets this forth, he makes the individual a world in itself, a class, an eternal prototype; and he who has grasped the essential character needs not to fear hardness and severity, for these are the conditions of life. Nature, that in her completeness appears as the utmost benignity, we see, in each particular, aiming even primarily and principally at severity, seclusion and reserve. As the whole creation is the work of the utmost externization and renunciation [*Entäusserung*], so the artist must first deny himself and descend into the Particular, without shunning isolation, nor the pain, the anguish of Form.

Nature, from her first works, is throughout characteristic; the energy of fire, the splendor of light, she shuts up in hard stone, the tender soul of melody in severe metal; even on the threshold of Life, and already meditating organic shape, she sinks back overpowered by the might of Form, into petrifaction.

The life of the plant consists in still receptivity, but in what exact and severe outline is this passive life inclosed! In the animal kingdom the strife between Life and Form seems first properly to begin; her first works Nature hides in hard shells, and, where these are laid aside, the animated world attaches itself again through its constructive impulse to the realm of crystallization. Finally she comes forward more boldly and freely, and vital, important characteristics show themselves, being the same through whole classes. Art, however, cannot begin so far down as Nature. Though Beauty is spread everywhere, yet there are various grades in the appearance and unfolding of the Essence, and thus of Beauty. But Art demands a certain fulness, and desires not to strike a single note or tone, nor even a detached accord, but at once the full symphony of Beauty.

Art, therefore, prefers to grasp immediately at the highest and most developed, the human form. For since it is not given it to embrace the immeasurable whole, and as in all other creatures only single fulgurations, in Man alone full entire Being appears without abatement, Art is not only permitted but required

to see the sum of Nature in Man alone. But precisely on this
account—that she here assembles all in one point—Nature repeats her whole multiformity, and pursues again in a narrower
compass the same course that she had gone through in her wide
circuit.

Here, therefore, arises the demand upon the artist first to be
true and faithful in detail, in order to come forth complete and
beautiful in the whole. Here he must wrestle with the creative
spirit of Nature (which in the human world also deals out character and stamp in endless variety), not in weak and effeminate,
but stout and courageous conflict.

Persevering exercise in the study of that by virtue of which
the characteristic in things is a positive principle, must preserve
him from emptiness, weakness, inward inanity, before he can
venture to aim, by ever higher combination and final melting together of manifold forms, to reach the extremest beauty in works
uniting the highest simplicity with infinite meaning.

Only through the perfection of form can Form be made to
disappear; and this is certainly the final aim of Art in the Characteristic. But as the apparent harmony that is even more easily
reached by the empty and frivolous than by others, is yet inwardly vain; so in Art the quickly attained harmony of the exterior, without inward fulness. And if it is the part of theory and
instruction to oppose the spiritless copying of beautiful forms,
especially must they oppose the tendency toward an effeminate
characterless Art, which gives itself, indeed, higher names, but
therewith only seeks to hide its incapacity to fulfill the fundamental conditions.

IV. THE EVOLUTION OF THE GRACEFUL
IN ART

In Nature and Art the Essence strives first after actualization,
or exhibition of itself in the Particular. Thus in each the utmost
severity is manifested at the commencement; for without bound,
the boundless could not appear; without severity, gentleness
could not exist; and if unity is to be perceptible, it can only be

through particularity, detachment, and opposition. In the beginning, therefore, the creative spirit shows itself entirely lost in the Form, inaccessibly shut up, and even in its grandeur still harsh. But the more it succeeds in uniting its entire fulness in one product, the more it gradually relaxes from its severity; and where it has fully developed the form, so as to rest contented and self-collected in it, it seems to become cheerful and begins to move in gentle lines. This is the period of its fairest maturity and blossom, in which the pure vessel has arrived at perfection; the spirit of Nature becomes free from its bonds, and feels its relationship to the soul. By a gentle morning blush stealing over the whole form, the coming soul announces itself; it is not yet present, but everything prepares for its reception by the delicate play of gentle movements; the rigid outlines melt and temper themselves into flexibility; a lovely essence, neither sensuous nor spiritual, but which cannot be grasped, diffuses itself over the form, and intwines itself with every outline, every vibration of the frame.

This essence, not to be seized, as we have already remarked, but yet perceptible to all, is what the language of the Greeks designated by the name *Charis,* ours as Grace.

Wherever, in a fully developed form, Grace appears, the work is complete on the side of Nature; nothing more is wanting; all demands are satisfied. Here, already, soul and body are in complete harmony; Body is Form, Grace is Soul, although not Soul in itself, but the Soul of Form, or the Soul of Nature.

Art may linger, and remain stationary at this point; for already, on one side at least, its whole task is finished. The pure image of Beauty arrested at this point is the Goddess of Love.

But the beauty of the Soul in itself, joined to sensuous Grace, is the highest apotheosis of Nature. . . .

For the representation of the Soul there are again gradations in Art, according as it is joined with the merely Characteristic, or in visible union with the Charming and Graceful.

Who perceives not already, in the tragedies of Æschylus, the presence of that lofty morality which is predominant in the works of Sophocles? But in the former it is enveloped in a bitter rind, and passes less into the whole work, since the bond of sensuous Grace is still wanting. But out of this severity, and the still rude charms of earlier Art, could proceed the grace of Sophocles, and with it the complete fusion of the two elements, which leaves us doubtful whether it is more moral or sensuous Grace that enchants us in the works of this poet.

The same is true of the plastic productions of the early and severe style, in comparison with the gentleness of the later.

If Grace, besides being the transfiguration of the spirit of Nature, is also the medium of connection between moral Goodness and sensuous Appearance, it is evident how Art must tend from all points toward it as its centre. This Beauty, which results from the perfect inter-penetration of moral Goodness and sensuous Grace, seizes and enchants us when we meet it, with the force of a miracle. For, whilst the spirit of Nature shows itself everywhere else independent of the Soul, and, indeed, in a measure opposed to it, here, it seems, as if by voluntary accord, and the inward fire of divine love, to melt into union with it; the remembrance of the fundamental unity of the essence of Nature and the essence of the Soul comes over the beholder with sudden clearness—the conviction that all antagonism is only apparent, that Love is the bond of all things, and pure Goodness the foundation and substance of the whole Creation.

Here Art, as it were, transcends itself, and again becomes means only. On this summit sensuous Grace becomes in turn only the husk and body of a higher life; what was before a whole is treated as a part, and the highest relation of Art and Nature is reached in this—that it makes Nature the medium of manifesting the soul which it contains.

V. THE TASK OF CONTEMPORARY ART

The requirement that Art, like everything living, should commence from the first rudiments, and, to renew its youth, constantly return to them, may seem a hard doctrine to an age that has so often been assured that it has only to take from works of Art already in existence the most consummate Beauty, and thus, as at a step, to reach the final goal. Have we not already the Excellent, the Perfect? How then should we return to the rudimentary and unformed?

Had the great founders of modern Art [3] thought thus, we should never have seen their miracles. Before them also stood the creations of the ancients, round statues and works in relief, which they might have transferred immediately to their canvas. But such an appropriation of a Beauty not self-won, and therefore unintelligible, would not satisfy an artistic instinct that aimed throughout at the fundamental, and from which the Beautiful was again to create itself with free original energy. They were not afraid, therefore, to appear simple, artless, dry, beside those exalted ancients; nor to cherish Art for a long time in the undistinguished bud, until the period of Grace had arrived. . . .

But what prospect does the present time offer for an Art springing from a vigorous germ, and growing up from the root? For it is in a great measure dependent on the character of its time; and who would promise the approbation of the present time to such earnest beginnings, when Art, on the one hand, scarcely obtains equal consideration with other instruments of prodigal luxury, and, on the other, artists and amateurs, with entire want of ability to grasp Nature, praise and demand the Ideal?

Art springs only from that powerful striving of the inmost powers of the heart and the spirit, which we call Inspiration. Everything that from difficult or small beginnings has grown up to great power and height, owes its growth to Inspiration. Thus spring empires and states, thus arts and sciences. But it is not the power of the individual that accomplishes this, but the Spirit alone, that diffuses itself over all. For Art especially is dependent on the tone of the public mind, as the more delicate plants on atmosphere and weather; it needs a general enthusiasm for Sublimity and Beauty, like that which, in the time of the Medici, as a warm breath of spring, called forth at once and together all those great spirits. . . .

To different ages are given different inspirations. Can we expect none for this age, since the new world now forming itself, as it exists in part already outwardly, in part inwardly and in the hearts of men, can no longer be measured by any standard of previous opinion, and since everything, on the contrary, loudly demands higher standards and an entire renovation?

[3] *i.e.,* Giotto and his immediate successors. (Ed.)

Should not the sense to which Nature and History have more livingly unfolded themselves, restore to Art also its great arguments? The attempt to draw sparks from the ashes of the Past, and fan them again into universal flame, is a vain endeavor. Only a revolution in the ideas themselves is able to raise Art from its exhaustion; only new Knowledge, new Faith, can inspire it for the work by which it can display, in a renewed life, a splendor like the past.

Johann Friedrich von Schiller

[1759–1805]

◆◈◆

T. S. ELIOT's BELIEF that criticism written by successful poets deserves special consideration is particularly appropriate for Schiller. One of the greatest German writers, Schiller achieved success in lyric poetry, history, and verse drama. His deep interest in philosophy is apparent in his poetry and overflowed in a series of critical prefaces, essays, and speculative works on the nature of art, not to mention his perennially fascinating correspondence with Goethe. Perhaps his most famous critical work is the essay "On Naive and Sentimental Poetry" (1795) in which he attempts to differentiate between the type of genius represented by Homer and Goethe, a genius which imitates nature directly without the need of philosophical analysis, and the genius of modern poets like himself who tend to reflect on and idealize their materials. Other significant essays include "The Ground of our Pleasure in Tragic Subjects" (1792), "On the Sublime" and "On the Pathetic" (1793), and "On Grace and Dignity" (1794), in which the influences of Winckelmann and of Schiller's own didactic tendencies are apparent.

Schiller's most considered statement, and ultimately his most influential one, is his *Letters on the Aesthetic Education of Man* (1793–95). The aesthetic faculty becomes for Schiller an outlet for man's desire for freedom. Like Kant, Schiller believed that beauty is a unique category of experience, unrelated to the determinate laws of nature and to the equally determinate laws of morality, Kant's categorical imperatives. The phenomenal world is a fusion of the formalizing impulse of the mind (*Formtrieb*) and the mind's receptivity to matter (*Stofftrieb*). The aesthetic experience is a free play of the imagination with and in the world of appearance (*Freiheit in der Erscheinung*), and the impulse generating this activity is the play-impulse (*Spieltrieb*). The play impulse is the expression of man's humanity. Its result is a purified form of joy in life, and it acts as a civilizing force in human culture.

Schiller's influence on Goethe has always been recognized. Although his influence on later writers has not been traced in detail, it has persisted. Matthew Arnold used Schiller's concept of artistic joy to explain the suppression of *Empedocles* in the *Preface* to the 1853 edition of his poems. The idea of art as play has frequently been revived, recently in Johan Huizinga's *Homo Ludens*.

Schiller's aesthetic and critical essays are available in the first volume of *The Works of Schiller,* ed. Dole (Boston, 1902). See also *Letters on the Aesthetic Education of Man,* trans. and intro. by Reginald Snell (New Haven, 1954), and *Selections from the Correspondence between Schiller and Goethe,* ed. J. Robertson (Boston, 1898). For comment see: V. Basch, *La Poétique de Schiller* (Paris, 1911); W. Bolze, *Schillers philosophische Begründung der Aesthetik der Tragödie* (Leipzig, 1913); F. Ewen, *The Prestige of Schiller in England, 1788–1859* (New York, 1932); R. Weirich, *Schillers Auffassung von der Kunst . . . und ihre Bedeutung für die Französische Literatur des 19. und 20. Jahrhunderts* (Wurzburg, 1936); W. Witte, *Schiller* (Oxford, 1949).

The present selections are from the translation of *Letters on the Aesthetic Education of Man* in the Dole *Works of Schiller,* cited above.

LETTERS ON THE AESTHETIC EDUCATION OF MAN

I. GREEK VS. MODERN CULTURE

AT THE PERIOD of Greek culture, which was an awakening of the powers of the mind, the senses and the spirit had no distinctly separated property; no division had yet torn them asunder, leading them to partition in a hostile attitude, and to mark off their limits with precision. Poetry had not as yet become the adversary of wit, nor had speculation abused itself by passing into quibbling. In cases of necessity both poetry and wit could exchange parts, because they both honoured truth only in their special way. However high might be the flight of reason, it drew matter in a loving spirit after it, and while sharply and stiffly defining it, never mutilated what it touched. It is true the Greek mind displaced humanity, and recast it on a magnified scale in the glorious circle of its gods; but it did this not by dissecting human nature, but by giving it fresh combinations, for the whole of human nature was represented in each of the gods. How different is the course followed by us moderns! We also displace and magnify individuals to form the image of the species, but we do this in a fragmentary way, not by altered combinations, so that it is necessary to gather up from different individuals the elements that form the species in its totality. It would almost appear as if the powers of mind express themselves with us in real life or empirically as separately as the psychologist distinguishes them in the representation. For we see not only individual subjects, but whole classes of men, uphold their capacities only in part, while the rest of their faculties scarcely show a germ of activity, as in the case of the stunted growth of plants.

I do not overlook the advantages to which the present race, regarded as a unity and in the balance of the understanding, may lay claim over what is best in the ancient world; but it is obliged to engage in the contest as a compact mass, and measure itself as a whole against a whole. Who among the moderns could step forth, man against man, and strive with an Athenian for the prize of higher humanity?

Whence comes this disadvantageous relation of individuals coupled with great advantages of the race? Why could the individual Greek be qualified as the type of his time; and why can no modern dare to offer himself as such? Because all-uniting nature imparted its forms to the Greek, and an all-dividing understanding gives our forms to us.

It was culture itself that gave these wounds to modern humanity. The inner union of human nature was broken, and a destructive contest divided its harmonious forces directly; on the one hand an enlarged experience and a more distinct thinking necessitated a sharper separation of the sciences, while, on the other hand, the more complicated machinery of states necessitated a stricter sundering of ranks and occupations. Intuitive and speculative understanding took up a hostile attitude in opposite fields, whose borders were guarded with jealousy and distrust; and by limiting its operation to a narrow sphere, men have made unto themselves a master who is wont not unfrequently to end by subduing and oppressing all the other faculties. Whilst on the one hand a luxuriant imagination creates ravages in the plantations that have cost the intelligence so much labour; on the other hand, a spirit of abstraction suffocates the fire that might have warmed the heart and inflamed the imagination.

II. THE SENSE INSTINCT AND THE FORM INSTINCT (*STOFFTRIEB* AND *FORMTRIEB*)

This twofold labour or task, which consists in making the necessary pass into reality *in us* and in making *out of us* reality subject to the law of necessity, is urged upon us as a duty by two opposing forces, which are justly styled impulsions or instincts, because they impel us to realise their object. The first of these impulsions, which I shall call the *sensuous instinct,* issues from the physical existence of man, or from sensuous nature; and it is this instinct which tends to enclose him in the limits of time, and to make of him a material being. . . .

This instinct extends its domains over the entire sphere of the finite in man, and as form is only revealed in matter, and the absolute by means of its limits, the total manifestation of human nature is connected on a close analysis with the sensuous instinct. But though it is only this instinct that awakens and develops what exists virtually in man, it is nevertheless this very instinct which renders his perfection impossible. It binds down to the world of sense by indestructible ties the spirit that tends higher, and it calls back to the limits of the present, abstraction which had its free development in the sphere of the infinite. . . .

The second impulsion, which may be named the *formal instinct,* issues from the absolute existence of man, or from his rational nature, and tends to set free, and bring harmony into the diversity of its manifestations, and to maintain personality notwithstanding all the changes of state. As this personality, being an absolute and indivisible unity, can never be in contradiction with itself, as *we are ourselves,* for ever, this impulsion, which tends to maintain personality, can never exact in one time anything but what it exacts and requires for ever. It therefore decides for always what it decides now, and orders now what it orders for ever. Hence it embraces the whole series of times, or what comes to the same thing, it suppresses time and change. It wishes the real to be necessary and eternal, and it wishes the eternal and the necessary to be real; in other terms, it tends to truth and justice.

III. THE PLAY INSTINCT (*SPIELTRIEB*)

The sensuous impulsion excludes from its subject all autonomy and freedom; the formal impulsion excludes all dependence and passivity. But the exclusion of freedom is physical necessity; the exclusion of passivity is moral necessity. Thus the two impulsions subdue the mind: the former to the laws of nature, the latter to the laws of reason. It results from this that the instinct of play, which unites the double action of the two other instincts, will content the mind at once morally and physically. Hence, as it suppresses all that is contingent, it will also suppress all coercion, and will set man free physically and morally. When we welcome with effusion some one who deserves our contempt, we feel painfully that *nature is constrained.* When we have a hostile feeling against a person who commands our esteem, we feel painfully the *constraint of reason.* But if this person inspires us with interest, and also wins our esteem, the constraint of feeling vanishes together with the constraint of reason, and we begin to love him, that is to say, to play, to take recreation, at once with our inclination and our esteem.

Moreover, as the sensuous impulsion controls us physically, and the formal impulsion morally, the former makes our formal constitution contingent, and the latter makes our material constitution contingent, that is to say, there is contingence in the agreement of our happiness with our perfection, and reciprocally. The instinct of play, in which both act in concert, will render both our formal and our material constitution contingent; accordingly, our perfection and our happiness in like manner. . . . In proportion that it will lessen the dynamic influence of feeling and passion, it will place them in harmony with rational ideas, and by taking from the laws of reason their moral constraint, it will reconcile them with the interest of the senses.

IV. BEAUTY THE OBJECT OF
THE PLAY INSTINCT

The object of the sensuous instinct, expressed in a universal conception, is named Life in the widest acceptation; a conception that expresses all material existence and all that is immediately present in the senses. The object of the formal instinct, expressed in a universal conception, is called shape or form, as well in an exact as in an inexact acceptation; a conception that embraces all formal qualities of things and all relations of the same to the thinking powers. The object of the play instinct, represented in a general statement, may therefore bear the name *living form;* a term that serves to describe all aesthetic qualities of phenomena, and what people style, in the widest sense, *beauty.*

Beauty is neither extended to the whole field of all living things nor merely enclosed in this field. A marble block, though it is and remains lifeless, can nevertheless become a living form by the architect and sculptor; a man, though he lives and has a form, is far from being a living form on that account. For this to be the case, it is necessary that his form should be life, and that his life should be a form. As long as we only think of his form, it is lifeless, a mere abstraction; as long as we only feel his life, it is without form, a mere impression. It is only when his form lives in our feeling, and his life in our understanding, he is the living form, and this will everywhere be the case where we judge him to be beautiful. . . .

But, perhaps the objection has for some time occurred to you, is not the beautiful degraded by this, that it is made a mere play, and is it not reduced to the level of frivolous objects which have for ages passed under that name? Does it not contradict the conception of the reason and the dignity of beauty, which is nevertheless regarded as an instrument of culture, to confine it to the work of being a mere play, and does it not contradict the empirical conception of play, which can coexist with the exclusion of all taste, to confine it merely to beauty?

But what is meant by a *mere play,* when we know that in all conditions of humanity that very thing is play, and *only* that is play which makes man complete, and develops simultaneously his twofold nature? What you style *limitation,* according to your representation of the matter, according to my views, which I have justified by proofs, I name *enlargement.* Consequently I should have said exactly the reverse: man is serious *only* with the agreeable, with the good, and with the perfect, but he *plays* with beauty. In saying this we must not indeed think of the plays that are in vogue in real life, and which commonly refer only to his material state. But in real life we should also seek in vain for the beauty of which we are here speaking. The actually present beauty is worthy of the really, of the actually present play-impulse; but by the ideal of beauty, which is set up by the reason, an ideal of the play-instinct is also presented, which man ought to have before his eyes in all his plays.

Therefore, no error will ever be incurred if we seek the ideal of beauty on the same road on which we satisfy our play-impulse. We can immediately understand why the ideal form of a Venus, of a Juno, and of an Apollo, is to be sought not at Rome, but in Greece, if we contrast the Greek population, delighting in the bloodless athletic contests of boxing, racing, and intellectual rivalry at Olympia, with the Roman people gloating over the agony of a gladiator. Now the reason pronounces that the beautiful must not only be life and form, but a living form, that is, beauty, inasmuch as it dictates to man the twofold law of absolute formality and absolute reality. Reason also utters the decision that man shall only *play* with beauty, and he *shall only play* with *beauty*.

For, to speak out once for all, man only plays when in the full meaning of the word he is a man, and *he is only completely a man when he plays*. This proposition, which at this moment perhaps appears paradoxical, will receive a great and deep meaning if we have advanced far enough to apply it to the twofold seriousness of duty and of destiny. I promise you that the whole edifice of æsthetic art and the still more difficult art of life will be supported by this principle. But this proposition is only unexpected in science; long ago it lived and worked in art, and in the feeling of the Greeks, her most accomplished masters; only they removed to Olympus what ought to have been preserved on earth. Influenced by the truth of this principle they effaced from the brow of their gods the earnestness and labour which furrow the cheeks of mortals, and also the hollow lust that smoothes the empty face. They set free the ever serene from the chains of every purpose, of every duty, of every care, and they made *indolence* and *indifference* the envied condition of the godlike race; merely human appelations for the freest and highest mind. As well the material pressure of natural laws as the spiritual pressure of moral laws lost itself in its higher idea of necessity, which embraced at the same time both worlds, and out of the union of these two necessities issued true freedom. Inspired by this spirit the Greeks also effaced from the features of their ideal, together with *desire or inclination,* all traces of *volition,* or, better still, they made both unrecognisable, because they knew how to wed them both in the closest alliance. It is neither charm, nor is it dignity, which speaks from the glorious face of Juno Ludovici; it is neither of these, for it is both at once. While the female god challenges our veneration the godlike woman at the same time kindles our love. But while in ecstasy we give ourselves up to the heavenly beauty, the heavenly self-repose awes us back. The whole form rests and dwells in itself—a fully complete creation in itself—and as if she were out of space, without advance or resistance; it shows no force contending with force, no opening through which time could break in. Irresistibly carried away and attracted by her womanly charm, kept off at a distance by her godly dignity, we also find ourselves at length in the state of the greatest repose, and the result is a wonderful impression for which the understanding has no idea and language no name.

V. BEAUTY AND UTILITY

The mind can be determined—is determinable—only in as far as it is not determined; it is, however, determinable also, in as far as it is not exclusively determined; that is, if it is not confined in its determination. The former is only a want of determination —it is without limits, because it is without reality; but the latter, the æsthetic determinableness, has no limits, because it unites all reality. . . .

Man is therefore *nothing* in the æsthetic state, if attention is given to the single result, and not to the whole faculty, and if we regard only the absence or want of every special determination. We must therefore do justice to those who pronounce the beautiful, and the disposition in which it places the mind, as entirely indifferent and unprofitable, in relation to *knowledge* and *feeling.* They are perfectly right; for it is certain that beauty gives no separate, single result, either for the understanding or for the will; it does not carry out a single intellectual or moral object; it discovers no truth, does not help us to fulfil a single duty, and in *one* word, is equally unfit to found the character or to clear the head. Accordingly, the personal worth of a man, or his dignity, as far as this can only depend on himself, remains entirely undetermined by æsthetic culture, and nothing further is attained than that, on the *part* of *nature*, it is made profitable for him to make of himself what he will; that the freedom to be what he ought to be is restored perfectly to him.

But by this something infinite is attained. But as soon as we remember that freedom is taken from man by the one-sided compulsion of nature in feeling, and by the exclusive legislation of the reason in thinking, we must consider the capacity restored to him by the æsthetical disposition, as the highest of all gifts, as the gift of humanity. I admit that he possesses this capacity for humanity, before every definite determination in which he may be placed. But, as a matter of fact, he loses it with every determined condition into which he may come; and if he is to pass over to an opposite condition, humanity must be in every case restored to him by the æsthetic life.

VI. THE EFFECTS OF ART

This high indifference and freedom of mind, united with power and elasticity, is the disposition in which a true work of art ought to dismiss us, and there is no better test of true æsthetic excellence. If after an enjoyment of this kind we find ourselves specially impelled to a particular mode of feeling or action, and unfit for other modes, this serves as an infallible proof that we have not experienced *any pure æsthetic* effect, whether this is owing to the object, to our own mode of feeling—as generally happens—or to both together.

As in reality no purely æsthetical effect can be met with—for man can never leave his dependence on material forces—the excellence of a work of art can only consist in its greater approximation to its ideal of æsthetic purity, and however high we may raise the freedom of this effect we shall always leave it with a particular disposition and a particular bias. Any class of productions or separate work in the world of art is noble and excellent in proportion to the universality of the disposition and the unlimited character of the bias thereby presented to our mind. This truth can be applied to works in various branches of art, and also to different works in the same branch. We leave a grand musical performance with our feelings excited, the reading of a noble poem with a quickened imagination, a beautiful statue or building with an awakened understanding; but a man would not choose an opportune moment who attempted to invite us to abstract thinking after a high musical enjoyment, or to attend to a prosaic affair of common life after a high poetical enjoyment, or to kindle our imagination and astonish our feelings directly after inspecting a fine statue or edifice. The reason of this is that music, *by its matter,* even when most spiritual, presents a greater affinity with the senses than is permitted by æsthetic liberty; it is because even the most happy poetry, having *for its medium* the arbitrary and contingent play of the imagination, always shares in it more than the intimate necessity of the really beautiful allows; it is because the best sculpture touches on severe science *by what is determinate in its conception.* However, these particular affinities are lost in proportion as the works of these three kinds of art rise to a greater elevation, and it is a natural and necessary consequence of their perfection that, without confounding their objective limits, the different arts come to resemble each other more and more in the action *which they exercise on the mind.* At its highest degree of ennobling, music ought to become a form, and act on us with the calm power of an antique statue; in its most elevated perfection the plastic art ought to become music, and move us by the immediate action exercised on the mind by the senses; in its most complete development poetry ought both to stir us powerfully like music, and like plastic art to surround us with a peaceful light. In each art the perfect style consists exactly in knowing how to remove specific limits, while sacrificing at the same time the particular advantages of the art, and to give it by a wise use of what belongs to it specially a more general character.

Nor is it only the limits inherent in the specific character of each kind of art that the artist ought to overstep in putting his hand to the work; he must also triumph over those which are inherent in the particular subject of which he treats. In a really beautiful work of art the substance ought to be inoperative, the form should do everything; for by the form the whole man is acted on; the substance acts on nothing but isolated forces. Thus, however vast and sublime it may be, the substance always exercises a restrictive action on the mind, and true æsthetic liberty can only be expected from the form. Consequently the true search of the matter consists in *destroying matter by the form;* and the triumph of art is great in proportion as it overcomes matter, and maintains its sway over those who enjoy its work.

VII. ART AND NATURE

Whilst man, in his first physical condition, is only passively affected by the world of sense, he is still entirely identified with it; and for this reason the external world, as yet, has no objective existence for him. When he begins in his æsthetic state of mind to regard the world objectively, then only is his personality severed from it, and the world appears to him an objective reality, for the simple reason that he has ceased to form an identical portion of it.

That which first connects man with the surrounding universe is the power of reflective contemplation. Whereas desire seizes at once its object, reflection removes it to a distance and renders it inalienably her own by saving it from the greed of passion. The necessity of sense which he obeyed during the period of mere sensations, lessens during the period of reflection; the senses are for the time in abeyance; even ever-fleeting time stands still whilst the scattered rays of consciousness are gathering and shape themselves; an image of the infinite is reflected upon the perishable ground. As soon as light dawns in man, there is no longer night outside of him; as soon as there is peace within him the storm lulls throughout the universe, and the contending forces of nature find rest within prescribed limits. Hence we cannot wonder if ancient traditions allude to these great changes in the inner man as a revolution in surrounding nature, and sym-

bolise thought triumphing over the laws of time, by the figure
of Zeus, which terminates the reign of Saturn.

As long as man derives sensations from a contact with nature,
he is her slave; but as soon as he begins to reflect upon her objects and laws he becomes her lawgiver. Nature, which previously ruled him as a power, now expands before him as an object.
What is objective to him can have no power over him, for in
order to become objective it has to experience his own power.
As far and as long as he impresses a form upon matter, he cannot be injured by its effect; for a spirit can only be injured by
that which deprives it of its freedom. Whereas he proves his own
freedom by giving a form to the formless; where the mass rules
heavily and without shape, and its undefined outlines are for
ever fluctuating between uncertain boundaries, fear takes up its
abode; but man rises above any natural terror as soon as he
knows how to mould it, and transform it into an object of his art.
As soon as he upholds his independence toward phenomenal natures he maintains his dignity toward her as a thing of power,
and with a noble freedom he rises against his gods. They throw
aside the mask with which they had kept him in awe during his
infancy, and to his surprise his mind perceives the reflection of
his own image. The divine monster of the Oriental, which roams
about changing the world with the blind force of a beast of prey,
dwindles to the charming outline of humanity in Greek fable;
the empire of the Titans is crushed, and boundless force is tamed
by infinite form.

VIII. ART AND APPEARANCE

It is nature herself which raises man from reality to appearance by endowing him with two senses which only lead him to
the knowledge of the real through appearance. In the eye and
the ear the organs of the senses are already freed from the per-
secutions of nature, and the object with which we are immediately in contact through the animal senses is remoter from us.
What we see by the eye differs from what we feel; for the understanding to reach objects overleaps the light which separates us

yield to the reins of love. For this purpose taste throws a veil over physical necessity, offending a free mind by its coarse nudity, and dissimulating our degrading parentage with matter by a delightful illusion of freedom. Mercenary art itself rises from the dust; and the bondage of the bodily, at its magic touch, falls off from the inanimate and animate. In the æsthetic state the most slavish tool is a free citizen, having the same rights as the noblest; and the intellect which shapes the mass to its intent must consult it concerning its destination. Consequently, in the realm of æsthetic appearance, the idea of equality is realised, which the political zealot would gladly see carried out socially. It has often been said that perfect politeness is only found near a throne. If thus restricted in the material, man has, as elsewhere appears, to find compensation in the ideal world.

Does such a state of beauty in appearance exist, and where? It must be in every finely harmonised soul; but as a fact, only in select circles, like the pure ideal of the Church and state—in circles where manners are not formed by the empty imitations of the foreign, but by the very beauty of nature; where man passes through all sorts of complications in all simplicity and innocence, neither forced to trench on another's freedom to preserve his own, nor to show grace at the cost of dignity.

from them. In truth, we are passive to an object: in sight and hearing the object is a form we create. . . .

The instinct of play likes appearance, and directly it is awakened it is followed by the formal imitative instinct which treats appearance as an independent thing. Directly man has come to distinguish the appearance from the reality, the form from the body, he can separate, in fact he has already done so. Thus the faculty of the art of imitation is given with the faculty of form in general. The inclination that draws us to it reposes on another tendency which I cannot examine in detail here. The exact period when the aesthetic instinct, or that of art, develops, depends entirely on the attraction that mere appearance has for men.

As every real existence proceeds from nature as a foreign power, whilst every appearance comes in the first place from man as a percipient subject, he only uses his absolute sight in separating semblance from essence, and arranging according to subjective law. With an unbridled liberty he can unite what nature has severed, provided he can imagine his union, and he can separate what nature has united, provided this separation can take place in his intelligence. Here nothing can be sacred to him but his own law: the only condition imposed upon him is to respect the border which separates his own sphere from the existence of things or from the realm of nature.

This human right of ruling is exercised by man in the art of appearance; and his success in extending the empire of the beautiful, and guarding the frontiers of truth, will be in proportion with the strictness with which he separates form from substance: for if he frees appearance from reality, he must also do the converse.

But man possesses sovereign power only in the world of appearance, in the unsubstantial realm of imagination, only by abstaining from giving being to appearance in theory, and by giving it being in practice. It follows that the poet transgresses his proper limits when he attributes being to his ideal, and when he gives this ideal aim as a determined existence. For he can only reach this result by exceeding his right as a poet, that of encroaching by the ideal on the field of experience, and by pretending to determine real existence in virtue of a simple possibility, or else he renounces his right as a poet by letting experience encroach on the sphere of the ideal, and by restricting possibility to the conditions of reality.

It is only by being frank or disclaiming all reality, and by being independent or doing without reality, that the appearance is æsthetical. Directly it apes reality or needs reality for effect, it is nothing more than a vile instrument for material ends, and can prove nothing for the freedom of the mind. Moreover, the object in which we find beauty need not be unreal if our judgment disregards this reality; for if it regards this the judgment is no longer æsthetical.

IX. IMAGINATION

The imagination, like the bodily organs, has in man its free movement and its material play, a play in which, without any reference to form, it simply takes pleasure in its arbitrary power, and in the absence of all hinderance. These plays of fancy, inasmuch as form is not mixed up with them, and because a free succession of images makes all their charm, though confined to man, belong exclusively to animal life, and only prove one thing —that he is delivered from all external sensuous constraint— without our being entitled to infer that there is in it an independent plastic force.

From this play of *free association* of ideas, which is still quite material in nature, and is explained by simple natural laws, the imagination, by making the attempt of creating a free form, passes at length at a jump to the æsthetic play: I say at one leap, for quite a new force enters into action here; for here, for the first time, the legislative mind is mixed with the acts of a blind instinct, subjects the arbitrary march of the imagination to its eternal and immutable unity, causes its independent permanence to enter in that which is transitory, and its infinity in the sensuous. Nevertheless, as long as rude nature, which knows of no other law than running incessantly from change to change, will yet retain too much strength, it will oppose itself by its different caprices to this necessity; by its agitation to this permanence; by its manifold needs to this independence, and by its insatiability to this sublime simplicity. It will be also troublesome

to recognize the instinct of play in its first trials, s sensuous impulsion, with its capricious humour a appetites, constantly crosses. It is on that account tha taste, still coarse, seize that which is new and s disordered, the adventurous and the strange, the the savage, and fly from nothing so much as from simplicity. It invents grotesque figures, it likes ra sitions, luxurious forms, sharply-marked changes, acu a pathetic song. That which man calls beautiful at thi that which excites him, that which gives him matter; which excites him to give his personality to the object, tha gives matter to a *possible plastic operation*, for otherwise it not be the beautiful for him. A remarkable change has the taken place in the form of his judgments; he searches for objects, not because they affect him, but because they fu him with the occasion of acting; they please him, not bec they answer to a want, but because they satisfy a law wh speaks in his breast, although quite low as yet.

X. TASTE

Taste does not suffer any superior or absolute authority, and the sway of beauty is extended over appearance. It extends up to the seat of reason's supremacy, suppressing all that is material. It extends down to where sensuous impulse rules with blind compulsion, and form is undeveloped. Taste ever maintains its power on these remote borders, where legislation is taken from it. Particular desires must renounce their egotism, and the agreeable, otherwise tempting the senses, must in matters of taste adorn the mind with the attraction of grace.

Duty and stern necessity must change their forbidding tone, only excused by resistance, and do homage to nature by a nobler trust in her. Taste leads our knowledge from the mysteries of science into the open expanse of common sense, and changes a narrow scholasticism into the common property of the human race. Here the highest genius must leave its particular elevation, and make itself familiar to the comprehension even of a child. Strength must let the Graces bind it, and the arbitrary lion must

Johann Wolfgang von Goethe

[1749–1832]

THE MAN WHOSE NAME is almost synonymous with German culture and whose *Faust* is the supreme expression of the romantic world-view produced surprisingly little formal criticism. Yet what he produced is consistently worth reading. In contrast to Schiller, Goethe is a practical critic. He avoids theory in favor of down-to-earth remarks about specific poems and authors. Since his views changed several times during his life, he can be accused of inconsistency, but he preferred being inconsistent to being dogmatic. His best-known sustained criticism is the analysis of *Hamlet* woven into the narrative of his novel *Wilhelm Meister*. His mature critical ideas are expressed in the *Conversations with Eckermann* which took place between 1822 and 1832.

Goethe's perceptiveness, his culture, his rejection of all that is parochial in criticism, and his concern for the relationship between literature and life have made him a major force in criticism. His influence is especially strong among humanistic critics. Sante-Beuve called him "the greatest critic of all times;" and to Matthew Arnold he was "the supreme critic." These opinions persist in the work of the "new humanists," Irving Babbitt, Norman Foerster, and their followers.

Goethe's *Conversations* were translated by John Oxenford in 1850, and this translation has often been reprinted. The bulk of his criticism is assembled in J. E. Spingarn, *Goethe's Literary Essays* (New York, 1921). For comment see: J. Carré, *Goethe en Angleterre* (Paris, 1920); E. Cassirer, *Rousseau, Kant, Goethe* (Princeton, 1945); B. Fairley, *A Study of Goethe* (Oxford, 1947); A. McKillop, "Goethe and Literary Criticism," *Rice Institute Pamphlet*, XIX (1932); T. Mann, *Freud, Goethe, Wagner* (New York, 1937); J. Orrick, *Matthew Arnold and Goethe* (London, 1928); G. Pollak, *International Perspective in Criticism* (New York, 1914); K. Viëtor, *Goethe, the Thinker* (Cambridge, 1950).

The present selections are from the *Conversations*, trans. by Oxenford, cited above.

CONVERSATIONS WITH ECKERMANN

I. WORLD LITERATURE

WITHIN the last few days I have read many and various things; especially a Chinese novel, which occupies me still, and seems to me very remarkable. The Chinese think, act, and feel almost exactly like ourselves; and we soon find that we are perfectly like them, excepting that all they do is more clear, more pure and decorous than with us. . . .

I am more and more convinced that poetry is the universal possession of mankind, revealing itself everywhere, and at all times, in hundreds and hundreds of men. One makes it a little better than another, and swims on the surface a little longer than another—that is all. Herr von Matthisson must not think he is the man, nor must I think that I am the man; but each must say to himself that the gift of poetry is by no means so very rare, and that nobody need think very much of himself because he has written a good poem.

But, really, we Germans are very likely to fall too easily into this pedantic conceit, when we do not look beyond the narrow circle which surrounds us. I therefore like to look about me in foreign nations, and advise every one to do the same. National literature is now rather an unmeaning term; the epoch of World Literature is at hand, and every one must strive to hasten its approach. But, while we thus value what is foreign, we must not bind ourselves to anything in particular, and regard it as a model. We must not give this value to the Chinese, or the Servian, or Calderon, or the Nibelungen; but if we really want a pattern, we must always return to the ancient Greeks, in whose works the beauty of mankind is constantly represented. All the rest we must look at only historically, appropriating to ourselves what is good, so far as it goes.

II. THE POET'S MISSION

To write military songs, and sit in a room! That would have suited me! To have written them in the bivouac, when the horses at the enemy's outposts are heard neighing at night, would have been well enough; however, that was not my life and not my business, but that of Theodor Körner. His war-songs suit him perfectly. But to me, who am not of a warlike nature, and who have no warlike sense, war-songs would have been a mask which would have fitted my face very badly.

I have never affected anything in my poetry. I have never uttered anything which I have not experienced, and which has not urged me to production. I have only composed love-songs when I have loved. How could I write songs of hatred without hating! And, between ourselves, I did not hate the French, although I thanked God that we were free from them. How could I, to whom culture and barbarism are alone of importance, hate a nation which is among the most cultivated of the earth, and to which I owe so great a part of my own culture?

Altogether, national hatred is something peculiar. You will always find it strongest and most violent where there is the lowest degree of culture. But there is a degree where it vanishes altogether, and where one stands to a certain extent *above* nations, and feels the weal or woe of a neighboring people, as if it had happened to one's own. This degree of culture was conformable to my nature, and I had become strengthened in it long before I had reached my sixtieth year.

It is better for us moderns to say with Napoleon, "Politics are Destiny." But let us beware of saying, with our latest literati, that politics are poetry, or a suitable subject for the poet. The English poet Thomson wrote a very good poem on the Seasons, but a very bad one on Liberty, and that not from want of poetry in the poet, but from want of poetry in the subject.

If a poet would work politically, he must give himself up to a party; and so soon as he does that he is lost as a poet; he must bid farewell to his free spirit, his unbiased view, and draw over his ears the cap of bigotry and blind hatred.

The poet, as a man and citizen, will love his native land; but the native land of his *poetic* powers and poetic action is the good, noble, and beautiful, which is confined to no particular province or country, and which he seizes upon and forms wherever he finds it. Therein is he like the eagle, who hovers with free gaze over whole countries, and to whom it is of no consequence whether the hare on which he pounces is running in Prussia or in Saxony.

And, then, what is meant by love of one's country? what is meant by patriotic deeds? If the poet has employed a life in battling with pernicious prejudices, in setting aside narrow views, in enlightening the minds, purifying the tastes, ennobling the feelings and thoughts of his countrymen, what better could he have done? how could he have acted more patriotically?

III. POETRY AND IDEAS

Idea! as if I knew anything about it. I had the life of Tasso, I had my own life; and whilst I brought together two odd figures with their peculiarities, the image of Tasso arose in my mind, to which I opposed, as a prosaic contrast, that of Antonio, for whom also I did not lack models. The further particulars of court life and love affairs were at Weimar as they were in Ferrara; and I can truly say of my production, *it is bone of my bone, and flesh of my flesh.*

The Germans are, certainly, strange people. By their deep thoughts and ideas, which they seek in everything and fix upon everything, they make life much more burdensome than is necessary. Only have the courage to give yourself up to your impressions, allow yourself to be delighted, moved, elevated, nay, instructed and inspired for something great; but do not imagine all is vanity, if it is not abstract thought and idea.

Then they come and ask what idea I meant to embody in my *Faust.* As if I knew myself and could inform them. *From heaven, through the world, to hell,* would indeed be something; but this is no idea, only a course of action. And further, that the devil loses the wager, and that a man, continually struggling from difficult errors towards something better, should be redeemed, is an effective, and to many, a good enlightening thought; but it is no idea which lies at the foundation of the whole and of every individual scene. It would have been a fine thing, indeed, if I had strung so rich, varied, and highly diversified a life as I have brought to view in *Faust* upon the slender string of one pervading idea.

It was, on the whole, not in my line, as a poet, to strive to embody anything *abstract.* I received in my mind *impressions,* and those of a sensuous, animated, charming, varied, hundredfold kind, just as a lively imagination presented them; and I had, as a poet, nothing more to do than artistically to round off and elaborate such views and impressions, and by means of a lively representation so to bring them forward that others might receive the same impression in hearing or reading my representation of them.

If I however wished, as a poet, to represent any idea, I did it in short poems, where a decided unity could prevail, as, for instance, in the *Metamorphosis of Animals,* that of *Plants,* the poem *Legacy,* and many others. The only production of greater extent, in which I am conscious of having labored to set forth a pervading idea, is probably my *Elective Affinities.* This novel has thus become comprehensible to the intellect; but I will not say that it is therefore better. I am rather of the opinion that the more incommensurable, and the more incomprehensible to the intellect, a poetic production is, so much the better it is.

IV. POETRY AND REALITY

The world is so great and rich, and life so full of variety, that you can never want occasions for poems. But they must all be occasional poems; that is to say, reality must give both impulse and material for their production. A particular case becomes universal and poetic by the very circumstance that it is treated by a poet. All my poems are occasional poems, suggested by real life, and having therein a firm foundation. I attach no value to poems snatched out of the air.

Let no one say that reality wants poetical interest; for in this the poet proves his vocation, that he has the art to win from a common subject an interesting side. Reality must give the motive, the points to be expressed, the kernel, as I may say; but to work out of it a beautiful, animated whole, belongs to the poet. You know Fürnstein, called the Poet of Nature; he has

written the prettiest poem possible on the cultivation of hops.
I have now proposed to him to make songs for the different
crafts of working-men, particularly a weaver's song, and I am
sure he will do it well, for he has lived among such people from
his youth; he understands the subjects thoroughly, and is therefore master of his material. That is exactly the advantage of
small works; you need only choose those subjects of which you
are master. With a great poem, this cannot be: no part can be
evaded; all which belongs to the animation of the whole, and is
interwoven into the plan, must be represented with precision. In
youth, however, the knowledge of things is only one-sided. A
great work requires many-sidedness, and on that rock the young
author splits.

V. POETRY AND HISTORY

Manzoni wants nothing except to know what a good poet he
is, and what rights belong to him as such. He has too much respect for history, and on this account always adds explanations
to his pieces, in which he shows how faithful he has been to
detail. Now, though his facts may be historical, his characters
are not so, any more than my Thoas and Iphigenia. No poet has
ever known the historical characters which he has painted; if
he had, he could scarcely have made use of them. The poet must
know what effects he wishes to produce, and regulate the nature
of his characters accordingly. If I had tried to make Egmont as
history represents him, the father of a dozen children, his light-
minded proceedings would have appeared very absurd. I needed
an Egmont more in harmony with his own actions and my poetic
views; and this is, as Clara says, *my* Egmont.

What would be the use of poets, if they only repeated the
record of the historian? The poet must go further, and give us,
if possible, something higher and better. All the characters of
Sophocles bear something of that great poet's lofty soul; and it
is the same with the characters of Shakespeare. This is as it
ought to be. Nay, Shakespeare goes farther, and makes his
Romans Englishmen; and there, too, he is right; for otherwise
his nation would not have understood him.

Here again the Greeks were so great that they regarded
fidelity to historic facts less than the treatment of them by the
poet. We have a fine example in Philoctetes, which subject has
been treated by all three of the great tragic poets, and lastly and
best by Sophocles. This poet's excellent play has, fortunately,
come down to us entire, while of the Philoctetes of Æschylus
and Euripides only fragments have been found, although sufficient to show how they have managed the subject. If time
permitted, I would restore these pieces, as I did the Phäeton
of Euripides; it would be to me no unpleasant or useless task.

In this subject the problem was very simple, namely, to bring
Philoctetes, with his bow, from the island of Lemnos. But the
manner of doing this was the business of the poet, and here
each could show the power of his invention, and one could
excel another. Ulysses must fetch him; but shall he be recognized by Philoctetes or not? and if not, how shall he be disguised? Shall Ulysses go alone, or shall he have companions, and
who shall they be? In Æschylus the companion is unknown; in
Euripides, it is Diomed; in Sophocles, the son of Achilles. Then,
in what situation is Philoctetes to be found? Shall the island
be inhabited or not? and, if inhabited, shall any sympathetic soul
have taken compassion on him or not? And so with a hundred
other things, which are all at the discretion of the poet, and in
the selection and omission of which one may show his superiority
in wisdom to another. This is the important point, and the poets
of today should do like the ancients. They should not be always
asking whether a subject has been used before, and look to
south and north for unheard-of adventures, which are often barbarous enough, and merely make an impression as incidents. But
to make something of a simple subject by a masterly treatment
requires intellect and great talent, and these we do not find.

VI. CLASSICISM AND ROMANTICISM

A new expression occurs to me which does not ill define the
state of the case. I call the classic *healthy*, the romantic *sickly*.
In this sense, the *Nibelungenlied* is as classic as the *Iliad*, for
both are vigorous and healthy. Most modern productions are

romantic, not because they are new, but because they are weak, morbid, and sickly; and the antique is classic, not because it is old, but because it is strong, fresh, joyous, and healthy. If we distinguish "classic" and "romantic" by these qualities, it will be easy to see our way clearly.

This is a pathological work; a superfluity of sap is bestowed on some parts which do not require it, and drawn out of those which stand in need of it. The subject was good, but the scenes which I expected were not there; while others, which I did not expect, were elaborated with assiduity and love. This is what I call pathological, or "romantic," if you would rather speak according to our new theory.

The French now begin to think justly of these matters. Both classic and romantic, say they, are equally good. The only point is to use these forms with judgment, and to be capable of excellence. You can be absurd in both, and then one is as worthless as the other. This, I think, is rational enough, and may content us for a while.

The idea of the distinction between classical and romantic poetry, which is now spread over the whole world, and occasions so many quarrels and divisions, came originally from Schiller and myself. I laid down the maxim of objective treatment in poetry, and would allow no other; but Schiller, who worked quite in the subjective way, deemed his own fashion the right one, and to defend himself against me, wrote the treatise upon *Naïve and Sentimental Poetry*. He proved to me that I myself, against my will, was romantic, and that my *Iphigenia*, through the predominance of sentiment, was by no means so classical and so much in the antique spirit as some people supposed.

The Schlegels took up this idea, and carried it further, so that it has now been diffused over the whole world; and every one talks about classicism and romanticism—of which nobody thought fifty years ago.

VII. FRENCH ROMANTICISM

Extremes are never to be avoided in any revolution. In a political one nothing is generally desired in the beginning but the abolition of abuses; but before people are aware, they are deep in bloodshed and horror. Thus the French, in their present literary revolution, desired nothing at first but a freer form; however, they will not stop there, but will reject the traditional contents together with the form. They begin to declare the representation of noble sentiments and deeds as tedious, and attempt to treat of all sorts of abominations. Instead of the beautiful subjects from Grecian mythology, there are devils, witches, and vampires, and the lofty heroes of antiquity must give place to jugglers and galley slaves. This is piquant! This is effective! But after the public has once tasted this highly seasoned food, and has become accustomed to it, it will always long for more, and that stronger. A young man of talent, who would produce an effect and be acknowledged, and who is great enough to go his own way, must accommodate himself to the taste of the day—nay, must seek to outdo his predecessors in the horrible and frightful. But in this chase after outward means of effect, all profound study, and all gradual and thorough development of the talent and the man from within, is entirely neglected. And this is the greatest injury which can befall a talent, although literature in general will gain by this tendency of the moment.

The extremes and excrescences which I have described will gradually disappear; but this great advantage will finally remain—besides a freer form, richer and more diversified subjects will have been attained, and no object of the broadest world and the most manifold life will be any longer excluded as unpoetical. I compare the present literary epoch to a state of violent fever, which is not in itself good and desirable, but of which improved health is the happy consequence. That abomination which now often constitutes the whole subject of a poetical work will in future only appear as a useful expedient; aye, the pure and the noble, which is now abandoned for the moment, will soon be resought with additional ardor.

VIII. MÉRIMÉE AND HUGO

Mérimée has treated these things very differently from his fellow-authors. These poems, it is true, are not deficient in various horrible motifs, such as churchyards, nocturnal crossroads,

ghosts and vampires; but the repulsive themes do not touch the
intrinsic merit of the poet. On the contrary, he treats them from
a certain objective distance, and, as it were, with irony. He goes
to work with them like an artist, to whom it is an amusement to
try anything of the sort. He has, as I have said before, quite
renounced himself, nay, he has even renounced the Frenchman, and that to such a degree that at first these poems of Guzla
were deemed real Illyrian popular poems, and thus little was
wanting for the success of the imposition he had intended.

Mérimée, to be sure, is a splendid fellow! Indeed, more power
and genius are generally required for the objective treatment of
a subject than is supposed. So Lord Byron, also, notwithstanding
his predominant personality, has sometimes had the power of
renouncing himself altogether, as may be seen in some of his
dramatic pieces, particularly in his *Marino Faliero*. In this piece
one quite forgets that Lord Byron, or even an Englishman,
wrote it. We live entirely in Venice, and entirely in the time
in which the action takes place. The personages speak quite
from themselves, and from their own condition, without having
any of the subjective feelings, thoughts, and opinions of the
poet. That is as it should be. Of our young French romantic
writers of the exaggerating sort, one cannot say as much. What
I have read of them—poems, novels, dramatic works—have all
borne the personal coloring of the author, and none of them
ever make me forget that a Parisian—that a Frenchman—wrote
them. Even in the treatment of foreign subjects one still remains
in France and Paris, quite absorbed in all the wishes, necessities,
conflicts, and fermentations of the present day.

[Victor Hugo] has a fine talent, but quite entangled in the
unhappy romantic tendency of his time, by which he is seduced
to represent, together with what is beautiful, also that which
is most insupportable and hideous. I have lately been reading
his *Notre Dame de Paris*, and required no little patience to support the horror with which this reading has inspired me. It is
the most abominable book that ever was written! Besides, one
is not even indemnified for the torture one has to endure by the
pleasure one might receive from a truthful representation of
human nature or human character. His book is, on the contrary,
utterly destitute of nature and truth! The so-called characters
whom he brings forward are not human beings with living flesh

and blood, but miserable wooden puppets, which he deals with as he pleases, and which he causes to make all sorts of contortions and grimaces just as he needs them for his desired effects. But what an age it must be which not only renders such a book possible and calls it into existence, but even finds it endurable and delightful.

IX. ORIGINALITY

The Germans cannot cease to be Philistines. They are now squabbling about some distichs, which are printed both in Schiller's works and mine, and fancy it is important to ascertain which really belongs to Schiller and which to me; as if anything could be gained by such investigation—as if the existence of such things were not enough. Friends like Schiller and myself, intimate for years, with the same interests, in habits of daily intercourse, and under reciprocal obligations, live so completely in one another that it is hardly possible to decide to which of the two the particular thoughts belong.

We have made many distiches together; sometimes I gave the thought, and Schiller made the verse; sometimes the contrary was the case; sometimes he made one line, and I the other. What matters the mine and thine? One must be a thorough Philistine, indeed, to attach the slightest importance to the solution of such questions.

People are always talking about originality; but what do they mean? As soon as we are born, the world begins to work upon us, and this goes on to the end. And, after all, what can we call our own except energy, strength, and will? If I could give an account of all that I owe to great predecessors and contemporaries, there would be but a small balance in my favor.

However, the time of life in which we are subjected to a new and important personal influence is, by no means, a matter of indifference. That Lessing, Winckelmann, and Kant were older than I, and that the first two acted upon my youth, the latter on my advanced age,—this circumstance was for me very important. Again, that Schiller was so much younger than I, and engaged in his freshest strivings just as I began to be weary of the world—just, too, as the brothers von Humboldt and Schlegel were beginning their career under my eye—was of the greatest importance. I derived from it unspeakable advantages.

What seduces young people is this. We live in a time in which so much culture is diffused that it has communicated itself, as it were, to the atmosphere which a young man breathes. Poetical and philosophic thoughts live and move within him, he has sucked them in with his very breath, but he thinks they are his own property, and utters them as such. But after he has restored to the time what he has received from it, he remains poor. He is like a fountain which plays for a while with the water with which it is supplied, but which ceases to flow as soon as the liquid treasure is exhausted.

X. DRAMATIC CONSTRUCTION

When a piece makes a deep impression on us in reading, we think that it will do the same on the stage, and that such a result can be obtained with little trouble. But this is by no means the case. A piece that is not originally, by the intent and skill of the poet, written for the boards, will not succeed; but whatever is done to it will always remain something unmanageable. What trouble have I taken with my *Goetz von Berlichingen!* Yet it will not quite do as an acting play; it is too long; and I have been forced to divide it into two parts, of which the last is indeed theatrically effective, while the first is to be looked upon as a mere introduction. If the first part were given only once as an introduction, and then the second repeatedly, it might succeed. It is the same with *Wallenstein;* the *Piccolomini* does not bear repetition, but *Wallenstein's Death* is always seen with delight.

The construction of a play must be symbolical; that is to say, each incident must be significant in itself, and lead to another still more important. The *Tartuffe* of Molière is, in this respect, a great example. Only think what an introduction is the first scene! From the very beginning everything is highly significant, and leads us to expect something still more important which is to come. The beginning of Lessing's *Minna von Barnhelm* is also admirable; but that of *Tartuffe* is absolutely unique: it is the greatest and best thing that exists of the kind.

In Calderon you find the same perfect adaptation to the theatre. His pieces are throughout fit for the boards; there is not a touch in them which is not directed towards the required effect. Calderon is a genius who had also the finest understanding.

Shakespeare wrote his plays direct from his own nature. Then, too, his age and the existing arrangements of the stage made no demands upon him; people were forced to put up with whatever he gave them. But if Shakespeare had written for the court of Madrid, or for the theatre of Louis XIV, he would probably have adapted himself to a severer theatrical form. This, however, is by no means to be regretted, for what Shakespeare has lost as a theatrical poet he has gained as a poet in general. Shakespeare is a great psychologist, and we learn from his pieces what really moves the hearts of men.

XI. SHAKESPEARE

We cannot talk about Shakespeare; everything is inadequate. I have touched upon the subject in my *Wilhelm Meister*, but that is not saying much. He is not a theatrical poet; he never thought of the stage; it was far too narrow for his great mind: nay, the whole visible world was too narrow.

He is even too rich and too powerful. A productive nature ought not to read more than one of his dramas in a year if it would not be wrecked entirely.

I did well to get rid of him by writing *Goetz* and *Egmont*, and Byron did well by not having too much respect and admiration for him, but going his own way. How many excellent Germans have been ruined by him and Calderon!

Shakespeare gives us golden apples in silver dishes. We get, indeed, the silver dishes by studying his works; but, unfortunately, we have only potatoes to put into them.

Macbeth is Shakespeare's best acting play, the one in which he shows most understanding with respect to the stage. But would you see his mind unfettered, read *Troilus and Cressida*, where he treats the materials of the *Iliad* in his own fashion.

Part II

POSITIVISM
AND
HUMANISM

Charles-Augustin Sainte-Beuve

[1804–1869]

SAINTE-BEUVE IS perhaps the best known and certainly the most widely quoted of French nineteenth-century critics. Praised by writers as diverse as Matthew Arnold and Hippolyte Taine, he became during his lifetime the *arbiter elegantium* of European letters. Yet if we seek in his criticism for a consistent literary theory, we are disappointed. By his own admission he began his career as an ardent romanticist, passed through a period of impressionism, and ended as a humanist with a strong sympathy for classicism. The problem of defining his critical principles is further complicated by the fact that he had an intense, lifelong interest in the social and biographical elements which help mold the literary work. His major study, *Port Royal* (1840 and later; 5 vols.), is history rather than criticism. Much of his discussion of literature is biographical with a self-conscious emphasis on psychology, its ultimate object being to create a "natural history of souls" comparable to other natural sciences. Therefore, Sainte-Beuve has often been called a founder of scientific—especially psychological—criticism. Taine acknowledged his debt to Sainte-Beuve in the "Introduction" to the *History of English Literature*.

Despite his influence on scientific criticism, it seems fair, today, to group Sainte-Beuve with the humanists rather than the literary scientists. He welcomed speculation of all kinds, but he opposed critical dogmas, believing that any system, if rigidly adhered to, eventually blinds the critic. While logic is important, it must be supplemented by the equally important principle of literary taste. Taste is partially a matter of instinct, but it must be cultivated by wide reading and familiarity with the great traditions of European culture. Finally, the literary critic should remain impersonal. He should avoid the romantic tendency to make criticism into an art form or a record of personal experiences.

Among Sainte-Beuve's most significant critical works are *Causeries du lundi* (15 vols.; Paris, 1851–62); *Nouveaux lundis* (13 vols.; Paris, 1863–70); *Portraits contemporains* (5 vols.; Paris, 1869–71); and *Portraits littéraires* (3 vols.; Paris, 1862–64). English translations of selected essays include *Essays,* trans. by Elizabeth Lee (London, 1892); *Monday-Chats,* ed. William Matthews (Chicago, 1877); and *Selected Essays,* ed. John Effinger, Jr. (Boston, 1895). Comment is extensive. See esp. I. Babbitt, *Masters of Modern French Criticism* (Boston, 1912); V. Giraud, *Sainte-Beuve critique* (Paris, 1902); G. Harper, *Sainte-Beuve* (Philadelphia, 1909); L. MacClintock, *Sainte-Beuve's Critical Theory and Practice after 1849* (Chicago, 1920); and G. Michaut, *Sainte-Beuve* (Paris, 1921).

   The present selection is from the *Essays,* trans. by Elizabeth Lee, cited above.

WHAT IS A CLASSIC?

A DELICATE QUESTION, to which somewhat diverse solutions might be given according to times and seasons. An intelligent man suggests it to me, and I intend to try, if not to solve it, at least to examine and discuss it face to face with my readers, were it only to persuade them to answer it for themselves, and, if I can, to make their opinion and mine on the point clear. And why, in criticism, should we not, from time to time, venture to treat some of those subjects which are not personal, in which we no longer speak of some one but of some thing? Our neighbours, the English, have well succeeded in making of it a special division of literature under the modest title of "Essays." It is true that in writing of such subjects, always slightly abstract and moral, it is advisable to speak of them in a season of quiet, to make sure of our own attention and of that of others, to seize one of those moments of calm moderation and leisure seldom granted our amiable France; even when she is desirous of being wise and is not making revolutions, her brilliant genius can scarcely tolerate them.

   A classic, according to the usual definition, is an old author canonised by admiration, and an authority in his particular style. The word *classic* was first used in this sense by the Romans. With them not all the citizens of the different classes were properly called *classici,* but only those of the chief class, those who possessed an income of a certain fixed sum. Those who possessed a smaller income were described by the term *infra classem,* below the pre-eminent class. The word *classicus* was used in a figurative sense by Aulus Gellius, and applied to writers; a writer of worth and distinction, *classicus assiduusque scriptor,* a writer who is of account, has real property, and is not lost in the proletariate crowd. Such an expression implies an age sufficiently advanced to have already made some sort of valuation and classification of literature.

At first the only true classics for the moderns were the ancients. The Greeks, by peculiar good fortune and natural enlightenment of mind, had no classics but themselves. They were at first the only classical authors for the Romans, who strove and contrived to imitate them. After the great periods of Roman literature, after Cicero and Virgil, the Romans in their turn had their classics, who became almost exclusively the classical authors of the centuries which followed. The middle ages, which were less ignorant of Latin antiquity than is believed, but which lacked proportion and taste, confused the ranks and orders. Ovid was placed above Homer, and Boetius seemed a classic equal to Plato. The revival of learning in the fifteenth and sixteenth centuries helped to bring this long chaos to order, and then only was admiration rightly proportioned. Thenceforth the true classical authors of Greek and Latin antiquity stood out in a luminous background, and were harmoniously grouped on their two heights.

Meanwhile modern literatures were born, and some of the more precocious, like the Italian, already possessed the style of antiquity. Dante appeared, and, from the very first, posterity greeted him as a classic. Italian poetry has since shrunk into far narrower bounds; but, whenever it desired to do so, it always found again and preserved the impulse and echo of its lofty origin. It is no indifferent matter for a poetry to derive its point of departure and classical source in high places; for example, to spring from Dante rather than to issue laboriously from Malherbe.

Modern Italy had her classical authors, and Spain had every right to believe that she also had hers at a time when France was yet seeking hers. A few talented writers endowed with originality and exceptional animation, a few brilliant efforts, isolated, without following, interrupted and recommenced, did not suffice to endow a nation with a solid and imposing basis of literary wealth. The idea of a classic implies something that has continuance and consistence, and which produces unity and tradition, fashions and transmits itself, and endures. It was only after the glorious years of Louis XIV that the nation felt with tremor and pride that such good fortune had happened to her. Every voice informed Louis XIV of it with flattery, exaggeration, and emphasis, yet with a certain sentiment of truth. Then arose a singular and striking contradiction: those men of whom Perrault was the chief, the men who were most smitten with the marvels of the age of Louis the Great, who even went the length of sacrificing the ancients to the moderns, aimed at exalting and canonising even those whom they regarded as inveterate opponents and adversaries. Boileau avenged and angrily upheld the ancients against Perrault, who extolled the moderns—that is to say, Corneille, Molière, Pascal, and the eminent men of his age, Boileau, one of the first, included. Kindly La Fontaine, taking part in the dispute in behalf of the learned Huet, did not perceive that, in spite of his defects, he was in his turn on the point of being held as a classic himself.

Example is the best definition. From the time France possessed her age of Louis XIV and could contemplate it at a little distance, she knew, better than by any arguments, what to be classical meant. The eighteenth century, even in its medley of things, strengthened this idea through some fine works, due to its four great men. Read Voltaire's *Age of Louis XIV*, Montesquieu's *Greatness and Fall of the Romans*, Buffon's *Epoch of Nature*, the beautiful pages of reverie and natural description of Rousseau's *Savoyard Vicar*, and say if the eighteenth century, in these memorable works, did not understand how to reconcile tradition with freedom of development and independence. But at the beginning of the present century and under the Empire, in sight of the first attempts of a decidedly new and somewhat adventurous literature, the idea of a classic in a few resisting minds, more sorrowful than severe, was strangely narrowed and contracted. The first Dictionary of the Academy (1694) merely defined a classical author as "a much-approved ancient writer, who is an authority as regards the subject he treats." The Dictionary of the Academy of 1835 narrows that definition still more, and gives precision and even limit to its rather vague form. It describes classical authors as those "who have become *models* in any language whatever," and in all the articles which follow, the expression, *models, fixed rules* for composition and style, *strict rules* of art to which men must conform, continually recur. That definition of *classic* was evidently made by the respectable Academicians, our predecessors, in face and sight of what was then called *romantic*—that is to say, in sight of the enemy. It seems to me time to renounce those timid and restrictive definitions and to free our mind of them.

A true classic, as I should like to hear it defined, is an author who has enriched the human mind, increased its treasure, and caused it to advance a step; who has discovered some moral and not equivocal truth, or revealed some eternal passion in that heart where all seemed known and discovered; who has expressed his thought, observation, or invention, in no matter what form, only provided it be broad and great, refined and sensible, sane and beautiful in itself; who has spoken to all in his own peculiar style, a style which is found to be also that of the whole world, a style new without neologism, new and old, easily contemporary with all time.

Such a classic may for a moment have been revolutionary; it may at least have seemed so, but it is not; it only lashed and subverted whatever prevented the restoration of the balance of order and beauty.

If it is desired, names may be applied to this definition which I wish to make purposely majestic and fluctuating, or in a word, all-embracing. I should first put there Corneille of the *Polyeucte, Cinna,* and *Horaces.* I should put Molière there, the fullest and most complete poetic genius we have ever had in France. Goethe, the king of critics, said:—

Molière is so great that he astonishes us afresh every time we read him. He is a man apart; his plays border on the tragic, and no one has the courage to try and imitate him. His *Avare,* where vice destroys all affection between father and son, is one of the most sublime works, and dramatic in the highest degree. In a drama every action ought to be important in itself, and to lead to an action greater still. In this respect *Tartuffe* is a model. What a piece of exposition the first scene is! From the beginning everything has an important meaning, and causes something much more important to be foreseen. The exposition in a certain play of Lessing that might be mentioned is very fine, but the world only sees that of *Tartuffe* once. It is the finest of the kind we

possess. Every year I read a play of Molière, just as from time to time
I contemplate some engraving after the great Italian masters.

I do not conceal from myself that the definition of the classic
I have just given somewhat exceeds the notion usually ascribed
to the term. It should, above all, include conditions of uniform-
ity, wisdom, moderation, and reason, which dominate and contain all the others. Having to praise M. Royer-Collard, M. de
Rémusat said—"If he derives *purity of taste, propriety of terms,
variety of expression,* attentive care in *suiting the action to the
thought,* from our classics, he owes to himself alone the distinctive character he gives it all." It is here evident that the part
allotted to classical qualities seems mostly to depend on harmony
and *nuances* of expression, on graceful and temperate style: such
is also the most general opinion. In this sense the pre-eminent
classics would be writers of a middling order, exact, sensible,
elegant, always clear, yet of noble feeling and airily veiled
strength. Marie-Joseph Chénier has described the poetics of those
temperate and accomplished writers in lines where he shows
himself their happy disciple:—

It is good sense, reason which does all,—virtue, genius, soul, talent,
and taste.—What is virtue? reason put in practice;—talent? reason expressed with brilliance;—soul? reason delicately put forth;—and genius is sublime reason.

While writing those lines he was evidently thinking of Pope,
Boileau, and Horace, the master of them all. The peculiar characteristic of the theory which subordinated imagination and
feeling itself to reason, of which Scaliger perhaps gave the first
sign among the moderns, is, properly speaking, the *Latin* theory,
and for a long time it was also by preference the *French* theory.
If it is used appositely, if the term *reason* is not abused, that
theory possesses some truth; but it is evident that it is abused,
and that if, for instance, reason can be confounded with poetic
genius and make one with it in a moral epistle, it cannot be the
same thing as the genius, so varied and so diversely creative in
its expression of the passions, of the drama or the epic. Where
will you find reason in the fourth book of the *Æneid* and the
transports of Dido? Be that as it may, the spirit which prompted
the theory, caused writers who ruled their inspiration, rather than

those who abandoned themselves to it, to be placed in the first rank of classics; to put Virgil there more surely than Homer, Racine in preference to Corneille. The masterpiece to which the theory likes to point, which in fact bring together all conditions of prudence, strength, tempered boldness, moral elevation, and grandeur, is *Athalie.* Turenne in his last two campaigns and Racine in *Athalie* are the great examples of what wise and prudent men are capable of when they reach the maturity of their genius and attain their supremest boldness.

Buffon, in his Discourse on Style, insisting on the unity of design, arrangement, and execution, which are the stamps of true classical works, said:—"Every subject is one, *and however vast it is, it can be comprised in a single treatise.* Interruptions, pauses, sub-divisions should only be used when many subjects are treated, when, having to speak of great, intricate, and dissimilar things, the march of genius is interrupted by the multiplicity of obstacles, and contracted by the necessity of circumstances: otherwise, far from making a work more solid, a great number of divisions destroys the unity of its parts; the book appears clearer to the view, but the author's design remains obscure." And he continues his criticism, having in view Montesquieu's *Spirit of Laws,* an excellent book at bottom, but subdivided: the famous author, worn out before the end, was unable to infuse inspiration into all his ideas, and to arrange all his matter. However, I can scarcely believe that Buffon was not also thinking, by way of contrast, of Bossuet's *Discourse on Universal History,* a subject vast indeed, and yet of such an unity that the great orator was able to comprise it in a single treatise. When we open the first edition, that of 1681, before the division into chapters, which was introduced later, passed from the margin into the text, everything is developed in a single series, almost in one breath. It might be said that the orator has here acted like the nature of which Buffon speaks, that "he has worked on an eternal plan from which he has nowhere departed," so deeply does he seem to have entered into the familiar counsels and designs of providence.

Are *Athalie* and the *Discourse on Universal History* the greatest masterpieces that the strict classical theory can present to its friends as well as to its enemies? In spite of the admirable

simplicity and dignity in the achievement of such unique productions, we should like, nevertheless, in the interests of art, to
expand that theory a little, and to show that it is possible to
enlarge it without relaxing the tension. Goethe, whom I like
to quote on such a subject, said:—

> I call the classical *healthy*, and the romantic *sickly*. In my opinion
> the Nibelungen song is as much a classic as Homer. Both are healthy
> and vigorous. The works of the day are romantic, not because they are
> new, but because they are weak, ailing, or sickly. Ancient works are
> classical not because they are old, but because they are powerful,
> fresh, and healthy. If we regarded romantic and classical from those
> two points of view we should soon all agree.

Indeed, before determining and fixing the opinions on that
matter, I should like every unbiased mind to take a voyage
round the world and devote itself to a survey of different literatures in their primitive vigour and infinite variety. What would
be seen? Chief of all a Homer, the father of the classical world,
less a single distinct individual than the vast living expression of
a whole epoch and a semi-barbarous civilisation. In order to
make him a true classic, it was necessary to attribute to him later
a design, a plan, literary invention, qualities of atticism and
urbanity of which he had certainly never dreamed in the luxuriant development of his natural aspirations. And who appear by
his side? August, venerable ancients, the Æschyluses and the
Sophocles, mutilated, it is true, and only there to present us with
a *débris* of themselves, the survivors of many others as worthy,
doubtless, as they to survive, but who have succumbed to the in-
juries of time. This thought alone would teach a man of impartial
mind not to look upon the whole of even classical literatures
with a too narrow and restricted view; he would learn that the
exact and well-proportioned order which has since so largely
prevailed in our admiration of the past was only the outcome
of artificial circumstances.

And in reaching the modern world, how would it be? The
greatest names to be seen at the beginning of literatures are those
which disturb and run counter to certain fixed ideas of what is
beautiful and appropriate in poetry. For example, is Shakespeare
a classic? Yes, now, for England and the world; but in the time

of Pope he was not considered so. Pope and his friends were the only pre-eminent classics; directly after their death they seemed so for ever. At the present time they are still classics, as they deserve to be, but they are only of the second order, and are for ever subordinated and relegated to their rightful place by him who has again come to his own on the height of the horizon.

It is not, however, for me to speak ill of Pope or his great disciples, above all, when they possess pathos and naturalness like Goldsmith: after the greatest they are perhaps the most agreeable writers and the poets best fitted to add charm to life. Once when Lord Bolingbroke was writing to Swift, Pope added a postscript, in which he said—"I think some advantage would result to our age, if we three spent three years together." Men who, without boasting, have the right to say such things must never be spoken of lightly: the fortunate ages, when men of talent could propose such things, then no chimera, are rather to be envied. The ages called by the name of Louis XIV or of Queen Anne are, in the dispassionate sense of the word, the only true classical ages, those which offer protection and a favourable climate to real talent. We know only too well how in our untrammelled times, through the instability and storminess of the age, talents are lost and dissipated. Nevertheless, let us acknowledge our age's part and superiority in greatness. True and sovereign genius triumphs over the very difficulties that cause others to fail: Dante, Shakespeare, and Milton were able to attain their height and produce their imperishable works in spite of obstacles, hardships, and tempests. Byron's opinion of Pope has been much discussed, and the explanation of it sought in the kind of contradiction by which the singer of *Don Juan* and *Childe Harold* extolled the purely classical school and pronounced it the only good one, while himself acting so differently. Goethe spoke the truth on that point when he remarked that Byron, great by the flow and source of poetry, feared that Shakespeare was more powerful than himself in the creation and realisation of his characters. "He would have liked to deny it; the elevation so free from egoism irritated him; he felt when near it that he could not display himself at ease. He never denied Pope, because he did not fear him; he knew that Pope was only a *low wall* by his side."

If, as Byron desired, Pope's school had kept the supremacy and a sort of honorary empire in the past, Byron would have been the first and only poet in his particular style; the height of Pope's wall shuts out Shakespeare's great figure from sight, whereas when Shakespeare reigns and rules in all his greatness, Byron is only second.

In France there was no great classic before the age of Louis XIV; the Dantes and Shakespeares, the early authorities to whom, in times of emancipation, men sooner or later return, were wanting. There were mere sketches of great poets, like Mathurin Regnier, like Rabelais, without any ideal, without the depth of emotion and the seriousness which canonises. Montaigne was a kind of premature classic, of the family of Horace; but for want of worthy surroundings, like a spoiled child, he gave himself up to the unbridled fancies of his style and humour. Hence it happened that France, less than any other nation, found in her old authors a right to demand vehemently at a certain time literary liberty and freedom, and that it was more difficult for her, in enfranchising herself, to remain classical. However, with Molière and La Fontaine among her classics of the great period, nothing could justly be refused to those who possessed courage and ability.

The important point now seems to me to be to uphold, while extending, the idea and belief. There is no receipt for making classics; this point should be clearly recognised. To believe that an author will become a classic by imitating certain qualities of purity, moderation, accuracy, and elegance, independently of the style and inspiration, is to believe that after Racine the father there is a place for Racine the son; dull and estimable *rôle*, the worst in poetry. Further, it is hazardous to take too quickly and without opposition the place of a classic in the sight of one's contemporaries; in that case there is a good chance of not retaining the position with posterity. Fontanes in his day was regarded by his friends as a pure classic; see how at twenty-five years' distance his star has set. How many of these precocious classics are there who do not endure, and who are so only for a while! We turn round one morning and are surprised not to find them standing behind us. Madame de Sévigné would wittily say they possessed but an *evanescent colour*. With regard to classics, the least expected prove the best and greatest: seek them rather in the vigorous genius born immortal and flourishing for ever. Apparently the least classical of the four great poets of the age of Louis XIV was Molière; he was then applauded far more than he was esteemed; men took delight in him without understanding his worth. After him, La Fontaine seemed the least classical: observe after two centuries what is the result for both. Far above Boileau, even above Racine, are they not now unanimously considered to possess in the highest degree the characteristics of an all-embracing morality?

Meanwhile there is no question of sacrificing or depreciating anything. I believe the temple of taste is to be rebuilt; but its reconstruction is merely a matter of enlargement, so that it may become the home of all noble human beings, of all who have permanently increased the sum of the mind's delights and possessions. As for me, who cannot, obviously, in any degree pretend to be the architect or designer of such a temple, I shall confine myself to expressing a few earnest wishes, to submit, as it were, my designs for the edifice. Above all I should desire not to exclude any one among the worthy, each should be in his place there, from Shakespeare, the freest of creative geniuses, and the greatest of classics without knowing it, to Andrieux, the last of classics in little. "There is more than one chamber in the mansions of my Father"; that should be as true of the kingdom of the beautiful here below, as of the kingdom of Heaven. Homer, as always and everywhere, should be first, likest a god; but behind him, like the procession of the three wise kings of the East, would be seen the three great poets, the three Homers, so long ignored by us, who wrote epics for the use of the old peoples of Asia, the poets Valmiki, Vyasa of the Hindoos, and Firdousi of the Persians: in the domain of taste it is well to know that such men exist, and not to divide the human race. Our homage paid to what is recognised as soon as perceived, we must not stray further; the eye should delight in a thousand pleasing or majestic spectacles, should rejoice in a thousand varied and surprising combinations, whose apparent confusion would never be without concord and harmony. The oldest of the wise men and poets, those who put human morality into maxims, and those who in simple fashion sung it, would converse together in *rare and gentle* speech, and would not be surprised at understanding each other's meaning at the very first word. Solon, Hesiod, Theognis, Job, Solomon, and why not Confucius, would welcome the cleverest moderns. La Rochefoucauld and La Bruyère, who, when listening to them, would say "they knew all that we know, and in repeating life's experiences, we have discovered nothing." On the hill, most easily discernible, and of most accessible ascent, Virgil, surrounded by Menander, Tibullus, Terence, Fénélon, would occupy himself in discoursing with them with great charm and divine enchantment: his gentle countenance would shine with an inner light, and be tinged with modesty; as on the day when entering the theatre at Rome, just as they finished reciting his verses, he saw the people rise with an unanimous movement and pay to him the same homage as to Augustus. Not far from him, regretting the separation from so dear a friend, Horace, in his turn, would preside (as far as so accomplished and wise a poet could preside) over the group of poets of social life who could talk although they sang,—Pope, Boileau, the one become less irritable, the other less fault-finding. Montaigne, a true poet, would be among them, and would give the finishing touch that should deprive that delightful corner of the air of a literary school. There would La Fontaine forget himself, and becoming less volatile would wander no more. Voltaire would be attracted by it, but while finding pleasure in it would not have patience to remain. A little lower down, on the same hill as Virgil, Xenophon, with a simple bearing, looking in no way like a general, but rather resembling a priest of the Muses, would be seen gathering round him the Attics of every tongue and of every nation, the Addisons, Pellissons, Vauvenargues—all who feel the value of an easy persuasiveness, an exquisite simplicity, and a gentle negligence mingled with ornament. In the centre of the place, in the portico of the principle temple (for there would be several in the enclosure), three great men would like to meet often, and when they were together, no fourth, however great, would dream of joining their discourse or their silence. In them would be seen beauty, proportion in greatness, and that perfect harmony which appears but once in the full youth of the world. Their three names have become the ideal of art—Plato, Sophocles, and Demosthenes. Those demi-gods honoured, we see a

numerous and familiar company of choice spirits who follow, the
Cervantes and Molières, practical painters of life, indulgent
friends who are still the first of benefactors, who laughingly embrace all mankind, turn man's experience to gaiety, and know
the powerful workings of a sensible, hearty, and legitimate joy.
I do not wish to make this description, which if complete would
fill a volume, any longer. In the middle ages, believe me, Dante
would occupy the sacred heights: at the feet of the singer of
Paradise all Italy would be spread out like a garden; Boccaccio
and Ariosto would there disport themselves, and Tasso would
find again the orange groves of Sorrento. Usually a corner would
be reserved for each of the various nations, but the authors
would take delight in leaving it, and in their travels would recognise, where we should least expect it, brothers or masters.
Lucretius, for example, would enjoy discussing the origin of the
world and the reducing of chaos to order with Milton. But both
arguing from their own point of view, they would only agree as
regards divine pictures of poetry and nature.

Such are our classics; each individual imagination may finish
the sketch and choose the group preferred. For it is necessary to
make a choice, and the first condition of taste, after obtaining
knowledge of all, lies not in continual travel, but in rest and ces-
sation from wandering. Nothing blunts and destroys taste so
much as endless journeyings; the poetic spirit is not the *Wandering Jew*. However, when I speak of resting and making choice,
my meaning is not that we are to imitate those who charm us
most among our masters in the past. Let us be content to know
them, to penetrate them, to admire them; but let us, the late-
comers, endeavour to be ourselves. Let us have the sincerity and
naturalness of our own thoughts, of our own feelings; so much
is always possible. To that let us add what is more difficult, elevation, an aim, if possible, towards an exalted goal; and while
speaking our own language, and submitting to the conditions of
the times in which we live, whence we derive our strength and
our defects, let us ask from time to time, our brows lifted towards
the heights and our eyes fixed on the group of honoured mortals:
what would they say of us?

But why speak always of authors and writings? Maybe an age
is coming when there will be no more writing. Happy those who

read and read again, those who in their reading can follow their
unrestrained inclination! There comes a time in life when, all
our journeys over, our experiences ended, there is no enjoyment
more delightful than to study and thoroughly examine the things
we know, to take pleasure in what we feel, and in seeing and
seeing again the people we love: the pure joys of our maturity.
Then it is that the word classic takes its true meaning, and is
defined for every man of taste by an irresistible choice. Then
taste is formed, it is shaped and definite; then good sense, if we
are to possess it at all, is perfected in us. We have neither more
time for experiments, nor a desire to go forth in search of pas-
tures new. We cling to our friends, to those proved by a long intercourse. Old wine, old books, old friends. We say to ourselves
with Voltaire in these delightful lines:—"Let us enjoy, let us
write, let us live, my dear Horace! . . . I have lived longer than
you: my verse will not last so long. But on the brink of the
tomb I shall make it my chief care—to follow the lessons of your
philosophy—to despise death in enjoying life—to read your writings full of charm and good sense—as we drink an old wine
which revives our senses."

In fact, be it Horace or another who is the author preferred,
who reflects our thoughts in all the wealth of their maturity, of
some one of those excellent and antique minds shall we request
an interview at every moment; of some one of them shall we ask
a friendship which never deceives, which could not fail us; to
some one of them shall we appeal for that sensation of serenity
and amenity (we have often need of it) which reconciles us with
mankind and with ourselves.

Hippolyte Taine

[1828–1893]

◆§§◆

TAINE's *History of English Literature* (1864) is the result of the fusion of two traditions. The first and most obvious is that of sociological criticism. This tradition, usually traced to Giambattista Vico's *New Science* (1725), is evident in such nineteenth-century works as Madame de Staël's *Literature in Its Relation to Social Institutions* (1800) and Sainte-Beuve's *Port-Royal* (1840 and later), and was encouraged by the scientific social theories of Auguste Comte. The second tradition is that of German idealism, which Taine absorbed from Hegel. From the first tradition he derived his theory of the influence of "race, environment, and epoch" on the literary work. From the second he derived his organic view of society and his theory of history as a dialectic in which each age (or literary "period") tends to give way to its anthesis, the whole process resulting in cultural evolution. Hegel also encouraged Taine to think of his approach as a means of describing the spiritual history of man, a fact often overlooked by readers who interpret the "Introduction" as an expression of simple environmental determinism.

Taine's influence is multifarious. It can be traced in all forms of historical criticism from the history of literary genres to the "history of ideas" as practiced by scholars such as Arthur Lovejoy. Reduced to narrower scope than he would have approved, his method is evident in the work of Marxist and Freudian critics.

Taine's *History* was translated by Henry van Laun in 1871, and this translation has often been reprinted. Other important works include *Essais de critique et d'histoire* (1858) and *Nouveaux essais de critique et d'histoire* (1865). For discussion see: I. Babbitt, *Masters of Modern French Criticism* (Boston, 1912); A. Cresson, *Hippolyte Taine* (Paris, 1951); L. Gates, "Taine's Influence as a Critic," *Studies and Appreciations* (New York, 1900); S. Kahn, *Science and Aesthetic Judgment* (New York, 1953); H. Levin, "Literature as an Institution," *Accent*, VI (1946), 159–68; H. Needham, *La Devéloppment de l'esthétique sociologique en france et en angleterre au XIXe siècle* (Paris, 1926); R. Wellek, "Hippolyte Taine's Theory and Criticism," *Criticism*, I (1959), 1–18.

The present selections are from the "Introduction" to the *History,* trans. by Henry van Laun (New York, 1902).

INTRODUCTION TO THE HISTORY OF ENGLISH LITERATURE

I. THE AIMS OF LITERARY HISTORY

HISTORY, within a hundred years in Germany, and within sixty years in France, has undergone a transformation, owing to a study of literatures.

The discovery has been made that a literary work is not a mere play of the imagination, the isolated caprice of an excited brain, but a transcript of contemporary manners and customs and the sign of a particular state of intellect. The conclusion derived from this is that, through literary monuments, we can retrace the way in which men felt and thought many centuries ago. This method has been tried and found successful.

We have meditated over these ways of feeling and thinking and have accepted them as facts of prime significance. We have found that they were dependent on most important events, that they explain these, and that these explain them, and that henceforth it was necessary to give them their place in history, and one of the highest. This place has been assigned to them, and hence all is changed in history—the aim, the method, the instrumentalities, and the conceptions of laws and of causes. It is this change as now going on, and which must continue to go on, that is here attempted to be set forth.

II. HISTORY AS THE STUDY OF MAN'S SPIRIT

On observing the visible man with your own eyes what do you try to find in him? The invisible man. These words which your ears catch, those gestures, those airs of the head, his attire and sensible operations of all kinds, are, for you, merely so many expressions; these express something, a soul. An inward man is hidden beneath the outward man, and the latter simply manifests the former. You have observed the house in which he lives, his furniture, his costume, in order to discover his habits and tastes, the degree of his refinement or rusticity, his extravagance or economy, his follies or his cleverness. You have listened to his conversation and noted the inflections of his voice, the attitudes he has assumed, so as to judge of his spirit, self-abandonment or gayety, his energy or his rigidity. You consider his writings, works of art, financial and political schemes, with a view to measure the reach and limits of his intelligence, his creative power and self-command, to ascertain the usual order, kind, and force of his conceptions, in what way he thinks and how he resolves. All these externals are so many avenues converging to one centre, and you follow these only to reach that centre; here is the real man, namely, that group of faculties and of sentiments which produces the rest. Behold a new world, an infinite world; for each visible action involves an infinite train of reasonings and emotions, new or old sensations which have combined to bring this into light and which, like long ledges of rock sunk deep in the earth, have cropped out above the surface and attained their level. It is this subterranean world which forms the second aim, the special object of the historian. If his critical education suffices, he is able to discriminate under every ornament in architecture, under every stroke of the brush in a picture, under each phrase of literary composition, the particular sentiment out of which the ornament, the stroke, and the phrase have sprung; he is a spectator of the inward drama which has developed itself in the breast of the artist or writer; the choice of words, the length or shortness of the period, the species of metaphor, the accent of a verse, the chain of reasoning— all are to him an indication; while his eyes are reading the text his mind and soul are following the steady flow and ever-changing series of emotions and conceptions from which this text has issued; he is working out its psychology. Should you desire to study this operation, regard the promoter and model of all the high culture of the epoch, Goethe, who, before composing his "Iphigenia" spent days in making drawings of the most perfect statues and who, at last, his eyes filled with the noble forms of antique scenery and his mind penetrated by the harmonious beauty of antique life, succeeded in reproducing internally, with such exactness, the habits and yearnings of Greek imagination as to provide us with an almost twin sister of the "Antigone" of Sophocles and of the goddesses of Phidias. This exact and demonstrated divination of bygone sentiments has, in our days, given a new life to history. There was almost complete ignorance of this in the last century; men of every race and of every epoch were represented as about alike, the Greek, the barbarian, the Hindoo, the man of the Renaissance and the man of the eighteenth century, cast in the same mold and after the same pattern, and after a certain abstract conception which served for the whole human species. There was a knowledge of man but not of men. There was no penetration into the soul itself; nothing of the infinite diversity and wonderful complexity of souls had been detected; it was not known that the moral organization of a people or of an age is as special and distinct as the physical structure of a family of plants or of an order of animals. History today, like zoölogy, has found its anatomy, and whatever branch of it is studied, whether philology, languages or mythologies, it is in this way that labor must be given to make it produce new fruit. Among so many writers who, since Herder, Ottfried Müller, and Goethe have steadily followed and rectified this great effort, let the reader take two historians and two works, one "The Life and Letters of Cromwell" by Carlyle, and the other the "Port Royal" of Sainte-Beuve. He will see how precisely, how clearly, and how profoundly we detect the soul of a man beneath his actions and works.

III. RACE, ENVIRONMENT, AND EPOCH

Three different sources contribute to the production of this elementary moral state, race, environment, and epoch. What we call race consists of those innate and hereditary dispositions which man brings with him into the world and which are generally accompanied with marked differences of temperament and of bodily structure. They vary in different nations. Naturally, there are varieties of men as there are varieties of cattle and horses, some brave and intelligent, and others timid and of limited capacity; some capable of superior conceptions and creations, and others reduced to rudimentary ideas and contrivances; some specially fitted for certain works, and more richly furnished with certain instincts, as we see in the better endowed species of dogs, some for running and others for fighting, some for hunting and others for guarding houses and flocks. We have here a distinct force; so distinct that, in spite of the enormous deviations which both the other motors impress upon it, we still recognize, and which a race like the Aryan people, scattered from the Ganges to the Hebrides, established under all climates, ranged along every degree of civilization, transformed by thirty centuries of revolutions, shows nevertheless in its languages, in its religions, in its literatures, and in its philosophies, the community of blood and of intellect which still today binds together all its offshoots. However they may differ, their parentage is not lost; barbarism, culture and grafting, differences of atmosphere and of soil, fortunate or unfortunate occurrences, have operated in vain; the grand characteristics of the original form have lasted, and we find that the two or three leading features of the primitive imprint are again apparent under the subsequent imprints with which time has overlaid them. There is nothing surprising in this extraordinary tenacity. Although the immensity of the distance allows us to catch only a glimpse in a dubious light of the origin of species,[1] the events of history throw sufficient light on events anterior to history to explain the almost unshaken solidity of primordial traits. At the moment of encountering them, fifteen, twenty, and thirty centuries before our era, in an Aryan, Egyptian, or Chinese, they represent the work of a much greater number of centuries, perhaps the work of many myriads of centuries. For, as soon as an animal is born it must adapt itself to its surroundings; it breathes in another way, it renews itself differently, it is otherwise stimulated according as the atmosphere, the food, and the temperature are different. A different climate and situation create different necessities and hence activities of a different kind; and hence, again, a system of different habits, and, finally a system of different aptitudes and instincts. Man, thus compelled to put himself in equilibrium with circumstances, contracts a corresponding tem-

[1] Darwin, "The Origin of Species." Prosper Lucas, "De l'Hérédité."

perament and character, and his character, like his temperament,
are acquisitions all the more stable because of the outward impression being more deeply imprinted in him by more frequent
repetitions and transmitted to his offspring by more ancient
heredity. So that at each moment of time, the character of a
people may be considered as a summary of all antecedent actions and sensations; that is to say, as a quantity and as a weighty
mass, not infinite,[2] since all things in nature are limited, but disproportionate to the rest and almost impossible to raise, since
each minute of an almost infinite past has contributed to render
it heavier, and, in order to turn the scale, it would require, on the
other side, a still greater accumulation of actions and sensations.
Such is the first and most abundant source of these master faculties from which historic events are derived; and we see at once
that if it is powerful it is owing to its not being a mere source,
but a sort of lake, and like a deep reservoir wherein other sources
have poured their waters for a multitude of centuries.

When we have thus verified the internal structure of a race
we must consider the environment in which it lives. For man is
not alone in the world; nature envelops him and other men surround him; accidental and secondary folds come and overspread
the primitive and permanent fold, while physical or social circumstances derange or complete the natural groundwork surrendered to them. At one time climate has had its effect. Although the history of Aryan nations can be only obscurely traced
from their common country to their final abodes, we can nevertheless affirm that the profound difference which is apparent between the Germanic races on the one hand, and the Hellenic and
Latin races on the other, proceeds in great part from the differences between the countries in which they have established
themselves—the former in cold and moist countries, in the depths
of gloomy forests and swamps, or on the borders of a wild ocean,
confined to melancholic or rude sensations, inclined to drunkenness and gross feeding, leading a militant and carnivorous life;
the latter, on the contrary, living amidst the finest scenery, alongside of a brilliant, sparkling sea inviting navigation and com-
merce, exempt from the grosser cravings of the stomach, disposed
at the start to social habits and customs, to political organiza-

[2] Spinosa, "Ethics," part iv, axiom.

tion, to the sentiments and faculties which develop the art
of speaking, the capacity for enjoyment and invention in the
sciences, in art, and in literature. At another time, political
events have operated, as in the two Italian civilizations: the first
one tending wholly to action, to conquest, to government, and to
legislation, through the primitive situation of a city of refuge, a
frontier emporium, and of an armed aristocracy which, import-
ing and enrolling foreigners and the vanquished under it, sets
two hostile bodies facing each other, with no outlet for its internal troubles and rapacious instincts but systematic warfare; the
second one, excluded from unity and political ambition on a
grand scale by the permanency of its municipal system, by the
cosmopolite situation of its pope and by the military intervention
of neighboring states, and following the bent of its magnificent
and harmonious genius, is wholly carried over to the worship of
voluptuousness and beauty. Finally, at another time, social conditions have imposed their stamp as, eighteen centuries ago, by
Christianity, and twenty-five centuries ago by Buddhism, when,
around the Mediterranean as in Hindostan, the extreme effects
of Aryan conquest and organization let to intolerable oppression, the crushing of the individual, utter despair, the whole
world under the ban of a curse, with the development of metaphysics and visions, until man, in this dungeon of despondency,
feeling his heart melt, conceived of abnegation, charity, tender
love, gentleness, humility, human brotherhood, here in the idea
of universal nothingness, and there under that of the fatherhood
of God. Look around at the regulative instincts and faculties implanted in a race; in brief, the turn of mind according to which it
thinks and acts at the present day; we shall find most frequently
that its work is due to one of these prolonged situations, to these
enveloping circumstances, to these persistent gigantic pressures
brought to bear on a mass of men who, one by one, and all
collectively, from one generation to another, have been unceasingly bent and fashioned by them, in Spain a crusade of
eight centuries against the Mohammedans, prolonged yet longer
even to the exhaustion of the nation through the expulsion of
the Moors, through the spoliation of the Jews, through the establishment of the Inquisition, through the Catholic wars; in
England, a political establishment of eight centuries which main-

tains man erect and respectful, independent and obedient, all
accustomed to struggling together in a body under the sanc-
tion of law; in France, a Latin organization which, at first imposed on docile barbarians, then levelled to the ground under the
universal demolition, forms itself anew under the latent workings of national instinct, developing under hereditary monarchs
and ending in a sort of equalized, centralized, administrative republic under dynasties exposed to revolutions. Such are the most
efficacious among the observable causes which mold the primitive man; they are to nations what education, pursuit, condition,
and abode are to individuals, and seem to comprise all, since
the external forces which fashion human matter, and by which
the outward acts on the inward, are comprehended in them.

There is, nevertheless, a third order of causes, for, with the
forces within and without, there is the work these have already
produced together, which work itself contributes towards producing the ensuing work; beside the permanent impulsion and
the given environment there is the acquired momentum. When
national character and surrounding circumstances operate it is
not on a *tabula rasa,* but on one already bearing imprints. According as this *tabula* is taken at one or at another moment so is
the imprint different, and this suffices to render the total effect
different. Consider, for example, two moments of a literature
or of an art, French tragedy under Corneille and under Voltaire,
and Greek drama under Æschylus and under Euripides, Latin
poetry under Lucretius and under Claudian, and Italian painting under Da Vinci and under Guido. Assuredly, there is no
change of general conception of either of these two extreme
points; ever the same human type must be portrayed or represented in action; the cast of the verse, the dramatic structure,
the physical form have all persisted. But there is this among
these differences, that one of the artists is a precursor and the
other a successor, that the first one has no model and the second
one has a model; that the former sees things face to face, and
that the latter sees them through the intermediation of the
former, that many departments of art have become more perfect,
that the simplicity and grandeur of the impression have diminished, that what is pleasing and refined in form has augmented—
in short, that the first work has determined the second. In this

respect, it is with a people as with a plant; the same sap at the same temperature and in the same soil produces, at different stages of its successive elaborations, different developments, buds, flowers, fruits, and seeds, in such a way that the condition of the following is always that of the preceding and is born of its death. Now, if you no longer regard a brief moment, as above, but one of those grand periods of development which embraces one or many centuries like the Middle Ages, or our last classic period, the conclusion is the same. A certain dominating conception has prevailed throughout; mankind, during two hundred years, during five hundred years, have represented to themselves a certain ideal figure of man, in mediæval times the knight and the monk, in our classic period the courtier and refined talker; this creative and universal conception has monopolized the entire field of action and thought, and, after spreading its involuntarily systematic works over the world, it languished and then died out, and now a new idea has arisen, destined to a like domination and to equally multiplied creations. Note here that the latter depends in part on the former, and that it is the former, which, combining its effect with those of national genius and surrounding circumstances, will impose their bent and their direction on new-born things. It is according to this law that great historic currents are formed, meaning by this, the long rule of a form of intellect or of a master idea, like that period of spontaneous creations called the Renaissance, or that period of oratorical classifications called the Classic Age, or that series of mystic systems called the Alexandrine and Christian epoch, or that series of mythological efflorescences found at the origins of Germany, India, and Greece. Here as elsewhere, we are dealing merely with a mechanical problem: the total effect is a compound wholly determined by the grandeur and direction of the forces which produce it. The sole difference which separates these moral problems from physical problems lies in this, that in the former the directions and grandeur cannot be estimated by or stated in figures with the same precision as in the latter. If a want, a faculty, is a quantity capable of degrees, the same as pressure or weight, this quantity is not measurable like that of the pressure or weight. We cannot fix it in an exact or approximative formula; we can obtain or give of it only a literary impression; we are reduced to noting and citing the prominent facts which make it manifest and which nearly, or roughly, indicate about what grade on the scale it must be ranged at. And yet, notwithstanding the methods of notation are not the same in the moral sciences as in the physical sciences, nevertheless, as matter is the same in both, and is equally composed of forces, directions and magnitudes, we can still show that in one as in the other, the final effect takes place according to the same law. This is great or small, according as the fundamental forces are great or small and act more or less precisely in the same sense, according as the distinct effects of race, environment and epoch combine to enforce each other or combine to neutralize each other. Thus are explained the long impotences and the brilliant successes which appear irregularly and with no apparent reason in the life of a people; the causes of these consist in internal concordances and contrarities.

IV. THE LAW OF MUTUAL DEPENDENCIES

There remains to be ascertained in what way these causes, applied to a nation or to a century, distribute their effects. Like a spring issuing from an elevated spot and diffusing its waters, according to the height, from ledge to ledge, until it finally reaches the low ground, so does the tendency of mind or of soul in a people, due to race, epoch, or environment, diffuse itself in different proportions, and by regular descent, over the different series of facts which compose its civilization.[3] In preparing the geographical map of a country, starting at its watershed, we see the slopes, just below this common point, dividing themselves into five or six principal basins, and then each of the latter into several others, and so on until the whole country, with its thousands of inequalities of surface, is included in the ramifications of this network. In like manner, in preparing the psychological map of the events and sentiments belonging to a certain human

---

[3] For this scale of coördinate effects consult, "Langues Sémitiques," by Renan, ch. 1; "Comparison des civilisations Grecque et Romaine," vol. i, ch. i, 3d ed., by Mommsen; "Conséquences de la démocratie," vol. iii, by De Tocqueville.

civilization, we find at the start five or six well determined provinces—religion, art, philosophy, the state, the family, and industries; next, in each of these provinces, natural departments, and then finally, in each of these departments, still smaller territories until we arrive at those countless details of life which we observe daily in ourselves and around us. If, again, we examine and compare together these various groups of facts we at once find that they are composed of parts and that all have parts in common. Let us take first the three principal products of human intelligence—religion, art, and philosophy. What is a philosophy but a conception of nature and of its primordial causes under the form of abstractions and formulas? What underlies a religion and an art if not a conception of this same nature, and of these same primordial causes, under the form of more or less determinate symbols, and of more or less distinct personages, with this difference, that in the first case we believe that they exist, and in the second case that they do not exist. Let the reader consider some of the great creations of the intellect in India, in Scandinavia, in Persia, in Rome, in Greece, and he will find that art everywhere is a sort of philosophy become sensible, religion a sort of poem regarded as true, and philosophy a sort of art and religion, dessicated and reduced to pure abstractions. There is, then, in the centre of each of these groups a common element, the conception of the world and its origin, and if they differ amongst each other it is because each combines with the common element a distinct element; here the power of abstraction, there the faculty of personifying with belief, and, finally, the talent for personifying without belief. Let us now take the two leading products of human association, the Family and the State. What constitutes the State other than the sentiment of obedience by which a multitude of men collect together under the authority of a chief? And what constitutes the Family other than the sentiment of obedience by which a wife and children act together under the direction of a father and husband? The Family is a natural, primitive, limited state, as the State is an artificial, ulterior, and expanded Family, while beneath the differences which arise from the number, origin, and condition of its members, we distinguish, in the small as in the large community, a like fundamental disposition of mind which brings them together

and unites them. Suppose, now, that this common element receives from the environment, the epoch, and the race peculiar
characteristics, and it is clear that all the groups into which it
enters will be proportionately modified. If the sentiment of
obedience is merely one of fear,[4] you encounter, as in most of the
Oriental states, the brutality of despotism, a prodigality of vigorous punishments, the exploitation of the subject, servile habits,
insecurity of property, impoverished production, female slavery,
and the customs of the harem. If the sentiment of obedience is
rooted in the instinct of discipline, sociability, and honor, you
find, as in France, a complete military organization, a superb
administrative hierarchy, a weak public spirit with outbursts of
patriotism, the unhesitating docility of the subject along with the
hotheadedness of the revolutionist, the obsequiousness of the
courtier along with the reverse of the gentleman, the charm of
refined conversation along with home and family bickerings, conjugal equality together with matrimonial incompatibilities under
the necessary constraints of the law. If, finally, the sentiment of
obedience is rooted in the instinct of subordination and in the
idea of duty, you perceive, as in Germanic nations, the security
and contentment of the household, the firm foundations of domestic life, the slow and imperfect development of worldly matters, innate respect for established rank, superstitious reverence
for the past, maintenance of social inequalities, natural and habitual deference to the law. Similarly in a race, just as there is a
difference of aptitude for general ideas, so will its religion, art,
and philosophy be different. If man is naturally fitted for broader
universal conceptions and inclined at the same time to their
derangement, through the nervous irritability of an overexcited
organization, we find, as in India, a surprising richness of gigantic religious creations, a splendid bloom of extravagant transparent epics, a strange concatenation of subtle, imaginative
philosophic systems, all so intimately associated and so inter-
penetrated with a common sap, that we at once recognize them,
by their amplitude, by their color, and by their disorder, as productions of the same climate and of the same spirit. If, on the
contrary, the naturally sound and well-balanced man is content

---

[4] "L'Esprit des Lois," by Montesquieu; the essential principles of the
three governments.

to restrict his conceptions to narrow bounds in order to cast them in more precise forms, we see, as in Greece, a theology of artists and narrators, special gods that are soon separated from objects and almost transformed at once into substantial personages, the sentiment of universal unity nearly effaced and scarcely maintained in the vague notion of destiny, a philosophy, rather than subtle and compact, grandiose and systemtic, narrow metaphysically but incomparable in its logic, sophistry, and morality, a poesy and arts superior to anything we have seen in lucidity, naturalness, proportion, truth, and beauty. If, finally, man is reduced to narrow conceptions deprived of any speculative subtlety, and at the same time finds that he is absorbed and completely hardened by practical interests, we see, as in Rome, rudimentary deities, mere empty names, good for denoting the petty details of agriculture, generation, and the household, veritable marriage and farming labels, and, therefore, a null or borrowed mythology, philosophy, and poesy. Here, as elsewhere, comes in the law of mutual dependencies. A civilization is a living unit, the parts of which hold together the same as the parts of an organic body. Just as in an animal, the instincts, teeth, limbs, bones, and muscular apparatus are bound together in such a way that a variation of one determines a corresponding variation in the others, and out of which a skilful naturalist, with a few bits, imagines and reconstructs an almost complete body, so, in a civilization, do religion, philosophy, the family scheme, literature and the arts form a system in which each local change involves a general change, so that an experienced historian, who studies one portion apart from the others, sees beforehand and partially predicts the characteristics of the rest. There is nothing vague in this dependence. The regulation of all this in the living body consists, first, of the tendency to manifest a certain primordial type, and, next, the necessity of its possessing organs which can supply its wants and put itself in harmony with itself in order to live. The regulation in a civilization consists in the presence in each great human creation of an elementary productor equally present in other surrounding creations, that is, some faculty and aptitude, some efficient and marked disposition, which, with its own peculiar character, introduces this with that into all operations in which it takes part, and which, according to its variations, causes variation in all the works in which it coöperates.

V. THE SIGNIFICANCE OF LITERARY HISTORY

The question as now stated is this: Given a literature, a philosophy, a society, an art, a certain group of arts, what is the moral state of things which produces it? And what are the conditions of race, epoch, and environment the best adapted to produce this moral state? There is a distinct moral state for each of these formations and for each of their branches; there is one for art in general as well as for each particular art; for architecture, painting, sculpture, music, and poetry, each with a germ of its own in the large field of human psychology; each has its own law, and it is by virtue of this law that we see each shoot up, apparently haphazard, singly and alone, amidst the miscarriages of their neighbors, like painting in Flanders and Holland in the seventeenth century, like poetry in England in the sixteenth century, like music in Germany in the eighteenth century. At this moment, and in these countries, the conditions for one art and not for the others are fulfilled, and one branch only has bloomed out amidst the general sterility. It is these laws of human vegetation which history must now search for; it is this special psychology of each special formation which must be got at; it is the composition of a complete table of these peculiar conditions that must now be worked out. There is nothing more delicate and nothing more difficult. Montesquieu undertook it, but in his day the interest in history was too recent for him to be successful; nobody, indeed, had any idea of the road that was to be followed, and even at the present day we scarcely begin to obtain a glimpse of it. Just as astronomy, at the bottom, is a mechanical problem, and physiology, likewise, a chemical problem, so is history, at bottom, a problem of psychology. There is a particular system of inner impressions and operations which fashions the artist, the believer, the musician, the painter, the nomad, the social man; for each of these, the filiation, intensity, and interdependence of

ideas and of emotions are different; each has his own moral
history, and his own special organization, along with some
master tendency and with some dominant trait. To explain
each of these would require a chapter devoted to a profound internal analysis, and that is a work that can scarcely be called
sketched out at the present day. But one man, Stendhal,
through a certain turn of mind and a peculiar education, has attempted it, and even yet most of his readers find his works
paradoxical and obscure. . . . And yet his works are those in
which we of the present day may find the most satisfactory
efforts that have been made to clear the road I have just striven
to describe. Nobody has taught one better how to observe
with one's own eyes, first, to regard humanity around us and
life as it is, and next, old and authentic documents; how to
read more than merely the black and white of the page; how to
detect under old print and the scrawl of the text the veritable
sentiment and the train of thought, the mental state in which
the words were penned. In his writings, as in those of Sainte-
Beuve and in those of the German critics, the reader will find
how much is to be derived from a literary document; if this
document is rich and we know how to interpret it, we will find in
it the psychology of a particular soul, often that of an age, and
sometimes that of a race. In this respect, a great poem, a good
novel, the confessions of a superior man, are more instructive
than a mass of historians and histories; I would give fifty volumes of charters and a hundred diplomatic files for the memoirs
of Cellini, the epistles of Saint Paul, the table-talk of Luther, or
the comedies of Aristophanes. Herein lies the value of literary
productions. They are instructive because they are beautiful;
their usefulness increases with their perfection; and if they provide us with documents, it is because they are monuments. The
more visible a book renders sentiments the more literary it is,
for it is the special office of literature to take note of sentiments.
The more important the sentiments noted in a book the higher
its rank in literature, for it is by representing what sort of a life
a nation or an epoch leads, that a writer rallies to himself the
sympathies of a nation or of an epoch. Hence, among the documents which bring before our eyes the sentiments of preceding
generations, a literature, and especially a great literature, is in-

comparably the best. It resembles those admirable instruments of remarkable sensitiveness which physicists make use of to detect and measure the most profound and delicate changes that occur in a human body. There is nothing approaching this in constitutions or religions; the articles of a code or of a catechism do no more than depict mind in gross and without finesse; if there are documents which show life and spirit in politics and in creeds, they are the eloquent discourses of the pulpit and the tribune, memoirs and personal confessions, all belonging to literature, so that, outside of itself, literature embodies whatever is good elsewhere. It is mainly in studying literatures that we are able to produce moral history, and arrive at some knowledge of the psychological laws on which events depend.

I have undertaken to write a history of a literature and to ascertain the psychology of a people; in selecting this one, it is not without a motive. A people had to be taken possessing a vast and complete literature, which is rarely found. There are few nations which, throughout their existence, have thought and written well in the full sense of the word. Among the ancients, Latin literature is null at the beginning, and afterward borrowed and an imitation. Among the moderns, German literature is nearly a blank for two centuries. Italian and Spanish literatures come to an end in the middle of the seventeenth century. Ancient Greece, and modern France and England, alone offer a complete series of great and expressive monuments. I have chosen the English because, as this still exists and is open to direct observation, it can be better studied than that of an extinct civilization of which fragments only remain; and because, being different, it offers better than that of France very marked characteristics in the eyes of a Frenchman. Moreover, outside of what is peculiar to English civilization, apart from a spontaneous development, it presents a forced deviation due to the latest and most effective conquest to which the country was subject; the three given conditions out of which it issues—race, climate, and the Norman conquest—are clearly and distinctly visible in its literary monuments; so that we study in this history the two most potent motors of human transformation, namely, nature and constraint, and we study them, without any break or uncertainty, in a series of authentic and complete monuments. I have tried to define these primitive motors, to show their gradual effects, and explain how their insensible operation has brought religions and literary productions into full light, and how the inward mechanism is developed by which the barbarous Saxon became the Englishman of the present day.

Ferdinand Brunetière

[1849–1906]

❦

A BRILLIANT CRITIC and an opponent of naturalism (in *Le Roman Naturaliste*, 1883), Brunetière became a leading spokesman for the historical method of criticism. Although admitting Taine's influence, he gave Darwin major credit for his evolutionary theory of literature. Among his many works the *Études critiques* (1880–98) and *L'Evolution des genres dans l'histoire de la littérature* (1890) are especially significant. The *Manual of the History of French Literature* (1897) is a good illustration of his method. In comparison to Taine's *History* it is objective, scholarly, and unblemished by Taine's tendency to exaggerate for the sake of drama or to illustrate a point. It remains today a useful introduction to its subject.

As the *Manual* illustrates, by the end of the nineteenth century the historical method had evolved far toward what is now known as historical scholarship. Other works illustrating the evolution of the historical method include August Boeckh, *Encyklopädie und Methodologie der Philologischen Wissenschaft* (1877); W. J. Courthope, *History of English Poetry* (1895–1905); and Georges Renard, *La Méthode scientifique de l'histoire littéraire* (1900). For discussion see: I. Babbitt, *Masters of Modern French Criticism* (Boston, 1912); A. Belis, *La Critique française à la fin du XIXe siècle* (Paris, 1926); E. Hocking, *Ferdinand Brunetière* (Madison, 1936).

The present selection is from the "Preliminary Notice" and "Preface to the English Edition" of the *Manual of the History of French Literature*, trans. by Ralph Derechef (New York, 1898).

PRELIMINARY NOTICE AND PREFACE TO MANUAL OF THE HISTORY OF FRENCH LITERATURE

IN WRITING this *Manual of the History of French Literature*, which is at the same time, I do not venture to say the promise,

94

but at least the "programme" of a more exhaustive and detailed "History," I have given attention to certain points, which will be noted I hope; but as there is a chance of their being overlooked —if I have been unsuccessful in making them clear—the reader will excuse my insisting upon them in this short preliminary notice.

In the first place, to the customary division into Centuries, and in each century into Branches—poetry set apart from prose; comedy in one section, the novel in a second, "eloquence" in a third—I have substituted the division into Literary Periods. For since the periods of physics or those of chemistry are not dated from the transition from one century to another, nor even from the beginning of the reign of a sovereign, what grounds are there to date in this way those of the history of a literature? Did writers reflect in the course of the year 1800 that they were about to belong to the nineteenth century; and are we to believe that they were at pains to differ from themselves in view of the advent of January 1, 1801? At the same time, the division into branches is in nowise less artificial or less arbitrary, supposing these branches to become differentiated, after the manner of species in the natural world, solely by the struggle, against one another, to which they are perpetually exposed. What, for instance, is tragi-comedy, if not the hesitation of the drama between the novel and the tragedy? And how shall we perceive this, if we separate the study of the novel from that of tragedy? The truth is, Literary Periods ought to be dated from only what are called literary events—the appearance of the *Lettres provinciales,* or the publication of the *Génie du Christianisme;* [1]— and this is not only in accordance with reality, but is also the only mode there is of giving the history of a literature that continuity of movement and life without which, in my opinion, there is no such thing as history.

In the second place—and with a view to making this continuity still clearer—I have not omitted to note these other influences on which it is the habit to lay weight, the influence of race or the influence of environment; however, as I hold that of all the in-

[1] The *Lettres provinciales* by Blaise Pascal first appeared in 1656; François-René de Chateaubriand's *Génie du Christianisme,* a herald of French romanticism, appeared in 1802. See below, pp. 292 ff. (Ed.)

fluences which make themselves felt in the history of a literature, the principal is that of *works on works,* I have made it my special concern to trace this influence and to follow its continuous action. We wish to be different from those who have preceded us in history: this design is the origin and determining cause of changes in taste as of literary revolutions; there is nothing metaphysical about it. The Pleiad of the sixteenth century wished to do "something different" from the school of Clément Marot. Racine in his *Andromaque* wished to do "something different" from Corneille in his *Pertharite;* and Diderot in his *Père de Famille* wished to do "something different" from Molière in his *Tartuffe.* The romanticists of our own time wished to do "something different" from the classicists. It is for this reason that I have not concerned myself with the other influences, except in so far as the succession of periods is not sufficiently explained by the influence of works on works. The useless multiplication of causes is to be avoided, and under the pretext that literature is the expression of society, the history of literature must not be confounded with that of manners. . . .

Again, this book being a Manual . . . I have so contrived these Notes, that each of them in its kind, and in its rather narrow but also most clearly defined scope, should be the outline or "summary" of a complete study, and naturally I have proportioned the dimensions of this study, as mathematically as I have been able, to the true importance of the writer who is its subject. I say "mathematically," because in such a matter there should be no intrusion of one's personal tastes; one does not write a History of French Literature for the purpose of giving expression in it to his own opinions, but, very much as he draws up the map of a large country, with a view to giving in it a correct idea of the relief, relations, and proportions of the constituent parts.

Further—always in order that the book might be more useful and a more efficacious and constant aid—I have given very special attention to the Bibliography of the subject. . . . In consequence, at the end of these notices will be found an almost complete enumeration of the *works,* and of the best editions, with their dates, of the *works* of each writer; while the notices begin with an enumeration of the principal *sources* of information to which reference can be made if desired. It is even incumbent on the student to refer to these sources: first, because he cannot neglect them without exposing himself to making discoveries that are not discoveries at all; and in the next place, because the very judgments formed upon the works of our writers by their contemporaries and by those who have come after them have become, as it were, incorporated with the idea we form of them ourselves. . . .

* * * *

It would doubtless be impossible for me to find a better or surer means of inviting the indulgence of English readers for the present Manual, than to offer it to them for what it is: an application of the doctrine of Evolution to the history of a great literature. In this way the work is placed, as it were, under the auspices of the great name of Charles Darwin, and while it is not for me to decide whether the illustrious author of the *Origin of Species* ranks, as has been maintained, but little below or perhaps on a level with Sir Isaac Newton in the history of modern European ideas, it is certain that for some forty years past his influence is everywhere to be traced. I shall be happy if English readers see it to be at work in the present volume. . . .

It is from the genealogical standpoint, then, that I have endeavoured to study in the history of French literature the perpetually changing succession of ideas, authors, and works; and if there be any novelty in this Manual it is constituted by this attitude.

I am aware that serious objection is taken to the employment of this method in history. To reply to many of the objections made would doubtless be beyond the scope of this short Preface, but among them is one graver, or apparently graver, than the others, and I must not pass over it entirely. What, it is said, is most interesting, or solely interesting perhaps, in the history of literature or art is the *individual*, Shakespeare or Molière, Milton or Bossuet, Pope or Boileau, Swift or Voltaire, Burke or Mirabeau, Tennyson or Lamartine, George Eliot or Honoré de Balzac; and I wholly share this opinion. Whether we study these writers in their works, or whether in their works it be they themselves that excite our preference, what interests us in them is what distinguishes them from all other writers, or what in them

is *irreducible* and *incommensurable*. In their own line they resemble themselves alone, a characteristic that is the cause of
their glory or renown. But is not this precisely the characteristic
that no method is capable of dealing with? And if we treat the
writers who possess it in conformity with the laws of the evolutionary hypothesis, is it not at the expense of the very originality
that is their pre-eminent quality? Do we not rob them of their
individuality by resolving it into its elements, and make away
with their singularity when we decompose it? At first sight it
seems that such is the case, but Darwin had answered the objection in advance; while inasmuch as it can scarcely be said
that he had the exigencies of the history of literature or art in
view when framing his reply, we have the more right to regard
it as convincing.

What, according to Darwin, is Natural Selection, and what
are the conditions under which it operates? He has told us explicitly, and indeed it is the definition of this power that his
disciples, in spite of his express declarations, have so often taken
to be a psychological *Entity*. In a given species, among all of
whose representatives the observer had hitherto detected none
but almost insignificant differences, *it is inevitable* that there
should at length appear a specimen *better endowed* than its
fellows—a bull, for instance, with exceptional horns, or a horse
of exceptional swiftness. Until this better endowed individual
has appeared there is no variation, and in consequence no ground
or adequate reason for the action of natural selection. . . .

Let us now apply this theory to the history of literature or art.
A given variety of literature, for instance, the English drama of
the sixteenth century, or the French comedy of the seventeenth
century, or the English novel of the eighteenth century, is in the
process of development, slowly organizing itself under the double
influence of the interior and exterior "environment." The movement is slow and the differentiation almost insensible. Suddenly,
and without its being possible to give a reason, a Shakespeare,
a Molière, or a Richardson appears, and forthwith not only is the
variety modified, but new species have come into being: psychological drama, the comedy of character, the novel of manners.
The superior adaptability and power of survival of the new
species are at once recognized and proved, indeed, in practice.

It is in vain that the older species attempt to struggle: their fate is sealed in advance. The successors of Richardson, Molière, and Shakespeare copy these unattainable models until, their fecundity exhausted—and by their fecundity I mean their aptitude for struggling with kindred and rival species—the imitation is changed into a routine which becomes a source of weakness, impoverishment, and death for the species. I shall not easily be persuaded that this manner of considering the history of literature or art is calculated to detract from the originality of great artists or great writers. On the contrary, as is doubtless perceived, it is precisely their individuality that is responsible for the constitution of new species, and in consequence for the evolution of literature and art.

Émile Zola

[1840–1902]

TAINE's *History of English Literature* is symptomatic of its age. Zola's *Experimental Novel* (1880) is equally symptomatic, for it is even more obviously based on the analogy between science and literature. Zola used the idea that human actions are determined by biological and environmental laws to formulate a program for the writing of novels. His program defines the literary movement known as Naturalism. Comte and Taine contributed to Zola's thought, but Darwin's *Origin of Species* (1859; French trans., 1862) was the decisive influence. Darwin's immense prestige helped to convert a general critical bias into a dogma espoused by critics and novelists with almost religious enthusiasm. Claude Bernard's *Introduction to the Study of Experimental Medicine,* with its emphasis on empiricism and its theory of experiment, provided Zola with the specific means of converting scientific thought into literary theory.

According to *The Experimental Novel,* man's actions are rigidly controlled. Free will is an illusion. The requirement that the novelist imitate life therefore becomes a requirement that he imitate the laws which determine the way life is lived. The novel is a laboratory in which the operation of these laws is observed.

In spite of the fact that his novels are less doctrinaire than his theory, Zola is the chief nineteenth-century spokesman for Naturalism. Other Naturalists include Guy de Maupassant, George Moore, Samuel Butler, Stephen Crane, Jack London, Theodore Dreiser, Gerhart Hauptmann, and Hermann Sudermann.

The standard translation of Zola's crticism is Belle M. Sherman, *The Experimental Novel and Other Essays* (New York, 1893). For discussion see: H. Edwards, "Zola and the American Critics," *American Literature,* IV (1932), 114–29; M. Josephson, *Zola and His Time* (New York, 1928); J. Matthews, *Les Deux Zola* (Geneva, 1957); W. Root, *German Criticism of Zola, 1875–1893* (New York, 1931); E. Stone, *What Was Naturalism?* (New York, 1958).

The present selection is from *The Experimental Novel,* trans. by Belle Sherman.

THE EXPERIMENTAL NOVEL
I. THE EXPERIMENTAL METHOD

IN MY LITERARY ESSAYS I have often spoken of the application of the experimental method to the novel and to the drama. The return to nature, the naturalistic evolution which marks the century, drives little by little all the manifestation of human intelligence into the same scientific path. Only the idea of a literature governed by science is doubtless a surprise, until explained with precision and understood. It seems to me necessary, then, to say briefly and to the point what I understand by the experimental novel.

I really only need to adapt, for the experimental method has been established with strength and marvelous clearness by Claude Bernard in his *Introduction à l'étude de la médecine expérimentale*. This work, by a savant whose authority is unquestioned, will serve me as a solid foundation. I shall here find the whole question treated, and I shall restrict myself to irrefutable arguments and to giving the quotations which may seem necessary to me. This will then be but a compiling of texts, as I intend on all points to intrench myself behind Claude Bernard. It will often be but necessary for me to replace the word "doctor" by the word "novelists," to make my meaning clear and to give it the rigidity of a scientific truth. . . .

To be more clear, I think it would be better to give a brief résumé of *L'Introduction* before I commence. The applications which I shall make of the texts will be better understood if the plan of the work and the matters treated are explained.

Claude Bernard, after having declared that medicine enters the scientific path with physiology as its foundation and by means of the experimental method, first explains the differences which exist between the sciences of observation and the sciences of experiment. He concludes, finally, that experiment is but provoked observation. All experimental reasoning is based on doubt, for the experimentalist should have no preconceived idea, in the face of nature, and should always retain his liberty of thought. He simply accepts the phenomena which are produced, when they are proved.

In the second part he reaches his true subject and shows
that the spontaneity of living bodies is not opposed to the employment of experiment. The difference is simply that an inanimate body possesses merely the ordinary, external environment,
while the essence of the higher organism is set in an internal
and perfected environment endowed with constant physico-
chemical properties exactly like the external environment;
hence there is an absolute determinism in the existing conditions of natural phenomena, for the living as for the inanimate
bodies. He calls determinism the cause which determines the
appearance of these phenomena. This nearest cause, as it is
called, is nothing more than the physical and material condition of the existence or manifestation of the phenomena. The
end of all experimental method, the boundary of all scientific
research, is then identical for living and for inanimate bodies;
it consists in finding the relations which unite a phenomenon
of any kind to its nearest cause, or, in other words, in determining the conditions necessary for the manifestation of this phenomenon. Experimental science has no necessity to worry itself about the "why" of things; it simply explains the "how."

After having explained the experimental considerations common to living beings and to inanimate, Claude Bernard passes to
the experimental considerations which belong specially to living
beings. The great and only difference is this, that there is presented to our consideration, in the organism of living beings, a
harmonious group of phenomena. He then treats of practical
experiments on living beings, of vivisection, of the preparatory
anatomical conditions, of the choice of animals, of the use of
calculation in the study of phenomena, and lastly of the physi-
ologist's laboratory.

Finally, in the last part of *L'Introduction*, he gives some examples of physiological experimental investigations in support
of the ideas which he has formulated. He then furnishes some
examples of experimental criticism in physiology. In the end
he indicates the philosophical obstacles which the experimental
doctor encounters. He puts in the first rank the false application of physiology to medicine, the scientific ignorance as well
as certain illusions of the medical mind. Further, he concludes
by saying that empirical medicine and experimental medicine,

not being incompatible, ought, on the contrary, to be inseparable one from the other. His last sentence is that experimental medicine adheres to no medical doctrine nor any philosophical system.

II. APPLICATION TO LITERATURE

The first question which presents itself is this: Is experiment possible in literature, in which up to the present time observation alone has been employed?

Claude Bernard discusses observation and experiment at great length. There exists, in the first place, a very clear line of demarcation, as follows: "The name of 'observer' is given to him who applies the simple or complex process of investigation in the study of phenomena which he does not vary, and which he gathers, consequently, as nature offers them to him; the name of 'experimentalist' is given to him who employs the simple and complex process of investigation to vary or modify, for an end of some kind, the natural phenomena, and to make them appear under circumstances and conditions in which they are not presented by nature." For instance, astronomy is a science of observation, because you cannot conceive of an astronomer acting upon the stars; while chemistry is an experimental science, as the chemist acts upon nature and modifies it. This, according to Claude Bernard, is the only true and important distinction which separates the observer from the experimentalist. . . .

To determine how much observation and experimenting there can be in the naturalistic novel, I only need to quote the following passages:

The observer relates purely and simply the phenomena which he has under his eyes. . . . He should be the photographer of phenomena, his observation should be an exact representation of nature. . . . He listens to nature and he writes under its dictation. But once the fact is ascertained and the phenomenon observed, an idea or hypothesis come into his mind, reason intervenes, and the experimentalist comes forward to interpret the phenomenon. The experimentalist is a man who, in pursuance of a more or less probable, but anticipated, explanation of observed phenomena, institutes an experiment in such a way that, according to all probability, it will furnish a result which will serve to confirm the hypothesis or preconceived idea. The moment that the result of the experiment manifests itself, the experimentalist finds himself face to face with a true observation which he has called forth and which he must ascertain, as all observation, without any preconceived idea. The experimentalist should then disappear, or rather transform himself instantly into the observer, and it is not until after he has ascertained the absolute results of the experiment, like that of an ordinary observation, that his mind comes back to reasoning, comparing, and judging whether the experimental hypothesis is verified or invalidated by these same results.

The mechanism is all there. It is a little complicated, it is true, and Claude Bernard is led on to say:

When all this passes into the brain of a savant who has given himself up to the study of a science as complicated as medicine still is, then there is such an entanglement between the result of observation and what belongs to experiment that it will be impossible and, besides, useless to try to analyze, in their inextricable *mélange,* each of these terms.

In one word, it might be said that observation "indicates" and that experiment "teaches."

Now, to return to the novel, we can easily see that the novelist is equally an observer and an experimentalist. The observer in him gives the facts as he has observed them, suggests the point of departure, displays the solid earth on which his characters are to tread and the phenomena to develop. Then the experimentalist appears and introduces an experiment, that is to say, sets his characters going in a certain story so as to show that the succession of facts will be such as the requirements of the determinism of the phenomena under examination call for. Here it is nearly always an experiment *"pour voir,"* as Claude Bernard calls it. The novelist starts out in search of a truth. I will take as an example the character of the Baron Hulot, in *Cousine Bette,* by Balzac. The general fact observed by Balzac is the ravages that the amorous temperament of a man makes in his home, in his family, and in society. As soon as he has chosen his subject, he starts from known facts; then he makes his experiment, and exposes Hulot to a series of trials, placing him amid certain surroundings in order to exhibit how the complicated machinery of his passions works. It is then evident that there is not only observation there, but that there is also experiment; as Balzac does not remain satisfied with photographing the facts collected by him, but interferes in a direct way to place his character in certain conditions, and of these he remains the master. The problem is to know what such a passion, acting in such a surrounding and under such circumstances, would produce from the point of view of an individual and of society; and an experimental novel, *Cousine Bette,* for example, is simply the report of the experiment that the novelist conducts before the eyes of the public. In fact, the whole operation consists in taking facts in nature, then in studying the mechanism of these facts, acting upon them by the modification of circumstances and surroundings without deviating from the laws of nature. Finally, you possess knowledge of the man, scientific knowledge of him, in both his individual and social relations.

Doubtless we are still far from certainties in chemistry and even physiology. Nor do we know any more the reagents which decompose the passions, rendering them susceptible of analysis. Often, in this essay, I shall recall in similar fashion this fact, that the experimental novel is still younger than experimental medicine, and the latter is but just born. But I do not intend to exhibit the acquired results, I simply desire to clearly expose a method. If the experimental novelist is still groping in the most obscure and complex of all the sciences, this does not prevent this science from existing. It is undeniable that the naturalistic novel, such as we understand it today, is a real experiment that a novelist makes on man by the help of observation. . . .

I shall still call your attention to another illustration of Claude Bernard, which struck me as very forcible: "The experimentalist is the examining magistrate of nature." We novelists are the examining magistrates of men and their passions.

But see what splendid clearness breaks forth when this conception of the application of the experimental method to the novel is adequately grasped and is carried out with all the scientific rigor which the matter permits today. A contemptible reproach which they heap upon us naturalistic writers is the

desire to be solely photographers. We have in vain declared
that we admit the necessity of an artist's possessing an individual
temperament and a personal expression; they continue to reply
to us with these imbecile arguments, about the impossibility of
being strictly true, about the necessity of arranging facts to
produce a work of art of any kind. Well, with the application
of the experimental method to the novel that quarrel dies out.
The idea of experiment carried with it the idea of modification. We start, indeed, from the true facts, which are our indestructible basis; but to show the mechanism of these facts it is
necessary for us to produce and direct the phenomena; this is
our share of invention, here is the genius in the book. Thus
without having recourse to the questions of form and of style,
which I shall examine later, I maintain even at this point that
we must modify nature, without departing from nature, when
we employ the experimental method in our novels. If we bear
in mind this definition, that "observation indicates and experiment teaches," we can even now claim for our books this great
lesson of experiment.

The writer's office, far from being lessened, grows singularly
from this point of view. An experiment, even the most simple,
is always based on an idea, itself born of an observation. As
Claude Bernard says: "The experimental idea is not arbitrary,
nor purely imaginary; it ought always to have a support in some
observed reality, that is to say, in nature." It is on this idea and
on doubt that he bases all the method. "The appearance of the
experimental idea," he says further on, "is entirely spontaneous
and its nature absolutely individual, depending upon the mind
in which it originates; it is a particular sentiment, a *quid pro-
prium*, which constitutes the originality, the invention, and the
genius of each one." Further, he makes doubt the great scientific lever. "The doubter is the true savant; he doubts only
himself and his interpretations; he believes in science; he even
admits in the experimental sciences a criterion or a positive principle, the determinism of phenomena, which is absolute in living
beings as in inanimate bodies." Thus, instead of confining the
novelist within narrow bounds, the experimental method gives
full sway to his intelligence as a thinker, and to his genius as a
creator. He must see, understand, and invent. Some observed

fact makes the idea start up of trying an experiment, of writing a novel, in order to attain to a complete knowledge of the truth. Then when, after careful consideration, he has decided upon the plan of his experiment, he will judge the results at each step with the freedom of mind of a man who accepts only facts conformable to the determinism of phenomena. He set out from doubt to reach positive knowledge; and he will not cease to doubt until the mechanism of the passion, taken to pieces and set up again by him, acts according to the fixed laws of nature. There is no greater, no more magnificent work for the human mind. We shall see, further on, the miseries of the scholastics, of the makers of systems, and those theorizing about the ideal, compared with the triumph of the experimentalists.

I sum up this first part by repeating that the naturalistic novelists observe and experiment, and that all their work is the offspring of the doubt which seizes them in the presence of truths little known and phenomena unexplained, until an experimental idea rudely awakens their genius some day, and urges them to make an experiment, to analyze facts, and to master them.

III. THE ROLE OF THE NOVELIST

Let us clearly define now what is meant by an experimental novelist. Claude Bernard gives the following definition of an artist: "What is an artist? He is a man who realizes in a work of art an idea or a sentiment which is personal to him." I absolutely reject this definition. On this basis if I represented a man as walking on his head, I should have made a work of art, if such happened to be my personal sentiments. But in that case I should be a fool and nothing else. So one must add that the personal feeling of the artist is always subject to the higher law of truth and nature. We now come to the question of hypothesis. The artist starts out from the same point as the savant; he places himself before nature, has an idea a priori, and works according to this idea. Here alone he separates himself from the savant, if he carries out his idea to the end without verifying its truth by the means of observation and experiment. Those who make use of experiment might well be called experimental artists; but then people will tell us that they are no longer artists, since such people regard art as the burden of personal error which the artist has put into his study of nature. I contend that the personality of the writer should only appear in the idea a priori and in the form, not in the infatuation for the false. I see no objection, besides, to its showing in the hypothesis, but it is necessary to clearly understand what you mean by these words.

It has often been said that writers ought to open the way for savants. This is true, for we have seen in *L'Introduction* that hypothesis and empiricism precede and prepare for the scientific state which is established finally by the experimental method. Man commenced by venturing certain explanations of phenomena, the poets gave expression to their emotions, and the savants ended by mastering hypotheses and fixing the truth. Claude Bernard always assigns the role of pioneers to the philosophers. It is a very noble role, and today it is the writers who should assume it and who should endeavor to fill it worthily. Only let it be well understood that each time that a truth is established by the savants the writers should immediately abandon their hypothesis to adopt this truth; otherwise they will remain deliberately in error without benefiting anyone. It is thus that science, as it advances, furnishes to us writers a solid ground upon which we should lean for support, to better enable us to shoot into new hypotheses. In a word, every phenomenon, once clearly determined, destroys the hypothesis which it replaces, and it is then necessary to transport your hypothesis one step further into the new unknown which arises. I will take a very simple example in order to make myself better understood; it has been proved that the earth revolves around the sun; what would you think of a poet who should adopt the old belief that the sun revolves around the earth? Evidently the poet, if he wishes to risk a personal explanation of any fact, should choose a fact whose cause is not already known. This, then, illustrates the position hypothesis should occupy for experimental novelists; we must accept determined facts, and not attempt to risk about them our personal sentiments, which would be ridiculous, building throughout on the territory that science has conquered; then before the unknown, but only then, exercising our intuition and suggesting the way to science, free to make mistakes, happy if we produce any data toward the solution of the problem. Here I stand at Claude Bernard's practical program, who is forced to accept empiricism as a necessary forerunner. In our experimental novel we can easily risk a few hypotheses on the questions of heredity and surroundings, after having respected all that science knows today about the matter. We can prepare the ways, we can furnish the results of observation, human data which may prove very useful. A great lyrical poet has written lately that our century is a century of prophets. Yes, if you wish it; only let it be well understood that these prophets rely neither upon the irrational nor the supernatural. If the prophets thought best to bring up again the most elementary notions, to serve up nature with a strange religious and philosophical sauce, to hold fast to the metaphysical man, to confound and obscure everything, the prophets, notwithstanding their genius in the matter of style, would never be anything but great gooses ignorant whether they would get wet if they jumped into the water. In our scientific age it is a very delicate thing to be a prophet, as we no longer believe in the truths of revelation, and in order to be able to foresee the unknown we must begin by studying the known.

The conclusion to which I wish to come is this: If I were to define the experimental novel I should not say, as Claude Bernard says, that a literary work lies entirely in the personal feeling, for the reason that in my opinion the personal feeling is but the first impulse. Later nature, being there, makes itself felt, or at least that part of nature of which science has given us the secret, and about which we have no longer any right to romance. The experimental novelist is therefore the one who accepts proven facts, who points out in man and in society the mechanism of the phenomena over which science is mistress, and who does not interpose his personal sentiments, except in the phenomena whose determinism is not yet settled, and who tries to test, as much as he can, this personal sentiment, this idea a priori, by observation and experiment.

I cannot understand how our naturalistic literature can mean anything else. I have only spoken of the experimental novel, but I am fairly convinced that the same method, after having triumphed in history and in criticism, will triumph everywhere, on the stage and in poetry even. It is an inevitable evolution. Literature, in spite of all that can be said, does not depend merely upon the author; it is influenced by the nature it depicts and by the man whom it studies. Now if the savants change their ideas of nature, if they find the true mechanism of life, they force us to follow them, to precede them even, so as to play our role in the new hypotheses. The metaphysical man is dead; our whole territory is transformed by the advent of the physiological man. No doubt "Achilles' Anger," "Dido's Love," will last forever on account of their beauty; but today we feel the necessity of analyzing anger and love, of discovering exactly how such passions work in the human being. This view of the matter is a new one; we have become experimentalists instead of philosophers. In short, everything is summed up in this great fact: the experimental method in letters, as in the sciences, is in the way to explain the natural phenomena, both individual and social, of which metaphysics, until now, has given only irrational and supernatural explanations.

Karl Marx

[1818–1893]

and

Friedrich Engels

[1820–1895]

⋙§⋚⋘

THE *Communist Manifesto* was published in 1848. Since then the fortunes of Marxist criticism have been closely associated with the fortunes of left-wing politics. For convenience Marxist criticism may be divided into two phases. The first phase, represented by critics such as William Morris and George Bernard Shaw, tends to be hortatory. Writers are urged to use literature to reform social injustice, a good deal of humanitarian sentiment is expressed, and there is some speculation about the possibility of literature "for the people"— folk literature, proletarian literature, and the like. This phase ended with the London Conference of 1903, at which the Bolsheviks split with the Mensheviks over the question of revolution versus gradual reform. Since 1903 Marxist criticism has become increasingly doctrinaire. The success of the Bolsheviks in Russia and the establishment of the Third Internationale (1919) prepared the way for explicitly Communist criticism. Marx's historical theories were applied to literary history in works like Christopher Caudwell's *Illusion and Reality* (1937) and Granville Hicks' *The Great Tradition* (1933). Contemporary writers were urged to consider themselves warriors in the class struggle—to depict the evils of capitalism, to compose proletarian novels, and to write in a style called "socialist realism." Writers who failed to observe these criteria were denounced as bourgeois, escapist, or fascist. The Communist party claimed the right of censorship, and the right of the Communist state to imprison unco-operative writers was defended.

It has often been observed that Marxist criticism suffers from schizophrenia. On the one hand Marxists support a deterministic historical theory according to which the writer is necessarily molded by the economic conditions of his society. On the other, they demand

111

that the writer produce "Communist" art regardless of his economic and social background. An equally obvious fault of Marxist criticism has been its willingness to subordinate elementary historical facts to propaganda.

In view of the many kinds of Marxist criticism and the sheer crudeness of so much of it, the fairest representation would seem to be the writings of Marx and Engels themselves. Neither was a literary critic, but both were widely read and made significant, often perceptive remarks about literature. Indeed, their comments were used by James T. Farrell in *A Note on Literary Criticism* (1936) to expose the absurdity of Communist apologists who claimed to be following their lead.

There is no satisfactory history of Marxist criticism. Among representative works are Nikolai Bukharin, "Poetry and Society," in Vivas and Krieger, *The Problems of Aesthetics* (New York, 1957); Christopher Caudwell, *Studies in a Dying Culture* (London, 1938); V. I. Lenin, "Party Organization and Party Literature," and "Five Essays on Leo Tolstoy," in *Dialectics*, V, VI (1938); and Leon Trotsky, *Literature and Revolution* (1923; repr., Ann Arbor, 1960). For comment see: P. Demetz, *Marx, Engels, und die Dichter* (Stuttgart, 1959); Z. Folejewski, "Socialist Realism in Western Literary Criticism," *Proceedings of the ICLA Congress* (Chapel Hill, 1959), II, 565–76; J. Freeman, intr., *Proletarian Literature* (New York, 1935); G. Steiner, "Marxism and the Literary Critic," *Encounter*, XI (1958), 33–43; E. Wilson, "Marxism and Literature," in *The Triple Thinkers* (New York, 1938).

The present selection is from *Literature and Art, by Karl Marx and Frederick Engels: Selections from Their Writings* (New York: International Publishers, 1947). Reprinted by permission.

LITERATURE AND ART

I. MODES OF PRODUCTION DETERMINE SOCIAL, POLITICAL, AND INTELLECTUAL PROCESSES

IN THE SOCIAL PRODUCTION which men carry on they enter into definite relations that are indispensable and independent of their will; these relations of production correspond to a definite stage of development of their material forces of production. The sum total of these relations of production constitutes the economic structure of society—the real foundation, on which rises a legal and political superstructure and to which correspond definite forms of social consciousness. The mode of production in material life determines the social, political, and intellectual life processes in general. It is not the consciousness of men that determines their being, but, on the contrary, their social being that determines their consciousness. At a certain stage of their development, the material forces of production in society come in conflict with the existing relations of produc- tion, or—what is but a legal expression for the same thing— with the property relations within which they have been at work before. From forms of development of the forces of production these relations turn into their fetters. Then begins an epoch of social revolution. With the change of the economic foundation the entire immense superstructure is more or less rapidly trans- formed. In considering such transformations a distinction should always be made between the material transformation of the economic conditions of production which can be determined with the precision of natural science, and the legal, political, religious, aesthetic, or philosophic—in short, ideological—forms in which men become conscious of this conflict and fight it out. Just as our opinion of an individual is not based on what he thinks of himself, so can we not judge of such a period of trans- formation by its own consciousness; on the contrary this con- sciousness must be explained rather from the contradictions of material life, from the existing conflict between the social forces of production and the relations of production. No social order ever disappears before all the productive forces for which there is room in it have been developed; and new higher relations of production never appear before the material conditions of their existence have matured in the womb of the old society itself.) Therefore, mankind always sets itself only such tasks as it can solve; since, looking at the matter more closely, we will always find that the task itself arises only when the material conditions necessary for its solution already exist or are at least in the process of formation. In broad outlines we can designate the Asiatic, the ancient, the feudal, and the modern bourgeois modes of production as so many epochs in the progress of the economic formation of society. The bourgeois relations of production are the last antagonistic form of the social process of production—antagonistic not in the sense of individual antagonism, but of one arising from the social conditions of life of the individuals; at the same time the productive forces developing in the womb of bourgeois society create the material conditions for the solution of that antagonism. This social formation constitutes, therefore, the closing chapter of the prehistoric stage of human society.

Karl Marx, "A Contribution to the Critique of Political Economy," *Selected Works*, Vol. I, pp. 356–57.

The production of ideas, of conceptions, of consciousness, is at first directly interwoven with the material activity and the material intercourse of men, the language of real life. Conceiving, thinking, the mental intercourse of men, appear at this stage as the direct efflux of their material behavior. The same applies to mental production as expressed in the language of the politics, laws, morality, religion, metaphysics of a people. Men are the producers of their conceptions, ideas, etc.—real, active men, as they are conditioned by a definite development of their productive forces and of the intercourse corresponding to these, up to its furthest forms. Consciousness can never be anything else than conscious existence, and the existence of men is their actual life-process. If in all ideology men and their circumstances appear upside down as in a *camera obscura*, this phenomenon arises just as much from their historical life-process as the inversion of objects on the retina does from their physical life-process.

In direct contrast to German philosophy which descends from heaven to earth, here we ascend from earth to heaven. That is to say, we do not set out from what men say, imagine, conceive, nor from men as narrated, thought of, imagined, conceived, in order to arrive at men in the flesh. We set out from real, active men, and on the basis of their real life-process we demonstrate the development of the ideological reflexes and echoes of this life-process. The phantoms formed in the human brain are also, necessarily, sublimates of their material life-process, which is empirically verifiable and bound to material premises. Morality, religion, metaphysics, all the rest of ideology and their corresponding forms of consciousness, thus no longer retain the semblance of independence. They have no history, no development; but men, developing their material production and their material intercourse, alter, along with this their real existence, their thinking and the products of their thinking. Life is not determined by consciousness, but consciousness by life. In the first method of approach the starting-point is consciousness taken as the living individual; in the second it is the real living individuals themselves, as they are in actual life, and consciousness is considered solely as *their* consciousness.

This method of approach is not devoid of premises. It starts out from the real premises and does not abandon them for a moment. Its premises are men, not in any fantastic isolation or abstract definition, but in their actual, empirically perceptible process of development under definite conditions. As soon as this active life-process is described, history ceases to be a collection of dead facts as it is with the empiricists (themselves still abstract), or an imagined activity of imagined subjects, as with the idealists.

Karl Marx and Frederick Engels, *The German Ideology,*
pp. 13–16.

II. A QUALIFICATION: ART IS SOMETIMES INDEPENDENT OF THE MATERIAL BASIS OF SOCIETY

It is well known that certain periods of highest development of art stand in no direct connection with the general development of society, nor with the material basis and the skeleton structure of its organization. Witness the example of the Greeks as compared with the modern nations or even Shakespeare. As regards certain forms of art, as, *e.g.*, the epos, it is admitted that they can never be produced in the world-epoch-making form as soon as art as such comes into existence; in other words, that in the domain of art certain important forms of it are possible only at a low stage of its development. If that be true of the mutual relations of different forms of art within the domain of art itself, it is far less surprising that the same is true of the relation of art as a whole to the general development of society. The difficulty lies only in the general formulation of these contradictions. No sooner are they specified than they are explained. Let us take for instance the relation of Greek art and of that of Shakespeare's time to our own. It is a well known fact that Greek mythology was not only the arsenal of Greek art, but also the very ground from which it had sprung. Is the view of nature and of social relations which shaped Greek imagination and Greek [art] possible in the age of automatic machinery, and railways, and locomotives, and electric telegraphs? Where does Vulcan come in as against Roberts & Co.; Jupiter, as against the lightning rod; and Hermes, as against the Credit Mobilier? All mythology masters and dominates and shapes the forces of nature in and through the imagination; hence it disappears as soon as man gains mastery over the forces of nature. What becomes of the Goddess Fame side by side with Printing House Square? Greek art presupposes the existence of Greek mythology, *i.e.*, that nature and even the form of society are wrought up in popular fancy in an unconsciously artistic fashion. That is its material. Not, however, any mythology taken at random, nor any accidental, unconsciously artistic elaboration of nature (including under the latter all objects, hence [also] society). Egyptian mythology could never be the soil or womb which would give birth to Greek art. But in any event [there had to be] a mythology. In no event [could Greek art originate] in a society which excludes any mythological explanation of nature, any mythological attitude towards it and which requires from the artist an imagination free from mythology.

Looking at it from another side: Is Achilles possible side by side with powder and lead? Or is the Iliad at all compatible with the printing press and steam press? Do not singing and reciting and the muses necessarily go out of existence with the appearance of the printer's bar, and do not, therefore, disappear the prerequisites of epic poetry?

But the difficulty is not in grasping the idea that Greek art and epos are bound up with certain forms of social development. It rather lies in understanding why they still constitute with us a source of aesthetic enjoyment and in certain respects prevail as the standard and model beyond attainment.

A man cannot become a child again unless he becomes childish. But does he not enjoy the artless ways of the child and must he not strive to reproduce its truth on a higher plane? Is not the character of every epoch revived perfectly true to nature in child nature? Why should the social childhood of mankind, where it had obtained its most beautiful development, not exert an eternal charm as an age that will never return? There are ill-bred children and precocious children. Many of the ancient nations belong to the latter class. The Greeks were normal children. The charm their art has for us does not conflict with the primitive character of the social order from which it had sprung. It is rather the product of the latter, and is rather due to the fact that the unripe social conditions under which the art arose and under which alone it could appear could never return.

Karl Marx, *A Contribution to the Critique of Political Economy*, pp. 309–12.

III. REALISM IN LITERATURE

Thank you very much for sending me your *City Girl* through Mr. Vizetelly.

I have read it with the greatest pleasure and avidity. It is, indeed, as my friend Eichkof, your translator, calls it, *ein kleines Kunstwerk* [a little work of art]; to which he adds what will be satisfactory to you, that consequently his translation must be almost literal, as any omission or attempted manipulation could only destroy part of the original's value.

What strikes me most in your tale, besides its realistic truth, is that it exhibits the courage of the true artist. Not only in the way you treat the Salvation Army, in your sharp repudiation of the conception of the self-satisfied philistines, who will learn from your story, perhaps for the first time, why the Salvation Army finds such support among the masses of the people, but

above all in the unembroidered form in which you have clothed
the fundamental basis of the whole book—the old, old story of
the proletarian girl seduced by a man from the middle class.
A mediocre writer would have attempted to disguise the trite
character of the plot under a heap of artificial details and embellishment, and his design would have been seen through, none-
theless. But you felt that you could tell an old story because you
were in a position to make it new by the truthfulness of your
presentation.

Your Mr. Grant is a masterpiece.

If I have any criticism to make, it is only that your story is not
quite realistic enough. Realism, to my mind, implies, besides truth
of detail, the truthful reproduction of typical characters under
typical circumstances. Now your characters are typical enough,
to the extent that you portray them. But the same cannot be said
of the circumstances surrounding them and out of which their
action arises. In *City Girl* the working class appears as a passive
mass, incapable of helping itself or even trying to help itself. All
attempts to raise it out of its wretched poverty come from the
outside, from above. This may have been a valid description
around 1800 or 1810 in the days of Saint Simon and Robert
Owen, but it cannot be regarded as such in 1887 by a man who
for almost fifty years has had the honor to participate in most
of the struggles of the fighting proletariat and has been guided
all the time by the principle that the emancipation of the working class ought to be the cause of the working class itself. The
revolutionary response of the members of the working class to
the oppression that surrounds them, their convulsive attempts—
semiconscious or conscious—to attain their rights as human beings, belong to history and may therefore lay claim to a place
in the domain of realism.

I am far from finding fault with your not having written a
purely socialist novel, a *Tendenzroman,* as we Germans call it,
to glorify the social and political views of the author. That is
not at all what I mean. The more the author's views are concealed the better for the work of art. The realism I allude to
may creep out even in spite of the author's views. Let me refer
to an example.

Balzac, whom I consider a far greater master of realism than all of the Zolas, past, present, or future, gives us in his *Comédie Humaine* a most wonderfully realistic history of French "society," describing, chronicle fashion, almost year by year from 1816 to 1848, the ever-increasing pressure of the rising bourgeoisie upon the society of nobles that established itself after 1815 and that set up again, as far as it could (*tant bien que mal*) the standard of the *veille politesse française* [old French manners]. He describes how the last remnants of this, to him, model society gradually succumbed before the intrusion of the vulgar moneyed upstart or was corrupted by him. How the *grande dame*, whose conjugal infidelities were but a mode of asserting herself, in perfect accord with the way she had been disposed of in marriage, gave way to the bourgeoisie, who acquired her husband for cash or cashmere. And around this central picture he groups a complete history of French society from which, even in economic details (for instance, the redistribution of real and private property after the French Revolution) I have learned more than from all the professional historians, economists and statisticians of the period together.

Well, Balzac was politically a legitimist; his great work is a constant elegy on the irreparable decay of good society; his sympathies are with the class that is doomed to extinction. But for all that, his satire is never keener, his irony never more bitter, than when he sets in motion the very men and women with whom he sympathizes most deeply—the nobles. And the only men of whom he speaks with undisguised admiration are his bitterest political antagonists, the republican heroes of the Cloître Saint Méry, the men who at that time (1830–36) were indeed representatives of the popular masses.

That Balzac was thus compelled to go against his own class sympathies and political prejudices, that he *saw* the necessity of the downfall of his favorite nobles and described them as people deserving no better fate; that he *saw* the real men of the future where, for the time being, they alone were to be found—that I consider one of the greatest triumphs of realism, and one of the greatest features in old Balzac.

I must own, in your defense, that nowhere in the civilized

world are the working people less actively resistant, more passively submitting to fate, more depressed than in the East End of London. And how do I know whether you have not had your reasons for contenting yourself, for once, with a picture of the passive side of working class life, leaving the active side for another work?

Frederick Engels, Letter to Margaret Harkness, April,
1888. Original in Marx-Engels-Lenin Institute, Moscow.

IV. ON CENSORSHIP AND THE INTEGRITY
OF THE WRITER

My property is *form*, it is my spiritual individuality. *The style is the man.* And how! The law allows me to write, but on the condition that I write in a style other than my own, I have the right to show the face of my spirit, but I must first set it in *the prescribed expression!* What man of honor would not blush at such presumption and prefer to hide his head under his toga? At least the toga suggests the head of Jupiter. The prescribed expression only means putting a good face on a bad situation.
You admire the delightful variety, the inexhaustible wealth of nature. You do not demand that a rose should have the same scent as a violet, but the richest of all, the spirit, is to be allowed to exist in *only one* form? I am a humorist, but the law orders me to write seriously. I am bold, but the law orders my style to be modest. Gray and more gray, that is the only authorized color of freedom. Every dewdrop in which the sun is reflected, glitters with an inexhaustible display of colors, but the sun of the spirit may break into ever so many different individuals and objects, yet it is permitted to produce only one color, the *official color.* The essential form of the spirit is *gaiety, light,* and you make *shadows* its only proper manifestation; it must be dressed only in black, and yet there are no black flowers. The essence of the spirit is always *truth itself,* and what do you make its essence? *Modesty.* Only the knave is modest, says Goethe; and you want to make such a knave out of the spirit? Or should the modesty be that modesty of genius of which Schiller speaks, then first

transform all your citizens and above all your censors into geniuses.

Karl Marx, "Ueber die neueste Preussische Zensurin-struktion," *MEGA*, Part I, Vol. I, p. 154.

The writer must, naturally, make a living in order to exist and write, but he must not exist and write in order to make a living. . . .

The writer in no way regards his works as a *means*. They are *ends in themselves;* so little are they a means for him and others that, when necessary, he sacrifices *his* existence to *theirs*, and, like the preacher of religion, he takes as his principle: "Obey God more than men," men among whom he is himself included along with his human needs and desires. On the other hand, imagine a tailor, from whom I order a Parisian frock coat, bringing me a Roman toga because it is more in accord with the external law of the beautiful! *The first freedom of the press consists in its not being a business.* The writer who debases it to a material means, deserves, as punishment for this inner lack of freedom, an external lack of freedom, namely censorship, or rather its existence is already his punishment.

Karl Marx, "Debaten ueber Pressfreiheit," *MEGA*, Part I, Vol. 1, pp. 222–23.

V. LITERATURE AND SOCIAL INSTITUTIONS IN ANCIENT GREECE

The history of the family dates from 1861, from the publication of Bachofen's *Mutterrecht*.[1] In this work the author advances the following propositions: (1) That originally man lived in a state of sexual promiscuity, to describe which Bachofen uses the mistaken term "hetaerism"; (2) that such promiscuity excludes any certainty of paternity, and that descent could therefore be reckoned only in the female line, according to mother-right, and that this was originally the case amongst all the peoples of antiquity; (3) that since women, as mothers,

[1] Mother-right (matriarchate).

were the only parents of the younger generation that were known with certainty, they held a position of such high respect and honor that it became the foundation, in Bachofen's conception, of a regular rule of women (gynaecocracy); (4) that the transition to monogamy, where the women belonged to one man exclusively, involved a violation of a primitive religious law (that is, actually a violation of the traditional right of the other men to this woman), and that in order to expiate this violation or to purchase indulgence for it the woman had to surrender herself for a limited period.

Bachofen finds the proofs of these assertions in innumerable passages of ancient classical literature, which he collected with immense industry. According to him, the development from "hetaerism" to monogamy and from mother-right to father-right is accomplished, particularly among the Greeks, as the consequence of an advance in religious conceptions, introducing into the old hierarchy of the gods, representative of the old outlook, new divinities, representative of the new outlook, who push the former more and more into the background. Thus, according to Bachofen, it is not the development of men's actual conditions of life, but the religious reflection of these conditions inside their heads, which has brought about the historical changes in the social position of the sexes in relation to each other. In accordance with this view, Bachofen interprets the *Oresteia* of Aeschylus as the dramatic representation of the conflict between declining mother-right and the new father-right that arose and triumphed in the heroic age. For the sake of her paramour, Aegisthus, Clytemnestra slays her husband, Agamemnon, on his return from the Trojan War; but Orestes, the son of Agamemnon and herself, avenges his father's murder by slaying his mother. For this act he is pursued by the Furies, the demonic guardians of mother-right, according to which matricide is the gravest and most inexpiable crime. But Apollo, who by the voice of his oracle had summoned Orestes to this deed, and Athena, who is called upon to give judgment—the two deities who here represent the new patriarchal order—take Orestes under their protection; Athena hears both sides. The whole matter of the dispute is briefly summed up in the debate which now takes place between Orestes and the Furies. Orestes contends that Clytemnestra has committed a double crime; she has slain *her* husband and thus she has also slain *his* father. Why should the Furies pursue him, and not her, seeing that she is by far the more guilty? The answer is striking: "She was *not kin by blood* to the man she slew."

The murder of a man not related by blood, even if he be the husband of the murderess, is expiable and does not concern the Furies; their office is solely to punish murder between blood relations, and of such murders the most grave and the most inexpiable, according to mother-right, is matricide. Apollo now comes forward in Orestes' defense; Athena calls upon the Areopagites—the Athenian jurors—to vote; the votes for Orestes' condemnation and for his acquittal are equal; Athena, as president, gives her vote for Orestes and acquits him. Father-right has triumphed over mother-right, the "gods of young descent," as the Furies themselves call them, have triumphed over the Furies; the latter then finally allow themselves to be persuaded to take up a new office in the service of the new order.

This new but undoubtedly correct interpretation of the *Oresteia* is one of the best and finest passages in the whole book, but it proves at the same time that Bachofen believes at least as much as Aeschylus did in the Furies, Apollo, and Athena; for, at bottom, he believes that the overthrow of mother-right by father-right was a miracle wrought during the Greek heroic age by these divinities. That such a conception, which makes religion the lever of world history, must finally end in pure mysticism, is clear. It is therefore a tough and by no means always a grateful task to plow through Bachofen's solid tome. But all that does not lessen his importance as a pioneer. He was the first to replace the vague phrases about some unknown primitive state of sexual promiscuity by proofs of the following facts: that abundant traces survive in old classical literature of a state prior to monogamy among the Greeks and Asiatics when not only did a man have sexual intercourse with several women, but a woman with several men, without offending against morality; that this custom did not disappear without leaving its traces in the limited surrender which was the price women had to pay for the right to monogamy; that therefore descent could originally be reckoned only in the female line, from mother to father; that far into the period of monogamy, with its certain or at least acknowledged paternity, the female line was still alone recognized, and that the original position of the mothers, as the only certain parents of their children, secured for them, and thus for their whole sex, a higher social position than women have ever enjoyed since. Bachofen did not put these statements as clearly as this, for he was hindered by his mysticism. But he proved them; and in 1861 that was a real revolution.

Frederick Engels, *The Origin of the Family, Private Property, and the State,* pp. 8–10.

VI. THE ARTIST UNDER CAPITALISM AND COMMUNISM

The exclusive concentration of artistic talent in a few individuals and its consequent suppression in the large masses is the result of the division of labor. Even if under certain social conditions everyone were an excellent painter, this would not prevent everyone from also being an original painter, so that here, too, the difference between "human" and "individual" work becomes sheer nonsense. The subordination of the artist to local and national narrowness which arises entirely out of the division of labor, and the subordination of the individual to a given art so that he is exclusively a painter, a sculptor, etc., and the very name sufficiently expresses the narrowness of his professional development and his dependence on the division of labor—in a communist organization of society all this disappears. In a communist organization of society there are no painters; at most there are people who, among other things, also paint.

Karl Marx and Frederick Engels, *The German Ideology,* Part II, *MEGA,* Part I, Vol. 5, p. 373.

VII. GOETHE'S RELATION TO HIS SOCIETY

Naturally we cannot speak in detail here of Goethe himself. We are calling attention to only one point. Goethe stands in his works in a double relation to the German society of his time. Sometimes he is hostile to it: he tries to escape its odiousness, as in the *Iphigenia* and in general during the Italian journey; he rebels against it as Goetz, Prometheus, and Faust; he pours out on it his bitterest scorn as Mephistopheles. Sometimes, on the contrary, he is friendly to it, accommodating, as in most of the *Tame Epigrams* and in many prose writings, celebrates it, as in the *Masquerades,* even defends it against the intruding historical movement, particularly in all the writings where he happens to speak of the French Revolution. It is not only single sides of German life that Goethe accepts, as opposed to others that are repugnant to him. More commonly it is the various moods in which he finds himself; it is the persistent struggle in himself between the poet of genius, disgusted by the wretchedness of his surroundings, and the Frankfurt alderman's cautious child, the privy councilor of Weimar, who sees himself forced to make a truce with it and to get used to it. Thus Goethe is now colossal, now petty; now a defiant, ironical, world-scorning genius, now a calculated, complacent, narrow philistine. Even Goethe was unable to overcome the wretchedness of German life; on the contrary, it overcame him, and this victory over the greatest German is the best proof that it cannot be conquered by the individual. Goethe was too universal, too active a nature, too fleshly to seek escape from this wretchedness in a flight, like Schiller's, to the Kantian ideal: he was too sharp-sighted not to see how this flight finally reduced itself to the exchange of a commonplace for a transcendental misery. His temperament, his energies, his whole spiritual tendency directed him towards practical life, and the practical life that he met with, was miserable. In this dilemma— to exist in a sphere of life that he must despise, and yet to be fettered to this sphere, as the only one in which he could fulfill himself—in this dilemma Goethe continually found himself, and the older he became, the more did the powerful poet retire, *de guerre lasse* [weary of war], behind the insignificant Weimar minister. We are not throwing it up to Goethe, *à la* Boerne and Menzel, that he was not a liberal, but that he could even be a philistine at times; not that he was incapable of any enthusiasm for German freedom, but that he sacrificed his occasionally irrepressible, sounder aesthetic feeling to a small-town aversion to every great contemporary historical movement; not that he was a courtier, but at the time when a Napoleon was cleaning out the vast Augean stables of Germany, he could manage with a ceremonial seriousness the most trivial affairs and the *menus plaisirs* [minute details] of one of the most trivial little German courts. In general, we are reproaching him neither from moral nor from partisan standpoints, but chiefly from aesthetic and historical standpoints; we are measuring Goethe neither by a moral, nor by a political, nor by a "human" standard. We cannot undertake here to represent Goethe in connection with his whole age, with his literary forerunners and contemporaries, in his development and social position. We are therefore limiting ourselves simply to the statement of the fact.

Frederick Engels, "Deutscher Sozialismus in Versen und Prosa, II," *MEGA,* Part I, Vol. 6, pp. 56–58.

VIII. PROLETARIAN LITERATURE

And in how great a measure the English proletariat has succeeded in attaining independent education is shown especially by the fact that the epoch-making products of modern philosophical, political, and poetical literature are read by working men almost exclusively. The bourgeois, enslaved by social conditions and the prejudices involved in them, trembles, blesses, and crosses himself before everything which really paves the way for progress; the proletarian has open eyes for it, and studies it with pleasure and success. In this respect the Socialists, especially, have done wonders for the education of the proletariat. They have translated the French materialists, Helvétius, Holbach, Diderot, etc., and disseminated them, with the best English works, in cheap editions. Strauss' *Life of Jesus* and Proudhon's *Property* also circulate among the working men only. Shelley, the genius, the prophet, Shelley, and Byron, with his glowing sensuality and his bitter satire upon our existing society, find most of their readers in the proletariat; the bourgeoisie owns only castrated editions, family editions, cut down in accordance with the hypocritical morality of today. The two great practical philosophers of latest date, Bentham and Godwin, are, especially the latter, almost exclusively the property of the proletariat; for though Bentham has a school within the Radical bourgeoisie, it is only the proletariat and the Socialists who have succeeded in developing his teachings a step forward. The proletariat has formed upon this basis a literature, which consists chiefly of journals and pamphlets, and is far in advance of the whole bourgeois literature in intrinsic worth.

Frederick Engels, *Condition of the Working Class in England in 1844*, pp. 239–40.

Leo Nikolaivich Tolstoy

[1828–1910]

ᴥᕥᕥᕥ

TOLSTOY'S VIOLENT ATTACK on what he considered the decadence of nineteenth-century literature is an extreme example of didactic criticism. Behind it is Tolstoy's vision of a classless society founded on Christian brotherhood. His doctrine of "infection," his insistence on sincerity, and his praise of folk literature are corollaries of the position. His most withering scorn is reserved for the French aesthetic school, but he also finds fault with Shakespeare, Kant, Marx, Nietzsche, Darwin, and a host of other writers including himself.

Obviously Tolstoy would not have been so dogmatic if he had not had such an intense faith in human potentialities. In Tolstoy's opinion, only that art which helps man toward fulfillment in Christian brotherhood is worth preserving. The rest is trivial or morally destructive. Many critics have shared this view, although few have carried it to such an extreme. William Dean Howells admired aspects of *What Is Art?*, and modern aestheticians like R. G. Collingwood, who treat art in affective terms, have referred sympathetically to the theory of "infection."

The present selections are from *What Is Art?*, trans. by Aylmer Maud (New York, 1899). A reprint with an introduction by Vincent Tomas has been published by the Liberal Arts Press, New York, 1960.

WHAT IS ART?

I. A DEFINITION OF ART

IN ORDER CORRECTLY to define art, it is necessary, first of all, to cease to consider it as a means to pleasure and to consider it as one of the conditions of human life. Viewing it in this way we cannot fail to observe that art is one of the means of intercourse between man and man.

Every work of art causes the receiver to enter into a certain kind of relationship both with him who produced, or is producing, the art, and with all those who, simultaneously, previously, or subsequently, receive the same artistic impression.

Speech, transmitting the thoughts and experiences of men, serves as a means of union among them, and art acts in a similar manner. The peculiarity of this latter means of intercourse, distinguishing it from intercourse by means of words, consists in this, that whereas by words a man transmits his thoughts to another, by means of art he transmits his feelings.

The activity of art is based on the fact that a man, receiving through his sense of hearing or sight another man's expression of feeling, is capable of experiencing the emotion which moved the man who expressed it. To take the simplest example: one man laughs, and another who hears becomes merry; or a man weeps, and another who hears feels sorrow. A man is excited or irritated, and another man seeing him comes to a similar state of mind. By his movements or by the sounds of his voice, a man expresses courage and determination or sadness and calmness, and this state of mind passes on to others. A man suffers, expressing his sufferings by groans and spasms, and this suffering transmits itself to other people; a man expresses his feeling of admiration, devotion, fear, respect, or love to certain objects, persons, or phenomena, and others are infected by the same feelings of admiration, devotion, fear, respect, or love to the same objects, persons, and phenomena.

And it is upon this capacity of man to receive another man's expression of feeling and experience those feelings himself, that the activity of art is based. . . .

The feelings with which the artist infects others may be most various—very strong or very weak, very important or very insignificant, very bad or very good: feelings of love for one's own country, self-devotion and submission to fate or to God expressed in a drama, raptures of lovers described in a novel, feelings of voluptuousness expressed in a picture, courage expressed in a triumphal march, merriment evoked by a dance, humor evoked by a funny story, the feeling of quietness transmitted by an evening landscape or by a lullaby, or the feeling of admiration evoked by a beautiful arabesque—it is all art.

If only the spectators or auditors are infected by the feelings which the author has felt, it is art.

To evoke in oneself a feeling one has once experienced, and having evoked it in oneself, then, by means of movements, lines, colors, sounds, or forms expressed in words, so to transmit that feeling that others may experience the same feeling—this is the activity of art.

Art is a human activity consisting in this, that one man consciously, by means of certain external signs, hands on to others feelings he has lived through, and that other people are infected by these feelings and also experience them.

Art is not, as the metaphysicians say, the manifestation of some mysterious Idea of beauty or God; it is not, as the aesthetical physiologists say, a game in which man lets off his excess of stored-up energy; it is not the expression of man's emotions by external signs; it is not the production of pleasing objects; and, above all, it is not pleasure; but it is a means of union among men, joining them together in the same feelings, and indispensable for the life and progress toward well-being of individuals and of humanity.

II. DECADENT ART

At first, at the very beginning of the separation of the exclusive art of the upper classes from universal art, its chief subject matter was the feeling of pride. It was so at the time of the Renaissance and after it, when the chief subject of works of art was the laudation of the strong—popes, kings, and dukes; odes and madrigals were written in their honor, and they were extolled in cantatas and hymns; their portraits were painted and their statues carved, in various adulatory ways. Next, the element of sexual desire began more and more to enter into art, and (with very few exceptions, and in novels and dramas almost without exception) it has now become an essential feature of every art product of the rich classes. . . .

From Boccaccio to Marcel Prévost, all the novels, poems, and verses invariably transmit the feeling of sexual love in its different forms. Adultery is not only the favorite, but almost the only theme of all the novels. A performance is not a performance unless, under some pretense, women appear with naked busts and limbs. Songs and romances—all are expressions of lust idealized in various degrees.

A majority of the pictures by French artists represent female nakedness in various forms. In recent French literature there is hardly a page or poem in which nakedness is not described, and in which, relevantly or irrelevantly, their favorite thought and word, *nu*, is not repeated a couple of times. There is a certain writer, René de Gourmond, who gets printed and is considered talented. To get an idea of the new writers, I read his novel, *Les Chevaux de Diomède*. It is a consecutive and detailed account of the sexual connections some gentleman had with various women. Every page contains lust-kindling descriptions. It is the same in Pierre Louys' book, *Aphrodite*, which met with success; it is the same in a book I lately chanced upon, Huysmans' *Certains*, and, with but few exceptions, it is the same in all the French novels. They are all the productions of people suffering from erotic mania. And these people are evidently convinced that as their whole life, in consequence of their diseased condition, is concentrated on amplifying various sexual abominations, therefore the life of all the world is similarly concentrated. And these people, suffering from erotic mania, are imitated throughout the whole artistic world of Europe and America. . . . I must pause to note the amazing celebrity of . . . Baudelaire and Verlaine, who are now accepted as being great poets. How the French, who had Chénier, Musset, Lamartine, and, above all, Hugo—and among whom quite recently flourished the so-called Parnassiens: Leconte de Lisle, Sully-Prudhomme, etc.—could attribute such importance to these two versifiers, who were far from skillful in form and most contemptible and commonplace in subject matter, is to me incomprehensible. The conception of life of one of them, Baudelaire, consisted in elevating gross egotism into a theory, and replacing morality by a cloudy conception of beauty and especially artificial beauty. Baudelaire had a preference, which he expressed, for a woman's face painted rather than showing its natural color, and for metal trees and a theatrical imitation of water rather than real trees and real water.

The life-conception of the other, Verlaine, consisted in weak profligacy, confession of his moral impotence, and, as an antidote to that impotence, in the grossest Roman Catholic idolatry. Both, moreover, were quite lacking in naïveté, sincerity, and simplicity, and both overflowed with artificiality, forced originality and self-assurance. So that in their least bad productions one sees more of M. Baudelaire or M. Verlaine than of what they were describing. But these two indifferent versifiers form a school and lead hundreds of followers after them.

There is only one explanation of this fact: it is that the art of the society in which these versifiers lived is not a serious, important matter of life, but is a mere amusement. And all amusements grow wearisome by repetition. And, in order to make wearisome amusement again tolerable, it is necessary to find some means to freshen it up. When, at cards, ombre grows stale, whist is introduced; when whist grows stale, écarté is substituted; when écarté grows stale, some other novelty is invented, and so on. The substance of the matter remains the same, only its form is changed. And so it is with this kind of art. The subject matter of the art of the upper classes growing continually more and more limited, it has come at last to this, that to the artists of these exclusive classes it seems as if everything has already been said and that to find anything new to say is impossible. And therefore, to freshen up this art they look out for fresh forms.

Baudelaire and Verlaine invent such a new form, furbish it up, moreover, with hitherto unused pornographic details, and—the critics and the public of the upper classes hail them as great writers.

This is the only explanation of the success, not of Baudelaire and Verlaine only, but of all the Decadents.

III. THE PERVERSITY OF CRITICISM

Professionalism is the first condition of the diffusion of false, counterfeit art.

The second condition is the growth in recent times of artistic criticism, i.e., the valuation of art not by everybody and, above all, not by plain men, but by erudite, that is, by perverted and at the same time self-confident individuals.

A friend of mine, speaking of the relation of critics to artists, half jokingly defined it thus: "Critics are the stupid who discuss the wise." However partial, inexact, and rude this definition may be, it is yet partly true and is incomparably more just than the definition which considers critics to be men who can explain works of art.

"Critics explain!" What do they explain?

The artist, if a real artist, has by his work transmitted to others the feeling he experienced. What is there, then, to explain?

If a work be good as art, then the feeling expressed by the artist—be it moral or immoral—transmits itself to other people. If transmitted to others, then they feel it, and all interpretations are superfluous. If the work does not infect people, no explanation can make it contagious. An artist's work cannot be interpreted. Had it been possible to explain in words what he wished to convey, the artist would have expressed himself in words. He expressed it by his art only because the feeling he experienced could not be otherwise transmitted. The interpretation of works of art by words only indicates that the interpreter is himself incapable of feeling the infection of art. And this is actually the case; for, however strange it may seem to say so, critics have always been people less susceptible than other men to the contagion of art. For the most part they are able writers, educated and clever, but with their capacity of being infected by art quite perverted or atrophied. And therefore their writings have always largely contributed, and still contribute, to the perversion of the taste of that public which reads them and trusts them. . . .

It is solely due to the critics, who in our times still praise rude, savage, and, for us, often meaningless works of the ancient Greeks: Sophocles, Euripides, Aeschylus, and especially Aristophanes; or, of modern writers, Dante, Tasso, Milton, Shakespeare; in painting, all of Raphael, all of Michael Angelo, including his absurd "Last Judgment"; in music, the whole of Bach and the whole of Beethoven, including his last period—thanks only to them have the Isbens, Maeterlincks, Verlaines, Mallarmés, Puvis de Chavannes, Klingers, Böcklins, Stucks, Schneiders, and in music the Wagners, Liszts, Berliozes, Brahmses, and Richard Strausses, etc., and all that immense mass of good-for-nothing imitators of these imitators become possible in our day.

IV. ART AND INFECTIOUSNESS

There is one indubitable indication distinguishing real art from its counterfeit, namely, the infectiousness of art. If a man, without exercising effort and without altering his standpoint on reading, hearing, or seeing another man's work, experiences a mental condition which unites him with that man and with other people who also partake of that work of art, then the object evoking that condition is a work of art. And however poetical, realistic, effectful, or interesting a work may be, it is not a work of art if it does not evoke that feeling (quite distinct from all other feelings) of joy and of spiritual union with another (the author) and with others (those who are also infected by it).

It is true that this indication is an *internal* one, and that there are people who have forgotten what the action of real art is, who expect something else from art (in our society the great majority are in this state), and that therefore such people may mistake for this aesthetic feeling the feeling of diversion and a certain excitement which they receive from counterfeits of art. But though it is impossible to undeceive these people, just as it is impossible to convince a man suffering from "Daltonism"[1] that green is not red, yet, for all that, this indication remains perfectly definite to those whose feeling for art is neither perverted nor atrophied, and it clearly distinguishes the feeling produced by art from all other feelings.

The chief peculiarity of this feeling is that the receiver of a true artistic impression is so united to the artist that he feels as if the work were his own and not someone else's—as if what it expresses were just what he had long been wishing to express. A real work of art destroys, in the consciousness of the receiver, the separation between himself and the artist—not that alone, but also between himself and all whose minds receive this work

[1] A kind of color blindness discovered by John Dalton.

of art. In this freeing of our personality from its separation and isolation, in this uniting of it with others, lies the chief character-istic and the great attractive force of art.

If a man is infected by the author's condition of soul, if he feels this emotion and this union with others, then the object which has effected this is art; but if there be no such infection, if there be not this union with the author and with others who are moved by the same work—then it is not art. And not only is infection a sure sign of art, but the degree of infectiousness is also the sole measure of excellence in art.

The stronger the infection, the better is the art as art, speak-ing now apart from its subject matter, i.e., not considering the quality of the feelings it transmits.

And the degree of the infectiousness of art depends on three conditions:

(1) On the greater or lesser individuality of the feeling transmitted;
(2) On the greater or lesser clearness with which the feeling is transmitted;
(3) On the sincerity of the artist, i.e., on the greater or lesser force with which the artist himself feels the emotion he transmits.

The more individual the feeling transmitted the more strongly does it act on the receiver; the more individual the state of soul into which he is transferred, the more pleasure does the receiver obtain, and therefore the more readily and strongly does he join in it.

The clearness of expression assists infection because the re-ceiver, who mingles in consciousness with the author, is the bet-ter satisfied the more clearly the feeling is transmitted, which, as it seems to him, he has long known and felt, and for which he has only now found expression.

But most of all is the degree of infectiousness of art increased by the degree of sincerity in the artist. As soon as the spectator, hearer, or reader feels that the artist is infected by his own production, and writes, sings, or plays for himself, and not merely to act on others, this mental condition of the artist infects the receiver; and contrariwise, as soon as the spectator, reader, or hearer feels that the author is not writing, singing, or playing for his own satisfaction—does not himself feel what he wishes

to express—but is doing it for him, the receiver, a resistance
immediately springs up, and the most individual and the newest
feelings and the cleverest technique not only fail to produce any
infection but actually repel.

V. ART AND RELIGION

Art is a spiritual organ of human life which cannot be destroyed, and therefore, notwithstanding all the efforts made by
people of the upper classes to conceal the religious ideal by
which humanity lives, that ideal is more and more clearly recognized by man, and even in our perverted society is more and
more often partially expressed by science and by art. During the
present century works of the higher kind of religious art have
appeared more and more frequently, both in literature and in
painting, permeated by a truly Christian spirit, as also works of
the universal art of common life accessible to all. So that even art
knows the true ideal of our times and tends toward it. On the
one hand, the best works of art of our times transmit religious
feelings urging toward the union and the brotherhood of man
(such are the works of Dickens, Hugo, Dostoevsky, and in painting of Millet, Bastien Lepage, Jules Breton, Lhermitte, and
others); on the other hand, they strive toward the transmission,
not of feelings which are natural to people of the upper classes
only, but of such feelings as may unite everyone without exception. There are as yet few such works, but the need of them is
already acknowledged. In recent times we also meet more and
more frequently with attempts at publications, pictures, concerts,
and theaters for the people. All this is still very far from accom-
plishing what should be done, but already the direction in which
good art instinctively presses forward to regain the path natural
to it can be discerned.

The religious perception of our time—which consists in ac-
knowledging that the aim of life (both collective and individual)
is the union of mankind—is already so sufficiently distinct that
people have now only to reject the false theory of beauty according to which enjoyment is considered to be the purpose of

art, and religious perception will naturally take its place as the guide of the art of our time.

And as soon as the religious perception, which already unconsciously directs the life of man, is consciously acknowledged, then immediately and naturally the division of art into art for the lower and art for the upper classes will disappear. There will be one common, brotherly, universal art, and first that art will naturally be rejected which transmits feelings incompatible with the religious perception of our time, feelings which do not unite, but divide men, and then that insignificant, exclusive art will be rejected to which an importance is now attached to which it has no right.

And as soon as this occurs, art will immediately cease to be what it has been in recent times, a means of making people coarser and more vicious, and it will become what it always used to be and should be, a means by which humanity progresses toward unity and blessedness.

Strange as the comparison may sound, what has happened to the art of our circle and time is what happens to a woman who sells her womanly attractiveness, intended for maternity, for the pleasure of those who desire such pleasures.

The art of our time and of our circle has become a prostitute. And this comparison holds good even in minute details. Like her it is not limited to certain times, like her it is always adorned, like her it is always salable, and like her it is enticing and ruinous.

A real work of art can only arise in the soul of an artist occasionally as the fruit of the life he has lived, just as a child is conceived by its mother. But counterfeit art is produced by artisans and handicraftsmen continually, if only consumers can be found.

Real art, like the wife of an affectionate husband, needs no ornaments. But counterfeit art, like a prostitute, must always be decked out.

The cause of the production of real art is the artist's inner need to express a feeling that has accumulated, just as for a mother the cause of sexual conception is love. The cause of counterfeit art, as of prostitution, is gain.

The consequence of true art is the introduction of a new feeling into the intercourse of life, as the consequence of a wife's love is the birth of a new man into life.

The consequences of counterfeit art are the perversion of man, pleasure which never satisfies, and the weakening of man's spiritual strength.

And this is what people of our day and of our circle should understand in order to avoid the filthy torrent of depraved and prostituted art with which we are deluged.

Part III

AESTHETICISM

Théophile Gautier

[1811–1872]

⋙⋘

MADEMOISELLE DE MAUPIN (1835) was written to order for Gautier's
publisher, who had requested a sensational novel. It took three years
to write and ended by being more artistic than sensational. As if to
remedy the defect, Gautier prefaced the novel with an essay denounc-
ing the age for its habit of regarding art as useful. A compound of serious criticism and brilliant showmanship, the Preface served the immediate purpose of publicizing the novel.

Today the Preface is interesting as a defense of "art for art's sake."
The Kantian principle of "purposiveness without purpose" is converted
into a weapon in the struggle to preserve art from the Philistines. The
battle continued to rage throughout the nineteenth century, and Gautier's points were frequently reiterated. The most important service
of Gautier and his fellow aesthetes was to prepare the way for the
Parnassiens and symbolists of the latter half of the nineteenth century.

Gautier's *Works* have been translated by F. C. de Sumichrast (Boston, 1900–1903). See especially volumes one (*Mademoiselle de Maupin* and the "Preface") and twelve (*Essays on Art and Criticism*). For
comment see: G. Matoré, *La Préface de Mademoiselle de Maupin*
(Paris, 1946); J. Richardson, *Théophile Gautier, His Life and Times*
(London, 1958).

The present selections from the Preface to *Mademoiselle de Maupin*
are translated by Professor Alfred Engstrom of the University of North
Carolina, Chapel Hill.

PREFACE TO MADEMOISELLE DE MAUPIN

ONE OF THE MOST ridiculous aspects of the glorious epoch in
which we have the good fortune to draw breath beside such men
as the treacherous Deutz and General Bugeaud is unquestionably
the rehabilitation of virtue undertaken by all the journals of
every hue—red, green, and tricolor.

Virtue is certainly very respectable, and we have no desire

to fail in our obligations to her—that good, worthy woman! God
forbid! We find her eyes shine brightly through her spectacles;
her stockings are drawn on neatly enough; she takes her snuff
from its golden box with all imaginable grace; and her little dog
curtseys like a dancing-master. We find all that. We even admit
that—considering her age—she is not unattractive and carries
the weight of her years lightly. She is a very agreeable grandmother, but she is still a grandmother. . . . It seems natural
to me, especially at age twenty, to prefer some neat little piece
of immorality who is coquettish, a good sport, her hair slightly
mussed, her skirt a trifle brief, tempting of foot and eye, her
cheek a little flushed, laughter on her lips, and her heart on her
sleeve. Journalists of the most monstrous virtue could hardly
disagree; and if they do, they probably don't think it. To think
one thing and write another happens every day, especially to
men of virtue.

I recall the low jokes made before the July revolution about
the unhappy and virginal Vicomte Sosthène de la Rochefoucauld,
who lengthened the dancers' dresses at the Opéra and with his
own patrician hands applied a modest daub of plaster to the
middle of all the statues. But the Vicomte Sosthène de la Rochefoucauld has been left far behind. Modesty has been brought to
far greater perfection since his time and has attained refinements
he would never have dreamed of.

Personally, I am not accustomed to examining the private parts
of statues, and like everyone else, I found the fig-leaf cut out
by the scissors of the beaux-arts deputy the most ridiculous object imaginable. But it seems that I was wrong, and the fig-
leaf is an institution of the most profound merit.

I have been told—though it seemed so strange that I refused
to believe it—that there were people who saw nothing in Michelangelo's "Last Judgment" but the episode of the licentious prel-
ates and veiled their eyes crying woe and desolation! . . .

I admit that I am not so virtuous as all that. Dorine, that saucy
maid, can go ahead and bare her plump breast to me. I certainly
won't pull my handkerchief from my pocket to cover it up. I
shall look upon her breast as upon her face; and if it is white
and shapely I shall take pleasure in the sight of it.—But I shall
not finger Elmire's dress to see if it is soft, and I shall not, like

wretched Tartuffe, thrust her down on the edge of the table while pretending to be a saint.

The great affectation of morality that is just now all the rage would be laughable if it were not so boring. Every newspaper column is becoming a pulpit, every journalist a preacher. All that is lacking is the tonsure and the priest's robe. The season is one of rain and homilies, and one defends himself against the combination by going out only in a carriage and by rereading *Pantagruel* between his bottle and pipe.

But good heavens! What a downpour! And what a fury! Who bit you? Why the devil do you shout so loud, and what has this poor fellow Vice done that you should bear him such ill will? And he such a good fellow, so easygoing, asking only to be amused and, if possible, not to bore others. Act with vice like the actor Serre with the gendarme in the play: embrace each other and end all this nonsense. Believe me, it will do you good.—For heaven's sake, you preachers, what would you do without vice? If people suddenly became virtuous you would be reduced to beggary overnight.

The theatres would close this very evening. What would you write your column about? No more Opera balls to take up space, no more novels to tear apart. For balls and plays and novels are the true pomps of Satan if one believes our holy mother the Church. The actress would send her rich lover packing and couldn't afford to continue paying your for your praise. People wouldn't subscribe any longer to your newspapers. They would read St. Augustine instead and go to church and say their rosaries. That might be all very fine, but *you* certainly wouldn't gain by it. If everyone were virtuous, where would you publish your articles on the immorality of the age? So you see, vice is good for something. . . .

One thing is certain and easy to demonstrate to sceptics. That is the critic's natural antipathy to the poet—the antipathy of the do-nothing toward the creator, of the drone toward the bee, of the gelding toward the stallion.

You don't become a critic until you have fully satisfied yourself that you can't become a poet. Before being reduced to the wretched role of cloak-warden or employee in a billiard room or tennis court, you wooed the Muse for a long time and tried to win her maidenhead. But you lacked the necessary vigor. Your breath gave out and you fell back, pale and emaciated, at the foot of Parnassus.

I understand your hatred. It is painful to see someone else sit at the feast to which you were not invited and sleep with the woman who has rejected you. I pity with all my heart the poor eunuch who has to be present at the joyous pleasures of the great lord.

He is admitted to the most private regions of the bedchamber. He ushers the Sultan's wives to their bath. He sees those lovely bodies all streaming with pearls and smoother than agates shining under the silvery waters of the great reservoirs. The most secret beauties are unveiled to him.

No one is embarrassed before him. He is a eunuch.

The Sultan caresses his favorite in the eunuch's presence and kisses her on her pomegranate mouth. In truth, the eunuch's position is utterly false and must cause him great embarrassment.

The same applies to the critic who sees the poet walking in poetry's garden with his nine fair odalisques and sporting idly in the shade of tall green laurel trees. It is hard for the critic not to pick up the stones of the highway and hurl them at the poet and hurt him behind his wall, if he is skillful enough to do it.

The critic who has produced nothing of his own is a coward. He is like an *abbé* who courts the wife of a layman: the layman cannot repay him in kind nor can he fight with him. . . .

It is absurd to say that a man is a drunkard because he describes an orgy or a *debauché* because he describes a debauch, just as it is absurd to pretend that a man is virtuous because he writes a book on ethics. One sees just the opposite every day. It is the character, not the author, who speaks in a work of fiction. If the hero is an atheist, that does not make the author one. The author make brigands talk and act like brigands, but that does not make him a brigand. If it did, Shakespeare, Corneille, and all the tragic writers would have had to be guillotined. They have murdered more people than Mandrin and Cartouche! Yet we have not guillotined them, and I do not think we will for a long time, no matter how virtuous and moral criticism may become. It is one of the manias of these little, narrow-minded dunces always to substitute the author for the work and to refer to a personality so as to introduce some poor touch of scandal into their miserable rhapsodies—which they know no one would read if they contained only the opinions of their writers.

It is impossible to understand the purpose of all these howls and barks and cries of rage. And why do small-scale Geoffreys turn into Don Quixotes of morality and veritable literary policemen who seize and cudgel in the name of virtue every idea they find in a book which has its headdress awry or its skirt tucked up a bit too high?

Whatever they say, the age is immoral (if the word has any real meaning, which is extremely doubtful); and we want no other proof than the quantity of immoral books it produces and the success they have. Books follow morals and not the other way around. The regency was responsible for Crébillon, Crébillon did not make the regency. Boucher's little shepherdesses had painted faces and bare breasts in imitation of the little marchionesses of their day. The paintings were made from the models, not the models from the paintings. I do not know who said or where that literature and the arts influence morals. Whoever he was, he was without doubt an idiot. It is as if one said that green peas make the spring come round. Green peas grow *because* it is spring just as cherries grow because it is summer. The trees bear the fruits, surely the fruits do not bear the trees, and this is an eternal and invariable law. The ages succeed one another and each bears its fruit, which is different from that of the preceding age. Books are the fruit of the ways that men behave.

Along with the moral journalists, under the rain of homilies as under a summer shower in a park, there has sprung up, between the boards of the Saint-Simonian [1] stage, a succession of little mushrooms of a curious new species whose natural history we are going to examine.

These are the utilitarian critics. Poor fellows whose noses were so short they could not put glasses on them and who could not even see as far as their noses.

[1] Claude Henri de Saint-Simon (1760–1825) was an early socialist and a philosopher whose theories prepared the way for those of Auguste Comte. Here and below Gautier cites him as the source of utilitarianism in literature and critical theory. (Ed.)

When an author threw down on their desk any sort of volume—
whether a novel or poetry—these gentlemen leaned back carelessly in their armchair, got it balanced on its hind feet, and,
teetering skillfully, assumed a pompous air and said: "What
good is this book? How can it be applied to improving the morals
and the well-being of the most numerous and poorest class of
men? What! Not a word about the needs of society? Nothing to
promote civilization and progress? Instead of making a great
synthesis of humanity and following throughout history the
phases of the idea of regeneration and providence, can one write
poems and novels that lead nowhere and do not advance one's
generation along the road to the future? In the presence of such
grave concerns can one be bothered with style or rhyme? What
good are style and rhyme and form to us? Those are fine matters
to worry about! (Poor foxes with their grapes.) Society is suffering; it is a prey to a great inner anguish (i.e.: No one wants
to buy the utilitarian papers). It is the poet's duty to seek out the
cause of this distress and cure it. He will find his way by sym-
pathizing heart and soul with humanity. (Philanthropic poets!
That would really be something rare and charming.) We await
this poet; we call to him with all our prayers. When he appears
the masses will acclaim him, and he will have palms and crowns
and the honors of the Prytaneum as guest of the State. . . ."

Great! But since we want our reader to stay awake to the very
end of this joyous preface, we will cut short our faithful imitation of the utilitarian style, which, by its nature, is pretty soporific
and might even profitably replace laudanum and Academy
speeches.

No, you imbeciles! No, you cretins and goitrous monsters! A
book does not make gelatine soup. A novel is not a pair of clumsy
boots. A sonnet is not a long-squirting syringe. A drama is not a
railroad. All of these being essentially civilizing things that make
humanity move along the path of progress.

By the bowels of all past, present, and future popes, No! And
two hundred thousand times, No!

You don't make a cotton cap with a metonymy or put on a
simile for a slipper. An antithesis cannot be used for an umbrella; and, unfortunately, a few motley rhymes cannot be worn
like a waistcoat over the belly. Personally, I am convinced that

an ode is too light a covering for the winter; and that one would
be no better dressed in a strophe, antistrophe, and epode than
that cynic's wife who had to get along with only her virtue for a
shirt, and went naked as your hand, according to the story. . . .

. . . I should really like to know, first of all, what precisely is
the meaning of that great, gawky noun with which the republican
or Saint-Simonian utilitarians daily stuff their empty columns,
and which they use as a shibboleth and a sacramental term:
Utility. What is this word, and to what does it apply?

There are two kinds of utilities, and the meaning of the word
is never anything but relative. What is useful for one is not for
another. You are a cobbler, I am a poet.—It is useful for me to
have my first and second verses rhyme. I find a rhyming dictionary very useful; you have no need for one to resole an old pair
of boots, and it is only fair to say that a cobbler's knife would not
be of much use to me in making an ode. Be that as it may, you
will object that a cobbler is much above a poet, and that one
can get along far better without the one than the other. Without pretending to disparage the illustrious profession of cobbler,
which I hold in equal honor with the profession of constitutional
monarch, I humbly admit that I should prefer to have my shoe
unsewn than my verse badly rhymed, and that I should rather
do without boots than poems. . . .

I know that there are men who prefer windmills to churches,
and physical to spiritual nourishment. I have no word for those
people. They deserve to be economists in this world, and the next.

Is there anything absolutely useful on this earth and in this
life of ours? First of all, there is not much use in our being on
earth and alive. I challenge the most learned of the band to say
what we are good for, if it isn't to refuse to subscribe to the
Constitutionnel or any other kind of journal.

If we admit a priori the practical value of our existence, what
is really essential for keeping us alive? Soup and a bit of meat
twice a day is all that we need to fill our bellies, in the strict
sense of the word. Man, for whom a coffin six feet long by two
feet wide is more than sufficient after his death, does not need
much room in life. A hollow cube seven to eight feet long in
every direction, with an air hole, a single cell of the hive, is all
that is necessary for a lodging and to keep the rain away. A

blanket suitably rolled about one's body will ward off the cold as well and better than the most elegant and best-tailored dress coat.

With these essentials, one can survive. They say that one can live on 25 sous a day. But merely to keep from dying is not living, and I fail to see how a city organized according to this idea of utility would be any more agreeable to live in than the cemetery of Père La Chaise.

Nothing that is beautiful is indispensable to life. One could suppress the flowers, and the world would not suffer materially from it; and yet who would be willing for there to be no more flowers? I should sooner give up potatoes than roses, and I suspect that there is not more than one utilitarian in the world capable of digging up a tulip bed to plant cabbages.

Of what use is the beauty of women? Provided that a woman is medically normal, in a condition to receive a man and to have children, she will always be good enough for the economists.

What good is music? Or painting? Who would be so mad as to prefer Mozart to a republican politician like M. Carel, or Michelangelo to the inventor of white mustard?

There is nothing truly beautiful except what is of no use: everything useful is ugly, for it is the expression of some need, and man's needs are ignoble and disgusting, like his poor, infirm nature. The most useful spot in a house is the bathroom.

As for me, if these gentlemen will forgive me, I am one of those for whom the superfluous is a necessity; and I prefer things and men in inverse ratio to the useful services they render me. I prefer to my useful chamber pot a Chinese jar, adorned with dragons and mandarins, that has no useful function whatever; and the talent that I hold highest is my inability to solve anagrams and charades. I would joyously renounce my rights of French citizenship to see an authentic painting by Raphael or a beautiful woman naked—say the Princess Borghese when she posed for Canova, or Julia Grisi entering her bath. . . .

The most fitting occupation for a civilized man seems to me to do nothing, or to smoke his pipe or cigar and meditate. I also esteem those who play skittles and those who make good verse. You see that utilitarian principles are quite different from mine, and that I shall never be an editor of a virtuous journal, unless I am converted, which would be ludicrous indeed.

Instead of establishing a Monthyon prize as a reward for virtue, I should prefer, like Sardanapalus, that great philosopher who has been so misunderstood, to give a huge reward to whoever invented a new pleasure; for enjoyment seems to me the goal of life, and the only useful thing in the world. God wished it so, for he made women, perfumes, light, beautiful flowers, good wines, spirited horses, greyhounds, and Angora cats. God did not say to his angels: "Have virtue," but "Have love"—and he gave us a mouth more sensitive than the rest of the skin to kiss women, eyes raised on high to see the light, a subtle sense of smell to breathe the soul of flowers, sinewy thighs to press the sides of stallions and to fly as swiftly as thought without railroads or steam-boilers; delicate hands to pass over the long heads of greyhounds, cats' velvety backs, and the smooth shoulders of girls without much virtue; and he, finally, has granted to us alone the triple and glorious privilege of drinking without being thirsty, striking a light, and making love in all seasons, an ability which distinguishes us from the brutes far more than the custom of reading newspapers and making deeds.

Good heavens! How stupid is this supposed perfectibility of the human race that is always being dinned into our ears! Truly, one could say that man is a machine susceptible of improvements, and that better-engaged wheelwork or a better-placed counterweight can make him function with greater comfort and ease. When someone has managed to provide man with a double stomach so that he can chew his cud like an ox; with eyes in the back of his head so that, like Janus, he can see those who are insulting him from behind and contemplate his *vileness* from a position less painful than that of the Callipygian Venus of Athens [*sic*]; and to plant wings on his shoulders so that he need not pay six sous to go anywhere by bus—when someone has created a new physical organ for his pleasure, well and good! The word perfectibility will then begin to mean something.

Despite all their fine improvements, what have people done that they did not do as well or better before the Flood? . . .

. . . The little houses in the suburbs belonging to the marquis of the regency are wretched country cottages in comparison with the villas of the Roman patricians of Baia, Capri and Tibur. Should not the Cyclopean magnificence of these great voluptuaries who built eternal monuments for ephemeral pleasures make us fall prostrate before the genius of antiquity, and obliterate forever from our dictionaries the word perfectibility?

Has anyone invented a single additional deadly sin? There are, sad to say, still only seven, as before. . . . —What does it matter whether we are ruled by a saber, a holy water sprinkler, or an umbrella! It is still a stick; and I am astonished that men who believe in progress keep on arguing about the choice of the cudgel that must tap them on the shoulder when it would be so much more progressive and so much less expensive to break it in two and hurl the pieces to all the devils.

The only one of you apostles of progress who has common sense is a madman, a great genius, an imbecile, a divine poet much superior to Lamartine, Hugo, and Byron; and that is Charles Fourier the Phalansterian, who is all these things in one. He alone had the logic and the boldness to push his consequences to their conclusion. He affirmed confidently that it would not be long before men had a tail fifteen feet long with an eye at the end. This, surely, is progress, and would permit man to do a thousand fine things he could never do before. . . .

Charles Fourier has invented as many species of animals as George Cuvier, the great naturalist . . . and he promises to create new pleasures and to develop man's organs and senses. He will make women more beautiful and more voluptuous, and men more vigorous and robust; he guarantees you children and proposes to reduce the number of inhabitants of the world so that everybody can be comfortable; which is much more reasonable than urging the working class to multiply, only to attack them with artillery in the streets when they multiply too much, and to send them cannon-balls in place of bread.

Progress is possible only in this way.

All the rest is a bitter mockery, a senseless sham which is not even good for duping idiotic simpletons. . . .

—Some centuries back there were Raphael and Michelangelo; today there is M. Paul Delaroche, and all because we are progressing. . . . In antiquity they had three or four thousand gods they believed in, and today we have only one in which we hardly believe at all; a strange kind of progress. Isn't Jupiter mightier and a better seducer than Don Juan? In truth, I do not know anything we have invented or even improved upon. . . .

In literary matters we have perhaps invented one thing—criticism of the future, criticism of what is to come. Think how charming that is and what a fine imagination it springs from. The formula is simple and can be told.—The book that is beautiful and praiseworthy is the one that has not yet been published. The one that *has* appeared is always detestable. Tomorrow's book will be superb; but the present is always today. This kind of criticism is like the barber who had a sign with the following words inscribed in large letters: SHAVING FREE HERE TO-MORROW. . . .

. . . But this critical formula is much superior to that which could be called retrospective and which consists in praising only old works of literature that no one reads any more and that don't disturb anybody, at the expense of modern books that people do read and that hurt human pride directly. . . .

Authors endure all this criticism with a magnanimity and forbearance that I find truly inconceivable. In the last analysis, who are these critics whose tone is so cutting and whose word is so terse that one would think them children of the gods? They are, quite simply, men we went to school with, whose studies have clearly been less profitable than ours, since they have not written anything of their own and, like veritable Stymphalean birds, can do nothing but defile and spoil the works of others.

Wouldn't a criticism of the critics be something worth attempting? For these hyperfastidious individuals who act so proud and hard to please are far from having our Holy Father's infallibility. There would be enough material on this subject to fill the bulkiest journal every day. Their silly blunders, their forged citations, their errors in French, their plagiarisms, their foolish repetitions, their hackneyed and vulgar pleasantries, their lack of ideas, intelligence and tact, their ignorance of the simplest matters that makes them quite willing to take Pyrée for a man and M. Delaroche for a painter, would furnish ample revenge to authors with no more work involved than underlining the appropriate passages in pencil and reproducing them verbatim. . . . If Chateaubriand, Lamartine, and other men of their quality wrote criticism, I should understand people's getting down on their knees and worshiping; but when Messrs. Z.K.Y.V.Q.X. (or any other letter from Alpha to Omega) pretend to be little Quintilians and rebuke you sharply in the name of morality and fine literature, I always become indignant and fly into a towering rage. . . .

Charles X was the only one who really understood the question. When he ordered the suppression of the newspapers he rendered a great service to the arts and to civilization. The newspapers are a kind of intermediary or go-between interposing themselves between the artists and the public, between the king and the people. We know what fine things have resulted from that. Their perpetual barking dulls inspiration and causes such suspicion that no one dares trust a poet or a government. The result is that royalty and poetry, the two greatest things in the world, become impossible, to the great injury of the peoples of the earth, who sacrifice their happiness for the low pleasure of reading every morning a few wretched sheets of wretched paper daubed with wretched ink and in a wretched style. There was no art criticism under Julian II, and I do not know of any *feuilleton* on Daniele da Volterra, Sebastiano del Piombo, Michelangelo, or Raphael; nor of any on Ghiberti delle Porte, or Benvenuto Cellini; and yet I think that, for men who had no newspapers, who didn't even know the word *art* or the word *artistic,* they had quite enough talent and did not perform too badly in their trade. The reading of newspapers prevents the development of true scholars and true artists; it is like a daily pollution that makes you nervous and weak as you climb into bed with the muses, those firm and exacting maidens who want their lovers to be fresh and vigorous. The newspaper is killing the book, just as the book has killed architecture, and just as artillery put an end to courage and muscular strength. People do not suspect what pleasures the newspapers deprive us of. They take away the maidenhood of everything; they keep one from having anything of his own—even a book; they take away the surprise of the theatre by telling all the dénouements in advance; they take away your pleasure in friendly chatter, in gossip, in prattle, in disparaging conversation, in making up a false tale or spreading a true one for a week in all the drawing rooms of society. In spite of ourselves, they fill our ears with ready-made judgments, and prejudice us against things we would otherwise enjoy. . . . If, once and forever, Louis-Philippe suppressed all the literary and political journals, I should be infinitely grateful to him for it, and I should immediately write him a fine, wild dithyramb in *vers libres* and in crossed rhymes, signed, "Your very humble and very faithful subject, etc." Let no one think that people wouldn't be concerned any more with literature: before the age of the newspapers, Paris was stirred up for a week over a single quatrain and for six months over the presentation of a new play.

It is true that without newspapers one would lose the advertisements and the eulogies at 30 sous a line, and notoriety would be slower and less spectacular. But I have conceived a very ingenious substitute for advertisements. If, between now and the appearance of my glorious novel, my gracious sovereign has suppressed the journals, I will certainly use my new idea, and I expect no end of wonders from it. When the great day arrives twenty-four criers on horseback in the livery of the publisher Renduel, with his address on their backs and chests and each carrying a flag embroidered on both sides with the title of the novel and preceded by drummers, will cry loudly and clearly through the town: "Today—not yesterday or tomorrow—they put on sale the admirable, inimitable, divine and super-divine novel of the famous Théophile Gautier—*Mademoiselle de Maupin*—which Europe and other parts of the earth, including Polynesia, have been impatiently awaiting for a year and more. It sells five hundred copies a minute and new printings follow one another every half hour; there have already been nineteen of them. A squad of the municipal guard is at the shopdoor to hold back the crowd and prevent disorders."—Surely that would be as good as a three-line advertisement in the *Débats* and the *Courrier Français* between the elastic pessaries, the crinoline collars, the incorruptible baby bottles, Regnault's pectoral paste, and the cures for leucorrhea.

May, 1834

Charles Pierre Baudelaire

[1821–1867]

❧§❧

IN 1846 BAUDELAIRE was a young man with a great deal of talent but no very clear theory of how to use it. His discovery of Edgar Allan Poe in that year marked a turning point in his career. As he wrote in 1860, he found in Poe's work "poems and short stories which I had conceived, but vaguely and in a confused and disorderly way, and which Poe had been able to finish perfectly." The result was five volumes of translations which span much of Baudelaire's creative life, from 1848 to 1865. What Baudelaire would have written without Poe's influence makes an interesting question, but one which is irrelevant to the history of modern criticism.

Baudelaire's essays on Poe, and particularly the *New Notes* of 1857, touch on principles which are central to his more independent criticism. Three aspects of Poe fascinated him. First, there was Poe the creative writer, addicted to the morbid and melancholy, and contemptuous of the democratic values of his age. Second, there was Poe the meticulous stylist. Finally, there was Poe the critic who combined faith in a transcendent world of ideal beauty with a theory of technique as rigorous as a demonstration in geometry. The combination of idealism with the search for a precise technique whereby the ideal may be symbolized is the most characteristic feature of Baudelaire's criticism. Allied to it is the idea, derived from Swedenborg, that "correspondence" exists between the ideal and the real and can be expressed by such devices as synesthesia and image-association. Baudelaire's most immediate influence was on the Parnassian group. He later influenced the symbolists, and through them his influence was transmitted to the twentieth century.

For Baudelaire's essays on Poe see L. and F. Hyslop, trans. and intr. *Baudelaire on Poe* (State College, Pa., 1952). Of the many discussions of Baudelaire and the symbolist movement, see especially: J. Chiari, *Symbolism from Poe to Mallarmé* (London, 1956); T. S. Eliot, "From Poe to Valéry," *Hudson Review*, II (1949), 327–42; E. Fiser, *Le symbole littéraire* (Paris, 1941); L. Lemonnier, *Edgar Poe et la critique française* (Paris, 1928); M. Raymond, *From Baudelaire to Surrealism* (New York, 1949); A. Symons, *The Symbolist Movement*

in Literature (London, 1911); P. Valéry, "Situation de Baudelaire," in
Variéte II (Paris, 1930).

The present selections are translated by Professor Alfred Engstrom
of the University of North Carolina.

Correspondences

Nature is a temple where living pillars
Sometimes let confused words come forth;
Man passes there through forests of symbols
That look upon him with familiar glances.

Like long echoes that fuse from far away
In a shadowy and deep union,
Vast as night and as light,
Perfumes, colors and sounds correspond.

There are perfumes cool as children's flesh,
Sweet as oboes, green as prairies,
—And others that are corrupt, rich and full of triumph,

Having the expansiveness of infinite things,
Like ambergris, musk, gum benjamin and incense,
That sing the ecstasies of the spirit and the senses.

NEW NOTES ON EDGAR ALLAN POE

I

LITERATURE OF DECADENCE! An empty phrase that one often hears
falling, sonorous as a great yawn, from the mouths of those
sphinxes without riddles that guard the sacred portals of classical
Esthetics. Whenever such an irrefutable oracle sounds off one
can be sure that it is in relation to a poem or a novel whose every
part is skillfully arranged for surprise, whose style is magnificently ornate, in which an impeccable hand has employed all
the resources of language and versification. When I hear the roar
of anathema—which, let me say in passing, generally falls on
some esteemed poet—I always want to reply: "Do you take me

for a barbarian like yourself, and do you think I can be amused in the same miserable way as you?" Then grotesque comparisons whirl in my mind; I have the impression that two women are presented to me; one is a rustic matron, repugnant in her health and virtue, without grace and with no charm in her glance, in brief, *one who draws all her qualities from simple nature;* the other is one of those beauties who dominate and haunt the memory, one who combines with a profound and original charm all that is eloquent in dress, who is mistress of her bearing, thoroughly conscious of her personality and completely self-possessed—with a voice that speaks like a well-tuned instrument, and with glances charged with intelligence and employed with perfect control. There would be no doubt as to my choice between these two, and yet there are pedantic sphinxes that would accuse me of a deficiency in classical honor. But, to put aside these allegories, I believe I may be permitted to inquire of these wise men whether they really comprehend the vanity and uselessness of their wisdom. The phrase *literature of decadence* implies that there is a series of stages in literatures—a puling period of infancy, a period of childhood, an adolescence, etc. I mean that this term presupposes something fatal and providential, like a decree from which there is no appeal. If so, it is completely unjust to reproach us for obeying the dictates of this mysterious law. All that I can make of the academic expression is that it is shameful to get any pleasure out of complying with this law, and that we are guilty if we rejoice in our destiny.—This sun which, a few hours ago, overwhelmed everything under its direct white light, will soon pour waves of varied colors over the western horizon. In the play of this setting sun, certain poetic minds will find new delights; they will find in it dazzling colonnades, cascades of melted metal, fiery paradises, a mournful splendor, the voluptuous pleasure of yearning, all the magical qualities of dream, all that opium brings back of memories. And for them the sunset will in fact appear as the marvelous allegory of a soul burdened with life that sinks behind the horizon, magnificently provided with thoughts and dreams.

But what the avowed professors have not considered is that, in the activity of life, there may arise complications and combinations entirely unanticipated by their scholarly wisdom. And then their inadequate jargon is found wanting, as in the case (which will perhaps recur many times in varying circumstances) of a nation which begins with decadence and thus starts at the point where other nations end.

As new literatures develop amidst the vast colonies of the present age, there will surely be spiritual accidents baffling to the academic mind. Young and old at the same time, America prattles and drivels with an astonishing volubility. Who could number its poets? They are innumerable. Its *blue stockings?* They fill the magazines. Its critics? You may be sure that America has pedants just as insistent as ours in calling the artist back endlessly to the ancient conceptions of beauty and in questioning a poet or a novelist on the morality of his purpose and the quality of his intentions. In America, even more than in this country, there are men of letters who don't know how to write; there is puerile, useless literary work; there are innumerable compilers, those who wearisomely repeat themselves, and those who plagiarize plagiarisms and criticize critics. In this bubbling up of mediocrities in a world dazzled by material improvements (a new kind of scandal that makes one realize the grandeur of peoples who are not doers), in this society that is so eager to be astonished, so in love with life, and especially a life full of excitement, there appeared a man who was great, not only through his metaphysical subtlety, through the sinister or enchanting beauty of his conceptions, through the rigor of his analysis, but great also, and no less great, as a *caricature.*—Here I must explain myself with some care; for recently an imprudent critic, in order to belittle Edgar Poe and to question the sincerity of my admiration, used the word *jongleur* that I had myself applied to the noble poet as a kind of praise.

From the womb of a greedy world hungry for material things, Poe soared into dreams. Stifled as he was by the American atmosphere, he wrote in the front of *Eureka:* "I offer this book to those who have put faith in dreams as in the only realities!" It was an admirable protest, and he made it *in his own way.* The author who, in *The Colloquy of Monos and Una,* lets loose torrents of scorn and disgust upon democracy, progress, and civilization, is the same author who, in order to combat the credulousness and the foolishness of his countrymen, proposed most emphatically the idea of the sovereignty of man and ingeniously devised hoaxes

most flattering to the pride of *modern man*. Seen in this light, Poe
seems to me like a slave seeking to make his master blush. Finally,
to express my thought even more precisely, Poe was always
great, not only in his noble conceptions, but even when he played
the role of buffoon.

II

For Poe was never a dupe! I do not believe that the man from
Virginia who calmly wrote in the full flood of democratic idealism: "The people have nothing to do with laws, except to obey
them," has ever been gulled by modern wisdom;—nor has the
author of "The nose of a mob is its imagination. By this, at any
time, it can be quietly led"—and a hundred other passages in
which mockery rains down as thick as grape-shot, but yet remains
careless and proud.—The Swedenborgians congratulate him for
his *Mesmeric Revelation*, like those innocent Illuminati of another
day who looked upon Cazotte's *Diable amoureux* as a revelation
of their mysteries; they thank the author for the great truths he
has just proclaimed—for they have discovered (O verifiers of
what cannot be verified!) that everything he stated is absolutely
true—although they admit that at first they suspected it might
very well be a mere fiction. Poe answers that, so far as he is concerned, he never had the slightest doubt about it.—Need I cite
again this little passage that leaps out at me from the page as,
for the hundredth time, I thumb through his amusing *Marginalia*,
which seem to reveal the innermost part of his mind: "The enormous multiplication of books in all branches of knowledge is one
of the greatest calamities of the present age! for it is one of the
most serious obstacles to the acquisition of any positive knowledge." An aristocrat by nature even more than by birth, a Virgin-
ian, a man from the South, a Byron who had strayed into a
wretched society, Poe always kept his philosophic calm, and,
whether he was defining the nose of the populace, or mocking
those who were inventing religious, or making game of libraries, he
remained what the true poet was and will always be—a truth in
strange garb, an apparent paradox, one who desires no intimacy

with the crowd and who runs as far as he can to the east when the fireworks are shot off in the west.

But most important of all: we shall observe that this author, the product of an age infatuated with itself, the child of a nation more infatuated with itself than any other, saw clearly, and imperturbably affirmed, the natural perversity of man. There is in man, he said, a mysterious force which modern philosophy does not want to consider; and yet, without this nameless force, without this primordial inclination, a multitude of human actions will remain unexplained and inexplicable. Such actions are attractive only *because* they are wicked and dangerous; they have the attraction of the abyss. This primitive, irresistible force is natural Perversity, which makes man unceasingly at the same time a killer of others and of himself, a murderer and an executioner;—for, he adds, with a remarkably satanic subtlety, the impossibility of finding a sufficiently reasonable motive for certain bad and dangerous actions could lead us to consider them as the result of suggestions from the Devil, if history and experience did not teach us that God often uses them for the establishment of order and the punishment of rogues;—*after having used these same rogues as his accomplices!* such is the phrase, I admit, that glides into my mind, with an implication as perfidious as it is inevitable. But at present I wish to consider only that great forgotten truth—the primordial perversity of man—and it is not without a certain satisfaction that I see some fragments of ancient wisdom returning to us from a country from which we did not expect them. It is a source of comfort that a few explosions of old truth burst like this in the face of all these flatterers of humanity, of all these coddlers and cajolers who repeat with every possible variation of tone: "I was born good, and you too, and all of us, were born good!" forgetting—no, pretending to forget, these upside-down egalitarians—that we were all born marked for evil!

What illusion could dupe this man who sometimes, under the painful compulsion of his environment, aimed so well against illusions? What scorn he had for pseudo-philosophy in his best days, when he was, as it were, gifted with vision! This poet, several of whose fictions seem wantonly made to confirm the supposed omnipotence of man, wished at times to purge himself. The day on which he wrote: "All certainty is in dreams," he

thrust back his own Americanism into the region of inferior
things; at other times, entering again into the true way of poets,
obedient doubtless to the inevitable truth that haunts us like a
demon, he breathed the ardent sighs of *the fallen angel that re-
members Heaven;* he mourned for the golden age and the lost
Paradise; he wept for all the magnificence of nature, *shrivelling
up before the hot blast of fiery furnaces;* and finally he wrote
down the admirable pages of *The Colloquy of Monos and Una,*
which would have charmed and disconcerted the impeccable
Joseph de Maistre.

It is he who said of socialism at a time when the latter did not
yet have a name, or when its name at least was not completely
popularized: "The world is infested, just now, by a new sect of
philosophers, who have not yet suspected themselves of forming
a sect, and who, consequently, have adopted no name. They are
the Believers in everything Old. Their High Priest, in the East,
is Charles Fourier—in the West, Horace Greeley; and high priests
they are to some purpose. The only common bond among the
sect is Credulity:—let us call it Insanity at once, and be done
with it. Ask any one of them *why* he believes this or that, and,
if he be conscientious (ignorant people usually are), he will make
you very much such a reply as Talleyrand made when asked why
he believed in the Bible. 'I believe in it first,' said he, 'because I
am Bishop of Autun; and secondly *because I know nothing about
it at all.*' What these philosophers call *argument* is a way they
have *de nier ce qui est et d'expliquer ce qui n'est pas.*" [1]

Progress, that great heresy of decrepitude, could not escape
Poe's attention. The reader will see, in various passages, the terms
he employed to characterize it. One would truly say, on seeing the
ardor of his attack, that he was seeking to avenge himself, as if
for some public humiliation or against some common nuisance.
How he would have laughed, with that scornful laugh of the poet
who is always aloof from the fatuous herd, if, as I did recently,
he had come upon this marvelous sentence, which makes one
think of buffoons and the wilful absurdities of mountebanks, and
which I found perfidiously on display in one of the most solemn
journals: *The continuous progress of science has very recently*

---

[1] Quoted from Poe's "Fifty Suggestions." (Ed.)

made possible the recovery of the secret lost and so long sought for of . . . (Greek fire, tempering of brass, whatever else has disappeared), *whose most successful applications date back to a barbarous and very ancient time! ! !*—There is a sentence that can be called a real find, a dazzling discovery, even in an age of *continuous progress;* but I believe that Poe's mummy Allamistakeo would not have failed to ask, with the tone, at once gentle and discreet, of one talking to his inferiors, whether it was also thanks to *continuous progress*—to the fatal, irresistible law of progress—that this famous secret had been lost.—Indeed, to abandon the tone of farce in discussing a subject that has about it as much of tears as of laughter, is it not a truly stupefying phenomenon to see a nation—several nations, and soon it will be all humanity—say to its wise men and its wizards: "I shall love you and make you great if you persuade me that we progress involuntarily, inevitably—even in our sleep; free us from responsibility, veil for us the humiliation of comparisons, falisfy history, and you can call yourselves the wisest of the wise"? Is it not a source of astonishment that so simple an idea as this does not spring up in all minds: that progress (in so far as there is any) increases suffering in proportion as it refines enjoyment, and that, if the epidermis of the peoples of the earth goes on becoming more delicate, they clearly pursue only a retreating goal—an *Italiam fugientem*—a conquest lost at every moment, a progress that is forever its own negation?

But these illusions, which are, moreover, selfish ones, originate in perversity and falsehood. They are will'-o'-the-wisps that arouse disdain in souls that love the eternal fire, like Edgar Poe, and that stir up hazy intelligences, like Jean-Jacques Rousseau, who, in place of philosophy have an injured sensibility eager for revolt. One cannot deny that Rousseau was right in what he said against the *depraved animal;* but the depraved animal has a right to reproach him for invoking simple nature. Nature creates nothing but monsters, and the whole problem is to come to an understanding of what is meant by *savages.* No philosopher will dare propose as models those corrupt, unhappy hordes, victims of the elements, the prey of wild beasts, creatures as incapable of fashioning arms as they are of conceiving the idea of a supreme spiritual power.

But, if one wishes to compare modern, civilized man with man in a state of savagery, or rather a so-called civilized nation with a nation in a savage state, that is to say deprived of all the ingenious inventions that make heroism unnecessary in the individual, who fails to see that all honor is due the savage? By his very nature, by necessity itself, he is encyclopedic, whereas civilized man finds himself confined within the infinitely small areas of his specialty. Civilized man invents the philosophy of progress to console himself for what he has given up and for his lowered state; while man in a state of savagery, feared and respected as a husband, as a warrior under compulsion to be brave, a poet in his hours of melancholy when the setting sun inspires him to sing of the past and his ancestors, approaches much nearer than civilized man to the threshold of the ideal. What shortcoming will we dare accuse him of? He has the priest, the magician, and the doctor. More than that, he has the dandy, the supreme incarnation of the idea of the beautiful carried over into material life, the one who dictates form and gives the rules for manners. His clothing, his ornaments, his arms, his calumet, bear witness to an inventive faculty that civilized men have long since lost. Shall we even think of comparing our dull eyes and our ears that have lost their perception to those keen eyes that pierce the mist, or to those ears *that would hear the grass grow?* And woman in a savage state, with her simple and childlike soul, an obedient wheedling animal, giving herself completely and knowing that she is only half of a destiny—shall we call her inferior to the American lady whom M. Bellegarigue (editor of *The Grocer's Advocate!*) thought to praise by saying that she was the ideal of the "kept woman"? This very woman, whose too-forward manners inspired in Edgar Poe—in Poe, so gallant, so respectful of beauty—the following sad lines:

The frightfully long money-pouches—'like the Cucumber called the Gigantic'—which have come in vogue among our belles—are *not* of Parisian origin, as many suppose, but are strictly indigenous here. The fact is, such a fashion would be quite out of place in Paris, where it is money *only* that women keep in a purse. The purse of an American lady, however, must be large enough to carry both her money and the soul of its owner.[2]

[2] From "Fifty Suggestions." (Ed.)

As for religion, I admit shamelessly that I prefer by a great deal the cult of the Celtic god Teutatès to that of Mammon; and the priest who offers to the cruel extortioner of human sacrifices victims who die *honorably*, victims who *want* to die, seems to me a being quite gentle and human in comparison to the man of finance who sacrifices whole populations for no interest but his own. At long intervals these things are still vaguely perceived, and I found once in an article of M. Barbey d'Aurevilly a philosophic exclamation of distress that sums up all that I should like to say on the subject: "Civilized peoples, you who are forever throwing stones at the uncivilized, soon you will not even deserve to be worshipers of idols!"

Such an environment—as I have already said, but cannot resist repeating—is hardly made for poets. What even the most democratic French mind understands by a State would never occur to an American. For any intelligent citizen of the old world, a political State has a center of activity that is its brain and the sun at the center of its system; it has ancient and glorious memories, poetic and military annals that go far back, an aristocracy, to which poverty, the daughter of revolutions, can only add a paradoxical splendor; but *this!* this mob of buyers and sellers, this nameless thing, this headless monster, this phenomenon deported beyond the Ocean, this State!—if a vast tavern, where the drinkers crowd in and discuss business over dirty tables, amidst the noisy babble of vulgar conversation, can be compared to a *salon,* to what we used formerly to call a salon, a republic of the mind presided over by beauty, I wish it well!

The role of man of letters will aways be hard to carry out, at once nobly and profitably, without being exposed to defamation, to the slander of the incompetent, to the envy of the rich—that envy which is their punishment!—to vengeful actions of bourgeois mediocrity. But what is difficult enough in a limited monarchy or in a well-ordered republic becomes all but impracticable in a sort of Bedlam where every police officer for public opinion enforces the law for the profit of his personal vices—or of his personal virtues, for it is all the same;—where a poet or a novelist of a region that has slaves is a detestable writer in the eyes of a critic who happens to be an abolitionist; where one cannot tell which is the greater scandal—the indecency of the cynicism

or the imperturbable religious hypocrisy. Burning chained Negroes, guilty of having felt their dark cheeks tingle from blushing
for their honor's sake; firing off a revolver in a theatre; establishing polygamy in the paradise of the West, which the savages
(the term seems unjust) had not yet soiled with such shameful
utopias; advertizing on walls, doubtless to consecrate the principle of limitless liberty, *a cure for nine-month illnesses*—these are
some of the salient features, some of the moral examples of the
noble country of Franklin, the inventor of sales-counter ethics, the
hero of a century devoted to material things. It is of value to call
attention unceasingly to these marvelous examples of brutality,
at a time when Americanomania has become almost a fashionable
passion, to such a point that an archbishop has been able to
promise us with a straight face that Providence would soon sum-
mon us to the enjoyment of this transatlantic ideal.

III

   Such a social environment of necessity engenders corresponding errors in matters of literature. It was against these errors that
Poe reacted as often as he could, and with all his strength. We
must not be astonished, therefore, that American writers, while
recognizing Poe's unusual power as a poet and as a storyteller,
always wanted to undermine his reputation as a critic. In a
country where the idea of utility, the idea most hostile in the
world to the idea of beauty, is pre-eminent and rises above everything else, the perfect critic will be the one who is the most
honorable, that is the one whose tendencies and desires come
closest to the tendencies and desires of his public—the one who,
mixing together all the talents and kinds of literary production,
will assign to them all a single aim—the one who will seek in a
book of poetry ways to improve the conscience of mankind.
Naturally, he will become proportionately less concerned about
the beauty of poetry and proportionately less shocked at imperfections and even downright faults in the writer's performance.
Edgar Poe, on the contrary, dividing the world of the mind into
pure intellect, taste, and *moral sense,*[3] applied his criticism ac-

   [3] In *The Poetic Principle.* (Ed.)

cording to whether the object of his analysis belonged to one or another of these three divisions. He was before everything else sensitive to the perfection of the over-all plan and to the precision of its execution; dismantling works of literature as if they were defective mechanisms (so far as the aims they sought to attain were concerned), noting carefully the faults of construction; and, when he passed to the detail of the work, to its plastic expression, in a word to its style, examining minutely, and without exception, the faults in prosody, the errors in grammar and all that mass of waste material that scatters its impurities over the best intentions and deforms the noblest conceptions when writers are incapable in their art.

For Poe, imagination is the queen of the faculties; but he means by imagination something greater than what the word signifies for ordinary readers. Imagination is not fantasy; nor is it sensibility, though it is hard to conceive of a man of imagination who would not be sensitive. The imagination is a faculty that is almost divine and that perceives from the very first moment, by ways other than those of the philosopher, the intimate and secret relations between things, their correspondences and analogies. The honors and functions that Poe confers upon the imagination give it so great a value (at least when one has well understood the author's meaning) that a learned man without imagination appears as no more than a pseudo-scholar, or at least as an incomplete one.

Among the literary domains in which imagination can obtain the most curious results and win, not the richest and most precious rewards (for those belong to poetry), but those that are most numerous and most varied, there is one for which Poe had a special preference—the Short Story. This form has the immense advantage over the lengthy novel that its brevity adds to the intensity of its effect. The reading of a Short Story, which can be accomplished at a single sitting, leaves a much more powerful memory in the mind than a reading that is broken up into parts and often interrupted by the turmoil of business and concern for worldly affairs. The unity of impression, the *totality* of effect, is an immense advantage that can give to this kind of composition a superiority all its own, to such an extent that a short story which is too short (though this is clearly a fault) is still better than one which is too long. The artist, if he has any skill, will not adopt his thoughts to the incidents; but, having deliberately conceived at his leisure an effect to be produced, he will invent the incidents and combine the events most suitable to lead to the desired effect. If the first sentence is not written with the object of preparing for this final impression, the work is a failure from the very beginning. There must not slip into the whole composition a single word that was not intended and that does not tend, directly or indirectly, to complete the premeditated design.

There is one particular through which the short story is superior even to the poem. Rhythm is necessary to developing the ideal beauty, which is the greatest and most noble aim of the poem. Now, the artifice of rhythm is an insurmountable obstacle to the minute development of thoughts and expressions which has truth for its object. For truth can often be the goal of the short story, and logical reasoning can be the best tool for construction of a perfect narrative in this form. That is why the short story, which does not have so lofty an elevation as pure poetry, can furnish products more varied and more easily appreciated by ordinary readers. Moreover, the author of a short story has at his disposal a multitude of tones and shades of language—the argumentative tone, the tone of sarcasm, the humorous tone—which poetry rejects, and which are like discords, insulting to the idea of pure beauty. And this is also what causes the author who pursues a simple goal of beauty in a short story to work at a great disadvantage, since he is deprived of rhythm, his most useful instrument. I know that, in all literatures, efforts have been made, and often successfully, to create tales that are purely poetic; Edgar Poe has himself written some very fine ones of this kind. But such efforts and struggles serve only to show the power of the right media adapted to corresponding goals, and I tend to believe that, with some authors, including the greatest that one could select, these heroic efforts arose from despair.

IV

That poets (using the word comprehensively, as including artists in general) are a *genus irritabile,* is well understood; but the *why* seems not to be commonly seen. An artist *is* an artist only by dint of his

exquisite sense of Beauty—a sense affording him rapturous enjoyment, but at the same time implying, or involving, an equally exquisite sense of Deformity or disproportion. Thus a wrong—an injustice—done a poet who is really a poet, excites him to degree which,
to ordinary apprehension, appears disproportionate with the wrong.
Poets *see* injustice—*never* where it does not exist—but very often
where the unpoetical see no injustice whatever. Thus the poetical
irritability has no reference to 'temper' in the vulgar sense, but merely
to a more than usual clear-sightedness in respect to wrong:—this
clear-sightedness being nothing more than a corollary from the vivid
perception of right—of justice—of proportion—in a word, of *tò kalón*.
But one thing is clear—that the man who is *not* 'irritable' (to the ordinary apprehension), is *no poet*.[4]

There speaks the poet himself, and thus he prepares an excellent and irrefutable apologia for all those of his race. Poe
carried this sensitiveness into literary affairs, and the extreme
importance that he attached to poetic matters often led him to
adopt a tone of superiority that offended weaklings. I believe I
have already remarked that many of the prejudices he had to
combat, false ideas, popular judgments that circulated about
him, have for a long time now infected the French press. It will
not be useless, therefore, to give a brief account of some of his
more important opinions on the composition of poetry. The
parallel errors in America and in France will make the application of Poe's theories very easy indeed.

But, first of all, I must say that, having made allowance for the
natural poet, for innate gifts, Poe provided for knowledge, work,
and analysis in a way that seemed exorbitant to arrogant men
who had no knowledge. Not only did he expend a great deal of
effort to bring under the control of his will the fugitive demon of
his happy moments, in order to recall at his pleasure those exquisite sensations, spiritual desires, and conditions of poetic
health that are so rare and so precious that one could truly
consider them as acts of grace outside of man and as visitations
from another world; but he also submitted inspiration to a
method and to the most severe analysis. The choice of a medium!
He returns to this unceasingly and insists with learned eloquence
upon suiting the medium to the desired effect, upon the use of

---

[4] From "Fifty Suggestions." (Ed.)

rhyme, upon perfecting the refrain, and upon adapting the rhythm to the sense of the poem. He declared that no one who cannot grasp the intangible is a poet; that he alone is a poet who is master of his memory, a sovereign ruler over words, and who keeps the registry of his own feelings always ready for perusal. Everything for the dénouement! he says over and over again. Even a sonnet needs a plan; and construction, the armature, so to speak, is the most important guarantee of the mysterious life of works of the mind.

I turn naturally to the article called *The Poetic Principle,* and I find there, at the very beginning, a vigorous protest against what one could call, so far as poetry is concerned, the heresy of length or dimension—the absurd value attributed to long poems. "A long poem does not exist; the phrase 'a long poem' is simply a flat contradiction in terms." In fact, a poem deserves its title only in so far as it excites and elevates the soul, and the positive value of a poem is by reason of this excitement and this elevation of the soul. But, by a pyschological necessity, all excitations are fugitive and transitory. This strange condition, into which the reader's soul has been, so to speak, *drawn* by force, will surely not last throughout the reading of a poem that exceeds the limits of the human capacity for enthusiasm.

This is clearly a condemnation of the epic poem. For a work of epic length cannot be considered poetic except in so far as one sacrifices unity, which is the vital condition of every work of art; and I do not mean unity of conception, but unity of impression, of *totality* of effect, as I once stated in comparing the novel with the short story. The epic poem, then, appears self-contradictory to us, so far as aesthetics is concerned. It is possible that former ages produced series of lyric poems that were later bound together by compilers into epics; but every *epic intention* clearly results from an imperfect sense of art. The time of these artistic anomalies is past, and it is even very doubtful that a long poem has ever been truly popular in the complete sense of the word.

We must add that too short a poem, one that fails to supply sufficient *pabulum* for the excitement that is aroused, and that fails to satisfy the reader's natural appetite, is also very inadequate. However brilliant and vivid its effect may be, it will not last; one's memory loses it; it is like a seal that has been pressed down too lightly and too quickly without having time enough to impress its image upon the wax.

But there is another heresy which, thanks to hypocrisy and the dullness and vulgarity of human minds, is much more to be feared and has chances of much longer survival—an error that has a tougher vitality—the heresy of the *didactic*, which includes as inevitable corollaries the heresies of *passion, truth,* and *ethics.* Many people imagine that the aim of poetry is to teach something or other, that it must either strengthen one's conscience, or perfect his behavior, or finally *demonstrate* something useful of any kind whatever. Edgar Poe insists that Americans have been special champions of this heterodox idea; but, unhappily, one does not have to go to Boston to meet this particular heresy. It besets us here at home, and every day batters in upon true poetry. However little one may wish to descend within his consciousness, to question his soul, to recall his memories of exaltation, poetry still has no goal but itself; it can have no other aim, and no poem will be so great, so noble, so truly worthy of being called a poem as the one that its author writes merely for the pleasure of writing it.

Please understand—I do not mean that poetry does not lend nobility to human behavior, or that it does not finally result in elevating man above the level of ordinary concerns; to say that would clearly be absurd. But I do say that if the poet has tried to teach a moral lesson, he has diminished his power as a poet; and it is not imprudent to wager that his work will be bad. Under penalty of collapse or death, poetry cannot be adapted to *science* or to *morality;* it does not have Truth for its object, it has only itself. The modes of demonstrating truth are different and are not found in the realm of art. Truth has nothing to do with song. Everything that makes a poet's song charming, graceful, irresistible, would deprive truth of its authority and its power. Cold, calm, impassive, the mind concerned with the demonstration of truth rebuffs the diamonds and flowers of the Muse; its disposition, then, is the absolute opposite of the poet's.

Pure Intellect has truth as its goal, taste shows us beauty, and the moral sense teaches us the nature of our obligations. It is true that an intermediate sense has intimate connections with the two extremes, and it is separated by so slight a distinction from

the moral sense that Aristotle had no qualms about including
some of its delicate operations with the virtues. Thus, what especially exasperates the man of taste at the sight of vice is its deformity, its lack of proportion. Vice impairs what is just and what
is true, and is revolting to the intellect and the conscience; but,
as a violation of harmony, as a dissonance, it will cause particular distress to certain poetic intelligences; and I see no cause
for scandal in considering every infraction of superior morality a
kind of violation of the rhythm and poetics of the universe.

It is this marvelous and immortal instinct for the beautiful that
makes us look upon the earth and what we see of it as a glimpse
of something to come, a correspondence linking us to another
world. Our insatiable thirst for everything that this life reveals
of the beyond is the most enduring proof of our immortality. It
is at once by and *through* poetry, by and *through* music, that the
soul catches a glimpse of the splendors beyond the grave; and
when an exquisite poem brings tears to one's eyes, these tears are
not proof of excessive joy but rather indication of an aroused
melancholy, a postulation of nerves, a nature exiled in imperfec-
tion and desirous of possessing at once, upon this earth, the
paradise that it has seen revealed.

Thus, the poetic principle is strictly and simply human aspiration towards a superior beauty, and the manifestation of this
principle is seen in an enthusiasm, an excitement of the soul—
an enthusiasm that is entirely independent of passion, which is
the heart's intoxication, and of truth, which serves as the food of
reason. For passion is *natural,* too natural not to introduce an
offensive, discordant tone into the domain of pure beauty, too
intimate and too violent not to offend the pure desires, gracious
melancholies, and noble despairs that dwell in the supernatural
regions of poetry.

This extraordinary elevation, this exquisite delicacy, this accent of immortality that Edgar Poe demands of the Muse, far
from making him less concerned with the details of execution, impelled him to endless improvement of his technical skill. Many
people, especially those who have read the strange poem called
The Raven, would be shocked if I reviewed the article in which
our poet, with apparent candor but with a subtle impertinence for
which I cannot blame him, explained in minute detail the method

he employed in writing his poem, the adaptation of the rhythm, the choice of a refrain—the shortest one he could find and the one with the most varied applications, and at the same time the one most representative of melancholy and despair, ornamented with the most sonorous of all rhymes (*nevermore*)— the choice of a bird that could imitate the human voice, but a raven—a bird famous in popular imagination for its baneful and fatal character—the choice of the most poetic of all tones, that of melancholy—and of the most poetic of all sentiments, love for a dead woman, etc.[5] "And," said Poe, "I shall not place the hero of my poem in poor surroundings, because poverty is commonplace and contrary to the idea of Beauty. . . ." The reader will discover in several of Poe's short stories curious symptoms of this immoderate taste for beautiful forms, especially for beautiful forms that are unusual, for ornate surroundings and oriental luxury.

I have said that this article seemed to me to show the marks of a subtle impertinence. Those who champion inspiration at all costs would not fail to find blasphemy and profanation in these ideas; but I believe that the article was written especially in their behalf. As insistently as certain writers affect a careless attitude, aiming with their eyes closed at the creation of a masterpiece, full of confidence in their lack of order, and expecting the letters hurled toward the ceiling to fall back on the floor in the shape of a poem, just so insistently Edgar Poe—one of the best inspired men of whom I know—made a point of concealing his spontaneity and of pretending to be completely unmoved and deliberate in his art. "I believe," he said, with an amusing pride that I do not find in bad taste, "that I can boast that no one point in [*The Raven's*] composition is referable either to accident or intuition; that the work proceeded, step by step, to its completion with the precision and rigid consequence of a mathematical problem." And I may say that it is only the fanciers of chance, those who consider inspiration a matter of fate, and the enthusiasts for blank verse, who could find anything strange in these *minutiae*. So far as art is concerned, no details are petty.

On the subject of blank verse, I shall add that Poe attached an

[5] Here and below the reference is to Poe's *Philosophy of Composition*. (Ed.)

extreme importance to rhyme, and that, to his analysis of the mathematical and musical pleasure which the mind draws from rhyme, he brought as much care and subtlety as he brought to all other subjects relating to the poet's craft. Just as he had demonstrated that the refrain can have infinitely varied applications, he sought also to renew, to increase the pleasure of rhyme by adding to it the unexpected element of *strangeness*, which is, as it were, the indispensable seasoning for all beauty. He often employed attractive repetitions of the same verse or of several verses, insistent repetitions of phrases simulating the obsessions of melancholy or of a fixed idea—he used the refrain pure and simple, but brought it into position in several different ways—he employed the variant refrain that gives an impression of indolence and distraction—he employed double and triple rhyme-schemes and also a kind of rhyme that introduces into modern poetry the surprises of leonine verse, but with greater precision and purpose.

It is clear that the worth of all these means can be verified only when they are set to work; and the dream of translating poems made as deliberately and with as much concentration as Poe's may be flattering, but must remain a dream. Poe wrote few poems; he sometimes expressed his regret at not being able to devote himself, not just more often but exclusively, to poetry, which he considered the noblest of all forms of writing. But his poetry has always a powerful effect. It is not the ardent effusion of Byron, or the soft, harmonious, distinguished melancholy of Tennyson, although, let us note in passing, Poe admired the latter almost like a brother. It is something deep and shining like a dream, something mysterious and perfect like crystal. I assume there is no need for me to add that American critics have often belittled Poe's poetry; very recently I found in a dictionary of American biographies an article in which it was accused of strangeness, in which the writer expressed fear that this muse in such sophisticated dress might form a literary school in the glorious fatherland of utilitarian morality, and where, finally, regret was expressed that Poe had not applied his talents to stating moral truths instead of wasting them in search of a perverse ideal and of pouring out in his verses a mysterious, but sensual voluptuousness.

We are familiar with this kind of literary fencing. The reproaches made by bad critics to good poets are everywhere the same. As I was reading this article I seemed to be reading a translation of one of those numerous indictments drawn up by Parisian critics against those of our poets who are most in love with perfection. It is easy to guess which writers are preferred among us, and every mind that is attracted to pure poetry will understand me when I say that, amidst our antipoetic race, Victor Hugo would be less admired if he were a perfect poet, and that he has been able to win forgiveness for all his lyric genius only through introducing into his poetry, by force and brutality, what Edgar Poe considered the chief modern heresy—*the heresy of the didactic.*

Paul Verlaine

[1844–1896]

and

Stephané Mallarmé

[1842–1898]

ঙৡৢ৯

THE FRENCH SYMBOLIST TRADITION reached maturity in the work of Rimbaud, Verlaine, and Mallarmé. Rimbaud was first and last a poet, but Verlaine and Mallarmé both contributed to symbolist critical theory. Generally, they emphasize different aspects of symbolism. Verlaine stressed what might be called the mystique of symbolism. Poetry is the evocation of ineffable moods and atmospheres. At its best it is nondiscursive, like a musical composition. Its language should suggest rather than delineate and should be emotive rather than logical. Verlaine realized these aims brilliantly in his own poetry, but adopted by second-rate followers like Maeterlinck they too often became an excuse for diffuse, vaguely "poetic" writing.

Mallarmé is the more important theorist. He too believed that poetry should be indirect, suggestive, and musical. But he insisted that poetic effects are the result of rigorous craftsmanship. Following the lead of his "great master, Edgar Poe," he taught that poetic techniques are as precise as those of mathematics. All parts of the poem should be the result of conscious calculation. Every term should be simultaneously an image, a thought, a feeling, and a symbol. The successful poem will convey the pure essence of its subject.

Mallarmé's published criticism is important, but his influence on his contemporaries was largely the result of his "Tuesday receptions," which were attended by the most promising young French and English poets of the day. Later symbolists include Verhaeren, Laforgue, and, more recently, Paul Valéry. The work of Yeats, Rilke, Eliot, and the surrealists illustrates the continuing vitality of the symbolist tradition.

In addition to the works cited for Baudelaire see: B. Cook, tr. and intr., *Mallarmé: Selected Prose Poems, Essays, and Letters* (Baltimore, 1956); W. Fowlie, *Mallarmé* (Chicago, 1953); G. Michaud, *Message*

Poétique du Symbolisme (Paris, 1947); E. Wilson, *Axel's Castle* (New York, 1931).

The present translation of Verlaine's *Art Poétique* has been made by Professor Alfred Engstrom of the University of North Carolina. The translation of Mallarmé's *Music and Literature* is from *Mallarmé: Selected Prose Poems, Essays, and Letters,* trans. by Bradford Cook (Baltimore: The Johns Hopkins Press, 1956), pp. 43–56. Used by permission of the publisher.

I

Art Poétique

Music before everything,
And for music use the uneven number of syllables,
Vaguer than other rhythms, more soluble in the air,
And with nothing in it that weighs down or alights.

Moreover, you must not go
Choosing your words without some scorn:
Nothing is dearer than the gray song
Where the Imprecise and the Precise are joined.

It is like fair eyes behind veils,
Or the great trembling light of noon,
Or, in a warm autumn sky,
The blue confusion of clear stars.

For we still want Nuance,
Not Color, only Nuance!
Oh! Nuance alone links
The dream to the dream and the flute to the horn!

Flee far away from murderous Jest,
Cruel Wit and the impure Laugh
That make the eyes of the Azure weep
—And all such low-kitchen garlic.

Take eloquence and wring its neck!
You will do well, while you are about it,

To tame rhyme a little:
Without some control, where won't it go?

O, who will tell the wrongs done to Rhyme!
What heedless child or what wild, black savage
Has forged for us this penny gem
That sounds hollow and false under the file?

Music again and always!
And let your verse be the thing in flight
That one senses fleeing from a soul as it goes
Towards other skies to other loves.

Let your verse be the lucky find
Scattered on the crisp wind of morning
That goes stirring the scent of mint and thyme . . .
And all the rest is literature.

II

MUSIC AND LITERATURE

LADIES AND GENTLEMEN: [1]

For a long time now, two nations alone—England and France
—have shown a common faith in the possibility of Literature.
Each has extended or withdrawn the torch, and thus the mutual
influence has been brightened. But my main topic and objective
this evening is not so much this interchange (although it is partly
on that account that I am with you now and speaking to you in
my native tongue) as, first of all, the very particular desire for
continuity of masterpieces. In no sense can genius fail to be exceptional. Like the jutting corner of a façade, it reaches unexpected heights; yet it does not create vast wild spaces (here,
again, it is exceptional), nor does it know abandon, but rather
maintains a sort of grouping, an admirable assemblage of lesser,
miniature shrines, colonnades, fountains—keeps them as spiritual
sites and so produces in perspective a special and continuous

[1] This essay was first delivered as a public lecture on March 1, 1894,
at Oxford. (Ed.)

palace whose doors are thrown open to the princely instincts in each of us. Thus national taste is born and, in the case of France and England, we linger in our pleasure over the choice between these rival architectures both similar and sublime.

I have been invited on your behalf to speak in some detail of our present literary situation. The time is especially appropriate. For I bring news—the most amazing and unprecedented news. We have been experimenting with verse.

Governments change; prosody remains ever intact; perhaps because during revolutions it goes unnoticed or because attack is not called for upon a dogma considered incapable of change.

There should be no delay in discussing this subject (think of the breathless guest, fresh from his travels, who has been witness to an extraordinary event; he will have no peace until he has poured forth his story). For verse is everything, from the moment we take pen in hand. As long as there is cadence, there will be style and versification. That is why the careful prose of discriminating writers—ornamental prose—can always be thought of as broken verse; it plays with its own tones and hidden rhymes, like a thyrsus of infinite complexity. Such is the flowering of what we have come to call the *prose-poem.*

Meanwhile, the ancient and regular verse stands by with its very strict, numerical, and simple nature.

There can be no doubt that we have now reached the point of separation between the two.

At the beginning of this century, the keen and powerful poetic instinct of the Romantics combined these elements and created flowing alexandrines with regular pauses and run-on lines. Now, however, the combination is breaking up into two separate wholes. Our recent search has apparently been brought to a close by the fortunate discovery of *free verse,* which I like to call an individual modulation; for every soul is a knot of rhythm.

The inevitable result was disagreement. Naturally, certain of the pioneering spirits ventured far afield and thought they had done with what we must call "official" verse. They had not, however; for it will be used on special occasions; their attempt at divorce was overbold, but it was the only one and it will be tempered.

Those who looked askance at the whole affair probably think it was a waste of time.

On the contrary.

For authentic works of art were born, quite apart from the fight over form; and even if their value goes unrecognized, let us prize the special silence which will take their place and thus provide much-needed rest for the ancient instrument of our music. On special occasions verse will always thunder. Yet it should be exceptional, despite the fact that all measured writing, as we have just observed, *is* verse by definition. Similarly, Literature should continue to be the rarest of phenomena, despite our common desire to perpetuate it throughout the ages. French verse in particular is a delicate instrument and should be used sparingly. But now, after the recent interval of silence and hesitation, eternal verse may once again rise up with all its perfect tonalities and flow renewed—rise, accompanied by its newest elements, to the sublime.

Here, then, was a purifying storm; and it is entirely to the credit of the recent generation that, in the midst of all confusion, the act of writing was studied through to its very origin. The greatest progress was made in their answer to a question which I should ask quite simply in the following way: is there a reason for writing at all? It is not *description* which can unveil the efficacy and beauty of monuments, seas, or the human face in all their maturity and native state, but rather *evocation, allusion, suggestion.* These somewhat arbitrary terms reveal what may well be a very decisive tendency in modern literature, a tendency which limits literature and yet sets it free. For what is the magic charm of art, if not this: that, beyond the confines of a fistful of dust or of all other reality, beyond the book itself, beyond the very text, it delivers up that volatile scattering which we call the Spirit, Who cares for nothing save universal musicality.

So now you are up to date on the most recent poetic "fever," its sudden jumps and noble hesitations.

But we cannot let it go at that; for surely I have come here to speak to you of something far greater than the mere renewal of rites and rhymes—something which I scarcely grasp myself; indeed, we may finally *fail* to grasp it; but let us hope at least to touch upon it. You bid me in your kindness to discuss my favorite

theme; and fully realizing, as I do, your expectations, I am re-
visited by that vague desire of bygone days (which, in my solitude, I could never fulfill) to devote some special evening to an
all-embracing discovery (from the heavens to the abyss) of that
struggle with the Ideal which certain of my contemporaries are
now waging—as others struggle with social problems, for example. And so, without further ado, let me ask a question which
may seem startling to an audience long since devoted to literary
elegance: does Literature exist? Exist in some form other than
that convention of classical periods which was the art of etching
and refining ideas in all fields? It is axiomatic that in order to perfect the building or the discovery, an architect, a jurist, or a
doctor must finally raise them to the level of discourse. In short,
everything which emanates from the human mind must be re-
integrated. The subject is generally immaterial.

Very few people have faced up to this problem which looms
large only late in life. I too have been tardy, and now I suddenly
hesitate, when I should rather wish to speak with full confidence
upon the subject. Perhaps this sort of inquiry has been compla-
cently avoided because it was considered dangerous by gifted
men who hastened to fulfill their promise—who feared its efficacy
might be lost if they questioned it too deeply. All purposes endure: we force them into life through faith or facile self-persua-
sion; and so, for *us,* they do live. (Consider the shepherd, whose
voice is echoed mockingly by neighboring rocks; yet, in his ear,
never echoed so.) Be that as it may, I still find contentment and
wisdom in shedding even a fading light on the basic reasons for
this vocation.

So, now, to come back to that startling question I asked a few
moments ago (when I boldly expressed my doubts about the
legitimate function of literature—whereas I should perhaps have
been content to wreathe its altar)—to come back to that sort of
indefinable attack I made (bereft though I am of the power to
make it), I would reply with conscious exaggeration (and now
you are forewarned): Yes, Literature *does* exist and, I may add,
exists alone and all-exclusively. Such, at least, is the best name
we can give to the achievement I speak of.

At any moment in history, a man may appear who will be fully
forgetful—and always remember that he will be *consciously* for-

getful—of the intellectual impedimenta of his contemporaries. Using the most elemental and elementary of means, he will try to discover (for example) the symphonic equation of the seasons of the year, the habits of a sunbeam or a cloud. He will make one or two observations analogous to the undulant heat or other inclemencies of the changing climate, which are the multiple sources of our passions. But in order to do so, he must re-create verse, carefully eliminate its excess matter, and show perfect reverence for the twenty-four letters of the alphabet. These he shall transform, through the miracle of infinity, into some special language of his own. Then, with some gesture, some ray of light, he shall give meaning to their symmetry. And so, at last, he will achieve that transfiguration and reach that supernatural height which are Poetry. This truly polished initiate of paradise will then possess—beyond all other wealth—the means to happiness: a principle for knowledge. And he will have a native land. Through his initiative, or through their own virtual power, these divine characters will become a work of art.

They are our heritage from the ancient books of magic, from our age-old wealth of mind; they provide us with a method of notation which spontaneously becomes Literature. A method— no! They are our *principle!* The turn of some special phrase or the meshes of a couplet are patterned on our understanding of them, and thus insights and relationships are born in us.

Except for study-sheets, rubrics, parchment, and such, I consider reading to be a hopeless occupation. So it is that all attempts at the manufacture of happiness have failed for lack of proper means. I know of cases in which even the most secret and careful of such means cannot, must not, satisfy us.

Something else! yes, it is as if the chance trembling of a page sought only hesitation and fluttered with impatience at the possibility of—something else. We know, of course, that we are subject to the absolute law which states that only what exists exists. Yet it would be obviously inconsistent to choose such an empty pretext as the basis for refusing all delusion, for we would then be refusing the very pleasure that we seek. The *beyond* is our means to that pleasure; I might almost say the "instrument" of our pleasure were it not repugnant to me to disassemble fiction in public (for it would be blasphemous to analyze the "mechanics" of literature and thus discover its chief cog—which is, in any case, nothingness). Yes, for me the miracle occurs when, in a dream of fiction, we seize the ideal which is absent here below, yet explosively present up above, and hurl it to some forbidden, thunderbolt height of heaven.

Why should we do this?

It is a game.

For just as we have the right to elicit emptiness from ourselves (hampered as we may be by reality too solidly, too preponderantly enthroned in us), so do we act that a sublime attraction may lovingly deliver us from that reality—and yet be filled with it and shed glittering lights upon it through empty space and in willful, solitary celebrations.

As for myself, I ask no less of literature. And now I am going to prove my point.

Nature exists; She will not be changed, although we may add cities, railroads, or other inventions to our material world.

Therefore, our eternal and only problem is to seize relationships and intervals, however few or multiple. Thus, faithful to some special vision deep within, we may extend or simplify the world at will.

To create is to conceive an object in its fleeting moment, in its absence.

To do this, we simply compare its facets and dwell lightly, negligently upon their multiplicity. We conjure up a scene of lovely, evanescent, intersecting forms. We recognize the entire and binding arabesque thus formed as it leaps dizzily in terror or plays disquieting chords; or, through a sudden digression (by no means disconcerting), we are warned of its likeness unto itself even as it hides. Then when the melodic line has given way to silence, we seem to hear such themes as are the very logic and substance of our soul. Yet whatever the agony may be in which the Monster writhes (as, through Her golden wounds, She pours the proof that She is always entire, always Herself), no vanquished throe may bend or cross the omnipresent Line which runs infinitely from point to point in Its creation of idea—creation perhaps unseen by man, mysterious, like some Harmony of perfect purity.

I am convinced that the constant grasp and realization of this ideal constitutes our obligation to Him Who once unleashed Infinity—Whose rhythm (as our fingers longingly seek it out among the keys of our verbal instrument) can be rendered by the fitting words of our daily tongue.

For in truth, what is Literature if not our mind's ambition (in the form of language) to define things; to prove to the satisfaction of our soul that a natural phenomenon corresponds to our imaginative understanding of it. And our hope, of course, is that we may ourselves be reflected in it.

I know that Music—at least in the usual sense of the word: that is, concert performances with strings, brass, wood winds, and occasionally libretti—has a similar though unexpressed ambition (She is never very confiding). And when, a moment ago, I was sketching those winding and mobile variations of the Idea which are the prerogative of the written word, some of you may have been reminded of certain orchestral phrasings in which we hear, first, a withdrawal to the shades, swirls and uneasy hesitation, and then suddenly the bursting, leaping, multiple ecstasy of Brilliance, like the approaching radiance of a sunrise. Yet this will all be useless until language, retempered and purified by the flight of song, has given it meaning.

So now we are reaching the end of our search. There can be— or rather there *must* be—an exchange following this triumphant contribution of Music: the written word must rise and Music must receive it for a brief plaintive space, else the efficacies of life will be blind to their own brilliance, hidden, and without release. I am asking for a total restoration, in perfect and neutral silence, whereby the mind may seek its own native land again: let us have quakes and slippings, unlimited and unerring trajectories, rich revery in sudden flight, delightful unfulfillment, some special lunge or synthesis. But let there be no sonorous tumult which could be resorbed in dreams.

The greatest and most magical writers have always realized this ambition.

These, then, will be the precise and reciprocal elements of Mystery in our possession (we can forget the old distinction between Music and Literature—the one purposely separated from the other in preparation for their ultimate meeting): Music will release the powers lying within that abstract center of hearing, and even of vision, which is Comprehension; while Comprehension, in all its spaciousness, will lend equal power to the printed page.

I suggest, at my own esthetic risk, the following conclusion (and if I were fortunate enough to win your silent approval of it, I should feel fully honored this evening): namely, that Music and Literature constitute the moving facet—now looming toward obscurity, now glittering unconquerably—of that single, true phenomenon which I have called Idea.

The one bends toward the other, submerges, then returns to the surface with its treasure; another dive, another fluctuation, and the entire cycle is created to perfection. For humanity in general, this will be done theatrically: they will sit unconsciously and hear a performance of their own greatness. The individual, on the other hand, will be enlightened by the book, his teacher and constant companion.

Now I can breathe more easily. I was not sure at the outset whether my subject would seem authentic or naturally acceptable, and I felt especially guilty about presenting it to you for the first time. But now that you have accepted my basic premise at least (as was obvious from your close and understanding attention to these hurrying, fateful, and seemingly impersonal thoughts which are new to me, but which may endure if there be general acquiescence), I have the sudden feeling that we are closer together; the clouds have dispersed. I should be delighted to chat with you informally, like friends whose only desire is to be together. Will you forgive me, then, if I linger over such a pleasure? My excuse must be the grave shadow that comes down from out of the nights of this city of yours (where only Thought is wakeful) and hovers in this room where revery seems so specially resonant. Now, I trust you will not feel that I have been "holding forth" in this little talk tonight, or simply adding to your regular courses by "teaching a lesson." Before I arrived, you may possibly have thought of me as a *chef d'école* (public opinion loses no time in applying that title to anyone who works alone and thus attracts a group of younger and more idealistic artists). Yet nothing could be further from the truth. But if you prefer to think of me as a recluse meditating in his favorite laboratory, like a mystagogue, or as an actor in reveries which still remain to be performed, then I would agree with you. But a sense of loyalty and even of duty must rouse us from these dreams; the more experienced must communicate their enthusiasms to the younger men. This custom is especially dear to me. For we have already agreed that there must be no interruption in the literary traditions of our countries—no disagreement between us. And since my own haunting desire is to graft those traditions to the prophetic dreams of our predecessors, I feel quite at home with you here this evening, standing before this group of famous men and gifted youths.

Now then, what better amusement can we find for the next few minutes than the comedy of errors and misunderstanding?

The worst misunderstanding, of course (but I know this isn't the case, and I merely indicate it now so as to have done with it), would be some unspoken disappointment on your part, ladies and patient listeners, because I have failed to murmur brilliant words of wisdom to a piano accompaniment or speak with authority of the books you read dreamily in your leisure hours. But then, whatever I said would be superfluous, since you all turn your writing talents to the fullest and most essential account. When I was on the train on my way here, I thought about the letters—unpublished masterpieces—which are the precious burden of postal bags and speeding locomotive. You are the chosen authors of that correspondence. And I reflect that when, with pen in hand, you turn to dreaming, eloquence, or charity, and magnetize some inward beauty in all its splendor, you need no black magic or science; you merely choose your white sheet of paper (gleaming like your smiles), you write, and there you are.

I should like to observe that the role of the poet is not entirely without its comic aspects.

In the public eye, he has become a pitiful prince banishing his own ghost from the sepulcher which should have buried him long since, and consigning it to legend and melodrama. And yet he is also the one we hold responsible for having confronted Society with an explosive and original idea.

Certain newspaper articles have been gossiping about my connection (oh, a very slight connection, really) with some scandal unleashed by a book which is apparently only the first installment of a general satire aimed at almost all the foremost minds of

our time. It is not entirely unamusing to note how often such
words as "idiot" and "madman" are used (and how seldom they
are softened to "cretin" or "lunatic") and hurled like so many
stones at a group of proud, obtrusive, feudal minds which are
apparently threatening all Europe. But of course I dare not make
fun of the good intentions of these scandal-mongers who are so
stirred up over symptoms which do not exist; after all, we can
never prevent people from making something out of nothing.
The trouble in this particular instance is that science has seen fit
to meddle with the problem—or else has been dragged into it.
Degeneration is the title of the book in question (*Entartung* in
the German); its author is M. Nordau. (I was determined to keep
my statements on a general level and to name nobody. I think
that I have just done so.) This popularizer has called our attention
to a "fact": Nature (he notes) does not produce spontaneous or
complete genius; instead, genius is in man generally and in no one
particularly; She would appear, in practice (and in some occult
and gratuitous fashion), to "compensate" for one exceptional
faculty bestowed on man by destroying another. Now I submit
that this is the kind of pseudo-righteous panacea and old wives'
tale that needs clear critical judgment and some measure of pity.
But to continue: this sickly genius (says Nordau) manages to
draw strength from his weakness and grows toward fulfillment of
his nature; in so doing, of course, he leaves enormous wreckage in
his wake, i.e., his fellow citizens, like so many hospital cases or
the "outs" on a voting list. Now M. Nordau's mistake is that he
treats everything as wreckage; so you can see that the subtleties
and arcana of physiology and destiny must not be entrusted to
clean-living foremen or honest metal fitters, whose hands are
somewhat too crude to treat them properly. A man like that goes
only half way, you see; and if he had only added a little insight
to his other faculties, he would have discovered this particular
phase of poor Mother Nature's sacred laws and therefore not
written his book at all.

A quite different brand of insult has appeared in the newspapers—in rather timid and mumbling fashion, which is strange.
For, after all, why shouldn't the slightest suspicion be shouted
through the streets? When the propaganda machines break down,
we get a brief glimpse of parliamentary procedure and, in the

process, the mob is rather pitifully confounded. I find the glimpse most interesting—but, unfortunately, it is only a glimpse, and the lesson thus taught so brief that the legislators can claim ignorance of the problem. In any case, I would challenge the addition of bullets and nails to the fray. These are only my own opinions, of course. Let me add that the idea of damning out-of-line writers who happen to be for—or against—blank verse is really quite ingenious. It little matters whether they stand in or above the battle in readiness for some special moment: in either case they are considered an insult to the newspaper columnist. Regardless of their treasure, they manage to heap disgrace (you would think they were dropping bombs) on the organization that does of course keep us posted (at great expense) on the capital's most recent apotheoses. Let's just be sure that that organization has neither first nor last say in the matter of those particular splendors which human language can find within itself. I wish we would stop insinuating and speak out loud and bold, saying that we approve the inviolability and seclusion of certain outstanding men. Whenever the masses are being herded indiscrimately toward self-interest, amusement, or convenience, it is essential that a very few disinterested persons should adopt an attitude of respectful indifference toward those common motivations and, by so doing, create a minority. And be it always understood that however broad and deep those differences may be which are created by the mad struggles of the citizenry, they must all ultimately agree that the reason for their internecine warfare is of prime importance. Now, since we can grant the need for such a minority—for this salt of the earth, this truest exception to the rule, these few chosen minds working and living here to absolute perfection—what name can best praise them? Are they laborers for love, strangers, laborers in vain? Or are they, more simply, men of letters?

I see that I have failed to brighten the rather sombre tones of our discussion; the dogmatic touch was still there, even though I tried to make fun of the man in the street with his wild attacks on anyone who is impractical enough to gather and preserve the riches of the spirit. Perhaps it was because of the disturbing atmosphere so inherent in my subject, or perhaps its

dark, persistent resonance. In any case, my firework seems to
have hung fire.

Which is probably just as well.

Seriously, I feel I can bring our discussion to a close now. And
while I have no sense of guilt about it, I am still amazed that we
had to examine poets in such an ambiguous light and subject
them to twin fires of unintelligence.

It will always be the pleasure and duty of the thoughtful critic
to see through the ups and downs of a changing present and
show the truly glorious artists in perspective. But in the meantime the disinterested poet, eschewing all virtuosity and bravado,
must project his vision of the world and use the languages of the
school, home, and market place which seem most fitting to that
purpose. Then poetry will be lifted to some frightening, waver-
ing, ecstatic pitch—like an orchestral wing spread wide in flight,
but with its talons still rooted deep within your earth. Wherever
you find it, you must deny the ineffable; for somehow it will
speak.

Thus if the common man, neighbor to us all, has the gift of
language on his lips and follows this very ordinary—or, rather,
extraordinary!—method; and if an unheard echo joins his song,
he will be able to communicate in the common vocabulary with
all pomp and light. For it is fitting that to each of us Truth be
revealed in Her native magnificence. And so, like a dutiful son
or taxpayer, he willingly contributes what he owes to the common treasure of the fatherland.

Because (I must insist upon this last point—it all stems from
that poetic Celebration we have been speaking about for the
past hour; and, rather than divide it into the elements of Music
and Literature, we can call it "Mystery" or perhaps "the evolu-
tive context of the Idea"—I must insist) *because* . . .

Throughout the centuries, *our earthly society has been seriously handicapped* because we have failed to consider brute
reality—city, government, laws—as a group of symbols. Or, to
put it another way, we have turned them into cemeteries and
thus destroyed the paradise they should be. We have made them
a terrace, hardly higher than the earth. But, despite all appearances, it is not on earth, nor in tolls and elections, that we can
find the lofty drama of the formalities which create a popular

cult; for these are rather the representatives of the great Law as It is miraculously instituted with all transparent purity.

Whenever you are in danger of losing this perspective, you must destroy all material substructures. Or, better still, stream fairy lights along them all—and see! Your thoughts must ask an image of your earth.

If, in days to come, a new religion rises up in France, it will be the heavenly instinct within each one of us, expanded to the dimensions of infinite joy. A relatively harmless and elementary example of this can be found on the political level; voting (even for oneself) will not be satisfying until it becomes that expansive, trumpeting hymn of joy in which no name is chosen; nor can revolutions quite provide the broil and tempest in which we must stream and sink if we would rise and be reborn as heroes.

I shall stop now, especially because I do not wish to go too far—for once, at least!—with this all-inclusive subject which is the art of letters; and also because, ineffectual as I am as a jester, Ladies and Gentlemen, I should prefer—I know that we are agreed in this—to avoid the folly that there would surely be in prophesying.

Henri Bergson

[1859–1941]

❧❧❧

BERGSON IS BEST KNOWN as a philosopher, the theorist of creative evolution, time, and the *élan vital*. However, much of his work has implications for literary criticism, and one of his essays, *Laughter* (1900), is an analysis of comedy which is still a fundamental work on the subject.

The aspects of Bergson's philosophy which apply to literature have been summarized by T. E. Hulme in two essays, "Bergson's Theory of Art" and "The Intensive Manifold," both published in *Speculations* (1924). Following Bergson, Hulme defines reality as "flux." Man comes to "know" reality in two ways. The first is analysis. It is useful, being the method of science, but it subordinates reality to its own purposes. The second way is by artistic intuition. In the "intensive manifold" of the art work (the term is Hulme's), reality is not distorted or manipulated. Consequently it is "known" in something like its pure state. The sections in *Laughter* which deal with art and reality and the contrast between tragedy and comedy illustrate the application of Bergson's ideas to literary criticism.

Bergson's most obvious influence has been on French critics. However he has also had an important following in England. In addition to discussing Bergson's theory, Hulme adapted it to the analysis of language in his *Notes on Language and Style* (pub. 1929). Through Hulme, Bergson contributed to the poetics of imagism.

Bergson's major works include *Creative Evolution,* trans. by A. Mitchell (London, 1911) and *Laughter,* trans. by Brereton and Rothwell (London, 1911). For comment see: T. E. Hulme, "Bergson's Theory of Art" and "The Intensive Manifold," both in *Speculations,* ed. H. Read (London, 1924); W. Sypher, "Introduction" and "Appendix" in *Comedy* (New York, 1956); A. Szathmary, *The Aesthetic Theory of Bergson* (Cambridge, 1937).

The present selections are from the book *Comedy* © 1956 by Wylie Sypher, which contained "Laughter" by Henri Bergson. Reprinted by permission of Doubleday & Company, Inc.

189

LAUGHTER

I. ART AND REALITY

WHAT IS the object of art? Could reality come into direct contact
with sense and consciousness, could we enter into immediate
communion with things and with ourselves, probably art would
be useless, or rather we should all be artists, for then our soul
would continually vibrate in perfect accord with nature. Our
eyes, aided by memory, would carve out in space and fix in time
the most inimitable of pictures. Hewn in the living marble of the
human form, fragments of statues, beautiful as the relics of antique statuary, would strike the passing glance. Deep in our souls
we should hear the strains of our inner life's unbroken melody,—
a music that is ofttimes gay, but more frequently plaintive and
always original. All this is around and within us, and yet no
whit of it do we distinctly perceive. Between nature and ourselves, nay, between ourselves and our own consciousness a veil
is interposed: a veil that is dense and opaque for the common
herd,—thin, almost transparent, for the artist and the poet. What
fairy wove that veil? Was it done in malice or in friendliness? We
had to live, and life demands that we grasp things in their relations to our own needs. Life is action. Life implies the acceptance only of the *utilitarian* side of things in order to respond to
them by appropriate reactions: all other impressions must be
dimmed or else reach us vague and blurred. I look and I think
I see, I listen and I think I hear, I examine myself and I think I
am reading the very depths of my heart. But what I see and hear
of the outer world is purely and simply a selection made by my
senses to serve as a light to my conduct; what I know of myself is
what comes to the surface, what participates in my actions. My
senses and my consciousness, therefore, give me no more than a
practical simplification of reality. In the vision they furnish me of
myself and of things, the differences that are useless to man are
obliterated, the resemblances that are useful to him are empha-
sised; ways are traced out for me in advance along which my
activity is to travel. These ways are the ways which all mankind
has trod before me. Things have been classified with a view to

the use I can derive from them. And it is this classification I perceive, far more clearly than the colour and the shape of things. Doubtless man is vastly superior to the lower animals in this respect. It is not very likely that the eye of a wolf makes any distinction between a kid and a lamb; both appear to the wolf as the same identical quarry, alike easy to pounce upon, alike good to devour. We, for our part, make a distinction between a goat and a sheep; but can we tell one goat from another, one sheep from another? The *individuality* of things or of beings escapes us, unless it is materially to our advantage to perceive it. Even when we do take note of it—as when we distinguish one man from another—it is not the individuality itself that the eye grasps, *i.e.* an entirely original harmony of forms and colours, but only one or two features that will make practical recognition easier.

In short, we do not see the actual things themselves; in most cases we confine ourselves to reading the labels affixed to them. This tendency, the result of need, has become even more pronounced under the influence of speech; for words—with the exception of proper nouns—all denote genera. The word, which only takes note of the most ordinary function and commonplace aspect of the thing, intervenes between it and ourselves, and would conceal its form from our eyes, were that form not already masked beneath the necessities that brought the word into existence. Not only external objects, but even our own mental states, are screened from us in their inmost, their personal aspect, in the original life they possess. When we feel love or hatred, when we are gay or sad, is it really the feeling itself that reaches our consciousness with those innumerable fleeting shades of meaning and deep resounding echoes that make it something altogether our own? We should all, were it so, be novelists or poets or musicians. Mostly, however, we perceive nothing but the outward display of our mental state. We catch only the impersonal aspect of our feelings, that aspect which speech has set down once for all because it is almost the same, in the same conditions, for all men. Thus, even in our own individual selves, individuality escapes our ken. We move amidst generalities and symbols, as within a tilt-yard in which our force is effectively pitted against other forces; and fascinated by action, tempted by it, for our own good, on to the field it has selected, we live in a zone midway be-

tween things and ourselves, externally to things, externally also
to ourselves. From time to time, however, in a fit of absent-
mindedness, nature raises up souls that are more detached from
life. Not with that intentional, logical, systematical detachment—
the result of reflection and philosophy—but rather with a natural
detachment, one innate in the structure of sense or consciousness,
which at once reveals itself by a virginal manner, so to speak, of
seeing, hearing, or thinking. Were this detachment complete, did
the soul no longer cleave to action by any of its perceptions, it
would be the soul of an artist such as the world has never yet
seen. It would excel alike in every art at the same time; or rather,
it would fuse them all into one. It would perceive all things in
their native purity: the forms, colours, sounds of the physical
world as well as the subtlest movements of the inner life. But this
is asking too much of nature. Even for such of us as she has made
artists, it is by accident, and on one side only, that she has lifted
the veil. In one direction only has she forgotten to rivet the perception to the need. And since each direction corresponds to
what we call a *sense*—through one of his senses, and through
that sense alone, is the artist usually wedded to art. Hence,
originally, the diversity of arts. Hence also the speciality of
predispositions. This one applies himself to colours and forms,
and since he loves colour for colour and form for form, since he
perceives them for their sake and not for his own, it is the inner
life of things that he sees appearing through their forms and
colours. Little by little he insinuates it into our own perception,
baffled though we may be at the outset. For a few moments at
least, he diverts us from the prejudices of form and colour that
come between ourselves and reality. And thus he realises the
loftiest ambition of art, which here consists in revealing to us
nature. Others, again, retire within themselves. Beneath the thousand rudimentary actions which are the outward and visible signs
of an emotion, behind the commonplace, conventional expression
that both reveals and conceals an individual mental state, it is
the emotion, the original mood, to which they attain in its un-
defiled essence. And then, to induce us to make the same effort
ourselves, they contrive to make us see something of what they
have seen: by rhythmical arrangement of words, which thus become organised and animated with a life of their own, they tell

us—or rather suggest—things that speech was not calculated to express. Others delve yet deeper still. Beneath these joys and sorrows which can, at a pinch, be translated into language, they grasp something that has nothing in common with language, certain rhythms of life and breath that are closer to man than his inmost feelings, being the living law—varying with each individual —of his enthusiasm and despair, his hopes and regets. By setting free and emphasising this music, they force it upon our attention; they compel us, willy-nilly, to fall in with it, like passers-by who join in a dance. And thus they impel us to set in motion, in the depths of our being, some secret chord which was only waiting to thrill. So art, whether it be painting or sculpture, poetry or music, has no other object than to brush aside the utilitarian symbols, the conventional and socially accepted generalities, in short, everything that veils reality from us, in order to bring us face to face with reality itself. It is from a misunderstanding on this point that the dispute between realism and idealism in art has risen. Art is certainly only a more direct vision of reality. But this purity of perception implies a break with utilitarian convention, an innate and specially localised disinterestedness of sense or consciousness, in short, a certain immateriality of life, which is what has always been called idealism. So that we might say, without in any way playing upon the meaning of the words, that realism is in the work when idealism is in the soul, and that it is only through ideality that we can resume contact with reality.

II. THE ESSENTIAL NATURE OF DRAMA

Dramatic art forms no exception to this law. What drama goes forth to discover and brings to light, is a deep-seated reality that is veiled from us, often in our own interests, by the necessities of life. What is this reality? What are these necessities? Poetry always expresses inward states. But amongst these states some arise mainly from contact with our fellow-men. They are the most intense as well as the most violent. As contrary electricities attract each other and accumulate between the two plates of the condenser from which the spark will presently flash, so, by simply bringing people together, strong attractions and repulsions take place followed by an utter loss of balance, in a word, by that electrification of the soul known as passion. Were man to give way to the impulse of his natural feelings, were there neither social nor moral law, these outbursts of violent feeling would be the ordinary rule in life. But utility demands that these outbursts should be foreseen and averted. Man must live in society, and consequently submit to rules. And what interest advises, reason commands: duty calls, and we have to obey the summons. Under this dual influence has perforce been formed an outward layer of feelings and ideas which make for permanence, aim at becoming common to all men, and cover, when they are not strong enough to extinguish it, the inner fire of individual passions. The slow progress of mankind in the direction of an increasingly peaceful social life has gradually consolidated this layer, just as the life of our planet itself has been one long effort to cover over with a cool and solid crust the fiery mass of seething metals. But volcanic eruptions occur. And if the earth were a living being, as mythology has feigned, most likely when in repose it would take delight in dreaming of these sudden explosions whereby it suddenly resumes possession of its innermost nature. Such is just the kind of pleasure that is provided for us by drama. Beneath the quiet humdrum life that reason and society have fashioned for us, it stirs something within us which luckily does not explode, but which it makes us feel in its inner tension. It offers nature her revenge upon society. Sometimes it makes straight for the goal, summoning up to the surface, from the depths below, passions that produce a general upheaval. Sometimes it follows a flank movement, as is often the case in contemporary drama; with a skill that is frequently sophistical it shows up the inconsistencies of society; it exaggerates the shams and shibboleths of the social law, and so indirectly, by merely dissolving or corroding the outer crust, it again brings us back to the inner core. But, in both cases, whether it weakens society or strengthens nature, it has the same end in view: that of laying bare a secret portion of ourselves, what might be called the tragic element in our character. This is indeed the impression we get after seeing a stirring drama. What has just interested us is not so much what we have been told about others as the glimpse we have caught of ourselves—a whole host of ghostly feelings, emotions and events that would fain have come into real existence, but, fortunately for us, did not. It also seems as if an appeal had been made within us to certain ancestral memories belonging to a faraway past—memories so deep-seated and so foreign to our present life that this latter, for a moment, seems something unreal and conventional, for which we shall have to serve a fresh apprenticeship. So it is indeed a deeper reality that drama draws up from beneath our superficial and utilitarian attainments; and this art has the same end in view as all the others.

III. THE CRITERION OF INDIVIDUALITY: TRAGEDY *VS.* COMEDY

Hence it follows that art always aims at what is *individual*. What the artist fixes on his canvas is something he has seen at a certain spot, on a certain day, at a certain hour, with a colouring that will never be seen again. What the poet sings of is a certain mood which was his, and his alone, and which will never return. What the dramatist unfolds before us is the life-history of a soul, a living tissue of feelings and events—something, in short, which has once happened and can never be repeated. We may, indeed, give general names to these feelings, but they cannot be the same thing in another soul. They are *individualised*. Thereby, and thereby only, do they belong to art; for generalities, symbols, or even types form the current coin of our daily perception. How, then, does a misunderstanding on this point arise?

The reason lies in the fact that two very different things have been mistaken for each other: the generality of things and that of the opinions we come to regarding them. Because a feeling is generally recognised as true, it does not follow that it is a general feeling. Nothing could be more unique than the character of Hamlet. Though he may resemble other men in some respects, it is clearly not on that account that he interests us most. But he is universally accepted and regarded as a living character. In this sense only is he universally true. The same holds good of all the other products of art. Each of them is unique, and yet, if it

bear the stamp of genius, it will come to be accepted by everybody. Why will it be accepted? And if it is unique of its kind, by
what sign do we know it to be genuine? Evidently, by the very
effort it forces us to make against our predispositions in order to
see sincerely. Sincerity is contagious. What the artist has seen we
shall probably never see again, or at least never see in exactly
the same way; but if he has actually seen it, the attempt he has
made to lift the veil compels our imitation. His work is an example which we take as a lesson. And the efficacy of the lesson
is the exact standard of the genuineness of the work. Consequently, truth bears within itself a power of conviction, nay, of
conversion, which is the sign that enables us to recognise it. The
greater the work and the more profound the dimly apprehended
truth, the longer may the effect be in coming, on the other hand,
the more universal will that effect tend to become. So the
universality here lies in the effect produced, and not in the cause.

Altogether different is the object of comedy. Here it is in the
work itself that the generality lies. Comedy depicts characters
we have already come across and shall meet with again. It takes
note of similarities. It aims at placing types before our eyes. It
even creates new types, if necessary. In this respect it forms a
contrast to all the other arts.

The very titles of certain classical comedies are significant in
themselves. Le Misanthrope, l'Avare, le Joueur, le Distrait, etc.,
are names of whole classes of people; and even when a character
comedy has a proper noun as its title, this proper noun is speedily
swept away, by the very weight of its contents, into the stream
of common nouns. We say "a Tartuffe," but we should never say
"a Phèdre" or "a Polyeucte."

Above all, a tragic poet will never think of grouping around
the chief character in his play secondary characters to serve as
simplified copies, so to speak, of the former. The hero of a tragedy
represents an individuality unique of its kind. It may be possible
to imitate him, but then we shall be passing, whether consciously
or not, from the tragic to the comic. No one is like him, because
he is like no one. But a remarkable instinct, on the contrary, im-
pels the comic poet, once he has elaborated his central character,
to cause other characters, displaying the same general traits, to
resolve as satellites round him. Many comedies have either a

plural noun or some collective term as their title. *"Les* Femmes savantes," *"Les* Précieuses ridicules," *"Le Monde* où l'on s'ennuie,"* etc., represent so many rallying points on the stage adopted by different groups of characters, all belonging to one identical type. It would be interesting to analyze this tendency in comedy. Maybe dramatists have caught a glimpse of a fact recently brought forward by mental pathology, viz. that cranks of the same kind are drawn by a secret attraction to seek each other's company. Without precisely coming within the province of medicine, the comic individual, as we have shown, is in some way absent-minded, and the transition from absent-mindedness to crankiness is continuous. But there is also another reason. If the comic poet's object is to offer us types, that is to say, characters capable of self-repetition, how can he set about it better than by showing us, in each instance, several different copies of the same model? That is just what the naturalist does in order to define a species. He enumerates and describes its main varieties.

This essential difference between tragedy and comedy, the former being concerned with individuals and the latter with classes, is revealed in yet another way. It appears in the first draft of the work. From the outset it is manifested by two radically different methods of observation.

Though the assertion may seem paradoxical, a study of other men is probably not necessary to the tragic poet. We find that some of the great poets have lived a retiring, homely sort of life, without having a chance of witnessing around them an outburst of the passions they have so faithfully depicted. But, supposing even they had witnessed such a spectacle, it is doubtful whether they would have found it of much use. For what interests us in the work of the poet is the glimpse we get of certain profound moods or inner struggles. Now, this glimpse cannot be obtained from without. Our souls are impenetrable to one another. Certain signs of passion are all that we ever apperceive externally. These we interpret—though always, by the way, defectively— only by analogy with what we have ourselves experienced. So what we experience is the main point, and we cannot become thoroughly acquainted with anything but our own heart—supposing we ever get so far. Does this mean that the poet has experienced what he depicts, that he has gone through the various

situations he makes his characters traverse, and lived the whole
of their inner life? Here, too, the biographies of poets would contradict such a supposition. How, indeed, could the same man
have been Macbeth, Hamlet, Othello, King Lear, and many
others? But then a distinction should perhaps here be made between the personality *we have* and all those we might have had.
Our character is the result of a choice that is continually being
renewed. There are points—at all events there seem to be—all
along the way, where we may branch off, and we perceive many
possible directions though we are unable to take more than one.
To retrace one's steps, and follow to the end the faintly distin-
guishable directions, appears to be the essential element in poetic
imagination. Of course, Shakespeare was neither Macbeth, nor
Hamlet, nor Othello; still, he *might have been* these several characters, if the circumstances of the case on one hand, and the con-
sent of his will on the other, had cause to break out into explosive
action what was nothing more than an inner prompting. We are
strangely mistaken as to the part played by poetic imagination
if we think it pieces together its heroes out of fragments filched
from right and left, as though it were patching together a harle-
quin's motley. Nothing living would result from that. Life cannot
be recomposed; it can only be looked at and reproduced. Poetic
imagination is but a fuller view of reality. If the characters
created by a poet give us the impression of life, it is only because
they are the poet himself,—a multiplication or division of the
poet,—the poet plumbing the depths of his own nature in so
powerful an effort of inner observation, that he lays hold of the
potential in the real, and takes up what nature has left as a mere
outline or sketch in his soul in order to make of it a finished
work of art.

Altogether different is the kind of observation from which
comedy springs. It is directed outwards. However interested a
dramatist may be in the comic features of human nature, he will
hardly go, I imagine, to the extent of trying to discover his own.
Besides, he would not find them, for we are never ridiculous
except in some point that remains hidden from our own consciousness. It is on others, then, that such observation must perforce be practised. But it will, for this very reason, assume a
character of generality that it cannot have when we apply it to

ourselves. Settling on the surface, it will not be more than skin-deep, dealing with persons at the point at which they come into contact and become capable of resembling one another. It will go no farther. Even if it could, it would not desire to do so, for it would have nothing to gain in the process. To penetrate too far into the personality, to couple the outer effect with causes that are too deep-seated, would mean to endanger, and in the end to sacrifice all that was laughable in the effect. In order that we may be tempted to laugh at it, we must localise its cause in some intermediate region of the soul. Consequently, the effect must appear to us as an average effect, as expressing an average of mankind. And, like all averages, this one is obtained by bringing together scattered data, by comparing analogous cases and extracting their essence; in short by a process of abstraction and generalisation similar to that which the physicist brings to bear upon facts with the object of grouping them under laws. In a word, method and object are here of the same nature as in the inductive sciences, in that observation is always external and the result always general.

And so we come back, by a roundabout way, to the double conclusion we reached in the course of our investigations. On the one hand, a person is never ridiculous except through some mental attribute resembling absent-mindedness, through something that lives upon him without forming part of his organism, after the fashion of a parasite; that is the reason this state of mind is observable from without and capable of being corrected. But, on the other hand, just because laughter aims at correcting, it is expedient that the correction should reach as great a number of persons as possible. This is the reason comic observation instinctively proceeds to what is general. It chooses such peculiarities as admit of being reproduced, and consequently are not indissolubly bound up with the individuality of a single person,— a possibly common sort of uncommonness, so to say,—peculiarities that are held in common. By transferring them to the stage, it creates works which doubtless belong to art in that their only visible aim is to please, but which will be found to contrast with other works of art by reason of their generality, and also of their scarcely confessed or scarcely conscious intention to correct and instruct. So we were probably right in saying that comedy lies

midway between art and life. It is not disinterested as genuine
art is. By organising laughter, comedy accepts social life as a
natural environment; it even obeys an impulse of social life. And
in this respect it turns its back upon art, which is a breaking away
from society and a return to pure nature.

IV. COMIC ABSURDITY AND DREAMS

Eager as we have been to discover the deep-seated cause of
the comic, we have so far had to neglect one of its most striking
phenomena. We refer to the logic peculiar to the comic character and the comic group, a strange kind of logic, which, in some
cases, may include a good deal of absurdity.

Théophile Gautier said that the comic in its extreme form was
the logic of the absurd. More than one philosophy of laughter
revolves round a like idea. Every comic effect, it is said, implies
contradiction in some of its aspects. What makes us laugh is
alleged to be the absurd realised in concrete shape, "a palpable
absurdity";—or, again, an apparent absurdity, which we swallow
for the moment only to rectify it immediately afterwards;—or,
better still, something absurd from one point of view though
capable of a natural explanation from another, etc. All these
theories may contain some portion of the truth; but, in the first
place, they apply only to certain rather obvious comic effects, and
then, even where they do apply, they evidently take no account
of the characteristic element of the laughable, that is, the *particular kind* of absurdity the comic contains when it does contain
something absurd. Is an immediate proof of this desired? You
have only to choose one of these definitions and make up effects
in accordance with the formula: twice out of every three times
there will be nothing laughable in the effect obtained. So we see
that absurdity, when met with in the comic, is not absurdity *in
general*. It is an absurdity of a definite kind. It does not create the
comic; rather, we might say that the comic infuses into it its own
particular essence. . . .

The behaviour of the intellect in a dream is exactly what we have
just been describing. The mind, enamoured of itself, now seeks
in the outer world nothing more than a pretext for realising its

imaginations. A confused murmur of sounds still reaches the ear, colours enter the field of vision, the senses are not completely shut in. But the dreamer, instead of appealing to the whole of his recollections for the interpretation of what his senses perceive, makes use of what he perceives to give substance to the particular recollection he favours: thus, according to the mood of the dreamer and the idea that fills his imagination at the time, a gust of wind blowing down the chimney becomes the howl of a wild beast or a tuneful melody. Such is the ordinary mechanism of illusion in dreams.

Now, if comic illusion is similar to dream illusion, if the logic of the comic is the logic of dreams, we may expect to discover in the logic of the laughable all the peculiarities of dream logic. Here, again, we shall find an illustration of the law with which we are well acquainted: given one form of the laughable, other forms that are lacking in the same comic essence become laughable from their outward resemblance to the first. Indeed, it is not difficult to see that any *play* of ideas may afford us amusement if only it bring back to mind, more or less distinctly, the play of dreamland.

We shall first call attention to a certain general relaxation of the rules of reasoning. The reasonings at which we laugh are those we know to be false, but which we might accept as true were we to hear them in a dream. They counterfeit true reasoning just sufficiently to deceive a mind dropping off to sleep. There is still an element of logic in them, if you will, but it is a logic lacking in tension and, for that very reason, affording us relief from intellectual effort. Many "witticisms" are reasonings of this kind, considerably abridged reasonings, of which we are given only the beginning and the end. Such play upon ideas evolves in the direction of a play upon words in proportion as the relations set up between the ideas become more superficial: gradually we come to take no account of the meaning of the words we hear, but only of their sound. It might be instructive to compare with dreams certain comic scenes in which one of the characters systematically repeats in a nonsensical fashion what another character whispers in his ear. If you fall asleep with people talking round you, you sometimes find that what they say gradually becomes devoid of meaning, that the sounds get distorted, as it were, and recombine in a haphazard fashion to form in your mind the strangest of meanings, and that you are reproducing between yourself and the different speakers the scene between Petit-Jean and The Prompter.

There are also *comic obsessions* that seem to bear a great resemblance to dream obsessions. Who has not had the experience of seeing the same image appear in several successive dreams, assuming a plausible meaning in each of them, whereas these dreams had no other point in common. Effects of repetition sometimes present this special form on the stage or in fiction: some of them, in fact, sound as though they belonged to a dream. It may be the same with the burden of many a song: it persistently recurs, always unchanged, at the end of every verse, each time with a different meaning.

Not infrequently do we notice in dreams a particular *crescendo*, a weird effect that grows more pronounced as we proceed. The first concession extorted from reason introduces a second; and this one, another of a more serious nature; and so on till the crowning absurdity is reached. Now, this progress towards the absurd produces on the dreamer a very peculiar sensation. Such is probably the experience of the tippler when he feels himself pleasantly drifting into a state of blankness in which neither reason nor propriety has any meaning for him. Now, consider whether some of Molière's plays would not produce the same sensation: for instance, *Monsieur de Pourceaugnac,* which, after beginning almost reasonably, develops into a sequence of all sorts of absurdities. Consider also the *Bourgeois gentilhomme,* where the different characters seem to allow themselves to be caught up in a very whirlwind of madness as the play proceeds. "If it is possible to find a man more completely mad, I will go and publish it in Rome." This sentence, which warns us that the play is over, rouses us from the increasingly extravagant dream into which, along with M. Jourdain, we have been sinking.

But, above all, there is a special madness that is peculiar to dreams. There are certain special contradictions so natural to the imagination of a dreamer, and so absurd to the reason of a man wide-awake, that it would be impossible to give a full and correct idea of their nature to anyone who had not experienced them. We allude to the strange fusion that a dream often effects between two persons who henceforth form only one and yet remain distinct. Generally one of these is the dreamer himself. He feels he has not ceased to be what he is; yet he has become someone else. He is himself, and not himself. He hears himself speak and sees himself act, but he feels that some other "he" has borrowed his body and stolen his voice. Or perhaps he is conscious of speaking and acting as usual, but he speaks of himself as a stranger with whom he has nothing in common; he has stepped out of his own self. Does it not seem as though we found this same extraordinary confusion in many a comic scene? I am not speaking of *Amphitryon,* in which play the confusion is perhaps suggested to the mind of the spectator, though the bulk of the comic effect proceeds rather from what we have already called a "reciprocal interference of two series." I am speaking of the extravagant and comic reasonings in which we really meet with this confusion in its pure form, though it requires some looking into to pick it out. For instance, listen to Mark Twain's replies to the reporter who called to interview him:

Question. Isn't that a brother of yours?
Answer. Oh! yes, yes, yes! Now you remind me of it, that *was* a brother of mine. That's William—*Bill* we called him. Poor old Bill!
Q. Why? Is he dead, then?
A. Ah! well, I suppose so. We never could tell. There was a great mystery about it.
Q. That is sad, very sad. He disappeared, then?
A. Well, yes, in a sort of general way. We buried him.
Q. Buried him! *Buried* him, without knowing whether he was dead or not?
A. Oh no! Not that. He was dead enough.
Q. Well, I confess that I can't understand this. If you buried him, and you knew he was dead—
A. No! no! We only thought he was.
Q. Oh, I see! He came to life again?
A. I bet he didn't.
Q. Well, I never heard anything like this. *Somebody* was dead. *Somebody* was buried. Now, where was the mystery?
A. Ah! that's just it! That's it exactly. You see, we were twins,—defunct and I,—and we got mixed in the bath-tub when we were only two weeks old, and one of us was drowned. But we didn't know which. Some think it was Bill. Some think it was me.

Q. Well, that *is* remarkable. What do *you* think?

A. Goodness knows! I would give whole worlds to know. This solemn, this awful tragedy has cast a gloom over my whole life. But I will tell you a secret now, which I have never revealed to any creature before. One of us had a peculiar mark,—a large mole on the back of his left hand: that was *me*. *That child was the one that was drowned!* . . . etc., etc.

A close examination will show us that the absurdity of this dialogue is by no means an absurdity of an ordinary type. It would disappear were not the speaker himself one of the twins in the story. It results entirely from the fact that Mark Twain asserts he is one of these twins, whilst all the time he talks as though he were a third person who tells the tale. In many of our dreams we adopt exactly the same method.

Benedetto Croce

[1866–1952]

୰ଌୗୖ

DURING HIS LONG CAREER Benedetto Croce became Italy's foremost aesthetician and literary critic. Despite many later qualifications and revisions, his *Aesthetic* (1901) remains a landmark of modern literary theory. Although clearly in the tradition of Kant and his successors, Croce retained a large measure of independence. He denied that space and time, Kant's primary a priori categories, are necessarily forms of intuition. He also shifted the emphasis of aesthetic criticism from the psychology of creation to the creative *expression*. His argument is pragmatic—that we only know of intuition through expression —but it has the far-reaching result of focusing attention on the work itself rather than the mind of the artist. For this reason Croce has often been invoked by the "new critics" to justify the technique of close reading. Finally, Croce was a student of literature as well as a theorist. His work is illuminated by his comprehensive knowledge of European literature and his awareness of the discoveries of contemporary scholars.

Croce's influence is pervasive but difficult to trace in detail. Joel Spingarn introduced his ideas in the United States in a lecture at Columbia University titled "The New Criticism" (1910). However, Spingarn later turned to impressionistic criticism. Croce's major service has been to confirm and reinforce the work of modern aesthetic critics, who have not always acknowledged their debt to him.

Croce's works include *Aesthetic,* trans. by Ainslie (London, 1909; rev. 1920); *Ariosto, Shakespeare, and Corneille,* trans. by Ainslie (London, 1920); "The Breviary of Aesthetic," *Rice Institute Pamphlets,* II (1915), 223–310; *The Defence of Poetry,* trans. by Carritt (Oxford, 1933); *La Poesia* (Bari, 1937); and *The Poetry of Dante,* trans. by Ainslie (London, 1922). For comment see: A. DeGennaro, "The Drama of the Aesthetics of Croce," JAAC, XV (1956), 117–21; M. Krieger, "Benedetto Croce and the Recent Poetics of Organicism," CL, XII (1955), 252–8; F. Martin, "On the Supposed Incompatibility of Expressionism and Formalism," JAAC, XV (1956), 94–9; G. Orsini, *Benedetto Croce* (Carbondale, 1961); F. Simoni, "The Philosophy of Benedetto Croce in the United States," JAAC, XI (1952), 7–14; E.

Wasiolek, "Croce and Contextualist Criticism," MP, XVII (1959), 44–54; and R. Wellek, "Benedetto Croce: Literary Critic and Historian," CL, V (1953), 75–82.

The present selections are reprinted from pp. 1–4, 7–18, 20–21, 25–6, 32–38 of *Aesthetic*, by Benedetto Croce, translated by Douglas Ainslie, by permission of Peter Owen, Ltd. and Farrar, Straus & Company, Inc. Published 1953 by The Noonday Press, a division of Farrar, Straus & Company, Inc.

AESTHETIC

I. INTUITION AND EXPRESSION

KNOWLEDGE has two forms: it is either *intuitive* knowledge or *logical* knowledge; knowledge obtained through the *imagination* or knowledge obtained through the *intellect;* knowledge of the *individual* or knowledge of the *universal;* of *individual things* or of the *relations* between them: it is, in fact, productive either of *images* or of *concepts*.

In ordinary life, constant appeal is made to intuitive knowledge. It is said that we cannot give definitions of certain truths; that they are not demonstrable by syllogisms; that they must be learnt intuitively. The politician finds fault with the abstract reasoner, who possesses no lively intuition of actual conditions; the educational theorist insists upon the necessity of developing the intuitive faculty in the pupil before everything else; the critic in judging a work of art makes it a point of honour to set aside theory and abstractions, and to judge it by direct intuition; the practical man professes to live rather by intuition than by reason.

But this ample acknowledgment granted to intuitive knowledge in ordinary life, does not correspond to an equal and adequate acknowledgment in the field of theory and of philosophy. There exists a very ancient science of intellectual knowledge, admitted by all without discussion, namely, Logic; but a science of intuitive knowledge is timidly and with difficulty asserted by but a few. Logical knowledge has appropriated the lion's share; and if she does not slay and devour her companion outright, yet yields to her but grudgingly the humble place of maidservant or doorkeeper.—What can intuitive knowledge be without the light of intellectual knowledge? It is a servant without a master; and though a master find a servant useful, the master is a necessity to the servant, since he enables him to gain his livelihood. Intuition is blind; intellect lends her eyes.

Now, the first point to be firmly fixed in the mind is that intuitive knowledge has no need of a master, nor to lean upon any one; she does not need to borrow the eyes of others, for she has excellent eyes of her own. Doubtless it is possible to find concepts mingled with intuitions. But in many other intuitions there is no trace of such a mixture, which proves that it is not necessary. The impression of a moonlight scene by a painter; the outline of a country drawn by a cartographer; a musical motive, tender or energetic; the words of a sighing lyric, or those with which we ask, command and lament in ordinary life, may well all be intuitive facts without a shadow of intellectual relation. But, think what one may of these instances, and admitting further the contention that the greater part of the intuitions of civilized man are impregnated with concepts, there yet remains to be observed something more important and more conclusive. Those concepts which are found mingled and fused with the intuitions are no longer concepts, in so far as they are really mingled and fused, for they have lost all independence and autonomy. They have been concepts, but have now become simple elements of intuition. The philosophical maxims placed in the mouth of a personage of tragedy or of comedy, perform there the function, not of concepts, but of characteristics of such personage; in the same way as the red in a painted face does not there represent the red colour of the physicists, but is a characteristic element of the portrait. The whole is that which determines the quality of the parts. A work of art may be full of philosophical concepts; it may contain them in greater abundance and they may there be even more profound than in a philosophical dissertation, which in its turn may be rich to overflowing with descriptions and intuitions. But notwithstanding all these concepts the total effect of the work of art is an intuition; and notwithstanding all those intuitions, the total effect of the philosophical dissertation is a concept. . . .

But to admit the independence of intuition as regards concept does not suffice to give a true and precise idea of intuition. An-

other error arises among those who recognize this, or who at
any rate do not explicitly make intuition dependent upon the intellect, to obscure and confuse the real nature of intuition. By
intuition is frequently understood *perception,* or the knowledge of
actual reality, the apprehension of something as *real.*

Certainly perception is intuition: the perceptions of the room
in which I am writing, of the ink-bottle and paper that are before
me, of the pen I am using, of the objects that I touch and make
use of as instruments of my person, which, if it write, therefore
exists;—these are all intuitions. But the image that is now passing
through my brain of a me writing in another room, in another
town, with different paper, pen and ink, is also an intuition. This
means that the distinction between reality and nonreality is ex-
traneous, secondary, to the true nature of intuition. If we
imagine a human mind having intuitions for the first time, it
would seem that it could have intuitions of actual reality only,
that is to say, that it could have perceptions of nothing but the
real. But since knowledge of reality is based upon the distinction
between real images and unreal images, and since this distinction
does not at the first moment exist, these intuitions would in truth
not be intuitions either of the real or of the unreal, not perceptions, but pure intuitions. Where all is real, nothing is real. The
child, with its difficulty of distinguishing true from false, history
from fable, which are all one to childhood, can furnish us with
a sort of very vague and only remotely approximate idea of this
ingenuous state. Intuition is the undifferentiated unity of the
perception of the real and of the simple image of the possible. In
our intuitions we do not oppose ourselves as empirical beings to
external reality, but we simply objectify our impressions, whatever they be.

Those, therefore, who look upon intuition as sensation formed
and arranged simply according to the categories of space and
time, would seem to approximate more nearly to the truth. Space
and time (they say) are the forms of intuition; to have an intuition is to place it in space and in temporal sequence. Intuitive
activity would then consist in this double and current function of
spatiality and temporality. But for these two categories must be
repeated what was said of intellectual distinctions, when found
mingled with intuitions. We have intuitions without space and

without time: the colour of a sky, the colour of a feeling, a cry
of pain and an effort of will, objectified in consciousness: these
are intuitions which we possess, and with their making space and
time have nothing to do. . . .

Intuition has sometimes been confused with simple sensation.
But since this confusion ends by being offensive to common
sense, it has more frequently been attenuated or concealed with
a phraseology apparently designed at once to confuse and to
distinguish them. Thus, it has been asserted that intuition is sensation, but not so much simple sensation as *association* of sensations. Here a double meaning is concealed in the word "association." Association is understood, either as memory, mnemonic
association, conscious recollection, and in that case the claim to
unite in memory elements which are not intuited, distinguished,
possessed in some way by the spirit and produced by consciousness, seems inconceivable: or it is understood as association of
unconscious elements, in which case we remain in the world of
sensation and of nature. But if with certain associationists we
speak of an association which is neither memory nor flux of sensations, but a *productive* association (formative, constructive, distinguishing); then our contention is admitted and only its name
is denied to it. For productive association is no longer association in the sense of the sensationalists, but *synthesis*, that is to say,
spiritual activity. Synthesis may be called association; but with
the concept of productivity is already posited the distinction
between passivity and activity, between sensation and intuition.

Other psychologists are disposed to distinguish from sensation
something which is sensation no longer, but is not yet intellectual
concept: the *representation* or *image*. What is the difference between their representation or image and our intuitive knowledge?
Everything and nothing: for "representation" is a very equivocal
word. If by representation be understood something cut off and
standing out from the psychic basis of the sensations, then representation is intuition. If, on the other hand, it be conceived as
complex sensation we are back once more in crude sensation,
which does not vary in quality according to its richness or
poverty, or according to whether the organism in which it appears is rudimentary or highly developed and full of traces of
past sensations. Nor is the ambiguity remedied by defining rep-

resentation as a psychic product of secondary degree in relation
to sensation, defined as occupying the first place. What does secondary degree mean here? Does it mean a qualitative, formal difference? If so, representation is an elaboration of sensation and
therefore intuition. Or does it mean greater complexity and complication, a quantitative, material difference? In that case intuition is once more confused with simple sensation.

And yet there is a sure method of distinguishing true intuition,
true representation, from that which is inferior to it: the spiritual
fact from the mechanical, passive, natural fact. Every true intuition or representation is also *expression*. That which does not
objectify itself in expression is not intuition or representation,
but sensation and mere natural fact. The spirit only intuites in
making, forming, expressing. He who separates intuition from
expression never succeeds in reuniting them.

Intuitive activity *possesses intuitions to the extent that it expresses them*. Should this proposition sound paradoxical, that is
partly because, as a general rule, a too restricted meaning is given
to the word "expression." It is generally restricted to what are
called verbal expressions alone. But there exist also nonverbal
expressions, such as those of line, colour, and sound, and to all of
these must be extended our affirmation, which embraces therefore every sort of manifestation of the man, as orator, musician,
painter, or anything else. But be it pictorial, or verbal, or musical,
or in whatever other form it appear, to no intuition can expression in one of its forms be wanting; it is, in fact, an inseparable
part of intuition. How can we really possess an intuition of a
geometrical figure, unless we possess so accurate an image of it
as to be able to trace it immediately upon paper or on the black-
board? How can we really have an intuition of the contour of a
region, for example of the island of Sicily, if we are not able to
draw it as it is in all its meanderings? Every one can experience
the internal illumination which follows upon his success in for-
mulating to himself his impressions and feelings, but only so far as
he is able to formulate them. Feelings or impressions, then, pass
by means of words from the obscure region of the soul into the
clarity of the contemplative spirit. It is impossible to distinguish
intuition from expression in this cognitive process. The one ap-

pears with the other at the same instant, because they are not two, but one.

The principal reason which makes our view appear paradoxical as we maintain it, is the illusion or prejudice that we possess a more complete intuition of reality than we really do. One often hears people say that they have many great thoughts in their minds, but that they are not able to express them. But if they really had them, they would have coined them into just so many beautiful, sounding words, and thus have expressed them. If these thoughts seem to vanish or to become few and meagre in the act of expressing them, the reason is that they did not exist or really were few and meagre. People think that all of us ordinary men imagine and intuit countries, figures, and scenes like painters, and bodies like sculptors; save that painters and sculptors know how to paint and carve such images, while we bear them unexpressed in our souls. They believe that any one could have imagined a Madonna of Raphael; but that Raphael was Raphael owing to his technical ability in putting the Madonna upon canvas. Nothing can be more false than this view. The world which as a rule we intuit is a small thing. It consists of little expressions, which gradually become greater and wider with the increasing spiritual concentration of certain moments. They are the words we say to ourselves, our silent judgments: "Here is a man, here is a horse, this is heavy, this is sharp, this pleases me," etc. It is a medley of light and colour, with no greater pictorial value than would be expressed by a haphazard splash of colours, from among which one could barely make out a few special, distinctive traits. This and nothing else is what we possess in our ordinary life; this is the basis of our ordinary action. It is the index of a book. The labels tied to things (it has been said) take the place of the things themselves. This index and these labels (themselves expressions) suffice for small needs and small actions. From time to time we pass from the index to the book, from the label to the thing, or from the slight to the greater intuitions, and from these to the greatest and most lofty. This passage is sometimes far from easy. It has been observed by those who have best studied the psychology of artists that when, after having given a rapid glance at any one, they attempt to obtain a real intuition of him, in order, for example, to paint his portrait, then this ordinary vision, that seemed so precise, so lively, reveals itself as little better than nothing. What remains is found to be at the most some superficial trait, which would not even suffice for a caricature. The person to be painted stands before the artist like a world to discover. Michael Angelo said, "One paints, not with the hands, but with the brain." Leonardo shocked the prior of the Convent of the Graces by standing for days together gazing at the "Last Supper," without touching it with the brush. He remarked of this attitude: "The minds of men of lofty genius are most active in invention when they are doing the least external work." The painter is a painter, because he sees what others only feel or catch a glimpse of, but do not see. We think we see a smile, but in reality we have only a vague impression of it, we do not perceive all the characteristic traits of which it is the sum, as the painter discovers them after he has worked upon them and is thus able to fix them on the canvas. We do not intuitively possess more even of our intimate friend, who is with us every day and at all hours, than at most certain traits of physiognomy which enable us to distinguish him from others. The illusion is less easy as regards musical expression; because it would seem strange to every one to say that the composer had added or attached notes to a motive which was already in the mind of him who is not the composer; as if Beethoven's Ninth Symphony were not his own intuition and his intuition the Ninth Symphony. Now, just as one who is deluded as to the amount of his material wealth is confuted by arithmetic, which states its exact amount, so he who nourishes delusions as to the wealth of his own thoughts and images is brought back to reality, when he is obliged to cross the *Pons Asinorum* of expression. Let us say to the former, count; to the latter, speak; or, here is a pencil, draw, express yourself.

Each of us, as a matter of fact, has in him a little of the poet, of the sculptor, of the musician, of the painter, of the prose writer: but how little, as compared with those who bear those names, just because they possess the most universal dispositions and energies of human nature in so lofty a degree! How little too does a painter possess of the intuitions of a poet! And how little does one painter possess those of another painter! Nevertheless, that little is all our actual patrimony of intuitions or representations. Beyond these are only impressions, sensations, feelings, impulses, emotions, or whatever else one may term what still falls short of the spirit and is not assimilated by man; something postulated for the convenience of exposition, while actually nonexistent, since to exist also is a fact of the spirit. . . .

II. INTUITION AND ART

We have frankly identified intuitive or expressive knowledge with the æsthetic or artistic fact, taking works of art as examples of intuitive knowledge and attributing to them the characteristics of intuition, and *vice versa*. But our identification is combated by a view held even by many philosophers, who consider art to be an intuition of an altogether special sort. "Let us admit" (they say) "that art is intuition; but intuition is not always art: artistic intuition is a distinct species differing from intuition in general by something *more*."

But no one has ever been able to indicate of what this something more consists. It has sometimes been thought that art is not a simple intuition, but an intuition of an intuition, in the same way as the concept of science has been defined, not as the ordinary concept, but as the concept of a concept. Thus man would attain to art by objectifying, not his sensations, as happens with ordinary intuition, but intuition itself. But this process of raising to a second power does not exist; and the comparison of it with the ordinary and scientific concept does not prove what is intended, for the good reason that it is not true that the scientific concept is the concept of a concept. If this comparison proves anything, it proves just the opposite. The ordinary concept, if it be really a concept and not a simple representation, is a perfect concept, however poor and limited. Science substitutes concepts for representations; for those concepts that are poor and limited it substitutes others, larger and more comprehensive; it is ever discovering new relations. But its method does not differ from that by which is formed the smallest universal in the brain of the humblest of men. What is generally called *par excellence* art, collects intuitions that are wider and more complex than those which we generally experience, but these intuitions are always of sensations and impressions.

Art is expression of impressions, not expression of expression.

For the same reason, it cannot be asserted that the intuition, which is generally called artistic, differs from ordinary intuition as intensive intuition. This would be the case if it were to operate differently on the same matter. But since the artistic function is extended to wider fields, yet does not differ in method from ordinary intuition, the difference between them is not intensive but extensive. The intuition of the simplest popular love-song, which says the same thing, or very nearly, as any declaration of love that issues at every moment from the lips of thousands of ordinary men, may be intensively perfect in its poor simplicity, although it be extensively so much more limited than the complex intuition of a love song by Leopardi.

The whole difference, then, is quantitative, and as such is in-different to philosophy, *scientia qualitatum*. Certain men have a greater aptitude, a more frequent inclination fully to express certain complex states of the soul. These men are known in or-dinary language as artists. Some very complicated and difficult expressions are not often achieved, and these are called works of art. The limits of the expression-intuitions that are called art, as opposed to those that are vulgarly called non-art, are empirical and impossible to define. If an epigram be art, why not a simple word? If a story, why not the news-jottings of the journalist? If a landscape, why not a topographical sketch? . . .

Nor can we admit that the word *genius* or artistic genius, as distinct from the nongenius of the ordinary man, possesses more than a quantitative signification. Great artists are said to reveal us to ourselves. But how could this be possible, unless there were identity of nature between their imagination and ours, and unless the difference were only one of quantity? It were better to change *poeta nascitur* into *homo nascitur poeta:* some men are born great poets, some small. The cult of the genius with all its attendant superstitions has arisen from this quantitative differ-ence having been taken as a difference of quality. It has been for-gotten that genius is not something that has fallen from heaven, but humanity itself. The man of genius who poses or is repre-sented as remote from humanity finds his punishment in becom-ing or appearing somewhat ridiculous. Examples of this are the *genius* of the romantic period and the *superman* of our time. The relation between matter and form, or between *content* and *form*, as is generally said, is one of the most disputed questions in Æsthetic. Does the æsthetic fact consist of content alone, or of form alone, or of both together? This question has taken on various meanings, which we shall mention, each in its place. But when these words are taken as signifying what we have above defined, and matter is understood as emotionality not æsthetically elaborated, or impressions, and form as intellectual activity and expression, then our view cannot be in doubt. We must, that is to say, reject both the thesis that makes the æsthetic fact to consist of the content alone (that is, the simple impressions), and the thesis which makes it to consist of a junction between form and content, that is, of impressions plus expressions. In the æsthetic fact, expressive activity is not added to the fact of the impressions, but these latter are formed and elaborated by it. The impressions reappear as it were in expression, like water put into a filter, which reappears the same and yet different on the other side. The æsthetic fact, therefore, is form, and nothing but form. . . .

The proposition that art is *imitation of nature* has also several meanings. Sometimes truths have been expressed or at least shadowed forth in these words, sometimes errors have been promulgated. More frequently, no definite thought has been expressed at all. One of the scientifically legitimate meanings occurs when "imitation" is understood as representation or intuition of nature, a form of knowledge. And when the phrase is used with this intention, and in order to emphasize the spiritual character of the process, another proposition becomes legitimate also: namely, that art is the *idealization* or *idealizing* imitation of nature. But if by imitation of nature be understood that art gives mechanical reproductions, more or less perfect duplicates of natural objects, in the presence of which is renewed the same tumult of impressions as that caused by natural objects, then the proposition is evidently false. The coloured waxen effigies that imitate the life, before which we stand astonished in the museums where such things are shown, do not give æsthetic intuitions. Illusion and hallucination have nothing to do with the calm domain of artistic intuition. But on the other hand if an artist paint the interior of a waxwork museum, or if an actor give a burlesque portrait of a man-statue on the stage, we have work of the spirit and artistic intuition. Finally, if photography have in it anything artistic, it will be to the extent that it transmits the intuition of the photographer, his point of view, the pose and grouping which he has striven to attain. And if photography be not quite an art, that is precisely because the element of nature in it remains more or less unconquered and ineradicable. Do we ever, indeed, feel complete satisfaction before even the best of photographs? Would not an artist vary and touch up much or little, remove or add something to all of them?

The statements repeated so often, that art is not knowledge, that it does not tell the truth, that it does not belong to the world of theory, but to the world of feeling, and so forth, arise from the failure to realize exactly the theoretic character of simple intuition. This simple intuition is quite distinct from intellectual knowledge, as it is distinct from perception of the real; and the statements quoted above arise from the belief that only intellectual cognition is knowledge. We have seen that intuition is knowledge, free from concepts and more simple than the so-called perception of the real. Therefore art is knowledge, form; it does not belong to the world of feeling or to psychic matter. The reason why so many æstheticians have so often insisted that art is *appearance* (*Schein*), is precisely that they have felt the necessity of distinguishing it from the more complex fact of perception, by maintaining its pure intuitiveness. And if for the same reason it has been claimed that art is *feeling* the reason is the same. For if the concept as content of art, and historical reality as such, be excluded from the sphere of art, there remains no other content than reality apprehended in all its ingenuousness and immediacy in the vital impulse, in its *feeling*, that is to say again, pure intuition. . . .

Another corollary of the conception of expression as activity is the *indivisibility* of the work of art. Every expression is a single expression. Activity is a fusion of the impressions in an organic whole. A desire to express this has always prompted the affirmation that the work of art should have *unity*, or, what amounts to the same thing, *unity in variety*. Expression is a synthesis of the various, or multiple, in the one.

The fact that we divide a work of art into parts, a poem into scenes, episodes, similes, sentences, or a picture into single figures and objects, background, foreground, etc., may seem opposed to this affirmation. But such division annihilates the work, as dividing the organism into heart, brain, nerves, muscles and so on, turns the living being into a corpse. It is true that there exist organisms in which division gives rise to other living beings, but in such a case we must conclude, maintaining the analogy between the organism and the work of art, that in the latter case too there are numerous germs of life each ready to grow, in a moment, into a single complete expression.

It may be said that expression sometimes arises from other expressions. There are simple and there are *compound* expressions. One must surely admit some difference between the *eureka*, with which Archimedes expressed all his joy at his discovery, and the expressive act (indeed all the five acts) of a regular tragedy. —Not in the least: expression always arises directly from impressions. He who conceives a tragedy puts into a crucible a great quantity, so to say, of impressions: expressions themselves, conceived on other occasions, are fused together with the new in a single mass, in the same way as we can cast into a melting furnace formless pieces of bronze and choicest statuettes. Those choicest statuettes must be melted just like the pieces of bronze, before there can be a new statue. The old expressions must descend again to the level of impressions, in order to be synthesized in a new single expression.

By elaborating his impressions, man *frees* himself from them. By objectifying them, he removes them from him and makes himself their superior. The liberating and purifying function of art is another aspect and another formula of its character as activity. Activity is the deliverer, just because it drives away passivity.

III. ART AND SCIENCE; FORM AND CONTENT; POETRY AND PROSE

The most lofty manifestations, the summits of intellectual and of intuitive knowledge shining from afar, are called, as we know, Art and Science. Art and Science, then, are different and yet linked together; they meet on one side, which is the æsthetic side. Every scientific work is also a work of art. The æsthetic side may remain little noticed when our mind is altogether taken

up with the effort to understand the thought of the man of
science and to examine its truth. But it is no longer unnoticed
when we pass from the activity of understanding to that of
contemplation and see that thought either develop itself before
us, limpid, exact, well-shaped, without superfluous or insufficient
words, with appropriate rhythm and intonation; or confused,
broken, embarrassed, tentative. Great thinkers are sometimes
called great writers, while other equally great thinkers remain
more or less fragmentary writers even if their fragments have
the scientific value of harmonious, coherent, and perfect works.

We pardon thinkers and men of science their literary mediocrity. The fragments, the flashes, console us for the whole, because it is far easier to recover the well-arranged composition
from the fragmentary work of genius, to liberate the flame latent
in the spark, than to achieve the discovery of genius. But how
can we pardon mediocre expression in pure artists? "*Mediocribus
esse poetis non di, non homines, non concessere columnae.*" The
poet or painter who lacks form, lacks everything, because he lacks
himself. Poetical material permeates the souls of all: the expression alone, that is to say, the form, makes the poet. And here
appears the truth of the view which denies all content to art,
just the intellectual concept being understood as content. In this
sense, when we take "content" as equal to "concept" it is most
true, not only that art does not consist of content, but also that
it has no content.

The distinction between *poetry and prose* also cannot be justified, save as that between art and science. It was seen in antiquity
that such distinction could not be founded on external elements,
such as rhythm and metre, or on rhymed or unrhymed form;
that it was, on the contrary, altogether internal. Poetry is the
language of feeling, prose of the intellect; but since the intellect
is also feeling, in its concreteness and reality, all prose has its
poetical side.

VI. CRITICAL FALLACIES: PROBABILITY, UNIVERSALS, THE THEORY OF GENRES

From the confusion between the demands of art in general and
the particular demands of history has resulted the theory (which

has lost ground today, but was once dominant) of the *probable* as the object of art. As is generally the case with erroneous propositions, the meaning of those who employed and employ the concept of probability has no doubt often been much more reasonable than their definition of the word. By probability used really to be meant the artistic *coherence* of the representation, that is to say, its completeness and effectiveness, its actual presence. If "probable" be translated "coherent," a very just meaning will often be found in the discussion, examples, and judgements of the critics who employ this word. An improbable personage, an improbable ending to a comedy, are really badly-drawn personages, badly-arranged endings, happenings without artistic motive. It has been said with reason that even fairies and sprites must have probability, that is to say, be really sprites and fairies, coherent artistic intuitions. Sometimes the word "possible" has been used instead of "probable." As we have already remarked in passing, this word possible is synonymous with the imaginable or intuitible. Everything truly, that is to say coherently, imagined, is possible. But also, by a good many critics and theorists, the probable was taken to mean the historically credible, or that historical truth which is not demonstrable but conjecturable, not true but probable. This was the character which these theorists sought to impose upon art. Who does not remember how great a part was played in literary history by criticism based on probability, for example, censure of *Jerusalem Delivered,* based upon the history of the Crusades, or of the Homeric poems, upon the probable customs of emperors and kings? Sometimes too the æsthetic reproduction of historical reality has been imposed upon art. This is another of the erroneous forms taken by the theory of the *imitation of nature.* Verism and naturalism also have afforded the spectacle of a confusion of the æsthetic fact with the processes of the natural sciences, by aiming at some sort of *experimental* drama or romance.

Confusions between the methods of art and those of the philosophic sciences have been far more frequent. Thus it has often been held to be the task of art to expound concepts, to unite an intelligible with a sensible, to represent *ideas* or *universals;* putting art in the place of science, that is, confusing the artistic function in general with the particular case in which it becomes æsthetico-logical.

The theory of art as supporting *theses,* of art considered as an individual representation exemplifying scientific laws, can be proved false in like manner. The example, as example, stands for the thing exemplified, and is thus an exposition of the universal, that is to say, a form of science, more or less popular or vulgarizing.

The same may be said of the æsthetic theory of the *typical,* when by type is understood, as it frequently is, the abstraction or the concept, and it is affirmed that art should make the *species* shine in the *individual.* If individual be here understood by typical, we have here too a merely verbal variation. To typify would signify, in this case, to characterize; that is, to determine and to represent the individual. Don Quixote is a type; but of what is he a type, save of all Don Quixotes? A type, so to speak, of himself. Certainly he is not a type of abstract concepts, such as the loss of the sense of reality, or of the love of glory. An infinite number of personages can be thought of under these concepts, who are not Don Quixotes. In other words, we find our own impressions fully determined and realized in the expression of a poet (for example in a poetical personage). We call that expression typical, which we might call simply æsthetic. Thus poetical or artistic universals have sometimes been spoken of, only to show that the artistic product is altogether spiritual and ideal.

Continuing to correct these errors, or to clear up misunderstandings, we shall also remark that the *symbol* has sometimes been given as the essence of art. Now, if the symbol be conceived as inseparable from the artistic intuition, it is a synonym for the intuition itself, which always has an ideal character. There is no double bottom to art, but one only; in art all is symbolical, because all is ideal. But if the symbol be conceived as separable— if the symbol can be on one side, and on the other the thing symbolized, we fall back again into the intellectualist error: the so-called symbol is the exposition of an abstract concept, an *allegory;* it is science, or art aping science. But we must also be just toward the allegorical. Sometimes it is altogether harmless. Given the *Gerusalemme liberata,* the allegory was imagined afterwards; given the *Adone* of Marino, the poet of the lascivious afterwards insinuated that it was written to show how "immoderate indulgence ends in pain"; given a statue of a beautiful woman, the sculptor can attach a label to the statue saying that it represents *Clemency* or *Goodness*. This allegory that arrives attached to a finished work *post festum* does not change the work of art. What then is it? It is an expression externally *added* to another expression. A little page of prose is added to the *Gerusalemme*, expressing another thought of the poet; a verse or a strophe is added to the *Adone*, expressing what the poet would like to make a part of his public believe; to the statue nothing but the single word: *Clemency* or *Goodness*.

But the greatest triumph of the intellectualist error lies in the theory of artistic and literary kinds, which still has vogue in literary treatises and disturbs the critics and the historians of art. Let us observe its genesis.

The human mind can pass from the æsthetic to the logical, just because the former is a first step in respect to the latter. It can destroy expression, that is, the thought of the individual, by thinking of the universal. It can gather up expressive facts into logical relations. We have already shown that this operation becomes in its turn concrete in an expression, but this does not mean that the first expressions have not been destroyed. They have yielded their place to the new æsthetico-logical expressions. When we are on the second step, we have left the first.

One who enters a picture-gallery, or who reads a series of poems, having looked and read, may go further: he may seek out the nature and the relations of the things there expressed. Thus those pictures and compositions, each of which is an individual inexpressible in logical terms, are gradually resolved into universals and abstractions, such as *costumes, landscapes, portraits, domestic life, battles, animals, flowers, fruit, seascapes, lakes, deserts; tragic, comic, pathetic, cruel, lyrical, epic, dramatic, chivalrous, idyllic facts,* and the like. They are often also resolved into merely quantitative categories, such as *miniature, picture, statuette, group, madrigal, ballad, sonnet, sonnet-sequence, poetry, poem, story, romance,* and the like.

When we think the concept *domestic life,* or *chivalry,* or *idyll,* or *cruelty,* or one of the quantitative concepts mentioned above, the individual expressive fact from which we started has been abandoned. From æsthetes that we were, we have changed into logicians; from contemplators of expression, into reasoners.

Certainly no objection can be made to such a process. In what other way could science arise, which, if it have æsthetic expressions presupposed in it, must yet go beyond them in order to fulfil its function? The logical or scientific form, as such, excludes the æsthetic form. He who begins to think scientifically has already ceased to contemplate æsthetically; although his thought assumes of necessity in its turn an æsthetic form, as has already been said, and as it would be superfluous to repeat.

Error begins when we try to deduce the expression from the concept, and to find in what takes its place the laws of the thing whose place is taken; when the difference between the second and the first step has not been observed, and when, in consequence, we declare that we are standing on the first step, when we are really standing on the second. This error is known as the *theory of artistic and literary kinds. . . .*

Even the most refined of such distinctions, which possess the most philosophic appearance, do not resist criticism; as when works of art are divided into subjective and objective kinds, into lyric and epic, into works of feeling and decorative works. In æsthetic analysis it is impossible to separate subjective from objective, lyric from epic, the image of feeling from that of things.

From the theory of artistic and literary kinds derive those erroneous modes of judgement and of criticism, thanks to which, instead of asking before a work of art if it be expressive and what it expresses, whether it speak or stammer or is altogether silent, they ask if it obey the *laws* of epic or of tragedy, of historical painting or of landscape. While making a verbal pretence of agreeing, or yielding a feigned obedience, artists have, however, really always disregarded these *laws of the kinds.* Every true work of art has violated some established kind and upset the ideas of the critics, who have thus been obliged to broaden the kinds, until finally even the broadened kind has proved too narrow, owing to the appearance of new works of art, naturally followed by new scandals, new upsettings and—new broadenings.

To the same theory are due the prejudices, owing to which at one time (is it really passed?) people used to lament that Italy had no tragedy (until one arose who bestowed such a wreath, which alone of adornments was wanting to her glorious locks), nor France the epic poem (until the *Henriade,* which slaked the thirsty throats of the critics). Eulogies accorded to the inventors of new kinds are connected with these prejudices, so much so, that in the seventeenth century the invention of the *mock-heroic* poem seemed an important event, and the honour of it was disputed, as though it were the discovery of America. But the works adorned with this name (the *Secchia rapita* and the *Scherno degli Dei*) were stillborn, because their authors (a slight drawback) had nothing new or original to say. Mediocrities racked their brains to invent new kinds artificially. The *piscatorial* eclogue was added to the *pastoral,* and finally the *military* eclogue. The *Aminta* was dipped and became the *Alceo.* Finally, there have been historians of art and literature, so much fascinated with these ideas of kinds, and they claimed to write the history, not of individual and real literary and artistic works, but of those empty phantoms, their kinds. They have claimed to portray, not the evolution of the *artistic spirit,* but the *evolution of kinds.*

The philosophical condemnation of artistic and literary kinds is found in the formulation and demonstration of what artistic activity has always done and good taste always recognized. What are we to do if good taste and the real fact, when reduced to formulas, sometimes assume the air of paradoxes?

It is not scientifically incorrect to talk of tragedies, comedies, dramas, romances, pictures of everyday life, battle-pieces, landscapes, seascapes, poems, versicles, lyrics, and the like, if it be only with a view to be understood, and to draw attention to certain groups of works, in general and approximately, to which, for one reason or another, it is desired to draw attention. To employ *words* and *phrases* is not to establish *laws* and *definitions.* The mistake only arises when the weight of a scientific definition is given to a word, when we ingenuously let ourselves be caught in the meshes of that phraseology. Pray permit me a comparison. The books in a library must be arranged in one way or another. This used generally to be done by a rough classification of subjects (among which the categories of miscellaneous and eccentric were not wanting); they are now generally arranged by sizes or by publishers. Who can deny the necessity and the utility of such arrangements? But what should we say if some one began seriously to seek out the literary laws of miscellanies and of eccentricities, of the Aldines or Bodonis, of shelf A or shelf B, that is to say, of those altogether arbitrary groupings whose sole object was their practical utility. Yet should any one attempt such an undertaking, he would be doing neither more nor less than those do who seek out the *æsthetic laws* which must in their belief control literary and artistic kinds.

Part IV

PSYCHOLOGY AND
ANTHROPOLOGY

Friedrich Nietzsche

[1844–1900]

AFTER A PERIOD of unpopularity, when he was frequently accused of being a forerunner of Nazism, Nietzsche is once again being recognized as one of the seminal minds of the nineteenth century. He was, above all, a reformer. He believed that Western culture is in the last stages of decay. He was scornful of scientific rationalism and Christianity and called for a heroic "transvaluation of values" which would initiate a new cultural epoch. Like many another reformer, he wished to enlist literature in his cause. He praised Wagner extravagantly, but later—especially after *Parsifal*—denounced him.

The Birth of Tragedy from the Spirit of Music (1872) was written under Wagner's influence and contains a preface to him. It was Nietzsche's first important work. In it he distinguished between the Dionysian impulse, which is primitive, arational, and healthgiving; and the Apollonian impulse, which is self-conscious, rational, and ultimately destructive. The Dionysian impulse is the source of the power of early Greek tragedy. The Apollonian impulse vitiates the tragedies of Euripides. Socrates is the symbol of Apollonian man. Socratic rationalism, in alliance with a cowardly Christian morality, dominates modern culture.

Stripped of its rhetoric Nietzsche's analysis of Greek tragedy anticipates to a remarkable degree contemporary interest in myth, archetypal symbolism, and the primitive roots of sophisticated literature. Writers as diverse as George Bernard Shaw, Eugene O'Neill, D. H. Lawrence, Thomas Mann, Susanne Langer, and Jean-Paul Sartre have confessed a debt to Nietzsche.

Nietzsche's *Complete Works* in translation have been edited by O. Levy (Edinburgh, 1909–14). The major works, including *The Birth of Tragedy*, are available in the Modern Library *Philosophy of Nietzsche* (New York, n.d.). For comment see: Erich Heller, *The Disinherited Mind* (Philadelphia, 1952); A. H. Knight, *Some Aspects of the Life and Work of Nietzsche* (Cambridge, 1933); A. Ludovici, *Nietzsche and Art* (Boston, 1912).

The present selection is from *The Birth of Tragedy from the Spirit of Music*, trans. by William A. Hausmann (Edinburgh, 1909).

THE BIRTH OF TRAGEDY

I. THE APOLLONIAN AND THE DIONYSIAN PRINCIPLES

WE SHALL HAVE GAINED much for the science of æsthetics, when once we have perceived not only by logical inference, but by the immediate certainty of intuition, that the continuous development of art is bound up with the duplexity of the *Apollonian* and the *Dionysian:* in like manner as procreation is dependent on the duality of the sexes, involving perpetual conflicts with only periodically intervening reconciliations. These names we borrow from the Greeks, who disclose to the intelligent observer the profound mysteries of their view of art, not indeed in concepts, but in the impressively clear figures of their world of deities. It is in connection with Apollo and Dionysus, the two art-deities of the Greeks, that we learn that there existed in the Grecian world a wide antithesis, in origin and aims, between the art of the shaper, the Apollonian, and the nonplastic art of music, that of Dionysus: both these so heterogeneous tendencies run parallel to each other, for the most part openly at variance, and continually inciting each other to new and more powerful births, to perpetuate in them the strife of this antithesis, which is but seemingly bridged over by their mutual term "Art"; till at last, by a metaphysical miracle of the Hellenic will, they appear paired with each other, and through this pairing eventually generate the equally Dionysian and Apollonian art-work of Attic tragedy.

In order to bring these two tendencies within closer range, let us conceive them first of all as the separate art-worlds of *dreamland* and *drunkenness;* between which physiological phenomena a contrast may be observed analogous to that existing between the Apollonian and the Dionysian. In dreams, according to the conception of Lucretius, the glorious divine figures first appeared to the souls of men, in dreams the great shaper beheld the charming corporeal structure of superhuman beings. . . .

This cheerful acquiescence in the dream-experience has likewise been embodied by the Greeks in their Apollo: for Apollo, as the god of all shaping energies, is also the soothsaying god. He, who (as the etymology of the name indicates) is the "shining one," the deity of light, also rules over the fair appearance of the inner world of fantasies. The higher truth, the perfection of these states in contrast to the only partially intelligible everyday world, ay, the deep consciousness of nature, healing and helping in sleep and dream, is at the same time the symbolical analogue of the faculty of soothsaying and, in general, of the arts, through which life is made possible and worth living. But also that delicate line, which the dream-picture must not overstep—lest it act pathologically (in which case appearance, being reality pure and simple, would impose upon us)—must not be wanting in the picture of Apollo: that measured limitation, that freedom from the wilder emotions, that philosophical calmness of the sculptor-god. His eye must be "sunlike," according to his origin; even when it is angry and looks displeased, the sacredness of his beauteous appearance is still there. And so we might apply to Apollo, in an eccentric sense, what Schopenhauer says of the man wrapt in the veil of Mâyâ: [1] *Welt als Wille und Vorstellung,* I. p. 416: "Just as in a stormy sea, unbounded in every direction, rising and falling with howling mountainous waves, a sailor sits in a boat and trusts in his frail barque: so in the midst of a world of sorrows the individual sits quietly supported by and trusting in his *principium individuationis.*" Indeed, we might say of Apollo, that in him the unshaken faith in this *principium* and the quiet sitting of the man wrapt therein have received their sublimest expression; and we might even designate Apollo as the glorious divine image of the *principium individuationis,* from out of the gestures and looks of which all the joy and wisdom of "appearance," together with its beauty, speak to us.

In the same work Schopenhauer has described to us the stupendous *awe* which seizes upon man, when of a sudden he is at a loss to account for the cognitive forms of a phenomenon, in that the principle of reason, in some one of its manifestations, seems to admit of an exception. Add to this awe the blissful ecstasy which rises from the innermost depths of man, ay, of nature, at this same collapse of the *principium individuationis,* and we shall gain an insight into the being of the *Dionysian,* which is brought within closest ken perhaps by the analogy of *drunkenness.* It is

[1] Cf. *World as Will and Idea,* trans. by Haldane and Kemp, I, 455ff.

either under the influence of the narcotic draught, of which the hymns of all primitive men and peoples tell us, or by the powerful approach of spring penetrating all nature with joy, that those Dionysian emotions awake, in the augmentation of which the subjective vanishes to complete self-forgetfulness. So also in the German Middle Ages singing and dancing crowds, ever increasing in number, were borne from place to place under this same Dionysian power. In these St. John's and St. Vitus's dancers we again perceive the Bacchic choruses of the Greeks, with their previous history in Asia Minor, as far back as Babylon and the orgiastic Sacæa. There are some, who, from lack of experience or obtuseness, will turn away from such phenomena as "folk-diseases" with a smile of contempt or pity prompted by the consciousness of their own health: of course, the poor wretches do not divine what a cadaverous-looking and ghastly aspect this very "health" of theirs presents when the glowing life of the Dionysian revellers rushes past them.

Under the charm of the Dionysian not only is the covenant between man and man again established, but also estranged, hostile, or subjugated nature again celebrates her reconciliation with her lost son, man. Of her own accord earth proffers her gifts, and peacefully the beasts of prey approach from the desert and the rocks. The chariot of Dionysus is bedecked with flowers and garlands: panthers and tigers pass beneath his yoke. Change Beethoven's "jubilee-song" into a painting, and, if your imagination be equal to the occasion when the awestruck millions sink into the dust, you will then be able to approach the Dionysian. Now is the slave a free man, now all the stubborn, hostile barriers, which necessity, caprice, or "shameless fashion" has set up between man and man, are broken down. Now, at the evangel of cosmic harmony, each one feels himself not only united, reconciled, blended with his neighbour, but as one with him, as if the veil of Mâyâ had been torn and were now merely fluttering in tatters before the mysterious Primordial Unity. In song and in dance man exhibits himself as a member of a higher community: he has forgotten how to walk and speak, and is on the point of taking a dancing flight into the air. His gestures bespeak enchantment. Even as the animals now talk, and as the earth yields milk and honey, so also something supernatural sounds forth from him:

he feels himself a god, he himself now walks about enchanted and elated even as the gods whom he saw walking about in his dreams. Man is no longer an artist, he has become a work of art: the artistic power of all nature here reveals itself in the tremors of drunkenness to the highest gratification of the Primordial Unity.

II. THE BIRTH OF TRAGEDY

It is an indisputable tradition that Greek tragedy in its earliest form had for its theme only the sufferings of Dionysus, and that for some time the only stage-hero therein was simply Dionysus himself. With the same confidence, however, we can maintain that not until Euripides did Dionysus cease to be the tragic hero, and that in fact all the celebrated figures of the Greek stage —Prometheus, Œdipus, etc.—are but masks of this original hero, Dionysus. The presence of a god behind all these masks is the one essential cause of the typical "ideality," so oft exciting wonder, of these celebrated figures. Some one, I know not whom, has maintained that all individuals are comic as individuals and are consequently untragic: from whence it might be inferred that the Greeks in general *could* not endure individuals on the tragic stage. And they really seem to have had these sentiments: as, in general, it is to be observed that the Platonic discrimination and valuation of the "idea" in contrast to the "eidolon," the image, is deeply rooted in the Hellenic being. Availing ourselves of Plato's terminology, however, we should have to speak of the tragic figures of the Hellenic stage somewhat as follows. The one truly real Dionysus appears in a multiplicity of forms, in the mask of a fighting hero and entangled, as it were, in the net of an individual will. As the visibly appearing god now talks and acts, he re- sembles an erring, striving, suffering individual: and that, in general, he *appears* with such epic precision and clearness, is due to the dream-reading Apollo, who reads to the chorus its Diony- sian state through this symbolic appearance. In reality, however, this hero is the suffering Dionysus of the mysteries, a god ex- periencing in himself the sufferings of individuation, of whom wonderful myths tell that as a boy he was dismembered by the

Titans and has been worshipped in this state as Zagreus: whereby is intimated that this dismemberment, the properly Dionysian *suffering*, is like a transformation into air, water, earth, and fire, that we must therefore regard the state of individuation as the source and primal cause of all suffering, as something objectionable in itself. From the smile of this Dionysus sprang the Olympian gods, from his tears sprang man. In his existence as a dismembered god, Dionysus has the dual nature of a cruel barbarised demon, and a mild pacific ruler. But the hope of the epopts looked for a new birth of Dionysus, which we have now to conceive of in anticipation as the end of individuation: it was for this coming third Dionysus that the stormy jubilation hymns of the epopts resounded. And it is only this hope that sheds a ray of joy upon the features of a world torn asunder and shattered into individuals: as is symbolised in the myth by Demeter sunk in eternal sadness, who *rejoices* again only when told that she may *once more* give birth to Dionysus. In the views of things here given we already have all the elements of a profound and pessimistic contemplation of the world, and along with these we have the *mystery doctrine of tragedy*: the fundamental knowledge of the oneness of all existing things, the consideration of individuation as the primal cause of evil, and art as the joyous hope that the spell of individuation may be broken, as the augury of a restored oneness.

It has already been intimated that the Homeric epos is the poem of Olympian culture, wherewith this culture has sung its own song of triumph over the terrors of the war of the Titans. Under the predominating influence of tragic poetry, these Homeric myths are now reproduced anew, and show by this metempsychosis that meantime the Olympian culture also has been vanquished by a still deeper view of things. The haughty Titan Prometheus has announced to his Olympian tormentor that the extremest danger will one day menace his rule, unless he ally with him betimes. In Æschylus we perceive the terrified Zeus, apprehensive of his end, in alliance with the Titan. Thus, the former age of the Titans is subsequently brought from Tartarus once more to the light of day. The philosophy of wild and naked nature beholds with the undissembled mien of truth the myths of the Homeric world as they dance past: they turn pale, they tremble before the lightning glance of this goddess—till the powerful fist of the Dionysian artist forces them into the service of the new deity. Dionysian truth takes over the entire domain of myth as symbolism of *its* knowledge, which it makes known partly in the public cult of tragedy and partly in the secret celebration of the dramatic mysteries, always, however, in the old mythical garb. What was the power, which freed Prometheus from his vultures and transformed the myth into a vehicle of Dionysian wisdom? It is the Heracleian power of music: which, having reached its highest manifestness in tragedy, can invest myths with a new and most profound significance, which we have already had occasion to characterise as the most powerful faculty of music. For it is the fate of every myth to insinuate itself into the narrow limits of some alleged historical reality, and to be treated by some later generation as a solitary fact with historical claims: and the Greeks were already fairly on the way to restamp the whole of their mythical juvenile dream sagaciously and arbitrarily into a historico-pragmatical *juvenile history*. For this is the manner in which religions are wont to die out: when of course under the stern, intelligent eyes of an orthodox dogmatism, the mythical presuppositions of a religion are systematised as a completed sum of historical events, and when one begins apprehensively to defend the credibility of the myth, while at the same time opposing all continuation of their natural vitality and luxuriance; when, accordingly, the feeling for myth dies out, and its place is taken by the claim of religion to historical foundations. This dying myth was now seized by the newborn genius of Dionysian music, in whose hands it bloomed once more, with such colours as it had never yet displayed, with a fragrance that awakened a longing anticipation of a metaphysical world. After this final effulgence it collapses, its leaves wither, and soon the scoffing Lucians of antiquity catch at the discoloured and faded flowers which the winds carry off in every direction. Through tragedy the myth attains its profoundest significance, its most expressive form; it rises once more like a wounded hero, and the whole surplus of vitality, together with the philosophical calmness of the Dying, burns in its eyes with a last powerful gleam.

III. THE DECAY OF TRAGEDY AND THE
SPIRIT OF SCIENCE

Here the question occupies us, whether the power by the
counteracting influence of which tragedy perished, has for all
time strength enough to prevent the artistic reawaking of
tragedy and of the tragic view of things. If ancient tragedy was
driven from its course by the dialectical desire for knowledge
and the optimism of science, it might be inferred that there is an
eternal conflict between *the theoretic* and *the tragic view of
things*, and only after the spirit of science has been led to its
boundaries, and its claim to universal validity has been destroyed
by the evidence of these boundaries, can we hope for a rebirth
of tragedy: for which form of culture we should have to use the
symbol of *the music-practising Socrates* in the sense spoken of
above. In this contrast, I understand by the spirit of science the
belief which first came to light in the person of Socrates,—the
belief in the fathomableness of nature and in knowledge as a
panacea.

He who recalls the immediate consequences of this restlessly
onward-pressing spirit of science will realise at once that *myth*
was annihilated by it, and that, in consequence of this annihila-
tion, poetry was driven as a homeless being from her natural ideal
soil. If we have rightly assigned to music the capacity to reproduce myth from itself, we may in turn expect to find the spirit of
science on the path where it inimically opposes this mythopoeic
power of music. This takes place in the development of the *New
Attic Dithyramb*, the music of which no longer expressed the inner essence, the will itself, but only rendered the phenomenon
insufficiently, in an imitation by means of concepts; from which
intrinsically degenerate music the truly musical natures turned
away with the same repugnance that they felt for the art-
destroying tendency of Socrates. The unerring instinct of Aristophanes surely did the proper thing when it comprised Socrates
himself, the tragedy of Euripides, and the music of the new
Dithyrambic poets in the same feeling of hatred, and perceived
in all three phenomena the symptoms of a degenerate culture. By
this New Dithyramb, music has in an outrageous manner been

made the imitative portrait of phenomena, for instance, of a battle or a storm at sea, and has thus, of course, been entirely deprived of its mythopoeic power. For if it endeavours to excite our delight only by compelling us to seek external analogies between a vital or natural process and certain rhythmical figures and characteristic sounds of music; if our understanding is expected to satisfy itself with the perception of these analogies, we are reduced to a frame of mind in which the reception of the mythical is impossible; for the myth as a unique exemplar of generality and truth towering into the infinite, desires to be conspicuously perceived. The truly Dionysian music presents itself to us as such a general mirror of the universal will: the conspicuous event which is refracted in this mirror expands at once for our consciousness to the copy of an eternal truth. Conversely, such a conspicuous event is at once divested of every mythical character by the tone-painting of the New Dithyramb; music has here become a wretched copy of the phenomenon, and therefore infinitely poorer than the phenomenon itself: through which poverty it still further reduces even the phenomenon for our consciousness, so that now, for instance, a musically imitated battle of this sort exhausts itself in marches, signal-sounds, etc., and our imagination is arrested precisely by these superficialities. Tone-painting is therefore in every respect the counterpart of true music with its mythopoeic power: through it the phenomenon, poor in itself, is made still poorer, while through an isolated Dionysian music the phenomenon is evolved and expanded into a picture of the world. It was an immense triumph of the non-Dionysian spirit, when, in the development of the New Dithyramb, it had estranged music from itself and reduced it to be the slave of phenomena. Euripides, who, albeit in a higher sense, must be designated as a thoroughly unmusical nature, is for this very reason a passionate adherent of the New Dithyrambic Music, and with the liberality of a freebooter employs all its effective turns and mannerisms.

In another direction also we see at work the power of this un-Dionysian, myth-opposing spirit, when we turn our eyes to the prevalence of *character representation* and psychological refinement from Sophocles onwards. The character must no longer be expanded into an eternal type, but, on the contrary, must operate

individually through artistic by-traits and shadings, through the
nicest precision of all lines, in such a manner that the spectator
is in general no longer conscious of the mighty nature-myth but
of the imitative power of the artist. Here also we observe the
victory of the phenomenon over the Universal, and the delight
in the particular quasi-anatomical preparation; we actually
breathe the air of a theoretical world, in which scientific knowledge is valued more highly than the artistic reflection of a universal law. The movement along the line of the representation
of character proceeds rapidly: while Sophocles still delineates
complete characters and employs myth for their refined development, Euripides already delineates only prominent individual
traits of character, which can express themselves in violent bursts
of passion; in the New Attic Comedy, however, there are only
masks with *one* expression: frivolous old men, duped panders,
and cunning slaves in untiring repetition. Where now is the
mythopoeic spirit of music? What is still left now of music is
either excitatory music or souvenir music, that is, either a stimu-
lant for dull and used-up nerves, or tone-painting. As regards the
former, it hardly matters about the text set to it: the heroes and
choruses of Euripides are already dissolute enough when once
they begin to sing; to what pass must things have come with his
brazen successors?

The new un-Dionysian spirit, however, manifests itself most
clearly in the *denouements* of the new dramas. In the Old
Tragedy one could feel at the close the metaphysical comfort,
without which the delight in tragedy cannot be explained at all;
the conciliating tones from another world sound purest, perhaps,
in the Œdipus at Colonus. Now that the genius of music has fled
from tragedy, tragedy is, strictly speaking, dead: for from whence
could one now draw the metaphysical comfort? One sought,
therefore, for an earthly unravelment of the tragic dissonance; the
hero, after he had been sufficiently tortured by fate, reaped a
well-deserved reward through a superb marriage or divine tokens
of favour. The hero had turned gladiator, on whom, after being
liberally battered about and covered with wounds, freedom was
occasionally bestowed. The *deus ex machina* took the place of
metaphysical comfort. I will not say that the tragic view of things
was everywhere completely destroyed by the intruding spirit of

the un-Dionysian: we only know that it was compelled to flee from art into the underworld as it were, in the degenerate form of a secret cult. Over the widest extent of the Hellenic character, however, there raged the consuming blast of this spirit, which manifests itself in the form of "Greek cheerfulness," which we have already spoken of as a senile, unproductive love of existence; this cheerfulness is the counterpart of the splendid "naïveté" of the earlier Greeks, which, according to the characteristic indicated above, must be conceived as the blossom of the Apollonian culture growing out of a dark abyss, as the victory which the Hellenic will, through its mirroring of beauty, obtains over suffering and the wisdom of suffering.

IV. THE LOSS OF MYTH AND THE STERILITY OF MODERN SOCIETY

He who wishes to test himself rigorously as to how he is related to the true æsthetic hearer, or whether he belongs rather to the community of the Socrato-critical man, has only to enquire sincerely concerning the sentiment with which he accepts the *wonder* represented on the stage: whether he feels his historical sense, which insists on strict psychological causality, insulted by it, whether with benevolent concession he as it were admits the wonder as a phenomenon intelligible to childhood, but relinquished by him, or whether he experiences anything else thereby. For he will thus be enabled to determine how far he is on the whole capable of understanding *myth*, that is to say, the concentrated picture of the world, which, as abbreviature of phenomena, cannot dispense with wonder. It is probable, however, that nearly every one, upon close examination, feels so disintegrated by the critico-historical spirit of our culture, that he can only perhaps make the former existence of myth credible to himself by learned means through intermediary abstractions. Without myth, however, every culture loses its healthy creative natural power: it is only a horizon encompassed with myths which rounds off to unity a social movement. It is only by myth that all the powers of the imagination and of the Apollonian dream are freed from their random rovings. The mythical figures have to be the invisibly omnipresent genii, under the care of which the young soul grows to maturity, by the signs of which the man gives a meaning to his life and struggles: and the state itself knows no more powerful unwritten law than the mythical foundation which vouches for its connection with religion and its growth from mythical ideas.

Let us now place alongside thereof the abstract man proceeding independently of myth, the abstract education, the abstract usage, the abstract right, the abstract state: let us picture to ourselves the lawless roving of the artistic imagination, not bridled by any native myth: let us imagine a culture which has no fixed and sacred primitive seat, but is doomed to exhaust all its possibilities, and has to nourish itself wretchedly from the other cultures—such is the Present, as the result of Socratism, which is bent on the destruction of myth. And now the mythless man remains eternally hungering among all the bygones, and digs and grubs for roots, though he have to dig for them even among the remotest antiquities. The stupendous historical exigency of the unsatisfied modern culture, the gathering around one of countless other cultures, the consuming desire for knowledge—what does all this point to, if not to the loss of myth, the loss of the mythical home, the mythical source? Let us ask ourselves whether the feverish and so uncanny stirring of this culture is aught but the eager seizing and snatching at food of the hungerer—and who would care to contribute anything more to a culture which cannot be appeased by all it devours, and in contact with which the most vigorous and wholesome nourishment is wont to change into "history and criticism"?

Sigmund Freud

[1856–1939]

FREUD WAS INTRODUCED to psychology by Dr. Josef Breuer in the 1880's. Breuer had developed a "cathartic method" of curing mental patients by hypnosis. After collaboration on *Studies in Hysteria* (1895), Freud and Breuer parted company because of Freud's conviction that sexual problems are at the root of most mental illness. From 1895 to 1905 Freud worked in almost complete isolation. In a brilliant series of studies beginning with *The Interpretation of Dreams* (1900) he demonstrated that the conscious mind is profoundly influenced by the unconscious, that childhood experiences, especially sexual ones, have a lasting influence on mature personality, and that mental disturbances can be alleviated by the recall of these experiences. To assist his patients Freud used dream-analysis, free-association, and lengthy consultations, techniques still basic in psychoanalysis.

Freud was deeply interested in literature. He believed that the great poets had often anticipated his findings. His essays abound with literary quotations and allusions. The Oedipus Complex, to which he traced "the beginnings of religion, ethics, society, and art," is named for the hero of Sophocles' *Oedipus Rex*. *The Interpretation of Dreams* (V, d) contains a remarkable analysis of *Oedipus Rex* and *Hamlet* in terms of the Oedipus Complex. Several of Freud's essays deal specifically with literature. Among the best known are *Delusion and Dream*, "Creative Writers and Day-Dreaming," "The Theme of the Three Caskets," and "A Childhood Recollection from Goethe's *Dichtung und Wahrheit*."

After World War I a vogue of Freudian criticism was established which reached its peak between 1930 and 1945. Much Freudian criticism is superficial. The serious works are predominantly biographical. They include Ernest Jones, *Hamlet and Oedipus* (1911); Van Wyck Brooks, *The Ordeal of Mark Twain* (1920); and Princess Marie Bonaparte, *Edgar Poe* (1930). A few Freudians have investigated nonpersonal aspects of literature; for example, C. S. Prescott, *The Poetic Mind* (1922) and Kenneth Burke, *The Philosophy of Literary Form* (1941). André Breton and his fellow surrealists converted

Freudian theory into a program for the composition of arational poetry.

Freud's *Complete Works*, in translation, have been published under the editorship of James Strachey (London, 1953ff.). Useful selections include *Basic Works*, trans. by Brill (New York, 1938); *Leonardo da Vinci* (New York, 1947); *Delusion and Dream and Other Essays*, intr. by Philip Rieff (Boston, 1956); *Freud: On Creativity and the Unconscious*, ed. by B. Nelson (New York, 1958). For comment see: Louis Fraiberg, *Psychoanalysis and American Literary Criticism* (Detroit, 1960); F. T. Hoffman, *Freudianism and the Literary Mind* (Baton Rouge, 1945); N. Holland, "Freud on Shakespeare," PMLA, LXXV (1960), 163–73; William Phillips, ed., *Art and Psychoanalysis* (New York, 1957); L. Trilling, "Freud and Literature," in *The Liberal Imagination* (New York, 1950).

The present selections are (i) "Creative Writers and Day-Dreaming," trans. by I. F. Duff, *The Complete Psychological Works*, ed. James Strachey (London: Hogarth Press), IX (1959), 145–53; and (ii) from "Some Character-Types Met with in Psychoanalytic Work," trans. by E. C. Mayne, *The Complete Psychological Works*, ed. Strachey (London: The Hogarth Press), XIV (1957), 316–31. Reprinted by permission.

CREATIVE WRITERS AND
DAY-DREAMING

WE LAYMEN have always been intensely curious to know—like the Cardinal who put a similar question to Ariosto [1]—from what sources that strange being, the creative writer, draws his material, and how he manages to make such an impression on us with it and to arouse in us emotions of which, perhaps, we had not even thought ourselves capable. Our interest is only heightened the more by the fact that, if we ask him, the writer himself gives us no explanation, or none that is satisfactory; and it is not at all weakened by our knowledge that not even the clearest insight into the determinants of his choice of material and into the nature of the art of creating imaginative form will ever help to make creative writers of *us*.

[1] Cardinal Ippolito d'Este was Ariosto's first patron, to whom he dedicated the *Orlando Furioso*. The poet's only reward was the question: "Where did you find so many stories, Lodovico?"

If we could at least discover in ourselves or in people like ourselves an activity which was in some way akin to creative writing! An examination of it would then give us a hope of obtaining the beginnings of an explanation of the creative work of writers. And, indeed, there is some prospect of this being possible. After all, creative writers themselves like to lessen the distance between their kind and the common run of humanity; they so often assure us that every man is a poet at heart and that the last poet will not perish till the last man does.

Should we not look for the first traces of imaginative activity as early as in childhood? The child's best-loved and most intense occupation is with his play or games. Might we not say that every child at play behaves like a creative writer, in that he creates a world of his own, or, rather, rearranges the things of his world in a new way which pleases him? It would be wrong to think he does not take that world seriously; on the contrary, he takes his play very seriously and he expends large amounts of emotion on it. The opposite of play is not what is serious but what is real. In spite of all the emotion with which he cathects his world of play, the child distinguishes it quite well from reality; and he likes to link his imagined objects and situations to the tangible and visible things of the real world. This linking is all that differentiates the child's 'play' from 'phantasying.'

The creative writer does the same as the child at play. He creates a world of phantasy which he takes very seriously—that is, which he invests with large amounts of emotion—while separating it sharply from reality. Language has preserved this relationship between children's play and poetic creation. It gives [in German] the name of '*Spiel*' ['play'] to those forms of imaginative writing which require to be linked to tangible objects and which are capable of representation. It speaks of a '*Lustspiel*' or '*Trauerspiel*' ['comedy' or 'tragedy': literally, 'pleasure play' or 'mourning play'] and describes those who carry out the representation as '*Schauspieler*' ['players': literally 'show-players']. The unreality of the writer's imaginative world, however, has very important consequences for the technique of his art; for many things which, if they were real, could give no enjoyment, can do so in the play of phantasy, and many excitements which, in themselves, are actually distressing, can become a source of pleasure for the hearers and spectators at the performance of a writer's work.

There is another consideration for the sake of which we will dwell a moment longer on this contrast between reality and play. When the child has grown up and has ceased to play, and after he has been labouring for decades to envisage the realities of life with proper seriousness, he may one day find himself in a mental situation which once more undoes the contrast between play and reality. As an adult he can look back on the intense seriousness with which he once carried on his games in childhood; and, by equating his ostensibly serious occupations of to-day with his childhood games, he can throw off the too heavy burden imposed on him by life and win the high yield of pleasure afforded by *humour*.[2]

As people grow up, then, they cease to play, and they seem to give up the yield of pleasure which they gained from playing. But whoever understands the human mind knows that hardly anything is harder for a man than to give up a pleasure which he has once experienced. Actually, we can never give anything up; we only exchange one thing for another. What appears to be a renunciation is really the formation of a substitute or surrogate. In the same way, the growing child, when he stops playing, gives up nothing but the link with real objects; instead of *playing*, he now *phantasies*. He builds castles in the air and creates what are called *day-dreams*. I believe that most people construct phantasies at times in their lives. This is a fact which has long been overlooked and whose importance has therefore not been sufficiently appreciated.

People's phantasies are less easy to observe than the play of children. The child, it is true, plays by himself or forms a closed psychical system with other children for the purposes of a game; but even though he may not play his game in front of the grown-ups, he does not, on the other hand, conceal it from them. The adult, on the contrary, is ashamed of his phantasies and hides them from other people. He cherishes his phantasies as his most intimate possessions, and as a rule he would rather confess his misdeeds than tell anyone his phantasies. It may come about that for that reason he believes he is the only person who invents such

[2] See *Wit and Its Relation to the Unconscious*, vii, 7.

phantasies and has no idea that creations of this kind are wide-spread among other people. This difference in the behaviour of a person who plays and a person who phantasies is accounted for by the motives of these two activities, which are nevertheless adjuncts to each other.

A child's play is determined by wishes: in point of fact by a single wish—one that helps in his upbringing—the wish to be big and grown up. He is always playing at being 'grown up,' and in his games he imitates what he knows about the lives of his elders. He has no reason to conceal this wish. With the adult, the case is different. On the one hand, he knows that he is expected not to go on playing or phantasying any longer, but to act in the real world; on the other hand, some of the wishes which give rise to his phantasies are of a kind which it is essential to conceal. Thus he is ashamed of his phantasies as being childish and as being unpermissible.

But, you will ask, if people make such a mystery of their phantasying, how is it that we know such a lot about it? Well, there is a class of human beings upon whom, not a god, indeed, but a stern goddess—Necessity—has allotted the task of telling what they suffer and what things give them happiness. These are the victims of nervous illness, who are obliged to tell their phantasies, among other things, to the doctor by whom they expect to be cured by mental treatment. This is our best source of knowledge, and we have since found good reason to suppose that our patients tell us nothing that we might not also hear from healthy people.

Let us make ourselves acquainted with a few of the characteristics of phantasying. We may lay it down that a happy person never phantasies, only an unsatisfied one. The motive forces of phantasies are unsatisfied wishes, and every single phantasy is the fulfilment of a wish, a correction of unsatisfying reality. These motivating wishes vary according to the sex, character, and circumstances of the person who is having the phantasy; but they fall naturally into two main groups. They are either ambitious wishes, which serve to elevate the subject's personality; or they are erotic ones. In young women the erotic wishes predominate almost exclusively, for their ambition is as a rule absorbed by erotic trends. In young men egoistic and ambitious wishes come to the fore clearly enough alongside of erotic ones. But we will not lay stress on the opposition between the two trends; we would rather emphasize the fact that they are often united. Just as, in many altar-pieces, the portrait of the donor is to be seen in a corner of the picture, so, in the majority of ambitious phantasies, we can discover in some corner or other the lady for whom the creator of the phantasy performs all his heroic deeds and at whose feet all his triumphs are laid. Here, as you see, there are strong enough motives for concealment; the well-brought-up young woman is only allowed a minimum of erotic desire, and the young man has to learn to suppress the excess of self-regard which he brings with him from the spoilt days of his childhood, so that he may find his place in a society which is full of other individuals making equally strong demands.

We must not suppose that the products of this imaginative activity—the various phantasies, castles in the air and daydreams—are stereotyped or unalterable. On the contrary, they fit themselves in to the subject's shifting impressions of life, change with every change in his situation, and receive from every fresh active impression what might be called a 'datemark.' The relation of a phantasy to time is in general very important. We may say that it hovers, as it were, between three times—the three moments of time which our ideation involves. Mental work is linked to some current impression, some provoking occasion in the present which has been able to arouse one of the subject's major wishes. From there it harks back to a memory of an earlier experience (usually an infantile one) in which this wish was fulfilled; and it now creates a situation relating to the future which represents a fulfilment of the wish. What it thus creates is a day-dream or phantasy, which carries about it traces of its origin from the occasion which provoked it and from the memory. Thus past, present, and future are strung together, as it were, on the thread of the wish that runs through them.

A very ordinary example may serve to make what I have said clear. Let us take the case of a poor orphan boy to whom you have given the address of some employer where he may perhaps find a job. On his way there he may indulge in a day-dream appropriate to the situation from which it arises. The content of his phantasy will perhaps be something like this. He is given a job, finds favour with his new employer, makes himself indispensable in the business, is taken into his employer's family, marries the charming young daughter of the house, and then himself becomes a director of the business, first as his employer's partner and then as his successor. In this phantasy, the dreamer has regained what he possessed in his happy childhood—the protecting house, the loving parents, and the first objects of his affectionate feelings. You will see from this example the way in which the wish makes use of an occasion in the present to construct, on the pattern of the past, a picture of the future.

There is a great deal more that could be said about phantasies; but I will only allude as briefly as possible to certain points. If phantasies become overluxuriant and overpowerful, the conditions are laid for an onset of neurosis or psychosis. Phantasies, moreover, are the immediate mental precursors of the distressing symptoms complained of by our patients. Here a broad bypath branches off into pathology.

I cannot pass over the relation of phantasies to dreams. Our dreams at night are nothing else than phantasies like these, as we can demonstrate from the interpretation of dreams. Language, in its unrivalled wisdom, long ago decided the question of the essential nature of dreams by giving the name of 'daydreams' to the airy creations of phantasy. If the meaning of our dreams usually remains obscure to us in spite of this pointer, it is because of the circumstance that at night there also arise in us wishes of which we are ashamed; these we must conceal from ourselves, and they have consequently been repressed, pushed into the unconscious. Repressed wishes of this sort and their derivatives are only allowed to come to expression in a very distorted form. When scientific work had succeeded in elucidating this factor of *dream-distortion*, it was no longer difficult to recognize that night-dreams are wish-fulfilments in just the same way as day-dreams—the phantasies which we all know so well.

So much for phantasies. And now for the creative writer. May we really attempt to compare the imaginative writer with the 'dreamer in broad daylight,' and his creations with day-dreams? Here we must begin by making an initial distinction. We must

separate writers who, like the ancient authors of epics and tragedies, take over their material ready-made, from writers who
seem to originate their own material. We will keep to the latter
kind, and, for the purposes of our comparison, we will choose not
the writers most highly esteemed by the critics, but the less
pretentious authors of novels, romances and short stories, who
nevertheless have the widest and most eager circle of readers
of both sexes. One feature above all cannot fail to strike us about
the creations of these story-writers: each of them has a hero who
is the centre of interest, for whom the writer tries to win our
sympathy by every possible means and whom he seems to place
under the protection of a special Providence. If, at the end of
one chapter of my story, I leave the hero unconscious and bleed-
ing from severe wounds, I am sure to find him at the beginning
of the next being carefully nursed and on the way to recovery;
and if the first volume closes with the ship he is in going down
in a storm at sea, I am certain, at the opening of the second
volume, to read of his miraculous rescue—a rescue without which
the story could not proceed. The feeling of security with which
I follow the hero through his perilous adventures is the same as
the feeling with which a hero in real life throws himself into the
water to save a drowning man or exposes himself to the enemy's
fire in order to storm a battery. It is the true heroic feeling, which
one of our best writers has expressed in an inimitable phrase:
"Nothing can happen to *me!*" It seems to me, however, that
through this revealing characteristic of invulnerability we can
immediately recognize His Majesty the Ego, the hero alike of
every day-dream and of every story.

Other typical features of these egocentric stories point to the
same kinship. The fact that all the women in the novel invariably
fall in love with the hero can hardly be looked on as a portrayal
of reality, but it is easily understood as a necessary constituent
of a day-dream. The same is true of the fact that the other characters in the story are sharply divided into good and bad, in
defiance of the variety of human characters that are to be observed in real life. The 'good' ones are the helpers, while the 'bad'
ones are the enemies and rivals, of the ego which has become
the hero of the story.

We are perfectly aware that very many imaginative writings

are far removed from the model of the naïve day-dream; and yet I cannot suppress the suspicion that even the most extreme deviations from that model could be linked with it through an uninterrupted series of transitional cases. It has struck me that in many of what are known as 'psychological' novels only one person—once again the hero—is described from within. The author sits inside his mind, as it were, and looks at the other characters from outside. The psychological novel in general no doubt owes its special nature to the inclination of the modern writer to split up his ego, by self-observation, into many part-egos, and, in consequence, to personify the conflicting currents of his own mental life in several heroes. Certain novels, which might be described as 'eccentric,' seem to stand in quite special contrast to the types of the day-dream. In these, the person who is introduced as the hero plays only a very small active part; he sees the actions and sufferings of other people pass before him like a spectator. Many of Zola's later works belong to this category. But I must point out that the psychological analysis of individuals who are not creative writers, and who diverge in some respects from the so-called norm, has shown us analogous variations of the day-dream, in which the ego contents itself with the role of spectator.

If our comparison of the imaginative writer with the day-dreamer, and of poetical creation with the day-dream, is to be of any value, it must, above all, show itself in some way or other fruitful. Let us, for instance, try to apply to these authors' works the thesis we laid down earlier concerning the relation between phantasy and the three periods of time and the wish which runs through them; and, with its help, let us try to study the connections that exist between the life of the writer and his works. No one has known, as a rule, what expectations to frame in approaching this problem; and often the connection has been thought of in much too simple terms. In the light of the insight we have gained from phantasies, we ought to expect the following state of affairs. A strong experience in the present awakens in the creative writer a memory of an earlier experience (usually belonging to his childhood) from which there now proceeds a wish which finds its fulfilment in the creative work. The work itself exhibits elements of the recent provoking occasion as well as of the old memory.

Do not be alarmed at the complexity of this formula. I suspect that in fact it will prove to be too exiguous a pattern. Nevertheless, it may contain a first approach to the true state of affairs; and, from some experiments I have made, I am inclined to think that this way of looking at creative writings may turn out not unfruitful. You will not forget that the stress it lays on childhood memories in the writer's life—a stress which may perhaps seem puzzling—is ultimately derived from the assumption that a piece of creative writing, like a day-dream, is a continuation of, and a substitute for, what was once the play of childhood.

We must not neglect, however, to go back to the kind of imaginative works which we have to recognize, not as original creations, but as the refashioning of ready-made and familiar material. Even here, the writer keeps a certain amount of independence, which can express itself in the choice of material and in changes in it which are often quite extensive. In so far as the material is already at hand, however, it is derived from the popular treasure-house of myths, legends, and fairy tales. The study of constructions of folk psychology such as these is far from being complete, but it is extremely probable that myths, for instance, are distorted vestiges of the wishful phantasies of whole nations, the *secular dreams* of youthful humanity.

You will say that, although I have put the creative writer first in the title of my paper, I have told you far less about him than about phantasies. I am aware of that, and I must try to excuse it by pointing to the present state of our knowledge. All I have been able to do is to throw out some encouragements and suggestions which, starting from the study of phantasies, lead on to the problem of the writer's choice of his literary material. As for the other problem—by what means the creative writer achieves the emotional effects in us that are aroused by his creations—we have as yet not touched on it at all. But I should like at least to point out to you the path that leads from our discussion of phantasies to the problems of poetical effects.

You will remember how I have said that the day-dreamer carefully conceals his phantasies from other people because he feels he has reasons for being ashamed of them. I should now add that even if he were to communicate them to us he could give us no pleasure by his disclosures. Such phantasies, when we learn them, repel us or at least leave us cold. But when a creative writer presents his plays to us or tells us what we are inclined to take to be his personal day-dreams, we experience a great pleasure, and one which probably arises from the confluence of many sources. How the writer accomplishes this is his innermost secret; the essential *ars poetica* lies in the technique of overcoming the feeling of repulsion in us which is undoubtedly connected with the barriers that rise between each single ego and the others. We can guess two of the methods used by this technique. The writer softens the character of his egoistic day-dreams by altering and disguising it, and he bribes us by the purely formal—that is, aesthetic—yield of pleasure which he offers us in the presentation of his phantasies. We give the name of an *incentive bonus,* or a *forepleasure,* to a yield of pleasure such as this, which is offered to us so as to make possible the release of still greater pleasure arising from deeper psychical sources. In my opinion, all the aesthetic pleasure which a creative writer affords us has the character of a forepleasure of this kind, and our actual enjoyment of an imaginative work proceeds from a liberation of tensions in our minds. It may even be that not a little of this effect is due to the writer's enabling us thenceforward to enjoy our own day-dreams without self-reproach or shame. This brings us to the threshold of new, interesting, and complicated enquiries; but also, at least for the moment, to the end of our discussion.

SOME CHARACTER-TYPES MET WITH IN PSYCHOANALYTIC WORK

THOSE WRECKED BY SUCCESS

Psychoanalytic work has furnished us with the thesis that people fall ill of a neurosis as a result of *frustration.* What is meant is the frustration of the satisfaction of their libidinal wishes, and some digression is necesary in order to make the thesis intelligible. For a neurosis to be generated there must be a conflict between a person's libidinal wishes and the part of his personality we call his ego, which is the expression of his instinct of self-preservation and which also includes his *ideals* of his personality. A pathogenic conflict of this kind takes place only when the libido tries to follow paths and aims which the ego has long since overcome and condemned and has therefore prohibited for ever; and this the libido only does if it is deprived of the possibility of an ideal ego-syntonic satisfaction. Hence privation, frustration of a real satisfaction, is the first condition for the generation of a neurosis, although, indeed, it is far from being the only one.

So much the more surprising, and indeed bewildering, must it appear when as a doctor one makes the discovery that people occasionally fall ill precisely when a deeply-rooted and long-cherished wish has come to fulfilment. It seems then as though they were not able to tolerate their happiness; for there can be no question that there is a casual connection between their success and their falling ill.

I had an opportunity of obtaining an insight into a woman's history, which I propose to describe as typical of these tragic occurrences. She was of good birth and well brought-up, but as quite a young girl she could not restrain her zest for life; she ran away from home and roved about the world in search of adventures, till she made the acquaintance of an artist who could appreciate her feminine charms but could also divine, in spite of what she had fallen to, the finer qualities she possessed. He took her to live with him, and she proved a faithful companion to him, and seemed only to need social rehabilitation to achieve complete happiness. After many years of life together, he succeeded in getting his family reconciled to her, and was then prepared to make her his legal wife. At that moment she began to go to pieces. She neglected the house of which she was now about to become the rightful mistress, imagined herself persecuted by his relatives, who wanted to take her into the family, debarred her lover, through her senseless jealousy, from all social intercourse, hindered him in his artistic work, and soon succumbed to an incurable mental illness.

On another occasion I came across the case of a most respectable man who, himself an academic teacher, had for many years cherished the natural wish to succeed the master who had initiated him into his own studies. When this older man retired, and his colleagues informed him that it was he who was chosen as successor, he began to hesitate, depreciated his merits, declared himself unworthy to fill the position designed for him, and fell into a melancholia which unfitted him for all activity for some years.

Different as these two cases are in other respects, they yet agree in this one point: the illness followed close upon the fulfilment of a wish and put an end to all enjoyment of it.

The contradiction between such experiences and the rule that what induces illness is frustration is not insoluble. It disappears if we make a distinction between an *external* and an *internal* frustration. If the object in which the libido can find its satisfaction is withheld *in reality*, this is an external frustration. In itself it is inoperative, not pathogenic, until an internal frustration is joined to it. This latter must proceed from the ego, and must dispute the access by the libido to other objects, which it now seeks to get hold of. Only then does a conflict arise, and the possibility of a neurotic illness, i.e. of a substitutive satisfaction reached circuitously by way of the repressed unconscious. Internal frustration is potentially present, therefore, in every case, only it does not come into operation until external, real frustration has prepared the ground for it. In those exceptional cases in which people are made ill by success, the internal frustration has operated by itself; indeed it has only made its appearance after an external frustration has been replaced by fulfilment of a wish. At first sight there is something strange about this; but on closer consideration we shall reflect that it is not at all unusual for the ego to tolerate a wish as harmless so long as it exists in phantasy alone and seems remote from fulfilment, whereas the ego will defend itself hotly against such a wish as soon as it approaches fulfilment and threatens to become a reality. The distinction between this and familiar situations in neurosis-formation is merely that ordinarily it is internal intensifications of the libidinal cathexis that turn the phantasy, which has hitherto been thought little of and tolerated, into a dreaded opponent; while in these cases of ours the signal for the outbreak of conflict is given by a real external change.

Analytic work has no difficulty in showing us that it is forces of conscience which forbid the subject to gain the long hoped-for advantage from the fortunate change in reality. It is a difficult task, however, to discover the essence and origin of these judging and punishing trends, which so often surprise us by their existence where we do not expect to find them. For the usual reasons [1] I shall not discuss what we know or conjecture on the point in relation to cases of clinical observation, but in relation to figures which great writers have created from the wealth of their knowledge of the mind.

We may take as an example of a person who collapses on reaching success, after striving for it with single-minded energy, the figure of Shakespeare's Lady Macbeth. Beforehand there is no hesitation, no sign of any internal conflict in her, no endeavour but that of overcoming the scruples of her ambitious and yet tender-minded husband. She is ready to sacrifice even her womanliness to her murderous intention, without reflecting on the decisive part which this womanliness must play when the question afterwards arises of preserving the aim of her ambition, which has been attained through a crime.

> Come, you spirits
> That tend on mortal thoughts, unsex me here
> . . . Come to my woman's breasts,
> And take my milk for gall, you murdering ministers!
> (Act I, Sc. 5.)

> . . . I have given suck, and know
> How tender 'tis to love the babe that milks me:
> I would, while it was smiling in my face,
> Have pluck'd my nipple from his boneless gums,
> And dashed the brains out, had I so sworn as you
> Have done to this.
> (Act I, Sc. 7.)

One solitary faint stirring of reluctance comes over her before the deed:

[1] i.e., Freud's desire to respect the confidences of his patients. (Ed.)

> . . . Had he not resembled
> My father as he slept, I had done it . . .
>
> (Act II, Sc. 2.)

Then, when she has become Queen through the murder of
Duncan, she betrays for a moment something like disappointment, something like disillusionment. We cannot tell why.

> . . . Nought's had, all's spent,
> Where our desire is got without content:
> 'Tis safer to be that which we destroy,
> Than by destruction dwell in doubtful joy.
>
> (Act III, Sc. 2.)

Nevertheless, she holds out. In the banqueting scene which
follows on these words, she alone keeps her head, cloaks her
husband's state of confusion, and finds a pretext for dismissing
the guests. And then she disappears from view. We next see her
in the sleepwalking scene in the last Act, fixated to the impressions of the night of the murder. Once again, as then, she seeks
to put heart into her husband:

Fie, my lord, fie! a soldier, and afeard? What need we fear who
knows it, when none can call our power to account?

> (Act V, Sc. 1.)

She hears the knocking at the door, which terrified her husband after the deed. But at the same time she strives to "undo
the deed which cannot be undone." She washes her hands,
which are bloodstained and smell of blood, and is conscious of
the futility of the attempt. She who had seemed so remorseless
seems to have been borne down by remorse. When she dies,
Macbeth, who meanwhile has become as inexorable as she had
been in the beginning, can only find a brief epitaph for her:

> She should have died hereafter;
> There would have been a time for such a word.
>
> (Act V, Sc. 5.)

And now we ask ourselves what it was that broke this character which had seemed forged from the toughest metal? Is it
only disillusionment—the different aspect shown by the accomplished deed—and are we to infer that even in Lady Macbeth

an originally gentle and womanly nature had been worked up to a concentration and high tension which could not endure for long, or ought we to seek for signs of a deeper motivation which will make this collapse more humanly intelligible to us?

It seems to me impossible to come to any decision. Shakespeare's *Macbeth* is a *pièce d'occasion,* written for the accession of James, who had hitherto been King of Scotland. The plot was ready-made, and had been handled by other contemporary writers, whose work Shakespeare probably made use of in his customary manner. It offered remarkable analogies to the actual situation. The 'virginal' Elizabeth, of whom it was rumoured that she had never been capable of childbearing and who had once described herself as 'a barren stock,' [2] in an anguished outcry at the news of James's birth, was obliged by this very childlessness of hers to make the Scottish king her successor. And he was the son of the Mary Stuart whose execution she, even though reluctantly, had ordered, and who, in spite of the clouding of their relations by political concerns, was nevertheless of her blood and might be called her guest.

The accession of James I was like a demonstration of the curse of unfruitfulness and the blessings of continuous generation. And the action of Shakespeare's *Macbeth* is based on this same contrast.

The Weird Sisters assured Macbeth that he himself should be king, but to Banquo they promised that his children should succeed to the crown. Macbeth is incensed by this decree of destiny. He is not content with the satisfaction of his own ambition. He wants to found a dynasty—not to have murdered for the benefit of strangers. This point is overlooked if Shakespeare's play is regarded only as a tragedy of ambition. It is clear that Macbeth cannot live for ever, and thus there is but one way for him to invalidate the part of the prophecy which opposes him—namely, to have children himself who can succeed him. And he seems to expect them from his indomitable wife:

[2] Cf. *Macbeth,* Act III, Sc. 1:
>Upon my head they placed a fruitless crown,
>And put a barren sceptre in my gripe,
>Thence to be wrenched with an unlineal hand,
>No son of mine succeeding . . .

> Bring forth men-children only!
> For thy undaunted mettle should compose
> Nothing but males . . . .
>
> (Act I, Sc. 7.)

And equally it is clear that if he is deceived in this expectation he must submit to destiny; otherwise his actions lose all purpose and are transformed into the blind fury of one doomed to destruction, who is resolved to destroy beforehand all that he can reach. We watch Macbeth pass through this development, and at the height of the tragedy we hear Macduff's shattering cry, which has so often been recognized to be ambiguous and which may perhaps contain the key to the change in Macbeth:

> He has no children!
>
> (Act IV, Sc. 3.)

There is no doubt that this means: 'Only because he is himself childless could he murder my children.' But more may be implied in it, and above all it might lay bare the deepest motive which not only forces Macbeth to go far beyond his own nature, but also touches the hard character of his wife at its only weak point. If one surveys the whole play from the summit marked by these words of Macduff's, one sees that it is sown with references to the father-children relation. The murder of the kindly Duncan is little else than parricide; in Banquo's case, Macbeth kills the father while the son escapes him; and in Macduff's, he kills the children because the father has fled from him. A bloody child, and then a crowned one, are shown him by the witches in the apparition scene; the armed head which is seen earlier is no doubt Macbeth himself. But in the background rises the sinister form of the avenger, Macduff, who is himself an exception to the laws of generation, since he was not born of his mother but ripp'd from her womb.

It would be a perfect example of poetic justice in the manner of the talion if the childlessness of Macbeth and the barrenness of his Lady were the punishment for their crimes against the sanctity of generation—if Macbeth could not become a father because he had robbed children of their father and a father of his children, and if Lady Macbeth suffered the unsexing she had demanded of the spirits of murder. I believe Lady Macbeth's illness, the transformation of her callousness into penitence, could be explained directly as a reaction of her childlessness, by which she is convinced of her impotence against the decrees of nature, and at the same time reminded that it is through her own fault if her crime has been robbed of the better part of its fruits.

In Holinshed's *Chronicle* (1577), from which Shakespeare took the plot of *Macbeth*, Lady Macbeth is only once mentioned as the ambitious wife who instigates her husband to murder in order that she may herself become queen. There is no mention of her subsequent fate and of the development of her character. On the other hand, it would seem that the change of Macbeth's character into a bloodthirsty tyrant is ascribed to the same motives as we have suggested here. For in Holinshed *ten years* pass between the murder of Duncan, through which Macbeth becomes king, and his further misdeeds; and in these ten years he is shown as a stern but just ruler. It is not until after this lapse of time that the change begins in him, under the influence of the tormenting fear that the prophecy to Banquo may be fulfilled just as the prophecy of his own destiny has been. Only then does he contrive the murder of Banquo, and, as in Shakespeare, is driven from one crime to another. It is not expressly stated in Holinshed that it was his childlessness which urged him to these courses, but enough time and room is given for that plausible motive. Not so in Shakespeare. Events crowd upon us in the tragedy with breathless haste so that, to judge by the statements made by the characters in it, the course of its action covers about *one week*. This acceleration takes the ground from under all our constructions of the motives for the change in the characters of Macbeth and his wife. There is no time for a long-drawn-out disappointment of their hopes of offspring to break the woman down and drive the man to defiant rage; and the contradiction remains that though so many subtle interrelations in the plot, and between it and its occasion, point to a common origin of them in the theme of childlessness, nevertheless the economy of time in the tragedy expressly precludes a development of character from any motives but those inherent in the action itself.

What, however, these motives can have been which in so short a space of time could turn the hesitating, ambitious man into an unbridled tyrant, and his steely-hearted instigator into a sick woman gnawed by remorse, it is, in my view, impossible to guess. We must, I think, give up any hope of penetrating the triple layer of obscurity into which the bad preservation of the text, the unknown intention of the dramatist, and the hidden purport of the legend have become condensed. But I should not subscribe to the objection that investigations like these are idle in face of the powerful effect which the tragedy has upon the spectator. The dramatist can indeed, during the representation, overwhelm us by his art and paralyse our powers of reflection; but he cannot prevent us from attempting subsequently to grasp its effect by studying its psychological mechanism. Nor does the contention that a dramatist is at liberty to shorten at will the natural chronology of the events he brings before us, if by the sacrifice of common probability he can enhance the dramatic effect, seem to me relevant in this instance. For such a sacrifice is justified only when it merely interferes with probability,[3] and not when it breaks the causal connection; moreover, the dramatic effect would hardly have suffered if the passage of time had been left indeterminate, instead of being expressly limited to a few days.

One is so unwilling to dismiss a problem like that of *Macbeth* as insoluble that I will venture to bring up a fresh point, which may offer another way out of the difficulty. Ludwig Jekels, in a recent Shakespearean study,[4] thinks he has discovered a particular technique of the poet's, and this might apply to *Macbeth*. He believes that Shakespeare often splits a character up into two personages, which, taken separately, are not completely understandable and do not become so until they are brought together once more into a unity. This might be so with Macbeth and Lady Macbeth. In that case it would of course be pointless to regard her as an independent character and seek to discover the motives for her change, without considering the Macbeth who completes her. I shall not follow this clue any further, but

[3] As in Richard III's wooing of Anne beside the bier of the King whom he has murdered.
[4] This does not appear to have been published. In a later paper on *Macbeth*, Jekels (1917) barely refers to this theory, apart from quoting the present paragraph. In a still later paper, on 'The Psychology of Comedy,' Jekels (1926) returns to the subject, but again very briefly.

I should, nevertheless, like to point out something which strikingly confirms this view: the germs of fear which break out in Macbeth on the night of the murder do not develop further in *him* but in *her*. It is he who has the hallucination of the dagger before the crime; but it is she who afterwards falls ill of a mental disorder. It is he who after the murder hears the cry in the house: "Sleep no more! Macbeth does murder sleep . . ." and so "Macbeth shall sleep no more"; but we never hear that *he* slept no more, while the Queen, as we see, rises from her bed and, talking in her sleep, betrays her guilt. It is he who stands helpless with bloody hands, lamenting that "all great Neptune's ocean" will not wash them clean, while she comforts him: "A little water clears us of this deed"; but later it is she who washes her hands for a quarter of an hour and cannot get rid of the bloodstains: "All the perfumes of Arabia will not sweeten this little hand." Thus what he feared in his pangs of conscience is fulfilled in her; she becomes all remorse and he all defiance. Together they exhaust the possibilities of reaction to the crime, like two disunited parts of a single psychical individuality, and it may be that they are both copied from a single prototype.

If we have been unable to give any answer to the question why Lady Macbeth should collapse after her success, we may perhaps have a better chance when we turn to the creation of another great dramatist, who loves to pursue problems of psychological responsibility with unrelenting rigour.

Rebecca Gamvik, the daughter of a midwife, has been brought up by her adopted father, Dr. West, to be a freethinker and to despise the restrictions which a morality founded on religious belief seeks to impose on the desires of life. After the doctor's death she finds a position at Rosmersholm, the home for many generations of an ancient family whose members know nothing of laughter and have sacrificed joy to rigid fulfilment of duty. Its occupants are Johannes Rosmer, a former pastor, and his invalid wife, the childless Beata. Overcome by "a wild, uncontrollable passion"[5] for the love of the highborn Rosmer, Rebecca resolves to remove the wife who stands in her way, and to this end makes use of her "fearless, free will," which is re-

[5] Quotations are based on William Archer's English translation. (Ed.)

strained by no scruples. She contrives that Beata shall read a medical book in which the aim of marriage is represented to be the begetting of offspring, so that the poor woman begins to doubt whether her own marriage is justifiable. Rebecca then hints that Rosmer, whose studies and ideas she shares, is about to abandon the old faith and join the "party of enlightenment"; and after she has thus shaken the wife's confidence in her husband's moral integrity, gives her finally to understand that she, Rebecca, will soon leave the house in order to conceal the consequences of her illicit intercourse with Rosmer. The criminal scheme succeeds. The poor wife, who has passed for depressed and irresponsible, throws herself from the path beside the mill into the millrace, possessed by the sense of her own worthlessness and wishing no longer to stand between her beloved husband and his happiness.

For more than a year Rebecca and Rosmer have been living alone at Rosmersholm in a relationship which he wishes to regard as a purely intellectual and ideal friendship. But when this relationship begins to be darkened from outside by the first shadow of gossip, and at the same time tormenting doubts arise in Rosmer about the motives for which his wife put an end to herself, he begs Rebecca to become his second wife, so that they may counter the unhappy past with a new living reality (Act II). For an instant she exclaims with joy at his proposal, but immediately afterwards declares that it can never be, and that if he urges her further she will "go the way Beata went." Rosmer cannot understand this rejection; and still less can we, who know more of Rebecca's actions and designs. All we can be certain of is that her "no" is meant in earnest.

How could it come about that the adventuress with the "fearless, free will," who forged her way ruthlessly to her desired goal, should now refuse to pluck the fruit of success when it is offered to her? She herself gives us the explanation in the fourth Act: "*This* is the terrible part of it: that now, when all life's happiness is within my grasp—my heart is changed and my own past cuts me off from it." That is to say, she has in the meantime become a different being; her conscience has awakened, she has acquired a sense of guilt which debars her from enjoyment.

And what has awakened her conscience? Let us listen to her

herself, and then consider whether we can believe her entirely.
"It is the Rosmer view of life—or your view of life at any rate—
that has infected my will. . . . And made it sick. Enslaved it to
laws that had no power over me before. You—life with you—
has ennobled my mind."

This influence, we are further to understand, has only become
effective since she has been able to live alone with Rosmer: "In
quiet—in solitude—when you showed me all your thoughts
without reserve—every tender and delicate feeling, just as it
came to you—*then* the great change came over me."

Shortly before this she has lamented the other aspect of the
change: "Because Rosmersholm has sapped my strength. My old
fearless will has had its wings clipped here. It is crippled! The
time is past when I had courage for anything in the world. I
have lost the power of action, Rosmer."

Rebecca makes this declaration after she had revealed herself
as a criminal in a voluntary confession to Rosmer and Rector
Kroll, the brother of the woman she has got rid of. Ibsen has
made it clear by small touches of masterly subtlety that Rebecca
does not actually tell lies, but is never entirely straightforward.
Just as, in spite of all her freedom from prejudices, she has
understated her age by a year, so her confession to the two men
is incomplete, and as a result of Kroll's insistence it is supplemented on some important points. Hence it is open to us to
suppose that her explanation of her renunciation exposes one
motive only to conceal another.

Certainly, we have no reason to disbelieve her when she
declares that the atmosphere of Rosmersholm and her association with the highminded Rosmer have ennobled—and crippled
—her. She is here expressing what she knows and has felt. But
this is not necessarily all that has happened in her, nor need she
have understood all that has happened. Rosmer's influence may
only have been a cloak, which concealed another influence that
was operative, and a remarkable indication points in this other
direction.

Even after her confession, Rosmer, in their last conversation
which brings the play to an end, again beseeches her to be his
wife. He forgives her the crime she has committed for love of
him. And now she does not answer, as she should, that no for-

giveness can rid her of the feeling of guilt she has incurred from
her malignant deception of poor Beata; but she charges herself
with another reproach which affects us as coming strangely
from this freethinking woman, and is far from deserving the
importance which Rebecca attaches to it: "Dear—never speak
of this again! It is impossible! For you must know, Rosmer, I
have a—a past behind me." She means, of course, that she has
had sexual relations with another man; and we do not fail to
observe that these relations, which occurred at a time when she
was free and accountable to nobody, seem to her a greater
hindrance to the union with Rosmer than her truly criminal
behaviour to his wife.

Rosmer refuses to hear anything about this past. We can
guess what it was, though everything that refers to it in the play
is, so to speak, subterranean and has to be pieced together from
hints. But nevertheless they are hints inserted with such art that
it is impossible to misunderstand them.

Between Rebecca's first refusal and her confession something
occurs which has a decisive influence on her future destiny.
Rector Kroll arrives one day at the house on purpose to humiliate
Rebecca by telling her that he knows she is an illegitimate child,
the daughter of the very Dr. West who adopted her after her
mother's death. Hate has sharpened his perceptions, yet he does
not suppose that this is any news to her. "I really did not suppose you were ignorant of this, otherwise it would have been
very odd that you should have let Dr. West adopt you . . ." "And
then he takes you into his house—as soon as your mother dies.
He treats you harshly. And yet you stay with him. You know
that he won't leave you a halfpenny—as a matter of fact you
got only a case of books—and yet you stay on; you bear with
him; you nurse him to the last." . . . "I attribute your care for
him to the natural filial instinct of a daughter. Indeed, I believe
your whole conduct is a natural result of your origin."

But Kroll is mistaken. Rebecca had no idea at all that she
could be Dr. West's daughter. When Kroll began with dark
hints at her past, she must have thought he was referring to
something else. After she has gathered what he means, she can
still retain her composure for a while, for she is able to suppose
that her enemy is basing his calculations on her age, which she

had given falsely on an earlier visit of his. But Kroll demolishes this objection by saying: Well, so be it, but my calculation may be right, none the less; for Dr. West was up there on a short visit the year before he got the appointment." After this new information, she loses her self-possession. "It is not true!" She walks about wringing her hands. "It is impossible. You want to cheat me into believing it. This can never, never be true. It cannot be true. Never in this world!—" Her agitation is so extreme that Kroll cannot attribute it to his information alone.

KROLL: But, my dear Miss West—why in Heaven's name are you so terribly excited? You quite frighten me. What am I to think—to believe——?

REBECCA: Nothing. You are to think and believe nothing.

KROLL: Then you must really tell me how you can take this affair—this possibility—so terribly to heart.

REBECCA (*controlling herself*): It is perfectly simple, Rector Kroll. I have no wish to be taken for an illegitimate child.

The enigma of Rebecca's behaviour is susceptible of only one solution. The news that Dr. West was her father is the heaviest blow that can befall her, for she was not only his adopted daughter, but had been his mistress. When Kroll began to speak, she thought that he was hinting at these relations, the truth of which she would probably have admitted and justified by her emancipated ideas. But this was far from the Rector's intention; he knew nothing of the love-affair with Dr. West, just as she knew nothing of Dr. West's being her father. She *cannot* have had anything else in her mind but this love-affair when she accounted for her final rejection of Rosmer on the ground that she had a past which made her unworthy to be his wife. And probably, if Rosmer had consented to hear of that past, she would have confessed half her secret only and have kept silence on the more serious part of it.

But now we understand, of course, that this past must seem to her the more serious obstacle to their union—the more serious crime.

After she has learnt that she has been the mistress of her own father, she surrenders herself wholly to her now overmastering sense of guilt. She makes the confession to Rosmer and Kroll which stamps her as a murderess; she rejects for ever the happiness to which she has paved the way by crime, and prepares for departure. But the true motive of her sense of guilt, which results in her being wrecked by success, remains a secret. As we have seen, it is something quite other than the atmosphere of Rosmersholm and the refining influence of Rosmer.

At this point no one who has followed us will fail to bring forward an objection which may justify some doubts. Rebecca's first refusal of Rosmer occurs before Kroll's second visit, and therefore before his exposure of her illegitimate origin and at a time when she as yet knows nothing of her incest—if we have rightly understood the dramatist. Yet this first refusal is energetic and seriously meant. The sense of guilt which bids her renounce the fruit of her actions is thus effective before she knows anything of her cardinal crime; and if we grant so much, we ought perhaps entirely to set aside her incest as a source of that sense of guilt.

So far we have treated Rebecca West as if she were a living person and not a creation of Ibsen's imagination, which is always directed by the most critical intelligence. We may therefore attempt to maintain the same position in dealing with the objection that has been raised. The objection is valid: before the knowledge of her incest, conscience was already in part awakened in Rebecca; and there is nothing to prevent our making the influence which is acknowledged and blamed by Rebecca herself responsible for this change. But this does not exempt us from recognizing the second motive. Rebecca's behaviour when she hears what Kroll has to tell her, the confession which is her immediate reaction, leave no doubt that then only does the stronger and decisive motive for renunciation begin to take effect. It is in fact a case of multiple motivation, in which a deeper motive comes into view behind the more superficial one. Laws of poetic economy necessitate this way of presenting the situation, for this deeper motive could not be explicitly enunciated. It had to remain concealed, kept from the easy perception of the spectator or the reader; otherwise serious resistances, based on the most distressing emotions, would have arisen, which might have imperilled the effect of the drama.

We have, however, a right to demand that the explicit motive shall not be without an internal connection with the concealed one, but shall appear as a mitigation of, and a derivation from, the latter. And if we may rely on the fact that the dramatist's conscious creative combination arose logically from unconscious premises, we may now make an attempt to show that he has fulfilled this demand. Rebecca's feeling of guilt has its source in the reproach of incest, even before Kroll, with analytical perspicacity, has made her conscious of it. If we reconstruct her past, expanding and filling in the author's hints, we may feel sure that she cannot have been without some inkling of the intimate relation between her mother and Dr. West. It must have made a great impression on her when she became her mother's successor with this man. She stood under the domination of the Oedipus complex, even though she did not know that this universal phantasy had in her case become a reality. When she came to Rosmersholm, the inner force of this first experience drove her into bringing about, by vigorous action, the same situation which had been realized in the original instance through no doing of hers—into getting rid of the wife and mother, so that she might take her place with the husband and father. She describes with a convincing insistence how, against her will, she was obliged to proceed, step by step, to the removal of Beata.

You think then that I was cool and calculating and self-possessed all the time! I was not the same woman then that I am now, as I stand here telling it all. Besides, there are two sorts of will in us, I believe! I wanted Beata away, by one means or another; but I never really believed that it would come to pass. As I felt my way forward, at each step I ventured, I seemed to hear something within me cry out: No farther! Not a step farther! And yet I *could* not stop. I *had* to venture the least little bit farther. And only one hair's-breadth more. And then one more—and always one more. And then it happened.— That is the way such things come about.

That is not an embellishment, but an authentic description. Everything that happened to her at Rosmersholm, her falling in love with Rosmer and her hostility to his wife, was from the first a consequence of the Oedipus complex—an inevitable replica of her relations with her mother and Dr. West.

And so the sense of guilt which first causes her to reject

Rosmer's proposal is at bottom no different from the greater one which drives her to her confession after Kroll has opened her eyes. But just as under the influence of Dr. West she had become a freethinker and despiser of religious morality, so she is transformed by her love for Rosmer into a being of conscience and nobility. This much of the mental processes within her she herself understands, and so she is justified in describing Rosmer's influence as the motive for her change—the motive that had become accessible to her.

The practising psycho-analytic physician knows how frequently, or how invariably, a girl who enters a household as servant, companion, or governess, will consciously or unconsciously weave a day-dream, which derives from the Oedipus complex, of the mistress of the house disappearing and the master taking the newcomer as his wife in her place. *Rosmersholm* is the greatest work of art of the class that treats of this common phantasy in girls. What makes it into a tragic drama is the extra circumstance that the heroine's day-dream had been preceded in her childhood by a precisely corresponding reality.

After this long digression into literature, let us return to clinical experience—but only to establish in a few words the complete agreement between them. Psychoanalytic work teaches that the forces of conscience which induce illness in consequence of success, instead of, as normally, in consequence of frustration, are closely connected with the Oedipus complex, the relation to father and mother—as perhaps, indeed, is our sense of guilt in general.

Carl G. Jung

[1875–1961]

~~~~~

JUNG'S COLLABORATION with Freud began in 1906 while Jung was at the Burghölzli clinic in Switzerland. After meeting in 1908 the two remained close friends until 1912. In that year, Jung published his *Psychology of the Unconscious*, which Freud accused of having mystic tendencies. Freud's side of the quarrel is related in his "History of the Psychoanalytic Movement," and Jung's in "Freud and Jung—Contrasts," in *Modern Man in Search of a Soul* (1933). The quarrel persists today with clinical psychiatrists generally favoring Freud and artists and critics increasingly favoring Jung.

The central doctrine of Jung's "analytical psychology" is that of the Collective Unconscious. This is a form, pattern, or recurrent mode of viewing reality which is universal, a priori, and transmitted by heredity or some other mechanism. It manifests itself in archetypes which recur in the literature of all areas and regions. Jung's ideas have received a good deal of independent confirmation from the work of Sir James Frazer (*The Golden Bough*, 1890ff.) and the "Cambridge anthropologists" who followed him.

The collective unconscious is analogous to the Kantian imagination. Therefore, while Freud has appealed chiefly to critics in the scientific tradition, Jung has appealed to aesthetic critics. At present it seems fair to say that Jung is the dominant figure in psychological criticism.

Jung's *Collected Works*, in translation, are currently being issued by the Bollingen Foundation of New York. Several works have been published in paperbacked editions. For comment and further illustration of Jungian criticism see: J. Baird, *Call Me Ishmael* (Baltimore, 1956); M. Bodkin, *Archetypal Patterns in Poetry* (London, 1933); N. Frye, *The Anatomy of Criticism* (Princeton, 1957); H. Murray, ed., *Myths and Mythmaking* (New York, 1960).

The present selection is from Carl G. Jung, *Contributions to Analytical Psychology*, trans. by H. G. and Cary F. Baynes (London: Routledge and Kegan Paul, Ltd., 1928), pp. 225–49. Reprinted by permission of Bollingen Foundation, New York.

CONTRIBUTIONS TO ANALYTICAL PSYCHOLOGY

ON THE RELATION OF ANALYTICAL PSYCHOLOGY TO POETIC ART

NOTWITHSTANDING ITS manifold difficulties, the task of discussing the relation of analytical psychology to poetic art provides me with a not unwelcome occasion for defining my standpoint in regard to a much debated question; namely, the relation between psychology and art in general. In spite of their incommensurability both provinces are closely interrelated, and these connexions cannot remain unexplored. For they originate in the fact that art in practice is a psychological activity, and, in so far as this is the case, it actually requires a psychological consideration. Art, like every other human activity, proceeds from psychic motives, and from this angle, it is a proper object for psychology. But this conclusion also involves a very obvious limitation in the application of the psychological viewpoint: only that aspect of art which consists in the process of artistic form can be an object of psychology; whereas that which constitutes the essential nature of art must always lie outside its province. This other aspect, namely, the problem what is art in itself, can never be the object of a psychological, but only of an aesthetico-artistic method of approach.

A like distinction must also be made in the realm of religion; there also a psychological consideration is permissible only in respect of the emotional and symbolical phenomena of a religion, where the essential nature of religion is in no way involved, as indeed it cannot be. For were this possible, not religion alone, but art also could be treated as a mere subdivision of psychology. In saying this I do not mean to affirm that such an encroachment has not actually taken place. But whoever trespasses in this way clearly forgets that a similar fate can easily befall psychology, the specific value and essential quality of which is at once obliterated as soon as it is regarded as a mere brain activity, thus bringing it into line with other glandular activities as a mere subdivision of physiology. In actual fact, this depreciation has already occurred.

Art, by its very nature, is not science, and science is essentially not art; both provinces of the mind, therefore, have a reservation that is peculiar to them, and that can be explained only from themselves. Hence when we speak of the relation between psychology and art, we are treating only of that aspect of art which without encroachment can be submitted to a psychological manner of approach. Whatever psychology is able to determine about art will be confined to the psychological process of artistic activity, and will have nothing whatever to do with the innermost nature of art itself. It is as powerless in this respect as is the capacity of the intellect to present or even apprehend the nature of feeling. Moreover these two things could have no kind of existence as separate entities had not their essential difference long since challenged recognition. The fact that in the child, the "war of faculties" not yet having declared itself, we find artistic, scientific, and religious possibilities still slumbering tranquilly together; or that with the primitive, dispositions towards art, science, and religion still maintain an undifferentiated coexistence in the chaos of a magical mentality; or that, finally, with animals no trace of "mind" can as yet be discerned, but merely "natural instinct,"—all these facts hold no shadow of evidence for that essential unity in the nature of art and science which alone could justify a reciprocal subsumption, or in other words, a reduction of the one into the other. For if we go back far enough in the state of mental development for the essential differences of the individual provinces of the mind to have become altogether invisible, we have not thereby reached a deeper principle of their unity, but merely an earlier evolutionary state of undifferentiation in which neither province has yet any existence at all. But this elementary state is not a principle from which any conclusion regarding the nature of later and more highly developed states might be inferred, notwithstanding, as is of course always the case, that a direct descent can be demonstrated. The scientific attitude will naturally and constantly tend to overlook the nature of a differentiation in favour of its causal derivation, and will strive to subordinate the former to an idea that is certainly more general, but at the same time more elementary.

These reflections seem to me not inappropriate at the present time, for there have been frequent demonstrations of late of the way in which poetic art-works in particular may be submitted to an interpretation that is neither more nor less than a reduction to elementary conditions. Granted that the determinants of the artistic creation, the material and its individual treatment, for instance, can be traced back to the personal relations of the poet with his parents. Yet nothing is gained by this procedure for the understanding of his art, since we can perform the same reduction in every other possible case, and not the least in cases of pathological disorder. Neuroses and psychoses are also reducible to infantile relations with the parents, as are good and bad habits, convictions, qualities, passions, especial interests, and so forth. But we are surely not entitled to assume that all these very different things must, therefore, have one and the same explanation; for were this so, we should be driven to conclude that they were actually one and the same thing. Thus, if a work of art and a neurosis are explained in precisely similar terms, either the art-work must be a neurosis, or the neurosis a work of art. As a paradoxical play upon words such a *façon de parler* [manner of speaking] might pass muster, but a healthy human reason must assuredly revolt at the notion of art-work and neurosis being placed in the same category. To take the most extreme case, only an analysing physician viewing a neurosis through the spectacles of a professional bias could come to regard it as a work of art. But it would never occur to a thinking lay mind to confound art with a morbid phenomenon, in spite of the undeniable fact that the origin of a work of art must confess to similar psychological preconditions as a neurosis. This is only natural, since certain psychic preconditions are universally present, and furthermore, because of the relative similarity of human conditions of life these are constantly the same, whether in the case of a nervous intellectual, a poet, or a normal human being. All, doubtless, have had parents, all have a so-called father- and mother-complex, all have the onus of sexuality and, therewith, certain general and typical human difficulties. That one poet is influenced more by the relation to the father, another by the tie to the mother, while a third reveals unmistakable traces of repressed sexuality in his works—all this can be said equally well not only of every neurotic, but also of every normal human being. Hence nothing specific is thereby gained for the judgment of a work of art. At most our knowledge of the historic preconditions will have been somewhat broadened and deepened. The school of medical psychology inaugurated by Freud has certainly tended to inspire the literary historian to bring certain qualities of the individual work of art into relation with the personal and intimate life of the poet. But in so doing nothing more has been said than what the scientific treatment of poetic works had long since revealed, namely, the presence of certain threads, woven by the personal and intimate life of the poet—whether with or without conscious intention—into the fabric of his work. But the works of Freud may conceivably enable a more penetrating and exhaustive demonstration of these influences, reaching back even as far as earliest childhood, that so often affect the artistic creation.

When employed with taste and common sense, such treatment often provides an attractive general picture of the way in which the artistic creation is interwoven in the personal life of the artist, and also in a sense arises from it.

To this extent the so-called psycho-analysis of art-works differs in no essential way from a penetrating and skilfully shaded psychologico-literary analysis. The difference is at most a question of degree, although it may occasionally astound us by indiscreet conclusions and references that a rather more delicate touch, or a certain sense of tact might easily have avoided. This lack of delicacy in dealing with the all-too-human element, which seems to be a professional peculiarity of the medical psychologist, was perfectly understood by Mephistopheles: "So may you finger everything and welcome, round which another prowls for years and years"—although unfortunately not always to his own advantage. The possibility of daring conclusions may easily lead the way to flagrant lapses of taste. A slight touch of scandal often flavours a biography, but a little more becomes a nasty inquisitiveness, a catastrophe of good taste beneath the cloak of science. Our interest is unwittingly diverted from the work of art and gets lost in the mazy, labyrinthine confusion of psychic preconditions, the poet becomes a clinical case, even serving on occasion as a curious example of *psychopathia sexualis*. But therewith the psycho-analysis of the art-work has also turned aside from its objective, and the discussion has strayed into a province that is as broad as mankind, and not in the smallest degree specific for the artist; it therefore possesses even less relevance to his art.

This kind of analysis brings the work of art into the sphere of general human psychology, whence everything else besides art may proceed. An explanation of a work of art obtained in this way is just as great a futility as the statement that "every artist is a narcissist." Every man who pursues his own line to the limit of his powers is a "narcissist"—if indeed it is at all permissible to use a concept so specifically coined for the pathology of neuroses in this wider application—hence such a statement says nothing; it merely elicits surprise in the style of a *bon-mot*.

Because this kind of analysis is in no sense concerned with the art-work itself, but is always striving with the instinct of a mole to bury itself as quickly as possible in the murky background of the human psyche, it always finds itself in the same common earth that unites all mankind. Accordingly its explanations possess an indescribable monotony—that same tedious recital, in fact, which can daily be heard in certain medical consulting rooms.

The reductive method of Freud is purely a method of medical treatment that has for its object a morbid and unsuitable structure. This morbid structure has taken the place of normal accomplishment, and hence must be broken down before the way can be cleared for a sound adaptation. In this case the process of leading-back to a general human basis is entirely appropriate. But when applied to the work of art this method leads to the results depicted above. From beneath the shimmering robe of art it extracts the naked commonness of the elementary *homo sapiens,* to which species the poet also belongs. The golden semblance of sublime creation we were about to discuss is blotted out; for its essence is lost when we treat it with the corrosive method which has to be used for the deceptive phantasms of hysteria. The product obtained by this mordant technique is, of course, interesting and might conceivably possess the same kind of scientific value as for instance a post-mortem examination of the brain of Nietzsche, which might certainly teach us the particular atypical form of paralysis from which he died. But what would this have to do with Zarathustra? Whatever may have been its subterranean background, is this not a world in itself, beyond the human, all-too-human imperfections, beyond the world of migraine and cerebral atrophy?

I have spoken hitherto of Freud's reductive method without stating with any particularity in what the method consists. It has to do with a medico-psychological technique for the investigation of morbid psychic phenomena. This technique is exclusively occupied with ways and means for circumventing or peering through the conscious foreground in order to reach the so-called unconscious, or psychic background. It is based upon the assumption that the neurotic patient is repressing certain psychic contents from consciousness because of their incompatibility or inconsistency with conscious values. This incompatibilty is regarded as a moral one; accordingly, the repressed contents must bear a correspondingly negative character, namely, infantile-sexual, obscene, or even criminal. It is these qualities that render them so distasteful to consciousness. Since no man is perfect, it is clear that everyone must possess such a background whether the fact be admitted or not. Hence it can be disclosed in all cases if only we apply the technique of interpretation elaborated by Freud.

I cannot, of course, enter here into the details of the technique. A few intimations as to its nature must suffice. The unconscious background does not remain inactive, but betrays itself by certain characteristic effects upon the conscious contents. For example, it creates phantasy-products of a peculiar character, which are in most cases easily referable to certain subterranean sexual representations. Or it effects certain characteristic disturbances of the conscious process, which are likewise reducible to repressed contents. A most important source of the knowledge of unconscious contents is provided by dreams, which are direct products of the activity of the unconscious. The essential factor of Freud's reductive method consists in the fact, that it collects all the circumstantial evidence of the unconscious backgrounds, and, through the analysis and interpretation of this material, reconstructs the elementary, unconscious, instinctive processes. Those conscious contents which give us a clue, as it were, to the unconscious backgrounds are by Freud incorrectly termed symbols.

These are not true symbols, however, since, according to his teaching, they have merely the rôle of signs or symptoms of the background processes. The true symbol differs essentially from this, and should be understood as the expression of an intuitive perception which can as yet, neither be apprehended better, nor expressed differently. When, for example, Plato expresses the whole problem of the theory of cognition in his metaphor of the cave, or when Christ expresses the idea of the Kingdom of Heaven in his parables, these are genuine and true symbols; namely, attempts to express a thing, for which there exists as yet no adequate verbal concept. If we were to interpret Plato's metaphor in the manner of Freud we should naturally come to the uterus, and we should have proved that even the mind of Plato was deeply stuck in the primeval levels of "infantile sexuality." But in doing so we should also remain in total ignorance of what Plato actually created from the primitive antecedents of his philosophical intuition; we should, in fact, carelessly have overlooked his most essential product, merely to discover that he had "infantile" phantasies like every other mortal. Such a conclusion could possess value only for the man who regards Plato as a superhuman being, and who is therefore able to find a certain satisfaction in the fact that even Plato was also a man. But who would have to regard Plato as a god? Surely only a man who is afflicted by the tyranny of infantile phantasies, in other words, a neurotic mentality. For such a one the reduction to universal human truths is profitable on medical grounds. But this would have nothing whatever to do with the meaning of the Platonic parable.

I have purposely lingered over the relation between medical psycho-analysis and the work of art, because I want to emphasize the point that this kind of psycho-analysis is, at the same time, also the Freudian doctrine. Freud himself by his rigid dogmatism has seen to it that the two fundamentally different things should be regarded by the public as identical. Yet this technique may be employed with benefit in certain medical cases without any corresponding necessity to exalt it to the level of a doctrine. Indeed against this doctrine we are bound to raise vigorous objections. The assumptions it rests upon are quite arbitrary. In no sense, for example, are neuroses exclusively based upon sexual repression, and the same holds good for the psychoses. There is no foundation for saying that dreams merely contain repressed wishes the incompatibility of which requires them to be disguised by a hypothetical dream-censor. The Freudian technique, in so far as it remains under the influence of its own one-sided and, therefore, erroneous hypotheses, is patently arbitrary.

Before analytical psychology can do justice to the work of art it must entirely rid itself of medical prejudice; for the art-work is not a morbidity, and therefore demands a wholly different orientation from the medical. The physician must naturally seek the prime cause of a sickness in order to eradicate it, if possible, by the roots; but just as naturally must the psychologist adopt an exactly opposite attitude towards the work of art. He will not raise the question, which for the art-work is quite superfluous, concerning its undoubted general antecedents, its basic human determinants; but he will inquire into the meaning of the work, and will be concerned with its preconditions only in so far as they are necessary for the understanding of its meaning. Personal causality has as much and as little to do with the work of art, as the soil with the plant that springs from it. Doubtless we may learn to understand some peculiarities of the plant by becoming familiar with the character of its habitat. And for the botanist this is, of course, an important component of his knowledge. But nobody will maintain that he has thereby recognized all the essentials relating to the plant itself. The personal orientation that is demanded by the problem of personal causality is out of place in the presence of the work of art, just because the work of art is not a human being, but essentially suprapersonal. It is a thing and not a personality; hence the personal is no criterion for it. Indeed the especial significance of the genuine art-work lies in the fact, that it has successfully rid itself of the restraints and blind alleys of the personal and breathes an air infinitely remote from the transitoriness and short-winded excursions of the merely personal.

I must confess from my own experience that it is by no means easy for the physician to lay aside his professional spectacles when considering the work of art, and at the same time to clear his judgment of the current biological causality. But I have come to learn that although a psychology with a purely biological orientation can with a certain measure of justification be applied to men, it can never be applied to the true work of art, and still less to man as creator. A purely causalistic psychology is only able to reduce every human individuality to a member of the species *homo sapiens*, since its entire range is limited to what is either transmitted or derived. But the art-work is not merely transmitted or derived—it is a creative reorganization of those very determinants to which a causalistic psychology must always reduce it. The plant is not a mere product of the soil; but a living creative process centered in itself, the essence of which has nothing to do with the character of the soil. In the same way the art-work must be regarded as a creative formation, freely making use of every precondition. Its meaning and its own individual particularity rests in itself, and not in its preconditions. In fact one might almost describe it as a being that uses man and his personal dispositions merely as a cultural medium or soil, disposing his powers according to its own laws, while shaping itself to the fulfilment of its own creative purpose.

But here I am anticipating somewhat, since I have in mind a particular class of art-work which I must first introduce. For not every work of art is produced under this constellation. There are works, verse as well as prose writings, that proceed wholly from the author's intention and resolve to produce this or that effect. In this case the author submits his material to a definite treatment that is both directed and purposeful; he adds to it and subtracts from it, emphasizing one effect, modifying another, laying on this colour here, that there, with the most careful weighing of their possible effects, and with constant observance of the laws of beautiful form and style. To this labour the author brings his keenest judgment, and selects his expression with the most complete freedom. In his view his material is only material, and entirely subject to his artistic purpose; he wills to present this and nothing else. In this activity the poet is simply identical with the creative process, whether he has willingly surrendered himself as the head of the creative movement, or whether this has so entirely seized upon him as a tool or instrument that all consciousness of the fact has escaped him. He is the creative process itself, standing completely in it and undifferentiated from it with all his aims and all his powers. There is no need, I think, to bring before you examples of this identity, either from the history of literature or from the poets' own confessions.

Doubtless, also, I am saying nothing new when I speak of the other class of art-works, that flow more or less spontaneous and perfect from the author's pen. They come as it were fully arrayed into the world, as Pallas Athene sprang from the head of Zeus. These works positively impose themselves upon the author; his hand is, as it were, seized, and his pen writes things that his mind perceives with amazement. The work brings with it its own form; what he would add to it is declined, what he does not wish to admit is forced upon him. While his consciousness stands disconcerted and empty before the phenomenon, he is overwhelmed with a flood of thought and images which it was never his aim to beget and which his will would never have fashioned. Yet in spite of himself he is forced to recognize that in all this his self is speaking, that his innermost nature is revealing itself, uttering things that he would never have entrusted to his tongue. He can only obey and follow the apparently foreign impulse, feeling that his work is greater than himself, and therefore has a power over him that he is quite unable to command. He is not identical with the process of creative formation; he is himself conscious of the fact that he stands as it were underneath his work, or at all events beside it, as though he were another person who had fallen within the magic circle of an alien will.

When we are speaking of the psychology of a work of art, before all else we must bear in mind these two entirely different possibilities of the origin of a work, since much that is of the greatest importance for psychological judgment hangs upon this discrimination. This antithesis was also sensed by Schiller; he sought, as we know, to embrace it with the concept, sentimental and naïve. The choice of his expression is probably based upon the fact that he had mainly the poetic activity in view. Psychologically we term the former kind introverted, the latter extraverted. The introverted attitude is characterized by an upholding of the subject with his conscious ends and aims against the claims and pretensions of the object; the extraverted attitude, on the contrary, is distinguished by a subordination of the subject to the claims of the object. In my view, Schiller's dramas give a good idea of the introverted attitude to material, as do most of his poems. The material is mastered by the aim of the poet. For the opposite attitude the second part of *Faust* gives us a good illustration. Here the material distinguishes itself by its refractory obstinacy. A still more striking example is Nietzsche's *Zarathustra* wherein the author himself observes how "one became two."

You will perhaps have discerned in the foregoing presentation that a considerable displacement of psychological standpoint has taken place, for now I am no longer speaking of the poet as a person, but of the creative process that moves him. The accent of interest has been shifted to the latter factor, while the former comes into consideration, as it were, only as a reacting object. When the consciousness of the author is not identical with the creative process this is at once clear, but in the first-mentioned instance the opposite appears at first to be the case. Here the author is apparently the creator himself, of his own free will and without the smallest compulsion. He is perhaps fully convinced of his own freedom, and will not be disposed to allow that his creation is not also his will, from which, in conjunction with his knowledge, he believes it to be exclusively derived.

Here we are faced with a question that we are quite unable to answer from what the poet himself tells us about the manner of his creating. It is really a scientific problem that psychology alone can solve. For it might also be the case, as I have already hinted, that the poet, while apparently creating consciously and spontaneously out of himself and producing only what he intends, is nevertheless, in spite of his consciousness, so caught up by the creative impulse that he is as little aware of an "alien" will, as the other type can be said to have any direct appreciation of his own will in the apparently foreign inspiration, and this notwithstanding the fact that it is manifestly the voice of his own self. In this case his conviction of the unconditioned freedom of his creating would be an illusion of consciousness—he fancies he is swimming, whereas an invisible stream bears him along.

In no sense is this doubt an airy phantasy; it is founded upon the experience of analytical psychology. For analytical investigation of the unconscious has disclosed an abundance of possibilities in which consciousness is not only influenced by the unconscious, but is actually led by it. The doubt therefore is justified. Yet where may we find evidence for the possible assumption that a conscious poet may also be taken captive by his work? The proof may be of two kinds, direct or indirect. Direct proof would be found in those cases where the poet, in what he believes he is saying, actually and patently says more than he himself is aware of. Many such instances could be cited. Indirect proof would be found in cases, where behind the apparent spontaneity of the production there stands a higher "must," that reveals the imperative nature of its demand if the creative activity is re-nounced voluntarily, or in those difficult psychic complications which immediately ensue in the event of an arbitrary interrup-tion of the artistic production.

Practical analysis of artists invariably shows not only the strength of the creative impulse springing from the unconscious, but also its splenetic and arbitrary character. We have only to turn to any of the biographies of the great artists to find abundant evidence of the way in which the creative urge works upon them; often it is so imperious that it actually absorbs every human impulse, yoking everything to the service of the work, even at the cost of health and common human happiness. The unborn work in the soul of the artist is a force of nature that effects its purpose, either with tyrannical might, or with that subtle cun-ning which nature brings to the achievement of her end, quite regardless of the personal weal or woe of the man who is the vehicle of the creative force. The creative energy lives and waxes in the man as a tree in the earth from which it takes its nourish-ment. It might be well, therefore, to regard the creative process as a living thing, implanted, as it were, in the souls of men. In terms of analytical psychology this is an autonomous complex. It is in fact a detached portion of the psyche that leads an inde-pendent psychic life withdrawn from the hierarchy of conscious-ness, and in proportion to its energic value or force, may appear as a mere disturbance of the voluntarily directed process of consciousness, or as a superordinated authority which may take the ego bodily into its service. The latter case, therefore, would be the poet who is identified with the creative process and who at once acquiesces whenever the unconscious "must" threatens. But the other poet to whom the creative element appears almost as a foreign power, is unable for one reason or another to ac-quiesce, and is, accordingly, caught by the "must" unawares.

It might be expected that this heterogeneity in its motivation would also be felt in a work of art. For in one case we have to do with a purposeful production that is accompanied and directed by consciousness, and to the making of which every consideration as to the form and effect intended has been freely given. Whereas in the other we are dealing with an event proceeding from unconscious nature; something that achieves its aim without the smallest contribution from human consciousness, and often imposing its form and effect quite arbitrarily in spite of the latter. Thus we should expect in the former case, that nowhere would the work transcend the limits of conscious understanding, that its effect would, as it were, be spent within the framework of the author's intention, and that in no way would its expression exceed the author's deliberate purpose. In the latter case we should have to conceive of something of a suprapersonal character that transcends the range of conscious understanding in the same degree as the author's consciousness is withheld from the development of his work. We should expect a certain strangeness of form and shape, thoughts that can only be apprehended by intuition, a language pregnant with meanings, expressions that would have the value of genuine symbols, because they are the best possible expressions of something as yet unknown—bridges thrown out towards an invisible shore.

These criteria are, on the whole, decisive. Wherever it is a question of an admittedly intended work with consciously selected material it should correspond to the first-named qualities, and similarly in the later case. The familiar example of Schiller's dramas, on the one hand, and the second part of *Faust,* on the other, or better still *Zarathustra*, should illustrate what has been said. I would not, however, pledge myself to place the work of an unknown poet into either of these classes without previously having made a rather searching inquiry into the poet's personal relation to his work. The knowledge as to whether a poet belongs to the introverted or to the extraverted type of man is not enough; since both types have the possibility of creating at one time in the extraverted, and, at another, in the introverted attitude. This can be observed with Schiller, in the difference between his poetical and his philosophical works; with Goethe in the contrast between his perfectly formed poems and his obvious strug-

gle in the shaping of his material in the second part of *Faust;*
with Nietzsche in the difference between his aphorisms and the
coherent stream of *Zarathustra.* The same poet may have quite
different attitudes towards his various works, and the particular
standard to be applied must be made dependent upon the particular relation prevailing at the time of production.

This question, as we now see, is infinitely complicated. But the
complication is still further aggravated when our judgment must
also include the above-mentioned considerations concerning the
case of the poet who is identical with the creative impulse. Should
it chance that the conscious and purposeful manner of production
with all its apparent consciousness of intention is nevertheless a
mere subjective illusion of the poet, then his work will also possess the same symbolical qualities, passing into the indefinable
and thus transcending contemporary consciousness. But in this
case these qualities would remain hidden; for the reader would
likewise be unable to reach beyond the limits of the author's
consciousness, which are themselves fixed by the spirit of his
time. He too moves within the limits of contemporary consciousness, with small hope of availing himself of some Archimedian
point outside the orbit of his world by which he could raise, as it
were, his contemporary consciousness off its hinges. For nothing
short of this would enable him to recognize the symbol in a work
of this kind; the symbol being the possibility and intimation of a
meaning higher and wider than our present powers of comprehension can seize.

This question, as we remarked, is somewhat delicate. Indeed,
I am raising it only that the possible significance of a work of
art might not be fettered or restricted by my typification, even
though apparently it intends neither to be nor to say anything
except what it obviously is and says. It happens moreover quite
frequently that a poet long dead is suddenly rediscovered. This
may occur when our conscious development has reached a higher
level, from which standpoint the ancient poet can tell us something new. It was always present in his work, but it remained a
hidden symbol that only a renewal of the spirit of the time permits us to read and to understand. It demanded other and fresher
eyes, just because the old ones could see in it only the things
they were accustomed to see. Experiences like these should

prompt us to be circumspect, since they give a certain justification for the view I developed above; whereas the admittedly symbolic work does not demand this subtlety. In its prophetic language it almost seems to say: I am really meaning more than I actually say, my meaning carries further than my words. Here we may lay our hand upon the symbol, although a satisfying solution of the riddle still escapes us. The symbol remains a perpetual reproach to our subsequent thoughts and feelings. Surely this explains the fact that the symbolical work is more stimulating, drives, as it were, more deeply into us, and therefore seldom permits us a purely aesthetic enjoyment of it. Whereas the work that is manifestly not symbolical appeals much more vividly to our aesthetic sensibility, because it offers us an harmonious vision of fulfilment.

But, you may ask, what contribution can analytical psychology make to the root-problem of artistic "creation," that is, the mystery of the creative energy? All that we have spoken of hitherto has been merely psychological phenomenology. Inasmuch as "no created mind can penetrate the inner soul of Nature," you will surely not expect the impossible from our psychology, namely, a valid explanation of that great mystery of life, that we immediately feel in the creative impulse. Like every other science psychology has only a modest contribution to make towards the better and deeper understanding of the phenomena of life; it is no nearer than its sisters to absolute knowledge.

We have spoken so much of the significance and meaning of the work of art, that one can hardly suppress the theoretical doubt whether in fact art does "signify." Perhaps art itself does not intend to "signify," contains no sort of "meaning," at least not in the sense in which we are now speaking of "meaning." Perhaps it is like nature, which simply is, without any intention to "signify." Is "meaning" necessarily more than mere interpretation "secreted" into it by the need of an intellect hungry for meaning? Art—one might say—is beauty, and therein it finds its true aim and fulfilment. It needs no meaning. The question of meaning holds nothing productive for art. When I enter the sphere of art I must certainly submit to the truth of this statement. But when we are speaking of the relation of psychology to the work of art we are standing outside the realm of art, and here it is impossible for us not to speculate. We must interpret;

we must find meaning in things, otherwise we should be quite
unable to think about them. We must resolve life and happenings,
all that fulfils itself in itself, into images, meanings, concepts;
and thereby we deliberately detach ourselves from the living
mystery. As long as we are caught up in the creative element itself we neither see nor understand; indeed we must not begin
to understand, for nothing is more damaging and dangerous to
immediate experience than cognition. But for the purpose of
cognition we must detach ourselves from the creative process and
regard it from without; only then does it become a picture that
expresses meanings. Then we not only may, but indeed must
speak of "meaning." And in so doing, what was before pure
phenomenon, becomes something that in association with other
phenomena has meaning; it plays a definite rôle, serves certain
ends, brings about effects fraught with meaning. And when we
can see all this we get the feeling of having understood and explained something. Thus is the need of science recognized.

When just now we likened the art-work to a tree growing from
the nourishing earth, we might with equal justice have chosen
the still more familiar metaphor of the child in its mother's womb.
But there is a certain lameness about all comparisons; in place
of metaphors, therefore, let us make use of the more precise
terminology of science. You will remember that I described the
work existing *in statu nascendi* [in the state of being born] as an
autonomous complex. This concept is used to distinguish all those
psychic formations which at first are developed quite unconsciously, and only from the moment when they attain threshold-
value are able to break through into consciousness. The association which they then make with consciousness has not the
importance of an assimilation, but rather of a perception; which
means to say, that the autonomous complex, although certainly
perceived, cannot be subjected to conscious control, whether in
the form of inhibition or of voluntary reproduction. The autonomy of the complex reveals itself in the fact that it appears or
vanishes when and in such guise as accords with its own intrinsic
tendency; it is independent of the option of consciousness. The
creative complex shares this peculiarity with every other autonomous complex. It is, moreover, at this point that the possibility
of an analogy with morbid psychic processes presents itself, for

the latter class (and mental disorders in particular) are especially distinguished by the appearance of autonomous complexes. The divine frenzy of the artist has a perilously real relation to morbid states without being identical with them. The analogy consists in the presence of an autonomous complex. The fact of such a presence, however, proves nothing either for or against the morbid hypothesis, since normal men have also to submit either temporarily or permanently to the tyranny of autonomous complexes. This fact is simply one of the normal peculiarities of the psyche, and for a man to be unaware of the existence of an autonomous complex merely betrays a rather high degree of unconsciousness. For instance every typical attitude that is to a certain extent differentiated shows a tendency to become an autonomous complex, and in the majority of cases actually becomes one. Every instinct too has more or less the character of an autonomous complex. In itself, therefore, there is nothing morbid in an autonomous complex, only its stored-up energy and its disturbing appearance on the scene may often involve suffering or illness.

How does an autonomous complex arise? From some cause or another—a closer investigation of which would at this point lead us too far afield—a hitherto unconscious region of the psyche is thrown into activity, and this activation undergoes a certain development and extension through the inclusion of related associations. The energy employed in this operation is naturally withdrawn from consciousness, unless the latter prefers to identify itself with the complex. But where this is not the case there results what Janet has termed an *"abaissement du niveau mental"* [abasement of the mental level]. The intensity of conscious interests and activities gradually fades, whereupon, either an apathetic inactivity—a condition very common with artists—or a regressive development of the conscious functions takes place, namely, a descent to their infantile or archaic prestages; hence something akin to a degeneration. The *"parties inférieures des fonctions"* [the lower elements of the functions] force themselves to the front, the instinctive rather than the ethical, the naïvely infantile instead of the deliberated and mature, the unadapted in place of the adapted. This also is shown in the lives of many artists. From the energy thus withdrawn from the conscious control of the personality the autonomous complex develops.

But in what does the autonomous creative complex consist? Of this we can know next to nothing so long as the completed work offers us no insight into its foundations. The work gives us a finished picture in the widest sense. This picture is accessible to analysis just in so far as we are able to appreciate it as a symbol. But if we are unable to discover any symbolic value in it, we have thereby ascertained that, for us at least, it means no more than what it obviously says—in other words, so far as we are concerned it is no more than it seems. I use the word "seems," because it is conceivable that our own bias forbids a wider appreciation of it. At all events in the latter case we can find no motive and no point of attack for analysis. In the former case, however, a phrase of Gerhart Hauptmann will come to our minds almost with the force of an axiom: "Poetry means the distant echo of the primitive word behind our veil of words." Translated into psychological language our first question should run: to what primordial image of the collective unconscious can we trace the image we see developed in the work of art?

This question demands elucidation in more than one respect. As already observed, the case I have assumed is that of a symbolical art-work; a work, therefore, of which the source is not to be found in the personal unconscious of the author, but in that sphere of unconscious mythology, the primordial contents of which are the common heritage of mankind. Accordingly, I have termed this sphere the collective unconscious, thus distinguishing it from a personal unconscious which I regard as the totality of those psychic processes and contents that are not only accessible to consciousness, but would often be conscious were they not subject to repression because of some incompatibility that keeps them artificially suppressed beneath the threshold of consciousness. From this sphere art also receives tributaries, dark and turbid though they be; but if they become a major factor they make the work of art a symptomatic rather than a symbolical product. This kind of art might conceivably be left without injury or regret to the Freudian purgative method.

In contrast to the personal unconscious, which in a sense is a relatively superficial layer immediately below the conscious threshold, the collective unconscious is quite unadapted for consciousness under normal conditions, and hence by no analytical technique can it be brought to conscious recollection, being neither repressed nor forgotten. In itself the collective unconscious cannot be said to exist at all; that is to say, it is nothing but a possibility, that possibility in fact which from primordial time has been handed down to us in the definite form of mnemic images, or expressed in anatomical formations in the very structure of the brain. It does not yield innate ideas, but inborn possibilities of ideas, which also set definite bounds to the most daring phantasy. It provides categories of phantasy-activity, ideas *a priori* as it were, the existence of which cannot be ascertained except by experience. In finished or shaped material they appear only as the regulative principle of its shaping, *i.e.*, only through the conclusion derived *a posteriori* from the perfected work of art are we able to reconstruct the primitive foundation of the primordial image. The primordial image or archetype is a figure, whether it be a daemon, man, or process, that repeats itself in the course of history wherever creative phantasy is freely manifested. Essentially, therefore, it is a mythological figure. If we subject these images to a closer investigation, we discover them to be the formulated resultants of countless typical experiences of our ancestors. They are, as it were, the psychic residua of numberless experiences of the same type. They depict millions of individual experiences in the average, presenting a kind of picture of the psychic life distributed and projected into the manifold shapes of the mythological pandemonium. These mythological forms, however, are in themselves themes of creative phantasy that still await their translation into conceptual language, of which there exist as yet only laborious beginnings. These concepts, for the most part still to be created, could provide us with an abstract scientific understanding of the unconscious processes that are the roots of the primordial images. Each of these images contains a piece of human psychology and human destiny, a relic of suffering or delight that has happened countless times in our ancestral story, and on the average follows ever the same course. It is like a deeply graven riverbed in the soul, in which the waters of life, that had spread hitherto with groping and uncertain course over wide but shallow surfaces, suddenly become

a mighty river. This happens when that particular chain of circumstances is encountered which from immemorial time has contributed to the laying down of the primordial image. The
moment when the mythological situation appears is always
characterized by a peculiar emotional intensity; it is as though
chords in us were touched that had never resounded before, or
as though forces were unloosed; of the existence of which we had
never even dreamed. The struggle of adaptation is laborious, because we have constantly to be dealing with individual, *i.e.* atypical conditions. No wonder then, that at the moment when a
typical situation occurs, we feel suddenly aware of an extraordinary release, as though transported, or caught up as by an
overwhelming power. At such moments we are no longer individuals, but the race; the voice of all mankind resounds in us.
The individual man is never able to use his powers to their fullest
range, unless there comes to his aid one of those collective presentations we call ideals that liberates in his soul all the hidden
forces of instinct, to which the ordinary conscious will alone can
never gain access. The most effective ideals are always more or
less transparent variants of the archetype. This is proved by the
fact that these ideals lend themselves so readily to allegorization,
e.g. the motherland as the mother. In this kind of figurative expression the allegory itself has not the smallest motive power;
this has its source in the symbolic value of the motherland-idea.
The corresponding archetype in this case is the so-called "*participation mystique*" [mystical participation] of the primitive with
the soil on which he dwells, and which alone contains the spirit of
his ancestors. Exile spells misery.

Every relation to the archetype, whether through experience
or the mere spoken word, is "stirring," *i.e.* it is impressive, it
calls up a stronger voice than our own. The man who speaks
with primordial images speaks with a thousand tongues; he
entrances and overpowers, while at the same time he raises the
idea he is trying to express above the occasional and the transitory into the sphere of the ever-existing. He transmutes personal
destiny into the destiny of mankind, thus evoking all those beneficent forces that have enabled mankind to find a rescue from
every hazard and to outlive the longest night.

That is the secret of effective art. The creative process, in so far as we are able to follow it at all, consists in an unconscious animation of the archetype, and in a development and shaping of this image till the work is completed. The shaping of the primordial image is, as it were, a translation into the language of the present which makes it possible for every man to find again the deepest springs of life which would otherwise be closed to him. Therein lies the social importance of art; it is constantly at work educating the spirit of the age, since it brings to birth those forms in which the age is most lacking. Recoiling from the unsatisfying present the yearning of the artist reaches out to that primordial image in the unconscious which is best fitted to compensate the insufficiency and onesidedness of the spirit of the age. The artist seizes this image, and in the work of raising it from the deepest unconsciousness he brings it into relation with conscious values, thereby transforming its shape, until it can be accepted by his contemporaries according to their powers.

The nature of the work of art permits conclusions to be drawn concerning the character of the period from which it sprang. What was the significance of realism and naturalism to their age? What was the meaning of romanticism, or Hellenism? They were tendencies of art which brought to the surface that unconscious element of which the contemporary mental atmosphere had most need. The artist as educator of his time—much could be said about that today.

People and times, like individual men, have their peculiar tendencies or attitudes. The very word "attitude" betrays the necessary onesidedness that every definite tendency postulates. Where there is direction there must also be exclusion. But exclusion means that certain definite psychic elements that could participate in life are denied their right to live through incompatibility with the general attitude. The normal man can endure the general tendency without much injury. But the man who takes to the bystreets and alleyways because, unlike the normal man, he cannot endure the broad highway, will be the first to discover those elements that lie apart from the main streets, and that await a new participation in life.

The artist's relative lack of adaptation becomes his real advantage; for it enables him to keep aloof from the highways, the better to follow his own yearning and to find those things of which the others are deprived without noticing it. Thus, as in the case of the single individual whose one-sided conscious attitude is corrected by unconscious reactions towards self-regulation, art also represents a process of mental self-regulation in the life of nations and epochs.

I am aware that I have only been able to give certain intuitive perceptions, and these only in the barest outlines. But I may perhaps hope that what I have been obliged to omit, namely, the concrete application to poetic works, has been furnished by your own thoughts, thus giving flesh and blood to my abstract intellectual frame.

Part V

NEW DIRECTIONS

Charles Maurras

[1868–1952]

CHARLES MAURRAS was a charter member of the *Action française* group which from 1899 to 1940 was the chief voice of the French right. Appalled by the decadence of the *fin de siècle* and the democratic tendencies of French society, he advocated the restoration of the French monarchy, an authoritarian system of government, a revival of religious influence, and an antiromantic movement in the arts. The influence of the *Action française* was greatest from 1908 to 1914 and during the 1930's. During the Second World War, Maurras collaborated with the Vichy regime. In 1945 he was convicted of treason and imprisoned until 1952, when he was released because of failing health.

Maurras has been an important force in modern criticism. The combination of authoritarianism, religious emphasis, and antiromanticism is echoed in T. S. Eliot's description of himself as a classicist in literature, an Anglo-Catholic in religion, and a royalist in politics. Maurras' attitude toward religion is ambivalent but characteristic of much subsequent rightist criticism. The value of religion lies not in its truth (in fact, it may very well be false), but in its usefulness as a myth which maintains the standards necessary to an orderly society. Maurras and the *Action française* were condemned by the Roman Catholic Church for maintaining this theory, but it continues to have advocates.

Among Maurras' works see especially: *L'Avenir de l'intelligence* (Paris, 1905); *Barbarie et poésie* (Paris, 1925); *Poésie et vérité* (Lyon, 1944). For comment see: G. Hupin, *Un grand défenseur de la civilisation: Charles Maurras* (Paris, 1956); L. Roudiez, *Maurras jusqu'à l'Action Française* (Paris, 1957); A. Thibaudet, *Les idées de Charles Maurras* (Paris, 1920). E. Tannenbaum, *The Action Française: Die-hard Reactionaries in Twentieth-Century France* (New York, 1962).

The present essay on Chateaubriand appeared first in 1898 and is almost a manifesto of ideas which Maurras and the *Action Française* group considered fundamental to their program. The notes to the essay are as significant as the essay itself. Because of their length they are here reprinted at the end of the essay proper. The translation is by Professor Alfred Engstrom of the University of North Carolina.

CHATEAUBRIAND; OR, ANARCHY

> Submissiveness is the basis
> of improvement. —Auguste Comte.

I ADMIRE ABOVE ALL the versatile aberration of the France of the old days. The Old Regime, the French State before 1789, whose religion is still preserved, was monarchial, hierarchical, trade unionist, and communal; and every individual lived under its maintenance and discipline. Chateaubriand was one of the first after Jean-Jacques Rousseau to cause men to recognize and be partial to the individual isolated and crippled, as it were, in the pride and boredom of his personal freedom.

Old France had its own peculiar constitution that had sprung from the races and soils of which it was composed. Chateaubriand's journeys to English lands, along with those of Voltaire and Montesquieu, mark the memorable dates of constitutional Anglomania. Chateaubriand never recovered from his first predilection for plagiarisms from the British system: liberalism, parliamentary government, and cabinet rule.

The spirit of old France was classical [See Note 1.], legalistic, philosophical, more sensitive to the relations between things than to the things themselves; and even in their most licentious tales, its writers submitted themselves to the control of reason. Like the Athenians of the fifth century, this race had attained the full development of human genius; had, in M. Boutmy's elegant expression, succeeded in substituting "logical behavior" for "intuitive behavior," the latter of which it left to the beasts and barbarians. Chateaubriand threw this genius for abstraction into confusion by making the imagination prevail over it, and by communicating to the language and to words a coloring of sensuality, a savor of the flesh [See Note 2.], a pleasure in what is physical, which no one had attempted before. At the same time he introduced the romantic art of the peoples of northern Europe. Although he later deplored the unnatural influence that these immature peoples acquired in France, he is the first to be responsible for it.

Old France professed the traditional Catholicism which, in its combination of Jewish visions, Christian feeling, and Hellenic and

Roman discipline, expresses the natural order of humanity. Chateaubriand neglected this powerful substance of doctrine. From the supposed Renaissance that he is praised for starting dates that "theological pantaloonery," that lack of seriousness in apologetics that amused the teachers of Ernest Renan. Upon close examination, it differs only by its picturesque gloss and its appeals to the senses from the sentimental deism [See Note 3.] propagated by the Germans and Swiss in the salon of Necker. Chateaubriand has been called "a Catholic Epicurean"; but he is not that at all. I should call him rather a wretched Protestant who has decked himself out in the pageantry of Rome. He has contributed almost as much as his compatriot Lamennais to our religious anarchy.

In a word, if the *Génie du Christianisme* gives Chateaubriand the semblance of a fierce adversary of the Revolution, he is in fact one of those who owe the most to it.

When, after taking leave of the savages of America, François-René de Chateaubriand returned to his country, it was covered with ruins that moved him profoundly. His first inclination was, it is true, to curse in a famous *Essay* what had just been lost in the upheaval of the Revolution. But, little by little, as his historical imagination regained control, he came to love when they were dead and lying prostrate institutions that he had fled even to the wilderness to avoid when they were in their prime. He gave them not tears, but pages so grandly and so pathetically lachrymose that their very sound caused him to weep.

He shed his tears in all good faith. His sincerity was excruciating. This artist brought to the concerts of his mournful flutes a state that was entirely his own and never changed: he insisted that his lament be sustained and his unhappiness nourished upon solid calamities—miseries that approached the absolute, and downfalls that were hopeless in their finality. His sympathy and his eloquence rejected incomplete misfortunes. The object of his attention had to be struck to the heart. But let one of the victims lamented by him in his poetry, when it had been wrapped and sewed up in its "purple shroud," make even the slightest motion of recovery—that is not fair at all; its recovery would offend him forever.

Thus when the French monarchy had the bad taste to come

back to life, it was well received! After the first complimentary words, made in hatred of Bonaparte—words that no good nobleman at the moment refused to his prince—Chateaubriand avenged as best he could the impertinent contradiction that the Restoration was inflicting upon his *Requiem* for the old order. Louis XVIII had no subject who was more troublesome; and his finest ministers had no more dangerous colleague.

Finally the explosion of 1830 sets him free, and we find our man perched upon a new ruin. Immediately, all the obligations of loyalism become not only easy but agreeable. He engages in intrigue, travels, makes declarations in print. "Madame, your son is my king!" The death of Napoleon II gives him great hopes: if the Duke of Bordeaux, too . . . ? But the Duke of Bordeaux flourishes. M. de Chateaubriand is denied the sweet pleasure of singing the great aria for the funeral service of the last king. He consoles himself by watching the disintegration of the last throne.

The legitimate monarchy is dead—such is the usual burden of his meditations—and the evidence of this temporary truth makes him feel once more secure; but yet, from time to time, he goes to the royal burial-vault, lifts the cloth, as it were, and puts his hands upon the fair, inanimate limbs. To keep them as best he can from being brought back to life, this one-time soldier of Condé overwhelms them with cutting benedictions and treacherous words of praise that are like dagger blows.

The literal truth is this. By Chateaubriand's special ways of *showing fear* of demagogy, socialism, or the coming of the European Republic, one realizes that he is calling for them with all his heart. To forecast certain calamities, especially in public, in a sarcastic, bitter, and careless tone, amounts in fact to making way for their arrival.

Surely this noble mind, so superior in intelligence to the Hugos, the Michelets, and the other romantics, did not envisage the new regime without some horror. But Chateaubriand delighted in horror. I might even be so bold as to say that, like Nero and the Marquis de Sade, he savored horror and enjoyed causing himself a certain amount of distress in connection with more acute pleasures.

His taste for historic calamities was well served to the last. He died in the agonized enjoyment of despair. The sound of the cannon of June, 1848, had hardly ceased. He had heard the gunshots of February. The necrologist of theocracies and monarchies who kept a register of the emperors, popes, kings, and great personages who had suffered disgrace or death before his eyes did not strike up the song of Simeon before he had entered on his tablets the exile of the Orleans princes and the political fall of Lamartine.

One of the race of wreckers and demolishers, a rapacious and lonely bird of prey, a lover of cemeteries, Chateaubriand never sought, in death and the past, what could be transmitted to another age—what was fruitful, full of tradition, eternal. His only pleasures were the past, seen merely as the past, and death, seen merely as death. Far from preserving anything, he was destructive when it suited his purpose, in order to provide himself with surer causes for sorrow. In all things, he saw only their power to arouse his emotions. At court, in camp, in public office, just as in his books, his sole interest is himself, the hermit of Combourg, the solitary of the American wilderness. He submitted the universe to his own concerns. This idol of conservative modern men is for us above all else the incarnate genius of Revolutions. He is this much more, perhaps, than Michelet. We should do him honor with wooden shoes on our feet, rigged out in the carmagnole, and with a red cockade in our revolutionary bonnet.

NOTE 1: "ON THE CLASSICAL SPIRIT"

"The spirit of Old France was classical."

A deplorable error, resulting perhaps from academic prepossessions, has led our teacher Taine to label as classical the spirit that prepared the way for the Revolution. If one reflects upon this matter, it is evident that classical antiquity had a very insignificant part in it. So far as classical books are concerned, the revolutionary bibliography scarcely includes more than Plato's *Republic* and Plutarch's *Lives;* and these are included only because Jean-Jacques Rousseau, the Father and Doctor of revolutionary ideas, borrowed phrases from them—phrases that were misleading in their implications.

Moreover, Plutarch was deeply informed and already penetrated in spite of himself by ideas of the Semitic people, for he was born almost at the moment when the inspiration of the East had changed the great spirit of the ancient world. As for Plato, of all the wise men of Greece he is the one who drew the most ideas and the most singular ideas from Asia; and he, more than all of his colleagues, has been commented upon and distorted by the Jews of Alexandria. What we call "Platonicism" and "Plutarchism" runs the risk, if one isolates it, of seriously misrepresenting the wisdom of Athens and of Rome. The two doctrines contain elements that are more barbarian than they are Graeco-Latin, and they are already "romantic."

But one can say that ancient Greece—with her physicists and geometricians, with her sophists, artists, and logician-poets, with Phidias, and with Aristotle, who opened a new world—laid the foundations of practical science, philosophy, and religion; and ancient Rome —with her statesmen, her historians, her moralists—exhibited so powerful a lesson of realistic politics that the English Parliament and the Capetian Monarchy did not surpass it. Nothing is left to anarchy in either the family or the city of the Ancients. The arbitrary whims of the leaders and the harsh prescriptions of the law are rigorously tempered and brought to compromise. The institution of slavery eliminates democracy's greatest difficulties; and, yet, the unfortunate history of the last half century of Athenian liberty, the repeated warnings of the Aristophaneses, Xenophons, Platos even, and of all the teachers of Attic genius, the swiftness of its destruction, and the thundering crash of its fall are powerful evidences in favor of aristocracies and other authoritarian administrations. Anyone who studies them feels himself rather ill-disposed towards the dogma of popular government.

In the modern era, Catholic philosophy is modeled on Aristotle; and Catholic politics appropriates for itself the methods of Roman politics. Such is the nature of the Classical tradition. The Classical spirit is the essence of the doctrines of superior men. It is a spirit of authority and of aristocracy. To call the spirit of the Revolution classical was then to deprive a word of its natural significance and to foster ambiguities.

The Revolution came from a completely different direction: the Bible of the Reformation, the statutes of the Republic of Geneva, the Calvinist theologians, the old individualistic ferment of Germania for which trilingual Switzerland already served as European interpreter; finally, the personal flights of a sensibility unrestrained either by hereditary customs or by vigorous studies or by healthy good sense— these are the humble causes of the ideas that sprang up in the mind of Rousseau. By the magic of his eloquence they gained entrance along with him into the old French society, where, far from engendering any classical state of mind, they destroyed a progressive and orderly spirit. Who will deny that Rousseau began the Romantic era?

NOTE 2: "THE SAVOR OF THE FLESH"

> "Chateaubriand threw this genius for abstraction into confusion by making the imagination prevail over it, and by communicating to the language and to words a coloring of sensuality, a savor of the flesh. . . ."

If I refrained here from literary criticism, I should not be able to develop the subject posed above. Moreover, my point is confirmed by attentive reading of any fine page of Chateaubriand. The sentences clearly seem formed to heighten the effect of certain expressions, certain words or even certain syllables of dazzling sensuality. Sensuality that has been made a word, a succession and arrangement of rich sounds—I could not define in any other way Chateaubriand's "great mystery of melancholy" or his "soft swelling of the waves." It is impossible to find anything more sensual: it is a physical caress on the sensitive nerve ends of lips and tongue, on the small fibres of our hearing organs. One would savor these words as if one were kissing their material elements in the air.

"Before Chateaubriand," I wrote in another place, "the word was a sign, an abstract sign that ceased to be one only by merest chance. Such a chance event had its own particular value, and no one ever tried to make it usual or even frequent; it was literally a lucky expression, a happy accident, in which one took delight without too much thought; for if it came to lose its accidental quality, one knew that it was losing its worth. In short, the reality-word, the color-word, the perfume-word, the sensation-word, the object-word might well come from the pen in fun or as a result of a mood; it was not in any way a conscious object of style. It was Chateaubriand who raised it to this new eminence. Chateaubriand is less concerned with what he says than with the moving, sonorous and picturesque shell around his works; and, since what he says is only a sequence of images, it is not to the order of images that he desires to direct our attention, but to the image itself, to the various individual images of which his statement is composed—that is, to the very nature of the words employed, since the images and the words are often exactly the same thing.

"A source of suffering and of pleasure, a living principle of all poetry, having personal virtues and intrinsic qualities that every writer since his time has tried to bring forward and stress—this is the ascendancy to which Chateaubriand has advanced the single word. Before him, syntax and style, the author's genius in language and thought, were in the forefront. Thanks to him, they have given place to vocabulary and descended to a rank of secondary importance. The results of this revolution have been continued, not only in Hugo and his contemporaries, but even in the work of that belated romantic whom we have just lost, M. Stéphane Mallarmé."

NOTE 3: "THE DEISTS"

> "Upon closer examination, it differs only by its picturesque gloss and its appeals to the senses from the sentimental deism propagated by the Germans and Swiss in the salon of Necker."

In spite of a very popular notion that predominates in France under Voltaire's influence, it is still questionable whether the idea of God, of a single God present in one's conscience, is always a beneficent and wise idea.

The positivists rightly call attention to the fact that this idea can result in anarchy. The individual, all too often in revolt against the general interests of the species and of the subgroupings of humanity (country, caste, city, family), frequently surrenders to it only through necessity, loneliness, and fear of destitution. But if one begins to think that in this conscience, which is by its very nature anarchical, one can establish direct relations with an absolute, infinite, and all-powerful Being, then the idea of the invisible and distant master will soon deprive the conscience of the respect that it owes to its visible and immediate masters. It will prefer to obey God rather than men. At every turn (not just once as Antigone justifiably did) it will invoke eternal and unwritten laws in order to free itself from the temporal laws that concern it most directly. It will defy without restraint the principles of the state and of reason. This mystical relationship encourages scepticism in theory and rebellion in practice; it persuades one that the divine inner power dictates every judgment that is insufficiently motivated by reason, and it inspires appetites that are in opposition to the established order. Such is the immense multiplier that the idea of God adds to individual caprice. Increased to the infinite, multiplied by the infinite, each egoism justifies itself in the name of God and everyone calls his personal obsession or his favorite sensation divine, be it Justice or Love, Mercy or Liberty.

There should be a single universal cry among moralists and politicians concerning the dangers of theistic hypocrisy. If it gives each individual some momentary fervor or energy, this is only apparent; this passing excitation of pride is not worth its bad effects, since it decomposes and dissolves all the elements of human community, not only the State and its various customs, but also science, and even thought. Thus, beyond the conditions of his elementary life, the individual loses the ornaments and pleasures of the higher order.

Even if one were neither moralist nor politician, he ought still to have a great horror of deism, however little taste he has. Deism robs the passions of their natural air, their simple and fair innocence. It corrupts them with a ridiculous metaphysics. Listen to Julie, Lélia, Emma, Elvire and the whole chorus of romantic women in love protest, in their lover's arms, that they have received him only because of an order from the Supreme Being!

It was the merit and the honor of Catholicism to *organize* the idea of God and to take this poison from it. On the road leading to God the Catholic finds legions of intermediaries: some are of this earth, others are supernatural, but the chain of both kinds is continuous. Heaven and earth are thoroughly peopled by them, as they were by the gods in former times.

This religion, in spite of its monotheistic foundation, thus restores to our world its natural character of multiplicity, harmony, and *composition*. Moreover, if God speaks in the secrecy of a Catholic heart, his words are controlled and, as it were, given the stamp of approval by learned men who are themselves in turn under the domination of a superior authority, the only one from whose decisions there is no appeal,[1] the infallible preserver of Catholic doctrine. Thus the spirit of fantasy and whim and the folly of literal interpretation are reduced to a minimum; the Pope is the only man who can, in the name of God, allow himself aberrations in thought and conduct, and everything around him is arranged in such a way as to prevent this.

In this admirable system each individual can communicate in person with God, on condition that he rise by this name to less personal

[1] This very authority recognizes in the chiefs and princes a divine anointing and election from which there springs the independence of these powers and the autonomy of the civil power. No one seems to me to have imagined any better arrangement than this since the regrettable split in the Christian era between the religious and civil orders.

thoughts and to nobler sentiments;[2] but the system does not allow the individual to attribute his own depravities to the infinite, or to authorize in its name his personal rebellions. The God of the Catholics preserves unchangeably the noble representation given him by the loftiest human minds. Senseless, lowly minds, held fast by dogma, are not free to choose for themselves a master of their making and in their image. The master remains superior to those who pray to him.

Finally, Catholicism proposes the only idea of God that is tolerable today in a civilized state. All others are likely to become dangerous to the public at large. Among the ancient Israelites the prophets, chosen by God apart from the priesthood, were causes of disorder and trouble. Since his national misfortunes have freed him from every regular sovereignty and often enough from every priestly control, the Jew, monotheistic and nurtured by the prophets, has become—as Bernard Lazare and James Darmesteter do not conceal from us—an agent of revolution. The Protestant proceeds strictly from the Jew in the progression monotheism, prophecy, and anarchy, at least so far as thought is concerned. Rousseau's Vicar from Savoy is a Protestant deist. In the States that have remained faithful to the spirit of the "so-called religious reform," and which have not turned, like northern Germany, to pure atheism,[3] or, like England, to a closer and closer copy of Catholicism, the idea of God endangers much more than it sustains.

[2] M. Laberthonnière, a liberal writer who is a confirmed enemy of the *Action Française* and only moderately respectful of the truth, has tried to draw from these reflections on inorganic deism a conclusion contrary to what was intended and what was said, but favorable to the wretched notions that this unhappy author imputes to us. According to him, we favor Catholic deism only as a ruling instrument put at the disposal, not even of the commonweal, but (and this entails a second falsehood) of a race of the Strong conceived in the manner of the barbarous Nietzsche. Unhappily for this ingenious and bold bit of nonsense, the phrase in which I show that the condition imposed upon Catholic deism was to rise, by God's name, *"to less personal thoughts and to nobler sentiments"*—that small phrase excludes from my idea every consideration of this order and overturns M. Laberthonnière's whole edifice. But no matter! This critic is not embarrassed by so slight a discrepancy. While he weighs with the utmost care every syllable expressed on the matter, questions it, plumbs its depths, tortures its smallest details, he has not a single glance or a single word for this very explicit phrase. . . . He has erased it from my text. And his book and his thesis, which would crumble otherwise, are erected wholly on this malignant omission.

[3] The atheistic Protestants, who still circulate among the affiliated deists, deny only the name of God. The majority attribute a metaphysical value to certain selected ideas, drawn from the natural order and from the place fixed by universal Logic. This error predisposes them to seditious action.

André Breton

[1894–   ]

❦

SURREALISM WAS one of several reactions to the hollowness and drabness of the era following World War I. It is related to *dada*, but unlike that movement has produced art and criticism of lasting value. The term was first used in connection with literature by Apollinaire in 1917. André Breton and Philippe Soupault popularized it during the early twenties, and Breton codified surrealist theory in the *First Surrealist Manifesto* (1924). Among "absolute surrealists" he named Aragon, Breton, Desnos, Éluard, and Soupault. Among the forerunners of surrealism he named Young (*Night Thoughts*), Swift, the Marquis de Sade, Poe, and Baudelaire.

According to Breton, surrealism is "Pure psychic automatism through which one seeks to express . . . the absolute functioning of thought . . . in the absence of all rational control and apart from any ethical or moral considerations. . . . Surrealism rests on a belief in the superior quality of certain forms of association heretofore neglected: in the omnipotence of the dream, in the disinterested play of thought. It tends to destroy all other psychic mechanisms and to substitute itself for them in the resolution of the principal problems of life." The first part of this definition recalls the romantic theory of imagination. The second part, with its emphasis on association and dream, is indebted to Freud, whose work Breton had encountered as a student of psychology. Marxism also influenced the surrealist movement between 1925 and 1930; but after 1930 the incompatibility of the two systems became increasingly apparent, and writers were forced to choose between them. Breton rejected Communism while Aragon and Éluard rejected surrealism.

For comment see: A. Balakian, *Literary Origins of Surrealism* (New York, 1947); A. Breton, *Le Manifeste du Surréalisme* (Paris, 1924); W. Fowlie, *Age of Surrealism* (New York, 1950); R. Groos and G. Truc, eds., *Petite anthologie poétique du surréalisme* (Paris, 1934); M. Nadeau, *Histoire du surréalisme* (Paris, 1934); H. Read, *Surrealism* (London, 1936).

The present selection is from André Breton, *Les Manifestes du Surréalisme* (Paris: Editions du Sagittaire, 1946), pp. 51–75, trans

by Professor James Patty of Washington and Lee University. Reprinted by permission.

SECRETS OF THE MAGIC ART
OF SURREALISM

HAVE WRITING MATERIALS brought to you after settling in a place as favorable as possible to your mind's concentration on itself. Put yourself in the most passive, receptive state that you can. Lay aside your genius, your talents, and those of everybody else. Tell yourself firmly that literature is one of the sorriest paths leading to anything. Write quickly without any preconceived subject, quickly enough so that you won't hold back and won't be tempted to reread. The first sentence will come all by itself, so true it is that at every moment there is a sentence alien to our conscious thought just waiting to be externalized. It is rather difficult to decide about the following sentence; it doubtless participates both in our conscious and unconscious activity, if we grant that having written the first one involves a minimum of perception. It will make little difference to you anyway; therein resides, for the most part, the interest of the surrealistic game. At any rate, punctuation is obviously opposed to the absolute continuity of the flow which concerns us, though it seem as necessary as the arrangement of the nodes on a vibrating violin string. Continue as long as you like. Trust to the inexhaustible nature of the murmur. If silence threatens to settle down because you commit some slight mistake—a lack of inattention, we might say—do not hesitate to break off at the line that is too clear. Following the word whose origin seems suspect to you, put any letter whatsoever, the letter *l* for example—always the letter *l*—and restore the arbitrary by imposing this letter as the initial one of the following word.

HOW NOT TO BE BORED IN COMPANY

This is very hard. Don't be at home to anyone, and, occasionally, when nobody has ignored your order not to be disturbed,

break off right in the middle of surrealistic activity, fold your arms and say: "That's all right; no doubt there are better things to do, or not do. It is difficult to remain interested in this life. How simple-minded! I am still disturbed by what goes on inside of me!" Or just any revolting banality.

HOW TO MAKE SPEECHES

Register on the day before an election, in the first country which sees fit to have recourse to this type of consultation. Every person has within him the raw material of an orator: the many-colored loin-cloths and glass beads called words. Through surrealism he will surprise despair in all its poverty. Some evening, on a platform, all by himself he will hack up the eternal heaven, that Skin of the Bear. He will promise so much that to keep his promises ever so little would be cause for consternation. He will give a slanted, derisive twist to the claims of a whole people. He will make the most irreducible adversaries commune in a secret passion, which will blow up nations. And thus he will succeed just by letting himself be swept up by the immense Word which melts into pity and rolls into hatred. Incapable of failure, he will play on the velvet of all failures. He will really be elected and the sweetest women will love him madly.

HOW TO WRITE PSEUDO-NOVELS

Whoever you are, if your heart so dictates, you will burn some laurel leaves and, without trying to keep this faint fire going, you will begin to write a novel. Surrealism will make it possible for you to do so; you will set the needle marked "Fair weather" on "Action," and the trick is turned. Lo and behold, here are characters with new bearings; in your writing their names are just a matter of capital letters and they will behave with the same nonchalance toward the active verbs as the impersonal pronoun *il* toward words like *pleut, y a, faut,* etc. They will have command over them, so to speak, and in those situations where observation, reflection, and the faculties of generalization have been of no help, rest assured that they will provide you with a thousand ideas which you did not have. Thus decked out with a small number of physical and mortal traits, these beings who actually owe you so little will henceforth hew to a certain line of conduct about which you need not bother yourself. The result will be a plot more or less artful in appearance, justifying point by point the moving or reassuring dénouement which leaves you cold. Your pseudo-novel will simulate a real novel remarkably well; you will be rich and people will join in recognizing that you have "something in your belly," since that is exactly where that "something" holds forth.

Of course, by a like procedure, providing you do not know what you will later realize, you can successfully devote yourself to pseudo-criticism.

HOW TO BE CLEARLY SEEN BY A WOMAN PASSING ALONG THE STREET

.   .   .   .
.   .   .   .
.   .   .   .
.   .   .   .

AGAINST DEATH

Surrealism will introduce you to the secret society of death. It will glove your hand, burying in it the deep *M* with which the word *Memory* begins. Don't neglect to make favorable arrangements about your will: for my part, I request that I be taken to the cemetery in a moving van. Have my friends destroy every last copy of the edition of my *Discourse on the Fire of Reality*.

❈   ❈   ❈   ❈   ❈   ❈   ❈   ❈   ❈

Language was given to man so that he could use it surrealistically. To the extent that he must make himself understood, he succeeds, somehow or other, in expressing himself and thereby making sure that certain functions—picked from among the very crudest—are carried out. Speaking and writing a letter offer him no real difficulty, provided, while doing it, he sets himself no goal above the average; in other words, provided he confines himself to conversing (for the pleasure of conversing) with someone. He feels no anxiety over the words which are going to come out, or over the sentence following the one he is now finishing. He will be capable of giving a point-blank answer to a very simple question. Lacking nervous *tics* contracted from dealing with others, he can spontaneously pass judgment on a small number of subjects; for that, he does not need to "turn his tongue over seven times" or to formulate anything in advance. Who has persuaded him that this faculty of spontaneity will do him nothing but harm when he sets out to establish more delicate relationships? He ought not to refuse to speak or write abundantly on anything. Listening to yourself or reading to yourself only interrupts marvelous, occult assistance. I am in no hurry to understand myself (Bah! I'll always understand myself). If some phrase or other of mine causes me momentarily a slight disappointment, I trust to the following sentence to redeem its inadequacies; I carefully refrain from starting it over again or polishing it up. Even the slightest loss of élan might prove fatal. Words or groups of words *which follow one another* practice the greatest solidarity among themselves. It is not up to me to favor some at the expense of others. There must be some miraculous compensation which intervenes—and it does intervene.

Not only does this unreserved language which I am seeking to justify forever, which I find adaptable to all the circumstances of life; not only does this language not deprive me of any of my powers, but it lends me an amazing lucidity—and in the field where I least expected any. I will go so far as to claim that it teaches me; and, in fact, I have occasionally used in a surrealistic way words whose meaning I had forgotten. I was able to verify afterwards that my use of them corresponded exactly to their definition. That would suggest that one does not "learn"—one only "relearns." In this way I mastered certain happy turns of phrase. And I say nothing of the *poetic awareness of objects,* which I was able to acquire only through oft-repeated spiritual contact with them.

The forms of surrealistic speech, however, are best adapted to dialogue. In dialogue, two minds confront one another; while one is giving of itself, the other is busy taking it in. But how does it take it in? To suppose that one assimilates the other would be to admit that one mind, for a time, can live entirely off the other, which is very unlikely. And, in fact, the attention one gives to the other is quite outward; it is free only to approve or reprove (usually the latter) with all the deference of which man is capable. Then too, this type of speech does not permit one to get to the heart of a subject. My attention, subjected to a solicitation which it cannot decently repel, treats contrary thought as an enemy. In current parlance, it nearly always "snaps up" the words and figures used by the other thought; it puts me in a position to take advantage of them in my answer by denaturing them. So true is this that in certain pathological mental states in which sensory difficulties completely dominate the attention of the patient, he continues to answer questions, but limits himself to grabbing the last word pronounced in his presence or the last surrealistic phrase of which he finds a trace in his mind:

"How old are you?—You." (Echolalia).

"What is your name?—Forty-five houses." (Ganser's symptom, or irrelevant answers).

Something of this disorder occurs in every conversation. Only the general striving for sociability and the deep-rooted habit we have in that direction succeed in disguising the fact from us for a while. The great weakness of books, too, is that they are forever joining battle with the minds of their best—I mean their most exacting—readers. In the very short dialogue which I improvized above between the doctor and the insane person, the latter has the best of it. Since by his answers he imposes himself on the attention of the examining doctor—and since he is not the one asking the questions. Does this mean that his thought is the stronger at that moment? Perhaps. He is free to take no further account of his age or his name.

Poetic surrealism, to which I am devoting this study, has so far endeavored to re-establish dialogue in its absolute truth, by freeing the two speakers from the obligation of politeness. Each of them simply pursues his soliloquy, without seeking to gain from it any particular dialectical pleasure or to impose in the least on his neighbor. The remarks made do not, as is usual, aim at the development of a thesis be it ever so negligible; they are as disjointed as possible. As for the reply which they are attempting to elicit, it is, in principle, of no interest whatsoever to the self-esteem of the person who spoke. Words and images are put forth only as springboards for the mind of the listener. Such is the intent of those pages in *Les champs magnétiques* (the first purely surrealistic work) grouped under the title "Barriers" in which Soupault and I reveal ourselves to be such impartial interlocutors.

❊

❊   ❊

Surrealism does not permit those who devote themselves to it to abandon it at their pleasure. Everything leads one to believe that it acts on the mind in the manner of drugs; like drugs it creates a certain state of need and can urge a man to terrible revolts. It is also, if you will, a quite artificial paradise, and the taste for it stems from Baudelaire's criticism in the same way as those other tastes described by him. Hence the analysis of the mysterious effects and special pleasures it can engender. In many ways, surrealism presents itself as a *new vice* which does not seem destined for only a few: like hashish, it has what it takes to satisfy all fastidious spirits. An analysis of its effects cannot fail to have its place in this study.

1. Surrealistic images operate like those opium images which man no longer evokes but which "offer themselves to him, spontaneously, despotically. He cannot dismiss them; for the will no longer has any power and no longer governs the faculties." [1] We have yet to discover if anyone has ever "evoked" images. If one sticks, as I do, to Reverdy's definition,[2] it does not seem possible deliberately to bring together what he calls "two remote realities." The coming together takes place or does not take place—

[1] Baudelaire.
[2] Pierre Reverdy, in *Nord-Sud*, March, 1918, maintained that true poetic imagery arises not from comparison, but from "the bringing together of two realities more or less remote from one another" and that the greater the disparity, the better the image. Breton agrees with Reverdy's definition but denies that the poet can consciously control the image-making process. (Ed.)

that is all. Personally, I deny categorically that such images in Reverdy as:

In the gutter there is a song flowing

or:

The day unfolded like a white tablecloth

or:

The world goes back into a sack

evince the slightest degree of premeditation. It is false, in my opinion, to claim that "the mind has seized the affinities" between the two juxtaposed realities. To begin with, it did not seize anything consciously. It was from the partly accidental coming together of the two terms that a special light flashed—the *light of the image,* to which we turn out to be infinitely sensitive. The value of the image depends on the beauty of the spark obtained; consequently, it is a function of the difference in potential between the two conductors. When this difference barely exists, as in comparison,[3] the spark is not produced. Now, in my view, it is not in the power of man to contrive the coming together of two widely separated realities. The principle of the association of ideas, it appears to us, is opposed to it. The alternative is to be reduced to an elliptical art, which Reverdy condemns just as I do. We must admit, then, that the two terms of the image are not deduced from one another by the mind *with a view* to producing the spark; that they are the simultaneous products of the activity which I call surrealistic; and reason limits itself to observing and appreciating the luminous phenomenon.

And just as the length of the spark gains from being produced through rarefied gases, so the surrealistic atmosphere created by mechanical writing, which I have insisted on putting within the reach of all, lends itself particularly to the production of the most beautiful images. One might even say that images appear, in the dizzying race, as the mind's only guideposts. The mind is gradually convinced of the supreme reality of these images. At first only submitting to them, it soon observes that they flatter its reason, thereby increasing its knowledge. It becomes aware of unlimited expanses in which its desires are manifested, in which the *pro*

---

[3] Cf. the imagery in Jules Renard.

and the *con* are forever being minimized, in which its darkness conceals its presence. It proceeds, borne along by those images which give it pleasure, which hardly leave it time to blow on the fire of its fingers. This is the most beautiful of nights, *the night of lightning;* compared to it, day is night.

The countless types of surrealistic images call for a classification which, for today, I do not propose to attempt. To group them according to their special affinities would take me too far afield. Basically, I want to account for their common virtue. For me— I cannot hide the fact—the strongest image is the one which presents the highest degree of arbitrariness; the one which takes the longest to translate into practical language: whether it contains an enormous dose of apparent contradiction; or one of its terms is curiously concealed; or, promising to be sensational, it seems to fizzle out (that is, it suddenly snaps shut the angle of its compass); or it draws from within itself an absurd *formal* justification; or it is in the nature of an hallucination; or it quite naturally lends the mask of the concrete to the abstract, or vice versa; or it implies the negation of some elementary physical property; or it sets off laughter. Here, in that order, are some examples:

The ruby of champagne. (Lautréamont).
Beautiful as the law of arrested development of the chest in adults whose propensity to growth is not in proportion to the quantity of molecules assimilated by their organism. (Lautréamont).
A church arose bursting like a bell. (Philippe Soupault).
In Rose Sélavy's slumber there is a dwarf from out of a well who comes and eats her bread at night. (Robert Desnos).
On the bridge the cat-headed dew was rocking. (André Breton).
A little to the left, in my guessed-at firmament, I perceive—but of course it's only a vapor of blood and murder—the brilliant lackluster of the perturbations of liberty. (Louis Aragon).
In the burning forest,
The lions were cool. (Roger Vitrac).
The color of a woman's stocking is not necessarily in the image of her eyes, which caused a philosopher, whom it is pointless to name, to say: "Cephalopoda have more reasons than quadrupeds to hate progress." (Max Morise).

Whether you like it or not, there is matter here to satisfy several requirements of the mind. All these images seem to testify that the mind is ripe for something other than the anodyne pleas-

ures it usually permits itself. This is the only way it has to turn
to its advantage the ideal quantity of events with which it is
laden.[4] These images indicate how much energy the mind usually
wastes and the price exacted by this waste. There is no harm
done if they end up by disconcerting the mind, for to do so is to
put it at a grave disadvantage. The sentences just quoted greatly
contribute to this effect. The mind which savors them has the
satisfaction of knowing that it is on the *right road;* on its own,
it could never be guilty of quibbling; moreover, it has nothing
to fear since it is sure to encircle everything.

2. The mind which plunges into surrealism relives, in exaltation, the best part of its childhood. Its experience is somewhat like
the assurance of a person who, as he drowns, reviews in less than
a minute all the frustration of his life. Someone may object that
this is not very encouraging. However, I have no desire to en-
courage those who make this objection. The memories of childhood and certain other memories give off a feeling of being undetermined and then of wandering, which I regard as the most
fruitful of all. Perhaps it is childhood which most nearly approaches "real life": childhood, after which man has at his disposal, over and above his travel permit, only a handful of free
passes; childhood when everything contributed to effective, risk-
free self-possession. Thanks to surrealism it seems these fortunate
opportunities have returned. It is as if you were again racing to
your salvation or doom. In the darkness you see a familiar and
precious terror. Thank God, it is still only Purgatory. With a
shudder you cross what the occultists call *perilous landscapes.* My
footsteps arouse vigilant monsters; they are not yet very hostile
to me, and I am not doomed since I am afraid of them. Here
are "the elephants with the heads of women and the flying lions"
which Soupault and I once trembled to encounter; here is the
"soluble fish" which still frightens me a little. SOLUBLE FISH—
Am *I* not the soluble fish? Since I was born under the sign of
Pisces and man is soluble in his own thought! The flora and
fauna of surrealism are inexpressible.

3. I do not believe in the forthcoming establishment of a sur-

[4] Let us not forget that, according to Novalis' formula, "There are
series of events running parallel to the real series. Men and circumstances
generally modify the ideal sequence of events so that it seems imperfect;
and their consequences too are equally imperfect. So it was with the
Reformation: instead of Protestantism came Lutheranism."

realistic "style." The qualities common to all surrealistic works, including those which I have just mentioned and many others which only a rigorous logical and grammatical analysis could make available to us, are not incompatible with a certain evolution of surrealistic prose in the course of time. Coming after a number of efforts in this direction to which I devoted myself for five years and which I indulgently regard as for the most part extremely disorganized, the little tales which form the sequel to this volume [5] provide striking proof of this. But I do not, for this reason, consider them especially worthy or especially unworthy to symbolize for the reader the psychic benefits of surrealism.

The techniques of surrealism, moreover, need to be expanded. Anything can be used to obtain the desirable sudden shock from certain associations. The *papiers collés* of Picasso and Braque have the same value as the introduction of a cliché into a literary exercise in the chastest style. It is even possible to give the title POEM to what can be obtained through the most arbitrary possible collection of lines and fragments of lines cut out of newspapers (We may observe syntax, if you like.): [6]

POÈME

Un éclat de rire
de saphir dans l'île de Ceylan

Les plus belles pailles

ONT LE TEINT FANÉ
SOUS LES VERROUS

[5] Collected under the title *Soluble Fish* in the first two editions (1924, 1929).

[6] One of two and one-half pages of examples is given here. The French is quoted to preserve the typography. In translation: "POEM// A burst of laughter/ of sapphire on the island of Ceylon// *The most beautiful straw/* HAS A FADED TINT/ UNDER BOLTS// in an isolated farm/ *FROM DAY TO DAY/* augments itself/ the agreeable// A CARRIAGE ROAD/ takes you to the edge of the unknown// coffee/ preaches for its saint/ THE DAILY CRAFTSMAN OF YOUR BEAUTY. (Ed.)

dans une ferme isolée
AU JOUR LE JOUR
s'aggrave
l'agréable

Une voie carrossable
vous conduit au bord de l'inconnu

le café
prêche pour son saint
L'ARTISAN QUOTIDIEN DE VOTRE BEAUTÉ

And examples could be multiplied. Theatre, philosophy, science, and criticism would also manage to find their place once more in this system. I hasten to add that the future *techniques* of surrealism do not interest me.

As I have clearly indicated, the applications of surrealism to action strike me as much more serious.[7] To be sure, I do not believe in the prophetic power of surrealistic speech. "What I say

[7] Whatever reservations I may have about responsibility in general and about the medico-legal considerations which determine an individual's degree of responsibility. . . . I would like to know how the first criminal acts of undoubtedly surrealist nature will be *judged*. Will the accused be acquitted or will he merely benefit from mitigating circumstances? It is too bad that journalistic crimes are now hardly ever punished; otherwise we would apparently witness a trial of this type: the accused has published a book which offends public morality; on a complaint from some of his "most respectable" fellow citizens he is also accused of libel; all sorts of other damaging charges have been placed against him, such as insulting the army, inciting to murder and rape, etc. Then, too, the accused immediately concurs with the accusation in "blasting" most of the ideas expressed. In his defense he merely says that he does not consider himself the author of his book; it is obviously just another surrealistic work which excludes all question of merit or lack of merit—he has merely copied a document without giving his own opinion, and he has no more connection with the circumstances than the presiding Judge.

What is true of the publication of a book will become true of countless other acts as soon as surrealistic methods begin to enjoy popularity. Then there will have to be a new morality to take the place of the current one, the source of all our ills.

is an oracle": [8] Yes, *as much as I please,* but what is an oracle, after all? [9] The piety of men does not fool me. The surrealistic voice which shook Cumae, Dodona, and Delphi is none other than the one which dictates to me my least violent speeches. My *time* cannot be its time; why should that voice help me solve the childish puzzle of my destiny? Unfortunately, I pretend to act in a world where, in order to account for its suggestions, I would be forced to resort to two sorts of interpreters: some to translate its pronouncements for me, others (who cannot be found) to impose on my fellow beings my interpretation of them. In this world in which I experience what I experience (take my word for it)— in this world, in short, damn it!—what do you expect me to do? Perhaps the surrealistic voice will fall silent. I am no longer at the stage of counting my disappearances. I will enter no more, not to the slightest degree, into the marvelous deduction of my years and days. I will be like Nijinsky, who was taken to the Ballets Russes last year and did not understand what sort of show he was witnessing. I will be alone, all alone in myself, indifferent to all the world's ballets. What I have done and what I have not done, I give to you.

And henceforth I feel a great desire to look down indulgently on the day-dream of science, a day-dream which is, ultimately, so vulgar. Radios? All right. Syphilis? If you like. Photography? I don't see any reason why not. Movies? Hurrah for the darkened halls. War? That really had us laughing. The telephone? Hello, yes. Youth! Charming white hair. Try to make me say thank you:

---

[8] Rimbaud.

[9] Nevertheless, NEVERTHELESS. . . . I must get it off my chest. Today, June 8, 1924, at about one o'clock, the voice whispered to me: "Béthune, Béthune." What can that mean? I know nothing about Béthune, and have only the faintest notion of the location of this place on the map of France, Béthune evokes nothing for me, not even a scene from *The Three Musketeers.* I ought to have set out for Béthune, where something was expecting me perhaps; but really, that would have been too obvious. Someone has told me that in a book by Chersterton [sic] there is a detective who, in order to find somebody he is looking for in a certain city, confines himself to searching from top to bottom those houses which, from the outside, reveal some slightly abnormal detail. This system is as good as any other.

Similarly, in 1919, Soupault would go into any number of impossible houses and ask the concierge if Philippe Soupault didn't live there. He would not have been surprised by an affirmative answer: he would have gone to knock on his door.

"Thank you." Thank you . . . If the common herd has great respect for things which are, really, laboratory experiments, it is
because these experiments have resulted in the invention of a
machine, the discovery of a serum—things by which the common
herd thinks it is directly benefited. It is sure that the experiment-
ers wanted to improve its lot. I do not know exactly what goes
into the ideals of the humanitarian scientist, but whatever it is,
it does not seem to me to involve very much kindness. I am speaking, of course, of the real scientists and not of the popularizers
of all sorts who get a license to practice. In this domain as in any
other, I believe in the pure surrealistic joy of the man who,
aware of the successive failure of all the others, will not admit
that he is beaten; who sets out from wherever he likes, and, by
any road except a *reasonable* one, arrives wherever he can. The
particular image which he may find opportune to point out his
progress and which may, perhaps, earn him public recognition,
I admit, holds no interest for me in itself. The equipment in
which he is necessarily entangled does not impress me either: his
glass tubes or my metallic pens. . . . As for his method, I hold
it as valid as mine. I have seen the discoverer of the cutaneous
reflex of the soles of the feet at work; he was manipulating his
subjects without pause; what he was doing was anything but an
"examination,"—*it was clear that he no longer trusted any plan.*
Now and again he would make an observation, distantly, without,
however, putting down his needle, and while his hammer kept on
moving. The treatment of the patients—he left that futile chore
to others. He was completely absorbed in his sacred fever.

Surrealism, as I envisage it, proclaims our absolute *noncon-
formity* loudly enough so that we need not drag it before the bar
of the real world as a witness for the defense. On the contrary, it
can only strengthen the case in favor of the state of utter distraction which we confidently hope to attain in this life. The
distraction of woman in Kant, the distraction "of grapes" in
Pasteur, the distraction of vehicles in Curie are profoundly symptomatic in this respect. The world is only relatively within the
grasp of thought, and such instances are merely the outstanding
episodes to date in a war of independence in which I am proud
to participate. Surrealism is the "invisible ray" which will make

it possible for us some day to triumph over our adversaries. "You are not trembling any more, carcass." This summer the roses are blue; the woods are glass. The earth draped in its greenery has as little effect on me as a ghost. Living and ceasing to live are imaginary solutions. Existence lies elsewhere.

Jean-Paul Sartre

[1905–   ]

۞

FRENCH EXISTENTIALISM draws on a variety of sources. Kierkegaard, Nietzsche, Heidegger, and Jaspers are among the most frequently mentioned. Its chief spokesman is Jean-Paul Sartre, who is equally distinguished as a philosopher (*Being and Nothingness,* 1943), a dramatist (*The Respectful Prostitute,* 1946), a novelist (*The Age of Reason,* 1945), and a critic (*Baudelaire,* 1945; the three collections of *Situations,* 1947, 1948, 1949). Since 1950 the existentialist movement has spread from France to Germany, England, Italy, the United States, and elsewhere. It has proved particularly attractive to writers and literary critics.

Existentialism begins with the assumption that all values are relative. It has no place for the ideal societies and religious myths of the humanists. On the other hand, man must act, and to act he must refer his actions to some value system. The result is an impossible paradox which is simultaneously painful and absurd. The solution proposed by Sartre—a solution which applies to writers with special force—is *engagement.* Becoming engaged in a particular situation permits man to achieve fulfillment, even nobility, despite his awareness of the absurdity of the goals toward which he is working. Existential criticism opposes "art for art's sake." Since it emphasizes acts of choice, it has encouraged much fruitful analysis of drama and the novel.

For existential criticism see A. Camus, *The Myth of Sisyphus* (New York, 1955); Sartre, *Literary Essays* (New York, 1957), and *What Is Literature?* (New York, 1957). For comment see: V. Erlich, "A Note on Sartre's Poetics," *Bucknell Review,* IX (1960), 123–9; H. Kuhn, *Encounter with Nothingness* (Urbana, 1949); C. Wilson, "Existential Criticism," *Chicago Review,* XIII (1959, 152–81.

The present selection is from *What Is Literature?,* trans. by Bernard Frechtman (New York: Philosophical Library, 1949), pp. 38–65. Reprinted by permission.

WHAT IS LITERATURE?

WHY WRITE?

Each has his reasons: for one, art is a flight; for another a means of conquering. But one can flee into a hermitage, into madness, into death. One can conquer by arms. Why does it have to be *writing*, why does one have to manage one's escapes and conquests by *writing?* Because, behind the various aims of authors, there is a deeper and more immediate choice which is common to all of us. We shall try to elucidate this choice, and we shall see whether it is not in the name of this very choice of writing that the self-commitment of writers must be required.

Each of our perceptions is accompanied by the consciousness that human reality is a 'revealer,' that is, it is through human reality that 'there is' being, or, to put it differently, that man is the means by which things are manifested. It is our presence in the world which multiplies relations. It is we who set up a relationship between this tree and that bit of sky. Thanks to us, that star which has been dead for millennia, that quarter moon, and that dark river are disclosed in the unity of a landscape. It is the speed of our car and our aeroplane which organizes the great masses of the earth. With each of our acts, the world reveals to us a new face. But, if we know that we are directors of being, we also know that we are not its producers. If we turn away from this landscape, it will sink back into its dark permanence. At least, it will sink back; there is no one mad enough to think that it is going to be annihilated. It is we who shall be annihilated, and the earth will remain in its lethargy until another consciousness comes along to awaken it. Thus, to our inner certainty of being 'revealers' is added that of being inessential in relation to the thing revealed.

One of the chief motives of artistic creation is certainly the need of feeling that we are essential in relationship to the world. If I fix on canvas or in writing a certain aspect of the fields or the sea or a look on someone's face which I have disclosed, I am conscious of having produced them by condensing relationships, by introducing order where there was none, by imposing the unity of mind on the diversity of things. That is, I feel myself essential in relation to my creation. But this time it is the created object which escapes me; I cannot reveal and produce at the same time. The creation becomes inessential in relation to the creative activity. First of all, even if it appears finished to others, the created object always seems to us in a state of suspension; we can always change this line, that shade, that word. Thus, it never *forces itself.* A novice painter asked his teacher, "When should I consider my painting finished?" And the teacher answered, "When you can look at it in amazement and say to yourself '*I'm* the one who did *that!'*"

Which amounts to saying 'never.' For it is virtually considering one's work with someone else's eyes and revealing what one has created. But it is self-evident that we are proportionally less conscious of the thing produced and more conscious of our productive activity. When it is a matter of pottery or carpentry, we work according to traditional patterns, with tools whose usage is codified; it is Heidegger's famous 'they' who are working with our hands. In this case, the result can seem to us sufficiently strange to preserve its objectivity in our eyes. But if we ourselves produce the rules of production, the measures, the criteria, and if our creative drive comes from the very depths of our heart, then we never find anything but ourselves in our work. It is we who have invented the laws by which we judge it. It is our history, our love, our gaiety that we recognize in it. Even if we should look at it without touching it any further, we never *receive* from it that gaiety or love. We put them into it. The results which we have obtained on canvas or paper never seem to us *objective.* We are too familiar with the processes of which they are the effects. These processes remain a subjective discovery; they are ourselves, our inspiration, our trick, and when we seek to *perceive* our work, we create it again, we repeat mentally the operations which produced it; each of its aspects appears as a result. Thus, in the perception, the object is given as the essential thing and the subject as the inessential. The latter seeks essentiality in the creation and obtains it, but then it is the object which becomes the inessential.

This dialectic is nowhere more apparent than in the art of writing, for the literary object is a peculiar top which exists only in movement. To make it come into view a concrete act called reading is necessary, and it lasts only as long as this act can last. Beyond that, there are only black marks on paper. Now, the writer cannot read what he writes, whereas the shoemaker can put on the shoes he has just made if they are his size, and the architect can live in the house he has built. In reading, one foresees; one waits. One foresees the end of the sentence, the following sentence, the next page. One waits for them to confirm or disappoint one's foresights. The reading is composed of a host of hypotheses, of dreams followed by awakenings, of hopes and deceptions. Readers are always ahead of the sentence they are reading in a merely probable future which partly collapses and partly comes together in proportion as they progress, which withdraws from one page to the next and forms the moving horizon of the literary object. Without waiting, without a future, without ignorance, there is no objectivity.

Now the operation of writing involves an implicit quasi-reading which makes real reading impossible. When the words form under his pen, the author doubtless sees them, but he does not see them as the reader does, since he knows them before writing them down. The function of his gaze is not to reveal, by brushing against them, the sleeping words which are waiting to be read, but to control the sketching of the signs. In short, it is a purely regulating mission, and the view before him reveals nothing except for slight slips of the pen. The writer neither foresees nor conjectures; he *projects*. It often happens that he awaits, as they say, the inspiration. But one does not wait for oneself the way one waits for others. If he hesitates, he knows that the future is not made, that he himself is going to make it, and if he still does not know what is going to happen to his hero, that simply means that he has not thought about it, that he has not decided upon anything. The future is then a blank page, whereas the future of the reader is two hundred pages filled with words which separate him from the end. Thus, the writer meets everywhere only *his* knowledge, *his* will, *his* plans, in short, himself. He touches only his own subjectivity; the object he creates is out of reach; he does not create it *for himself*. If he rereads himself, it is already too late. The sentence will never quite be a thing in his eyes. He goes to the very limits of the subjective but without crossing it. He appreciates the effect of a touch, of an epigram, of a well-placed adjective, but it is the effect they will have on others. He can judge it, not feel it. Proust never discovered the homosexuality of Charles, since he had decided upon it even before starting on his book. And if a day comes when the book takes on for its author a semblance of objectivity, it is because years have passed, because he has forgotten it, because its spirit is quite foreign to him, and doubtless he is no longer capable of writing it. This was the case with Rousseau when he reread the *Social Contract* at the end of his life.

Thus, it is not true that one writes for oneself. That would be the worst blow. In projecting one's emotions on paper, one barely manages to give them a languid extension. The creative act is only an incomplete and abstract moment in the production of a work. If the author existed alone he would be able to write as much as he liked; the work as *object* would never see the light of day and he would either have to put down his pen or despair. But the operation of writing implies that of reading as its dialectical correlative and these two connected acts necessitate two distinct agents. It is the joint effort of author and reader which brings upon the scene that concrete and imaginary object which is the work of the mind. There is no art except for and by others.

Reading seems, in fact, to be the synthesis of perception and creation.[1] It supposes the essentiality of both the subject and the object. The object is essential because it is strictly transcendent, because it imposes its own structures, and because one must wait for it and observe it; but the subject is also essential because it is required not only to disclose the object (that is, to make it possible for there to *be* an object) but also so that this object might exist absolutely (that is, to produce it). In a word, the reader is conscious of disclosing in creating, of creating by disclosing. In reality, it is not necessary to believe that reading is a mechanical operation and that signs make an impression upon him as light does on a photographic plate. If he is inattentive, tired, stupid, or thoughtless, most of the relations will escape him. He will never manage to 'catch on' to the object (in the sense in which we see that fire 'catches' or 'doesn't catch'). He will draw some phrases

---

[1] The same is true in different degrees regarding the spectator's attitude before other works of art (paintings, symphonies, statues, etc.).

out of the shadow, but they will seem to appear as random strokes. If he is at his best, he will project beyond the words a synthetic form, each phrase of which will be no more than a partial function: the 'theme,' the 'subject,' or the 'meaning.' Thus, from the very beginning, the meaning is no longer contained in the words, since it is he, on the contrary, who allows the significance of each of them to be understood; and the literary object, though realized *through* language, is never given *in* language. On the contrary, it is by nature a silence and an opponent of the word. In addition, the hundred thousand words aligned in a book can be read one by one so that the meaning of the work does not emerge. Nothing is accomplished if the reader does not put himself from the very beginning and almost without a guide at the height of this silence; if, in short, he does not invent it and does not then place there, and hold on to, the words and sentences which he awakens. And if I am told that it would be more fitting to call this operation a reinvention or a discovery, I shall answer that, first, such a reinvention would be as new and as original an act as the first invention. And, especially, when an object has never existed before, there can be no question of reinventing it or discovering it. For if the silence about which I am speaking is really the goal at which the author is aiming, he has, at least, never been familiar with it; his silence is subjective and anterior to language. It is the absence of words, the undifferentiated and lived silence of inspiration, which the word will then particularize, whereas the silence produced by the reader is an object. And at the very interior of this object there are more silences— which the author does not mention. It is a question of silences which are so particular that they could not retain any meaning outside the object which the reading causes to appear. However, it is these which give it its density and its particular face.

To say that they are unexpressed is hardly the word; for they are precisely the inexpressible. And that is why one does not come upon them at any definite moment in the reading; they are everywhere and nowhere. The quality of the marvellous in *Le Grand Meaulnes*, the grandioseness of *Armance*, the degree of realism and truth of Kafka's mythology, these are never given. The reader must invent them all in a continual exceeding of the written thing. To be sure, the author guides him, but all he does is guide him. The landmarks he sets up are separated by the void. The reader must unite them; he must go beyond them. In short, reading is directed creation.

On the one hand, the literary object has no other substance than the reader's subjectivity; Raskolnikov's waiting is *my* waiting which I lend him. Without this impatience of the reader he would remain only a collection of signs. His hatred of the police magistrate who questions him is my hatred which has been solicited and wheedled out of me by signs, and the police magistrate himself would not exist without the hatred I have for him via Raskolnikov. That is what animates him, it is his very flesh.

But on the other hand, the words are there like traps to arouse our feelings and to reflect them towards us. Each word is a path of transcendence; it shapes our feelings, names them, and attributes them to an imaginary personage who takes it upon himself to live them for us and who has no other substance than these borrowed passions; he confers objects, perspectives, and a horizon upon them.

Thus, for the reader, all is to do and all is already done; the work exists only at the exact level of his capacities; while he reads and creates, he knows that he can always go further in his reading, can always create more profoundly, and thus the work seems to him as inexhaustible and opaque as things. We would readily reconcile that 'rational intuition' which Kant reserved to divine Reason with this absolute production of qualities, which, to the extent that they emanate from our subjectivity, congeal before our eyes into impenetrable objectivities.

Since the creation can find its fulfilment only in reading, since the artist must entrust to another the job of carrying out what he has begun, since it is only through the consciousness of the reader that he can regard himself as essential to his work, all literary work is an appeal. To write is to make an appeal to the reader that he lead into objective existence the revelation which I have undertaken by means of language. And if it should be asked *to what* the writer is appealing, the answer is simple. As the sufficient reason for the appearance of the aesthetic object is never found either in the book (where we find merely solicitations to produce the object) or in the author's mind, and as his subjectivity, which he cannot get away from, cannot give a reason for the act of leading into objectivity, the appearance of the work of art is a new event which cannot *be explained* by anterior data. And since this directed creation is an absolute beginning, it is therefore brought about by the freedom of the reader, and by what is purest in that freedom. Thus, the writer appeals to the reader's freedom to collaborate in the production of his work.

It will doubtless be said that all tools address themselves to our freedom since they are the instruments of a possible action, and that the work of art is not unique in that. And it is true that the tool is the congealed outline of an operation. But it remains on the level of the hypothetical imperative. I may use a hammer to nail up a case or to hit my neighbour over the head. In so far as I consider it in itself, it is not an appeal to my freedom; it does not put me face to face with it; rather, it aims at using it by substituting a set succession of traditional procedures for the free invention of means. The book does not serve my freedom; it requires it. Indeed, one cannot address oneself to freedom as such by means of constraint, fascination, or entreaties. There is only one way of attaining it; first, by recognizing it, then, having confidence in it, and finally, requiring of it an act, an act in its own name, that is, in the name of the confidence that one brings to it.

Thus, the book is not, like the tool, a means for any end whatever; the end to which it offers itself is the reader's freedom. And the Kantian expression 'finality without end' [2] seems to me quite inappropriate for designating the work of art. In fact, it implies that the aesthetic object presents only the appearance of a finality and is limited to soliciting the free and ordered play of the imagination. It forgets that the imagination of the spectator has not only a regulating function, but a constitutive one. It does not play; it is called upon to recompose the beautiful object beyond the traces left by the artist. The imagination cannot revel in itself any more than can the other functions of the mind; it is always on the outside, always engaged in an enterprise. There would be finality without end if some object offered such a well-arranged composition that it would lead us to suppose that it has an end even though we cannot ascribe one to it. By defining the beautiful in this way one can—and this is Kant's aim—liken the beauty of art to natural beauty, since a flower, for example,

[2] An alternative translation of "purposiveness without purpose." (Ed.)

presents so much symmetry, such harmonious colours, and such
regular curves, that one is immediately tempted to seek a finalist
explanation for all these properties and to see them as just so
many means at the disposal of an unknown end. But that is exactly the error. The beauty of nature is in no way comparable to
that of art. The work of art *does not have* an end; there we agree
with Kant. But the reason is that it is an end. The Kantian formula does not account for the appeal which resounds at the
basis of each painting, each statue, each book. Kant believes that
the work of art first exists as fact and that it is then seen. Whereas,
it exists only if one *looks* at it and if it is first pure appeal, pure
exigence to exist. It is not an instrument whose existence is
manifest and whose end is undetermined. It presents itself as a
task to be discharged; from the very beginning it places itself
on the level of the categorical imperative. You are perfectly free
to leave that book on the table. But if you open it, you assume
responsibility for it. For freedom is not experienced by its enjoying its free subjective functioning, but in a creative act required
by an imperative. This absolute end, this imperative which is
transcendent yet acquiesced in, which freedom itself adopts as
its own, is what we call a value. The work of art is a value because it is an appeal.

If I appeal to my readers so that we may carry the enterprise
which I have begun to a successful conclusion, it is self-evident
that I consider him as a pure freedom, as an unconditioned activity; thus, in no case can I address myself to his passiveness,
that is, to try to *affect* him, to communicate to him, from the very
first, emotions of fear, desire, or anger. There are, doubtless,
authors who concern themselves solely with arousing these emotions because they are foreseeable, manageable, and because
they have at their disposal sure-fire means for provoking them.
But it is also true that they are reproached for this kind of thing,
as Euripides has been since antiquity because he had children
appear on the stage. Freedom is alienated in the state of passion;
it is abruptly engaged in partial enterprises; it loses sight of its
task, which is to produce an absolute end. And the book is no
longer anything but a means for feeding hate or desire. The
writer should not seek to *overwhelm;* otherwise he is in contradiction with himself; if he wishes to *make demands* he must

propose only the task to be fulfilled. Hence, the character of pure presentation which appears essential to the work of art. The reader must be able to make a certain aesthetic withdrawal. This is what Gautier foolishly confused with 'art for art's sake' and the Parnassians with the imperturbability of the artist. It is simply a matter of precaution, and Genet more justly calls it the author's politeness towards the reader. But that does not mean that the writer makes an appeal to some sort of abstract and conceptual freedom. One certainly creates the aesthetic object with feelings; if it is touching, it appears through our tears; if it is comic, it will be recognized by laughter. However, these feelings are of a particular kind. They have their origin in free- dom; they are loaned. The belief which I accord the tale is freely assented to. It is a Passion, in the Christian sense of the word, that is, a freedom which resolutely puts itself into a state of passiveness to obtain a certain transcendent effect by this sac- rifice. The reader renders himself credulous; he descends into credulity which, though it ends by enclosing him like a dream, is at every moment conscious of being free. An effort is some- times made to force the writer into this dilemma: 'Either one believes in your story, and it is intolerable, or one does not be- lieve in it, and it is ridiculous.' But the argument is absurd be- cause the characteristic of aesthetic consciousness is to be a belief by means of commitment, by oath, a belief sustained by fidelity to one's self and to the author, a perpetually renewed choice to believe. I can awaken at every moment, and I know it; but I do not want to; reading is a free dream. So that all feelings which are exacted on the basis of this imaginary belief are like partic- ular modulations of my freedom. Far from absorbing or mask- ing it, there are so many different ways it has chosen to reveal itself to itself. Raskolnikov, as I have said, would only be a shadow, without the mixture of repulsion and friendship which I feel for him and which makes him live. But, by a reversal which is the characteristic of the imaginary object, it is not his be- haviour which excites my indignation or esteem, but my indigna- tion and esteem which give consistency and objectivity to his behaviour. Thus, the reader's feelings are never dominated by the object, and as no external reality can condition them, they have their permanent source in freedom; that is, they are all generous

—for I call a feeling generous which has its origin and its end in freedom. Thus, reading is an exercise in generosity, and what the writer requires of the reader is not the application of an abstract freedom but the gift of his whole person, with his passions, his prepossessions, his sympathies, his sexual temperament, and his scale of values. Only this person will give himself generously; freedom goes through and through him and comes to transform the darkest masses of his sensibility. And as activity has rendered itself passive in order for it better to create the object, vice versa, passiveness becomes an act; the man who is reading has raised himself to the highest degree. That is why we see people who are known for their toughness shed tears at the recital of imaginary misfortunes; for the moment they have become what they would have been if they had not spent their lives hiding their freedom from themselves.

Thus, the author writes in order to address himself to the freedom of readers, and he requires it in order to make his work exist. But he does not stop there; he also requires that they return this confidence which he has given them, that they recognize his creative freedom, and that they in turn solicit it by a symmetrical and inverse appeal. Here there appears the other dialectical paradox of reading; the more we experience our freedom, the more we recognize that of the other; the more he demands of us, the more we demand of him.

When I am enchanted with a landscape, I know very well that it is not I who create it, but I also know that without me the relations which are established before my eyes among the trees, the foliage, the earth, and the grass would not exist at all. I know that I can give no reason for the appearance of finality which I discover in the assortment of hues and in the harmony of the forms and movements created by the wind. Yet, it exists; there it is before my eyes, and I can make something more out of what is already there. But even if I believe in God, I cannot establish any passage, unless it be purely verbal, between the divine, universal solicitude and the particular spectacle which I am considering. To say that He made the landscape in order to charm me or that He made me the kind of person who is pleased by it is to take a question for an answer. Is the marriage of this blue and that green deliberate? How can I know? The idea of

a universal providence is no guarantee of any particular intention, especially in the case under consideration, since the green of the grass is explained by biological laws, specific constants, and geographical determinism, while the reason for the blue of the water is accounted for by the depth of the river, the nature of the soil, and the swiftness of the current. The assorting of the shades, if it is willed, can only be something *thrown into the bargain;* it is the meeting of two causal series, that is to say, at first sight, a fact of chance. At best, the finality remains problematic. All the relations we establish remain hypotheses; no end is proposed to us in the manner of an imperative, since none is expressly revealed as having been willed by a creator. Thus, our freedom is never *called forth* by natural beauty. Or rather, there is an appearance of order in the whole which includes the foliage, the forms, and the movements, hence, the illusion of a calling forth which seems to solicit this freedom and which disappears immediately when one looks at it. Hardly have we begun to run our eyes over this arrangement, than the appeal disappears; we remain alone, free to tie up one colour with another or with a third, to set up a relationship between the tree and the water or the tree and the sky, or the tree, the water and the sky. My freedom becomes caprice. To the extent that I establish new relationships, I remove myself further from the illusory objectivity which solicits me. I *muse* about certain motifs which are vaguely outlined by the things; the natural reality is no longer anything but a pretext for musing. Or, in that case, because I have deeply regretted that this arrangement which was momentarily perceived was not offered to me by somebody and consequently is not *real*, the result is that I fix my dream, that I transpose it to canvas or in writing. Thus, I interpose myself between the finality without end which appears in the natural spectacles and the gaze of other men. I transmit it to them. It becomes human by this transmission. Art here is a ceremony of the *gift* and the gift alone brings about the metamorphosis. It is something like the transmission of titles and powers in the matriarchate where the mother does not possess the names, but is the indispensable intermediary between uncle and nephew. Since I have captured this illusion in flight, since I lay it out for other men and have disentangled it and rethought it for them, they can consider it with confidence.

It has become intentional. As for me, I remain, to be sure, at the border of the subjective and the objective without ever being able to contemplate the objective arrangement which I transmit. The reader, on the contrary, progresses in security. However far he may go, the author has gone further. Whatever connections he may establish among the different parts of the book—among the chapters or the words—he has a guarantee, namely, that they have been expressly willed. As Descartes says, he can even pretend that there is a secret order among parts which seem to have no connection. The creator has preceded him along the way, and the most beautiful disorders are effects of art, that is, again, order. Reading is induction, interpolation, extrapolation, and the basis of these activities rests on the reader's will, as for a long time it was believed that that of scientific induction rested on the divine will. A gentle force accompanies us and supports us from the first page to the last. That does not mean that we fathom the artist's intentions easily. They constitute, as we have said, the object of conjectures, and there is an *experience* of the reader; but these conjectures are supported by the great certainty we have that the beauties which appear in the book are never accidental. In nature, the tree and the sky harmonize only by chance; if, on the contrary, in the novel, the protagonists find themselves in a *certain* tower, in a *certain* prison, if they stroll in a *certain* garden, it is a matter both of the restitution of independent causal series (the character had a certain state of mind which was due to a succession of psychological and social events; on the other hand, he betook himself to a determined place and the layout of the city required him to cross a certain park) and of the expression of a deeper finality, for the park came into existence only *in order to* harmonize with a certain state of mind, to express it by means of things or to put it into relief by a vivid contrast, and the state of mind itself was conceived in connection with the landscape. Here it is causality which is appearance and which might be called 'causality without cause,' and it is the finality which is the profound reality. But if I can thus in all confidence put the order of ends under the order of causes, it is because by opening the book I am asserting that the object has its source in human freedom.

If I were to suspect the artist of having written out of passion and in passion, my confidence would immediately vanish, for it would serve no purpose to have supported the order of causes by the order of ends. The latter would be supported in its turn by a psychic causality and the work of art would end by re-entering the chain of determinism. Certainly I do not deny when I am reading that the author may be impassioned, nor even that he might have conceived the first plan of his work under the sway of passion. But his decision to write supposes that he withdraws somewhat from his feelings, in short, that he has transformed his emotions into free emotions as I do mine while reading him, that is, that he is in an attitude of generosity.

Thus, reading is a pact of generosity between author and reader. Each one trusts the other; each one counts on the other, demands of the other as much as he demands of himself. For this confidence is itself generosity. Nothing can force the author to believe that his reader will use his freedom; nothing can force the reader to believe that the author has used his. Both of them make a free decision. There is then established a dialectical going-and-coming; when I read, I make demands; if my demands are met, what I am then reading provokes me to demand more of the author, which means to demand of the author that he demand more of me. And, vice versa, the author's demand is that I carry my demands to the highest pitch. Thus, my freedom, by revealing itself, reveals the freedom of the other.

It matters little whether the aesthetic object is the product of 'realistic' art (or supposedly such) or 'formal' art. At any rate, the natural relations are inverted; that tree on the first plane of the Cézanne painting first appears as the product of a causal chain. But the causality is an illusion; it will doubtless remain as a proposition as long as we look at the painting, but it will be supported by a deep finality; if the tree is placed in such a way it is because the rest of the painting *requires* that this form and those colours be placed on the first plane. Thus, through the phenomenal causality, our gaze attains finality as the deep structure of the object, and, beyond finality, it attains human freedom as its source and original basis. Vermeer's realism is carried so far that at first it might be thought to be photographic. But if one considers the splendour of his texture, the pink and velvety glory of his little brick walls, the blue thickness of a branch of woodbine, the glazed darkness of his vestibules, the orange-coloured flesh of his faces, which are as polished as the stone of holy-water basins, one suddenly feels, in the pleasure that he experiences, that the finality is not so much in the forms or colours as in his material imagination. It is the very substance and temper of the things which here give the forms their reason for being. With this realist we are perhaps closest to absolute creation, since it is in the very passiveness of the matter that we meet the unfathomable freedom of man.

The work is never limited to the painted, sculpted, or narrated object. Just as one perceives things only against the background of the world, so the objects represented by art appear against the background of the universe. On the background of the adventures of Fabrice are the Italy of 1820, Austria, France, the sky and stars which the Abbé Blanis consults, and finally the whole earth. If the painter presents us with a field or a vase of flowers, his paintings are windows which are open on the whole world. We follow the red path which is buried among the wheat much farther than Van Gogh has painted it, among other wheat fields, under other clouds, to the river which empties into the sea, and we extend to infinity, to the other end of the world, the deep finality which supports the existence of the field and the earth. So that, through the various objects which it produces or reproduces, the creative act aims at a total renewal of the world. Each painting, each book, is a recovery of the totality of being. Each of them presents this totality to the freedom of the spectator. For this is quite the final goal of art: to recover this world by giving it to be seen as it is, but as if it had its source in human freedom. But, since what the author creates takes on objective reality only in the eyes of the spectator, this recovery is consecrated by the ceremony of the spectacle—and particularly of reading. We are already in a better position to answer the question we raised a while ago: the writer chooses to appeal to the freedom of other men so that, by the reciprocal implications of their demands, they may readapt the totality of being to man and may again enclose the universe within man.

If we wish to go still further, we must bear in mind that the writer, like all other artists, aims at giving his reader a certain feeling that is customarily called aesthetic pleasure, and which

I would very much rather call aesthetic joy, and that this feeling, when it appears, is a sign that the work is achieved. It is therefore fitting to examine it in the light of the preceding considerations. In effect, this joy, which is denied to the creator, in so far as he creates, becomes one with the aesthetic consciousness of the spectator, that is, in the case under consideration, of the reader. It is a complex feeling but one whose structures and condition are inseparable from one another. It is identical, at first, with the recognition of a transcendent and absolute end which, for a moment, suspends the utilitarian round of ends-means and means-ends,[3] that is, of an appeal or, what amounts to the same thing, of a value. And the positional consciousness which I take of this value is necessarily accompanied by the non-positional consciousness of my freedom, since my freedom is manifested to itself by a transcendent exigency. The recognition of freedom by itself is joy, but this structure of non-thetical consciousness implies another: since, in effect, reading is creation, my freedom does not only appear to itself as pure autonomy but as creative activity, that is, it is not limited to giving itself its own law but perceives itself as being constitutive of the object. It is on this level that the phenomenon specifically is manifested, that is, a creation wherein the created object is given *as object* to its creator. It is the sole case in which the creator gets any enjoyment out of the object he creates. And the word enjoyment which is applied to the positional consciousness of the word read indicates sufficiently that we are in the presence of an essential structure of aesthetic joy. This positional enjoyment is accompanied by the nonpositional consciousness of being essential in relation to an object perceived as essential. I shall call this aspect of aesthetic consciousness the feeling of security; it is this which stamps the strongest aesthetic emotions with a sovereign calm. It has its origin in the authentication of a strict harmony between subjectivity and objectivity. As, on the other hand, the aesthetic object is properly the world in so far as it is aimed at through the imaginary, aesthetic joy accompanies the positional consciousness that the world is a value, that is, a task proposed

---

[3] In *practical life* a means may be taken for an end as soon as one searches for it, and each end is revealed as a means of attaining another end.

to human freedom. I shall call this the aesthetic modification of the human project, for, as usual, the world appears as the horizon of our situation, as the infinite distance which separates us from ourselves, as the synthetic totality of the given, as the undifferentiated whole of obstacles and implements—but never as a demand addressed to our freedom. Thus, aesthetic joy proceeds to this level of the consciousness which I take of recovering and internalizing that which is non-ego *par excellence*, since I transform the given into an imperative and the fact into a value. The world is *my task*, that is, the essential and freely accepted function of my freedom is to make that unique and absolute object which is the universe come into being in an unconditioned movement. And, thirdly, the preceding structures imply a pact between human freedoms, for, on the one hand, reading is a confident and exacting recognition of the freedom of the writer, and, on the other hand, aesthetic pleasure, as it is itself experienced in the form of a value, involves an absolute exigence in regard to others; every man, in so far as he is a freedom, feels the same pleasure in reading the same work. Thus, all mankind is present in its highest freedom; it sustains the being of a world which is both *its* world and the 'external' world. In aesthetic joy the positional consciousness is an *image-making* consciousness of the world in its totality both as being and having to be, both as totally ours and totally foreign, and the more ours as it is the more foreign. The non-positional consciousness *really* envelops the harmonious totality of human freedoms in so far as it makes the object of a universal confidence and exigency.

To write is thus both to disclose the world and to offer it as a task to the generosity of the reader. It is to have recourse to the consciousness of others in order to make one's self be recognized as *essential* to the totality of being; it is to wish to live this essentiality by means of interposed persons; but, on the other hand, as the real world is revealed only by action, as one can feel oneself in it only by exceeding it in order to change it, the novelist's universe would lack depth if it were not discovered in a movement to transcend it. It has often been observed that an object in a story does not derive its density of existence from the number and length of the descriptions devoted to it, but from the complexity of its connections with the different characters. The more often the characters handle it, take it up, and put it down, in short, go beyond it towards their own ends, the more real will it appear. Thus, of the world of the novel, that is, the totality of men and things, we may say that in order for it to offer its maximum density the disclosure-creation by which the reader discovers it must also be an imaginary participation in the action; in other words, the more disposed one is to change it, the more alive it will be. The error of realism has been to believe that the real reveals itself to contemplation, and that consequently one could draw an impartial picture of it. How could that be possible, since the very perception is partial, since by itself the naming is already a modification of the object? And how could the writer, who wants himself to be essential to this universe, want to be essential to the injustice which this universe comprehends? Yet, he must be; but if he accepts being the creator of injustices, it is in a movement which goes beyond them towards their abolition. As for me who reads, if I create and keep alive an unjust world, I cannot help making myself responsible for it. And the author's whole art is bent on obliging me to *create* what he *discloses,* therefore to compromise myself. So both of us bear the responsibility for the universe. And precisely because this universe is supported by the joint effort of our two freedoms, and because the author, with me as medium, has attempted to integrate it into the human, it must appear truly *in itself,* in its very marrow, as being shot through and through with a freedom which has taken human freedom as its end, and if it is not really the city of ends that it ought to be, it must at least be a stage along the way; in a word, it must be a becoming and it must always be considered and presented not as a crushing mass which weighs us down, but from the point of view of its going beyond towards that city of ends. However bad and hopeless the humanity which it paints may be, the work must have an air of generosity. Not, of course, that this generosity is to be expressed by means of edifying discourses and virtuous characters; it must not even be premeditated, and it is quite true that fine sentiments do not make fine books. But it must be the very warp and woof of the book, the stuff out of which the people and things are cut; whatever the subject, a sort of essential lightness must appear everywhere and remind us that the work is never a natural datum, but an *exigence* and a *gift*. And if I am given this world with its injustices, it is not so that I may contemplate them coldly, but that I may animate them with my indignation, that I may disclose them and create them with their nature as injustices, that is, as abuses to be suppressed. Thus, the writer's universe will only reveal itself in all its depth to the examination, the admiration, and the indignation of the reader; and the generous love is a promise to maintain, and the generous indignation is a promise to change, and the admiration a promise to imitate; although literature is one thing and morality a quite different one, at the heart of the aesthetic imperative we discern the moral imperative. For, since the one who writes recognizes, by the very fact that he takes the trouble to write, the freedom of his readers, and since the one who reads, by the mere fact of his opening the book, recognizes the freedom of the writer, the work of art, from whichever side you approach it, is an act of confidence in the freedom of men. And since readers, like the author, recognize this freedom only to demand that it manifest itself, the work can be defined as an imaginary presentation of the world in so far as it demands human freedom. The result of which is that there is no 'gloomy literature,' since, however dark may be the colours in which one paints the world, one paints it only so that free men may feel their freedom as they face it. Thus, there are only good and bad novels. The bad novel aims to please by flattering, whereas the good one is an exigence and an act of faith. But above all, the unique point of view from which the author can present the world to those freedoms whose concurrence he wishes to bring about is that of a world to be impregnated always with more freedom. It would be inconceivable that this unleashing of generosity provoked by the writer could be used to authorize an injustice, and that the reader could enjoy his freedom while reading a work which approves or accepts or simply abstains from condemning the subjection of man by man. One can imagine a good novel being written by an American negro even if hatred of the whites were spread all over it, because it is the freedom of his race that he demands through this hatred. And, as he invites me to assume the attitude of generosity, the moment I feel myself a pure freedom I cannot bear to identify myself with a race of oppressors. Thus, I require of all freedoms that they demand the liberation of coloured people against the white race and against myself in so far as I am a part of it, but nobody can suppose for a moment that it is possible to write a good novel in praise of anti-Semitism.[4] For, the moment I feel that my freedom is indissolubly linked with that of all other men, it cannot be demanded of me that I use it to approve the enslavement of a part of these men. Thus, whether he is an essayist, a pamphleteer, a satirist, or a novelist, whether he speaks only of individual passions or whether he attacks the social order, the writer, a free man addressing free men, has only one subject—freedom.

Hence, any attempt to enslave his readers threatens him in his very art. A blacksmith can be affected by fascism in his life as a man, but not necessarily in his craft; a writer will be affected in both, and even more in his craft than in his life. I have seen writers, who before the war called for fascism with all their hearts, smitten with sterility at the very moment when the Nazis were loading them with honours. I am thinking of Drieu la Rochelle in particular; he was mistaken, but he was sincere. He proved it. He had agreed to direct a Nazi-inspired review. The first few months he reprimanded, rebuked, and lectured his countrymen. No one answered him because no one was free to do so. He became irritated; he no longer *felt* his readers. He became more insistent, but no sign appeared to prove that he had been understood. No sign of hatred, nor of anger either; nothing. He seemed to have lost his bearings, the victim of a growing distress. He complained bitterly to the Germans. His articles had been superb; they became shrill. The moment arrived when he struck his breast; no echo, except among the bought journalists whom he despised. He handed in his resignation, withdrew it, again spoke, still in the desert. Finally, he said nothing, gagged by the silence of others. He had demanded the enslavement of

4 This last remark may arouse some readers. If so, I'd like to know a single good novel whose express purpose was to serve oppression, a single good novel which has been written against Jews, negroes, workers, or colonial people. 'But if there isn't any, that's no reason why someone may not write one some day.' But you then admit that you are an abstract theoretician. You, not I. For it is in the name of your abstract conception of art that you assert the possibility of a fact which has ever come into being, whereas I limit myself to proposing an explanation for a recognized fact.

others, but in his crazy mind he must have imagined that it was voluntary, that it was still free. It came; the man in him congratulated himself mightily, but the writer could not bear it. While this was going on, others, who, happily, were in the majority, understood that the freedom of writing implies the freedom of the citizen. One does not write for slaves. The art of prose is bound up with the only régime in which prose has meaning, democracy. When one is threatened, the other is too. And it is not enough to defend them with the pen. A day comes when the pen is forced to stop, and the writer must then take up arms. Thus, however you might have come to it, whatever the opinions you might have professed, literature throws you into battle. Writing is a certain way of wanting freedom; once you have begun, you are committed, willy-nilly.

Jacques Maritain

[1882–   ]

❧❦❧

MARITAIN'S CAREER has been devoted to the reconciliation of aestheticism and religious value. He began his career as a disciple of Bergson. Despite his criticism of Bergson in *The Philosophy of Bergson* (1914), his debt remains extensive. *Art and Scholasticism* (1920) is an attempt to define the place of aesthetic values in the Thomistic system without doing violence to either art or religion. In his later work he has extended his ideas without basically changing them. The artist, according to Maritain, possesses the gift of "creative intuition." Like earlier aesthetic critics he recognizes that the artist must rely on his creative gift rather than on moral or logical preconceptions. However, creative intuition is only one of several faculties which comprise the whole man, and each of these faculties has its own legitimate claims. The artist must not abandon his humanity for the sake of his art, for if he does, the art, itself, will suffer. Maritain has developed this thesis brilliantly and with great tact. He remains today the leading representative of neo-Catholic criticism.

Among Maritain's works see: *Art and Faith* (New York, 1948); *Art and Scholasticism* (New York, 1937); *Creative Intuition in Art and Poetry* (New York, 1953); *The Responsibility of the Artist* (New York, 1960); *The Situation of Poetry* (New York, 1955). For comment see: W. Fowlie, *Jacob's Night: The Religious Renaissance in France* (New York, 1947); V. Simonsen, *L'Esthétique de Jacques Maritain* (Copenhagen, 1956).

The present selection is from *The Situation of Poetry*, trans. by Marshall Suther (New York: The Philosophical Library, 1955), pp. 52–70. Reprinted by permission.

THE SITUATION OF POETRY

CONCERNING POETIC KNOWLEDGE

ANCIENT AND MODERN philosophers have speculated a great deal about poetry; but, necessarily, from without. We admit—I tried

337

338 *New Directions*

to say why a moment ago—that it is in the 19th century, with the preparations made by the romantics, and above all with Baudelaire and Rimbaud, that poetry began *among the poets* to become deliberately and systematically conscious of itself. Every new consciousness is accompanied by a risk of perversion. The risk here was that poetry would want to escape from the line of the work-to-be-made in order to turn back upon the soul itself, thinking to fill the soul with pure knowledge and become its absolute.

Now it is quite true that one may be a poet without producing—without having yet produced—any work of art, but if one is a poet one is virtually turned towards operation. It is of the essence of poetry to be in the operative line, as a tree is in the line of producing fruit. But in becoming conscious of itself, poetry in some measures frees itself from the work-to-be-made, in the measure in which to know oneself is to turn back upon oneself.

At the same time poetry disengages its active principle in a pure state, I mean poetic knowledge itself, that indescribable and fecund experience which Plato called enthusiasm, and which the brief indications given above tried to characterize. And at that instant there awakens in poetry a desire hidden in its transcendental character and in its very spirituality, a metaphysical aspiration, to pass beyond, to transgress the limits which enclose it in a nature, at a certain degree on the scale of beings. At once poetry enters into conflict with art, with that art in whose way its nature condemns it to go: when art demands to form intellectively, according to a creative idea, poetry demands to suffer, to listen, to descend to the roots of being, to an unknown that no idea can circumscribe. "For *I* is an other," said Rimbaud,[1] and could one better define that engulfment in the *inhabited* subject which is poetic knowledge? An instant of vertigo is enough then. If poetry loses its footing, there it is, detached from its operative ends. It becomes a means of knowing; it no longer wants to create, but to know. When art demands to make, poetry, loosed from its natural ties, demands to know.

But knowledge—what a temptation, what an absolute! And

---

[1] Letter to Paul Demeny ("Lettre du Voyant"), 15 May, 1871, first published by Paterne Berrichon in *La Nouvelle Revue Française*, October, 1912.

such a knowledge, which engages the whole of man! And which gives the world to man in causing him to suffer the world! If, freed (or believing itself freed) from the relativities of art, poetry finds a soul which nothing else occupies, nothing confronting it, it is going to develop an appalling appetite to know, which will vampirise all that is metaphysical in man, and all that is carnal as well.

The experience of Rimbaud is decisive here. Whereas later, while appealing to Rimbaud, the surrealists were to try to use poetry as an instrument for their quasi-"scientific" curiosity, Rimbaud himself obeyed, he consciously and voluntarily obeyed the ultimate tyrannical exigencies of poetic knowledge let loose in its full state of savagery—it is that which made him search for all the treasures of the spirit in the forbidden byways of a heroic and "debauched" banditry.

A moment ago I quoted from the *Lettre du Voyant,* in which, precisely, while explaining that he is giving himself to knowledge, he declares in the same breath that he is "debauching" himself. Let us limit ourselves to this capital text, and to the evidence it offers us, the significance of which one's commentary would never exhaust.

"The first study of a man who wants to be a poet"—who *wants* to be a poet, says Rimbaud: taking consciousness, a deliberate undertaking, and there already the trap is hidden—"is knowledge of himself, complete. He seeks his soul, he inspects it, he tries it, learns it. As son as he knows it, he must cultivate it: that seems simple: in every brain a natural development is accomplished; so many *egotists* proclaim themselves authors; there are many more of them who attribute to themselves their intellectual progress! But it is a matter of making the soul monstrous: in the manner of the comprachicos, what! Imagine a man planting and cultivating warts on his face. I say it is necessary to *be a seer,* to make oneself a *seer.*

"The poet makes himself a *seer* by a long, immense, and reasoned *derangement* of *all the senses.* All the forms of love, of suffering, of madness; he searches in himself, he drains from himself all the poisons, that he may keep only their quintessences. Ineffable torture, in which he needs all the faith, all the superhuman force, in which he becomes among all the critical cases,

the great criminal, the great outcast—and the supreme Savant!—
For he arrives at the *unknown*—since he cultivates his soul, already richer than any! He arrives at the *unknown;* and when,
frantic, he would finish by losing the understanding of his visions,
he has seen them! Let him croak in the bouncing about by
unheard-of and unnameable things; there will come other horrible laborers: they will begin at the horizons where the other
gave way!" [2]

The conclusion, enunciated with an astonishing lucidity in
A Season in Hell, was inevitable. Poetry aiming, in order to
realize itself in full plenitude, to deliver itself from every condition
of existence, poetic knowledge exalting itself to the point of
claiming *absolute* life, engages itself in a dialectic which kills it.
It wants to be everything and give everything, the act, sanctity,
transubstantiation, the miracle; it has charge of humanity. And
whatever it does, it is limited by nature, in reality, to one line
only, a particular and very humble one indeed, to the line of art
and of the work-to-be-made. In the end there is nothing left but
to lapse into silence, to renounce the work and poetry at the same
time. Rimbaud not only stopped writing, he avenged himself on
poetry, applied himself to casting it from him as a monster.

✿   ✿   ✿

The preceding considerations suggest to us the idea that poetry
does not of *itself* accord with anything other than itself, not with
faith, nor with metaphysics, nor with sanctity: just as in general
nothing which reaches toward the infinite accords of itself with
anything else. It is folly, as we have just seen, to want it *alone* in
the soul. But *with the rest*—with all the other virtues and energies of the spirit, how should it get along? The fact is that all
these energies, in so far as they pertain to the transcendental universe, aspire like poetry to surpass their nature and to infinitise
themselves. They compose the one for the other a condition of
existence, they help one another exist, but all the while hating
one another (in a sense, for they love one another too), imposing limits on one another, seeking to reduce one another to
impotence. It is only in this conflict that they can exist and grow.

[2] Letter to Paul Demeny ("Lettre du Voyant"), cited above.

Art, poetry, metaphysics, prayer, contemplation, each one is wounded, struck traitorously in the best of itself, and that is the very condition of its living. *Man* unites them by force, weeping all his tears, dying every day, and thus he wins his peace and their peace.

The experience of Rimbaud was too complete and too hard for the lesson to be learned from it. In spite of Rimbaud, in spite of *A Season in Hell*, still attempting to enter by main force further into the consciousness of poetry, still persisting in this travail, and, what is more, making a glory of it, poets had to commit the same error of misdirection. But this time pretending to continue the trip up this blind alley, to go to the end of the world and beyond the world in a motionless vehicle: and can this not be accomplished by way of illusion, and thanks to a certain magic?

It is in its attempt to use poetry to fulfill the desires of man and his thirst for knowledge, and his need to see the face of the absolute, that surrealism has for us an exceptional historical interest.

According to the remark of M. Marcel Raymond cited above, "to attest that the game is not yet up, that all can perhaps be saved—that was the essential of the surrealist message." In short, the surrealists also have been victims of poetic knowledge. In the beginning for them, it was a matter above all of rediscovering, as Raïssa Maritain writes . . . "that river of the spirit which flows under all our customary activity, that profound authentic reality, foreign to all formulae, perceived in those 'minutes of abandonment to hidden forces' which vivify." [3] The fact was, I doubt not, that they had actually known those privileged instants of natural ecstasy in which the soul "reimmerses itself so to speak in its source, and from which it issues renewed and fortified" by the poetic experience. That experience they had, let that fortune not be denied them! It is what makes for the value and the tragedy of their adventure. They had it while turning away, by reflection, from the poetic work and from song, to engage themselves desperately in the circumvolutions of the consciousness. But they were caught in the trap. Wresting poetry almost completely from its natural finalities, they wanted to make of it a

[3] Raïssa Maritain, "Sense and Nonsense in Poetry," in *The Situation of Poetry*, p. 11.

means of speculative knowledge, an instrument of science, a method of metaphysical discovery.

And they not only confounded poetry with metaphysics; they confounded it with morality, and they confounded it with sanctity. They charged it thus with a burden it could not bear. What end, then, could its power of seduction serve, if not to astonish us with tricks, to open up to us a world of mere appearances and of tinsel?

Finally because they confounded the passivity of the poetic experience with that of psychic automatism, the surrealists believed that the means par excellence, or rather the unique source, of poetry was the delivering of images, the liberating of charges of emotion and dream accumulated in our animal subconscious filled with desires and signs. What then developed among the poets of that generation was a remarkable sharpness of instinct to confuse the traces and to disconcert the mind by means of surprise and the stimulative wounding of the imagination; and of how much more value is this allusive rapidity than the classic *discursus!* But in itself, if one remains at that point, it is only another technique, a feat of taste and of talent.

From all this, and from the history and the disappointment of the surrealist attempt, I conclude that errors can occur in the coming to consciousness of poetry, as in every human achievement of consciousness; that is one of the inevitable dangers, as we noted at the beginning of this essay, that the life and progress of the spirit carries with it in man.

To imagine, however, that coming to consciousness in itself, or progress in reflexivity, is a bad thing, a thing which by its nature tends to deform, would be to fall into a sort of Manichaean pessimism, which is, moreover, as false as possible, if it is true that reflexivity is, as I have said, a typical property of the spirit. In the very errors of coming to consciousness there are always coexistent discoveries.

Not to know what one is doing—it is thus, especially when it is a matter of self-forgetfulness due to a superior motion, that one makes the most beautiful things and performs the most generous acts. But not to know what one is doing—it is thus also that one commits the greatest crimes (and has the best chance also of being pardoned for them). All in all, other things being equal, it is better, however dangerous it be, and to whatever sanctions one expose oneself, to *know what one is doing*.

In any case, for that matter, we do not have the choice. When the naïve ages are past, they are *quite* past. The only resource left to us is a better and purer self-consciousness.

* * *

May I point out here the danger, which does not seem to me totally imaginary, of another possible error in the opposite direction? Among the normal reactions which take place against the experiences of these last years, it could happen—if we had to do with a simple phenomenon, as if of a pendulum, of action and reaction—that after having wished to give all to the subterranean powers of the world of images, one would turn, again in too *exclusive* a manner, and as if they alone counted, toward the powers, sometimes not less obscure, and the fecundity proper to the world of intelligence and discourse. And God preserve me from speaking ill of the intelligence! But it must not be mediocre, and in poetry it is far from being everything: error, said Pascal, comes from exclusion—that is the point I wish to make.

I add that in fact, when one invokes the primacy of the intelligence, not in order to seek out the internal hierarchies of the soul but in order to give passwords and collective instructions, it is not the intelligence as seeker of wisdom, the true intelligence (which is rarely met with), that profits from the operation; it is the facile and social intelligence, anti-metaphysical, empirical, and rationalizing, and which is found everywhere. And for this latter kind of intelligence poetry can very well on occasion express philosophical ideas, and sing *de natura rerum*—the foundation of the authority of such intelligence is neither metaphysical nor mystical, but only psychological, or even sociological.

If then things should take the course I have just indicated, by way of a simple reaction on the surface, we should run the risk of forgetting that though poetry cannot be confounded with metaphysics, it yet responds to a metaphysical need of the spirit of man, and is metaphysically justified. And though it cannot be confounded with sanctity, nor charged with the duties of sanctity, yet in its own line, which is not that of the good of man but rather of the good of the work, it involves a *kind* of sanctity, demands purifications and woes which are in a certain way symbolic of those of souls on the way toward the perfection of love. And we should run the risk of forgetting that the source of poetry is not the intelligence alone, from whatever depths it may surge up in certain men.

In brief, it could happen, on the pretext of latinity, and of the primacy of the reason (of a reason more or less rationalist), and in the name, if one may speak thus, of a Mediterranean catholicity, that a neo-classical reaction would ask poetry to *exhibit ideas and sentiments,* to charge itself with the rubbish of human notions in their verbosity and their natural meanness, and to fabricate *versified discourses* for the delectation of the formal intelligence. We should then see born a poetics "of abundance," of verbal abundance and of intellectual reduplication. And the word would again become master, the glory of the word, the endless and buzzing heroism of language—and all the stupidity of man.

Poetry is ontology, certainly, and even, according to the great saying of Boccaccio, poetry is theology. But in the sense that it finds its birth in the soul in the mysterious sources of being, and reveals them in some way by its own creative movement. Though the unconscious from which it proceeds is not, unless secondarily, the Freudian unconscious of instincts and images, it is, however, an unconscious more vital and deeper, the unconscious of the spirit at *its source*—hidden from the reasoning intelligence in that density of the soul where all the soul's powers have their common origin.

In short, it is toward the totality of his being that the poet is led back, if he is docile to the gift he has received, and consents to enter into the depths and let himself be laid bare. We think that this poetics of integrality, or rather of integration, not by an effort of voluntary concentration, but by the quietude of creative retreat and of poetic knowledge left to its own nature, is that which the present situation of poetry allows us to hope for— because it answers to the best and purest achievement of self-consciousness that one can expect from poetry today.

Let us transcribe here the witness of the poet who composed the first part of this book: "Born in a vital experience, life itself, poetry asks to be expressed by life-bearing signs, signs which conduct the one who receives them back to the ineffability of the original experience. Since in this contact all the sources of our faculties have been touched, the echo of it ought itself to be total . . ." "Song, poetry in all its forms, seeks to liberate a substantial experience . . . The brooding repose which is provided by such an experience acts as a refreshing bath, a rejuvenation and purification of the spirit . . . We cannot esteem too highly the profundity of the quiet which all our faculties then enjoy. It is a concentration of all the energies of the soul, but a peaceful, tranquil concentration, which involves no tension; the soul enters into its repose, in this place of refreshment and of peace superior to any feeling. It dies . . . but only to revive in exaltation and enthusiasm, in that state which is wrongly called 'inspiration,' because inspiration was nothing other, indeed, than this very repose itself, in which it escaped from sight. Now the mind, reinvigorated and enlivened, enters into a happy activity, so easy that everything seems to be given to it at once and, as it were, from outside. In reality, everything was there, in the shadow, hidden in the spirit and in the blood; everything that is going to be manifested in operation was there, but we knew it not. We knew neither how to discover it nor how to make use of it before having reimmersed ourselves in those tranquil depths." [4]

It is in no sense a matter of diminishing the role of the intelligence, nor the importance of intelligibility, of human experience, of conscious metaphysics involved in the poetic work, especially when that work is a tragedy for example, or a drama or epic. I say only that the fire of creative intuition must be hot enough to consume these materials, and not to be extinguished by them. Discursive lucidity is itself an integral part of the poetry of a Shakespeare, but the lucidity and all the logic, all the rationality and all the acquired knowledge, have been brought back to the secret source of refreshment and of peace of which we spoke a moment ago, in order to be transfigured and vivified there, and brought, if I may so express it, to the *creative state,* because they have all become poetic knowledge there. In that interior source the words of the tribe and the human notions lose

---

[4] Raïssa Maritain, "Sense and Nonsense in Poetry," in *The Situation of Poetry,* pp. 9 and 26.

that verbosity and that natural meanness which we referred to a few moments ago, because they undergo there, if I may so express it, a second birth.

Then, then alone, the poet has neither to escape from language nor submit himself to it, because the language is newly born in him and of him, as on the first morning of the terrestrial paradise.

All of these considerations suggest to us the conclusion that "in order that the life of the creative spirit grow without ceasing, conformably to its law, it is necessary that it deepen without ceasing the center of subjectivity where, in suffering the things of the world and those of the soul, it awakens to itself . . . Creation takes place at different levels in the substance of the soul— thereby each person shows what he is—and the more the poet grows, the more the level of the creative intuition descends into the density of his soul." [5] The more the poet at the same time simplifies himself, so much the more he rejects masks, consents to say what he is, feels the worth of human communion. The whole question for him is to have—along with a strong enough art (which can be learned)—a deep enough soul, which cannot be learned. Woe itself is not sufficient.

In an important study on melody, Arthur Lourié wrote a few years ago: "Modern music has lost the melodic element to the same degree that poetry has lost the lyric element." And what Lourié called melody here is an element of an order quite apart, which is developed in time but is not of time, and which is born of a breaking of the connections of time. "Melody, by itself," he writes further, "is not connected with any action, and does not lead to any action. It is like an end in itself. The *motif* serves to justify the action: the *theme* is a means of developing a thought. The *melody*, itself, serves no end. It gives liberation." That is to say that the melody is the very spirit of the music and the revelation of the intimate being of the musician. There is in poetry an element of the same nature, which is the spirit of poetry, and that revelation in act of the intimate person of the poet which is the same thing as poetic knowledge. I do not believe it to be true that modern poetry has lost that element. It

[5] *Frontières de la Poésie,* pp. 199–200.

has dissimulated it more or less, has been ashamed to avow it too loudly. But it is that element above all that it is trying to grasp in becoming conscious of itself.

There is at this moment in France a singular increase in poetry. I know some young poets who inspire me with a great confidence. I believe that their task will be to liberate the element of which we are speaking, that spring of living water born in the spiritual depths of the person, revealing, like melody, "the undisfigured essense of what is," and not "the lie imagined by its author."

The condition imposed—and it is dangerous enough to wound or to kill the seekers—is that the waters of that source be *true* enough, and well up from sufficient depth, to be able to carry away and transfigure the astonishing vegetation of images whose secret rites poetry has been learning for twenty years, but which by themselves are still only matter. If modern poetry must become more ontological, get into closer contact with being, with human and terrestrial reality (and perhaps also with divine reality), it is not by cares foreign to its nature and a well-intentioned zeal that it will accomplish this, but only through that lyric element which is almost as hidden as grace, hidden in the deepest of creative sources.

THREE PHILOSOPHICAL CONCLUSIONS

After this metaphysical description, we should like to propose briefly three more systematic conclusions.

In the first place: poetic knowledge is a knowledge *by affective connaturality* of the *operative* type, or tending to express itself in a work. It is not a knowledge "by mode of knowledge," it is a knowledge by mode of instinct or inclination, by mode of resonance in the subject, and which proceeds toward creating a work.

In such a knowledge it is the created object, the *work made*, the poem, the picture, the symphony, which plays the role of the mental word and of the *judgment* in speculative knowledge.[6]

[6] To eliminate all confusion, let it be noted that it is of *poetic knowledge* precisely understood, not of the *artistic habitus* that we are speaking here. The habitus of art produces its fruit in the practical *judgment* on the work to be made; poetic knowledge, in the *work done*.

It follows from this that poetic knowledge is not fully conscious except in the work made; it does not completely attain consciousness except in the work—in the work which in other ways materializes it and disperses it in some way in order to bring it back into a new unity, that of the thing posed in being.

Precisely as knowledge or experience (and more experience than knowledge), and taken separately from the production of the work, poetic knowledge is, in its essential character, unconscious—barely signalled to the consciousness by a shock which is at the same time emotional and intellectual, or by a spurt of song, which gives notice of its presence but does not at all express it.

We are here confronted by an unconscious of a special type. As we noted above, it is the unconscious of the spirit *at its source*, quite a different thing from the Freudian unconscious of images and instincts.

If on the other hand, it is remarked that the idea as such (in so far as it is distinguished from the judgment) is not necessarily conscious, one understands that it is with good reason that the ancients designated the intentional form of poetic knowledge not as a judgment but as an *idea*, as a factive or formative idea— which, inasmuch as it is nourished by poetic knowledge and vivified by the grace of poetry, is at the same time intuition and emotion.[7]

Our second conclusion concerns the relation of poetic knowledge to other kinds of knowledge by connaturality.

Leaving aside the knowledge by tendential or affective connaturality with the ends of human action, which is at the heart of *prudential* knowledge, we will distinguish three other kinds of knowledge by connaturality:

(1) A knowledge by intellectual connaturality with reality as *conceptualisable* and rendered proportionate in act to the human intellect. It goes along with the development of the *habitus* of

---

[7] If in their theory of the artistic idea the old schoolmen seem to have neglected this character—essential to the human creative intuition—of enveloping a knowledge by emotion and by affective connaturality, it is that they considered art and the creative activity above all as theologians, and concerned themselves with the analogical values according to which the activity of art is proper to God as well as to the human creature.

the intelligence; and it is from this knowledge that comes the *intuition*—intellectual and expressible in a mental work—of the philosopher, the scientist, of him who knows by mode of knowledge.

(2) A knowledge by either intellectual or affective connaturality with reality as *non-conceptualisable* and at the same time *contemplated,* in other words as non-objectifiable in notions and yet as a terminus of objective union. This is the knowledge of *contemplation:* whether it is a matter of a natural contemplation attaining, if that be possible, a transcendant reality inexpressible in itself in a human mental word, by means of a supra- or para-conceptual intellection; or of a supernatural contemplation attaining as object the divine reality inexpressible in itself in any created word, by means of the union of love (*amor transit in conditionem objecti*) and by a resonance in the subject, becomes a means of knowing.

(3) A knowledge by *affective* connaturality with reality as *non-conceptualisable* because *awakening to themselves the creative depths of the subject*—I mean by connaturality with reality according as reality comes to be buried in subjectivity itself in its quality of intellectually productive existence, and according as it is attained in its concrete and existential consonance with the subject *as subject*. This is *poetic* knowledge: radically factive or operative, since, being inseparable from the productivity of the spirit (owing to the fact that the connaturality which awakens it actuates the subject as subject, or as center of productive vitality and spiritual emanation), and being unable nevertheless to issue in a concept *ad intra,* it can only issue in a work *ad extra.*[8]

It seems likely that in the case of all those who have great in-

[8] The distinction of these two different modes (nos. 2 and 3) of transcending conceptualisation can be regarded as a free gloss of the following texts of Saint Thomas. "*Poetica scientia* est de his quae propter defectum veritatis non possunt a ratione capi; unde oportet quod quasi quibusdam similitudinibus ratio seducatur; *theologia* autem est de his quae sunt supra rationem; et ideo modus symbolicus utrique communis est, cum neutra rationi proportionetur." (I *Sent.* prol., q. 1, a. 5, ad 3.) "Sicut poetica non capiuntur in ratione humana, propter defectum veritatis quae est in eis; ita etiam ratio humana perfecte capere non potest divina, propter excedentem ipsorum veritatem. Ed ideo utrobique opus est repraesentatione per sensibiles figuras." (*Sum. Theol.,* I-II, 101, 2, ad 2.)

tuitive gifts there is an element of poetic knowledge, in the sense
that it underlies philosophic and scientific intuition and works
together with it, and that by a kind of inevitable psychological
resonance it also accompanies, be it only virtually, the natural
and supernatural contemplation of which it is an analogue. But
it is essentially distinct from the one and the other.

Being a knowledge by affective connaturality, the knowledge
of supernatural contemplation itself awakens in the soul the
poetic instinct, though it be in an entirely rudimentary and virtual
manner. That is why it is natural to the mystical experience to be
expressed lyrically. But in so far as it is expressed, and wells up
in song, it is that the mystical experience itself—when the contemplative is also a poet—has provoked in the depths of the subjectivity a present poetic knowledge of the realities mystically experienced; or it may be also that by virtue of the superabundance
of a perfect actuation it pours out gratuitously, without the least
operative tension, in words which can be richer in poetry than
the work of a poet, and which all the same, in the case in question, come not from a poetic knowledge, but from the excess of
a higher experience.

It is also to be remarked that poetic knowledge, like the knowledge of contemplation (when it express itself), employs simili-
tudes and symbols—in order to *seduce the reason,* as St. Thomas
says; [9] precisely because both of these kinds of knowledge have
to do, in different ways, with the non-conceptualisable.

But what we should like above all to remember is that being
in itself radically operative, oriented toward the creation of a
work, poetic knowledge does not liberate itself *in the mode of
knowledge* except in turning back upon itself in a reflexive consciousness in which it is detached in a way (in a purely virtual
way when everything remains normal) from its natural finalities.
It does not reveal itself thus to itself as knowledge and as appetite
for knowledge without running the risk in some measure of "perversion," or misdirection, of which we have spoken. And if this
misdirection occurs, if this separation from its natural ends takes
place really and effectively, poetic knowledge engenders an end-

[9] See I *Sent.*, prol., q. 1, a. 5, ad 3 (text cited in the previous note); and
In Johan., cap. 7, lect. 2.

less voracity to know—endless because resulting from turning aside from the natural ends.

And being unable to end either in a *work* (which it renounces and from which it turns away), or in a *speculative conceptualisation* (which is repugnant to it and for which it has not the means), it involves the spirit in a tragedy, strangely instructive and fecund in discoveries, but, in itself, monstrous.

In short, poetry *is* knowledge, incomparably: knowledge-experience and knowledge-emotion, existential knowledge, knowledge which is the germ of a work (and which does not know itself, and which it not *for* knowing). To make of it a *means of knowledge*, an instrument of knowledge, to take it out of its proper mode of being in order to procure that which it is, is to pervert it. In this sense it is a sin for the poet to eat of the fruit of the tree of knowledge. Let us add concerning the poets who have suffered most from this evil that their work, in so far as they have created works, is a victory over it, and all the more precious.

The third and last conclusion concerns the law of *transgression* of which we spoke a moment ago, and according to which all energies of a transcendental order aspire, inefficaciously, to go beyond the nature enclosed in a genus which they have in man, in order to follow the inclination of their transcendentality, and ultimately, tend toward pure act and infinitisation.

Taken as a transcendental and in its analogical polyvalence, a perfection of the transcendental order is not an essence, a specific nature; it is found in an essentially varied manner in a series of distinct specific essences. If here or there it follows the aspiration of its transcendentality taken as such, it aspires to go beyond these natures, it aspires in an inefficacious manner to pass beyond, to become in a certain way what it is in the pure Act.[10]

[10] St. Thomas (*Sum. Theol.*, I, 63, 3) explains that a thing constituted with a given nature (with a given nature enclosed in a species and a genus) cannot aspire to a superior specific nature, "sicut asinus non appetit esse equus: quia, si transferretur in gradum superioris naturae, jam ipsum non esset." But precisely the perfections of the transcendental order, not being enclosed in a species and a genus, do not lose their being when they pass from what they are in an inferior species to what they are in a superior species; on the contrary, they approach their "maximum" of being. That is why it is possible that in a given nature an energy of the transcendental order aspires in an inefficacious manner to pass in some way into what it is in a superior nature, and especially in the *Ipsum esse subsistens.*

An energy of transcendental order like that of metaphysics aspires in this way to the vision of God; an energy like that of mystical contemplation aspires to the divine liberty. It is only at the moment of becoming conscious of itself, when it discovers itself reflexively, that poetry also discovers such an aspiration within itself. This may tend toward pure creation (to create as God creates, that is the torment of certain great artists, who in the end, by force of wishing to be purely creators, and to owe nothing to the vision of the beings which God has had the indiscretion to make in front of them, have no other resource than that of artistically forcing and ravaging their art); or, on the contrary, if poetry detaches itself from its operative ends in the way we indicated a moment ago, if in becoming conscious of itself it takes a wrong direction, this aspiration will tend toward a kind of divine intuition or divine experience of the world and the soul, known as God knows them, from within, and within the essence of their Poet. And this will be the more violent in proportion as the poetic experience has been truly and really detached from its natural finalities.